Social History of Western Civilization

Volume I

Readings from the Ancient World to the Seventeenth Century

RICHARD M. GOLDEN

Clemson University

St. Martin's Press   **New York**

Acknowledgments

"Formation of Western Attitudes toward Women." Vern L. Bullough. From *The Subordinate Sex: A History of Attitudes Toward Women*. Urbana, Chicago, and London: 1973 by the Board of Trustees of the University of Illinois, pp. 19–3, 32–40.

"Slavery in the Ancient Near East." Isaac Mendelson. From *Biblical Archaeologist*, volume 9, December 1946, pages 74–88. Reprinted by permission of the American Schools of Oriental Research/ 4243 Spruce Street/ Philadelphia, PA 19104

"The Roots of Restriction: Women in Early Israel." Carol Meyers. From *Biblical Archaeologist*, volume 41, 1978, pages 91–103. Reprinted by permission of The American Schools of Oriental Research, publishers of the *Biblical Archaeologist*.

"The Semiotics of Food in the Bible." Jean Soler. From Forster, Robert and Orest Ranum, eds: *Food and Drink in History*. Baltimore/London: the Johns Hopkins University Press, 1979, pp. 126–38.

"Organized Greek Games." William J. Baker. From *Sports in the Western World*. Totowa, NJ: Rowman and Littlefield, 1982, pp. 14–23, 25–6.

"Marriage and the Family in Athens." W.K. Lacey. Reprinted form *The Family in Classical Greece*. 1968, Thames and Hudson. Used by permission of the publisher, Cornell University Press, pp. 100, 103–18.

"Classical Greek Attitudes to Sexual Behavior." K.J. Dover. In *Women in the Ancient World*. The Arethusa Papers, vol. 6, ed. by John Paradotto and J.P. Sullivan. 1984. Used by permission of the State University of New York Press.

"Roman Women." Gillian Clark. From *Greece and Rome* 28 (1981). Reprinted by permission of Oxford University Press.

"Gladiatorial Combat in Ancient Rome." Jérôme Carcopino. From *Daily Life in Ancient Rome: The People and the City at the Height of the Empire*, New Haven: Yale University Press, 1940, pp. 231–247

"Why Were the Early Christians Persecuted?" G.E.M. de Ste. Croix. World Copyright: The Past and Present Society, 175 Banbury Road, Oxford, England. This article is here reprinted in abridged form, and without the original footnote sequence, with the permission of the Society and the author, from *Past and Present: A Journal of Historical Studies*, no. 26 (November 1963). For further developments of the themes in this article see the debate that appeared in *Past and Present* no. 27 (April 1964).

Rural Economy and Country Life in the Medieval West, Georges Duby. Translated by Cynthia Postan. Reprinted by permission of the Unviersity of South Carolina Press, Columbia, South Carolina, 1968. Also with permission of Edward Arnold (Publishers) Ltd., 41 Bedford Square, London, WC1B 3DQ.

"The Life of the Nobility." Marc Bloch. From *Feudal Society*, Chicago: The University of Chicago Press, 1961, pp. 293–311.

Acknowledgments and copyrights continue at the back of the book, on page 312, which constitutes an extension of the copyright page.

Contents

Topical Table of Contents

Preface

Social History of Western Civilization is a two-volume reader for freshmen in Western Civilization courses. The twenty-five essays in each volume deal with social history because I believe that the most original and significant work of the past two decades has been in this area and because Western Civilization textbooks tend to slight social history in favor of the more traditional political, intellectual, and cultural history, though this bias is slowly changing. In the dozen years that I have taught Western Civilization, I have used many books, texts, and readers designed specifically for introductory courses. I decided to compile this reader because I perceived that other readers generally failed to retain student interest. My students found many of the essays in these other books boring, often because the selections assumed a degree of background knowledge that a typical student does not possess. To make this reader better suited to students, I have attempted to include essays that are not only important but readable as well. This has not been an easy task, for many significant history articles, which have been written solely for specialists, are, unfortunately, dull or simply too difficult for college undergraduates. I have gone through hundreds of articles searching for the few that are challenging, fascinating, important, and readable. Also, with readability in mind, I have translated foreign words and identified individuals and terms that students might not recognize. (All footnotes are my own unless otherwise indicated.) I, for one, cannot understand why anthologies intended for college students do not routinely translate foreign expressions, phrases, and book titles and, moreover, seem to take for granted that students will be familiar with Tertullian, Gustavus Adolphus, or Pearl Buck, to mention some examples.

A Western Civilization reader cannot be all things for all instructors and students, but I have consciously tried to make these two volumes useful for as many Western Civilization courses as possible, despite the widely varying ways in which such courses are taught. The readings in these volumes cover many geographical areas and a broad range of topics in social history. Some historians argue that Western civilization began with the Greeks, but I have included in Volume One a section on the Ancient Near East for the courses that begin there. Both volumes contain material on the seventeenth century; indeed, Volume Two includes in its first selections some material that precedes the seventeenth century. This chronological overlap is intentional because Western Civilization courses break differently according to the policies of instructors and institutions.

To show how the vast majority of articles in *Social History of Western Civilization* may be used in most Western Civilization courses, there is a correlation chart at the beginning of each volume that relates each essay to a relevant chapter in the major Western Civilization textbooks currently on the market. Though the textbooks do not always offer discrete discussions on all the subjects covered in the essays, they touch upon many of the subjects. As for the others, students will at least be able to place the articles in a historical context by reading the standard history of the period in the relevant textbook chapter and, more important, will gain fresh insight into that historical period. I have also provided introductions to the major periods in history for each volume as well as an introduction to each selection where I have asked pertinent questions in order to direct the students into the essays and to encourage them to think about the problems and issues they raise. These introductions do not contain summaries and so may not be substituted for the reading of the selections.

The preparation of this reader was more time-consuming than I had originally thought possible. There always seemed to be somewhere a more attractive article on every topic. Thus many people suggested essays to me, critiqued what I wrote, and helped in other ways as well. I thank Jay Crawford, Fara Driver, Phillip Garland, Leonard Greenspoon, Tully Hunter, Charles Lippy, Victor Matthews, Mike Sutton, and Carol Thomas. Especially generous in their time and comments were Robert Bireley, Elizabeth D. Carney, Suzanne A. Desan, Hilda Golden, Alan Grubb, Thomas Kuehn, Donald McKale, John A. Mears, Thomas F.X. Noble, and D.G. Paz. The staff of St. Martin's Press—Michael Weber, Vivian McLaughlin, Beverly Hinton, Kristen Heimstra, and Andrea Guidoboni—have been gracious, efficient, professional, and supportive.

Correlation Chart For Western Civilization Texts and Volume I of Social History of Western Civilization

Text	Vern L. Bullough, Formation of Western Attitudes toward Women	Isaac Mendelson, Slavery in the Ancient Near East	Carol Meyers, The Roots of Restriction: Women in Ancient Israel	Jean Soler, The Semiotics of Food in the Bible	William J. Baker, Organized Greek Games	WK. Lacey, Marriage and the Family in Athens	K.J. Dover, Classical Greek Attitudes to Sexual Behavior
Willis, *Western Civilization: A Brief Introduction* (1987)	1		1	1	2	2	2
Willis, *Western Civilization*, 4/e (1985)	1	1	1	1	2	2	2
Wallbank et al., *Civilization Past and Present*, 6e (1987)	1	1	1	1	2	2	2
Strayer & Gatzke, *The Mainstream of Civilization*, 4/e (1984)	1	1	1	1	2	2	2
Perry, et al., *Western Civilization: Ideas, Politics & Society* (1985)	1	1	2	2	3	3	3
Palmer & Colton, *A History of the Modern World*, 6/e (1984)					1	1	1
McNeill, *History of Western Civilization*, 6/e (1986)	I-A	I-A	I,A-5	I,A-5	II,A-3	II,A-4	II,A-4
McKay, Hill, Buckler, *A History of Western Society*, 3/e (1987)	1,2	1,2	2	2	3	3	3
Kagan, Ozment, Turner, *The Western Heritage*, 3/e (1987)	1	1	1	1	3	3	3
Harrison, Sullivan, Sherman, *A Short History of Western Civilization*, 6/e (1985)	1,2,3	1,2,3	2	2	6	6	6
Greer, *A Brief History of the Western World*, 5/e (1987)	1	1	1	1	2	2	2
Goff et al., *A Survey of Western Civilization* (1987)	1	1	1	1	2	2	3
Chambers et al., *The Western Experience*, 4/e (1987)	1	1	1	1	3	3	3
Burns et al., *Western Civilizations*, 10/e (1984)	2,3	3	4	4	6	6	6
Brinton et al., *A History of Civilization*, 6/e (1984)	1	1	1	1	2	2	2

	Gillian Clark, Roman Women	Jérôme Carcopino, Gladiatorial Combat in Ancient Rome	G.E.M. de Ste. Croix, Why Were the Early Christians Persecuted?	Georges Duby, Rural Economy and Country Life in the Medieval West	Marc Bloch, The Life of the Nobility	Jean Gimpel, Environment and Pollution
Willis, *Western Civilization: A Brief Introduction* (1987)	3	3	4	5	5	6
Willis, *Western Civilization*, 4/e (1985)	4	4	5	7	7	8
Wallbank *et al.*, *Civilization Past and Present*, 6e (1987)	3	3	5	8	8	9
Strayer & Gatzke, *The Mainstream of Civilization*, 4/e (1984)	4	4	4	9	9	11
Perry, *et al.*, *Western Civilization: Ideas, Politics & Society* (1985)	7	7	8	9	9	10
Palmer & Colton, *A History of the Modern World*, 6/e (1984)	1	1	1	3	3	3
McNeill, *History of Western Civilization*, 6/e (1986)	II-C,	II-C, II-D	II,D-2	II, B-1	III, B-1	III, B-2
McKay, Hill, Buckler, *A History of Western Society*, 3/e (1987)	5	6	6	10	10	11
Kagan, Ozment, Turner, *The Western Heritage*, 3/e (1987)	4,5	5	5	6,8	8	7
Harrison, Sullivan, Sherman, *A Short History of Western Civilization*, 6/e (1985)	11	10	12	17,18	17,18	18
Greer, *A Brief History of the Western World*, 5/e (1987)	3	3	4	5	5	5
Goff *et al.*, *A Survey of Western Civilization* (1987)	6	7,8	9	12	12	12
Chambers *et al.*, *The Western Experience*, 4/e (1987)	4,5	5	5	6	8	9
Burns *et al.*, *Western Civilizations*, 10/e (1984)	8	8	9	11	11	11
Brinton *et al.*, *A History of Civilization*, 6/e (1984)	3	3	4	5	5	7

David Herlihy, *Medieval Children*	7	11	9,11	12	5,6	18	8	10	III, B-2	3	9,10	11	9	8	6
Caroline Walker Bynum, *Fast, Feast, and Flesh: The Religious Significance of Food to Medieval Women*	7	12	11	13	6	22	7,8	10	III, B-2	4	9	11	11	8	6
Johan Huizinga, *The Vision of Death*	10	13	11	12	7	24	9	12	III, B-3	5	12	13	9	10	7
Norbert Elias, *The Development of the Concept of Civilté*	11	14	12	18	8	28,29	9	13	III, B-3	6	13	16	13	11	7
David Herlihy, *The Family in Renaissance Italy*	11	14	12	18	8	28	9	13	III, B-3	6	13	16	13	11	7
Henry Kamen, *Population Structures*	12	17	16	21	9	27	10	15	III, C-1	12	15	18,19	15	12	8
Alfred W Crosby Jr., *The Early History of Syphilis: A Reappraisal*	14	15	13	19	9	27	10	15	III C-1	11	15	18	18	13	9
Lucien Febvre, *Life in Renaissance France*	11	17	16	21	9	29	10	15	III, C-1	13	16	18	15	12	8
Geoffrey Parker, *Mutiny and Discontent in the Spanish Army of Flanders, 1572-1607*	13	16	15	21	10	31	11	15	III, C-1	14	16	18	15	14	9
Christina Larner, *Who Were the Witches?*	15	16	16	21	9	30	11	15	III, C-1	28,32	17	18	15	10	8
Natalie Z. Davis, *The Rites of Violence: Religious Riot in Sixteenth-Century France*	13	16	15	21	10	31	11	15	III, C-1	15	16	18	15	12,15	8
Michael MacDonald, *Insanity in Early Modern England*	15	17	17	24	10	37	13	16	III, C-2	34	18	21		15	11

Introduction

The social history of Western civilization seeks to include the complete fabric of human experience. Such comprehensiveness, like the quest for historical objectivity or the search for truth, is impossible to achieve. Nevertheless, the desire to learn about the totality of life differentiates social history from other subject areas such as military, intellectual, religious, cultural, diplomatic, biographical, economic, or art history. The social historian looks at groups or masses of people, at conditions that affected populations in everyday life. In part, this approach has been a reaction against biographies and the study of prominent people, usually military, political, or religious leaders, that dominated historical writing during the nineteenth century and the first half of the twentieth century. This history of élites ignores the vast majority of people and so implies that ordinary lives are unimportant. Hence, "history from the bottom up" seeks to rediscover previously neglected populations and lifestyles. But, ironically, social history, the history of aggregates, has sometimes become a history without names, that is, without the mention of individuals. Is it necessary to refer to anyone by name in discussing the agricultural system of the early Middle Ages or the effects of epidemics on human communities? On the other hand, discovering those "nameless" people and more intimate details constitutes the very humanness of history.

Though contempory problems should not be the sole criterion for a historian's choice of a topic, the subjects that form the backbone of social history still exist today, though in different forms. In other words, the social history of ancient civilizations or the Middle Ages is intrinsically of interest to us as citizens of the twentieth century because it is often relevant, though it must be emphasized that relevance is not a goal of the social historian. Rather, awareness of concerns in present society has often led to investigations of similar problems in the past. Thus primary topics in social history, all of which are discussed in this volume, include the family, marriage, children, death, disease, sports, violence, crime, women, persecution, food, sexuality, the environment, social behavior, religion, insanity, and the daily lives of various social groups. People in the past seem very different from us in Western civilization today; they thought and behaved in ways that appear alien to us, for the principles by which they ordered their universe are contrary to ours. The faceless masses, whom social historians are now beginning to see, fascinate precisely because they dealt with many of our problems—sex, for example—and our institutions—such as the family—in ways that from our vantage point seem superstitious, exotic, and neurotic. To appreciate social history, one must understand, not judge, and one must try to immerse oneself in the period studied and in the mentality of the people. The German poet Heinrich Heine said, "If one has no heart, one cannot write for the masses." To study the lives of the masses in history likewise requires heart; as the selections in this book reveal, the vast majority of people in past societies lived short, unhealthy lives, punctuated more often than not by violence, brutality, and exploitation. The study of social history needs empathy, the ability to place oneself in the hearts and minds of ordinary people in the past.

1

ANCIENT NEAR EAST

Where did Western civilization begin? Some argue that it began with the Greeks because they were so like us: they thought in terms of history, they reflected on the human predicament, and they questioned all areas of life. The Greeks invented history, drama, and philosophy and so were the first to tackle in a systematic way the perennial major questions basic to humanity: What is goodness, truth, beauty, justice, love. The Greeks were also the first to study nature as an autonomous and distinct entity, without reference to outside, supernatural forces. In history, science, and philosophy, the Greeks parted company with the earlier civilizations of the ancient Near East.

But a cogent argument could be made to include the ancient Near East in Western civilization. The cultures in what is today known as the Middle East, extending from Egypt to Iran, contributed writing, the alphabet, iron, astronomy, elements of common math, agriculture, monumental architecture, cities, codes of law, and, with the Hebrews, a religion of ethical monotheism. All these influenced Graeco-Roman civilization, and thus our own.

Filling the universe with exotic gods, the minds of most Near Eastern people seem alien to us. In social life and personal relationships, nevertheless, they bear affinities with the Western cultures that followed them. Slavery, for example, was a feature of every ancient society, dying out in the modern West only in 1865 and in the Middle East in the 1970s. The belief in the inferiority of women and even in their relative equality could be found in the Near East. Echoes of these convictions are heard in rancorous debates in the twentieth century. Some attitudes toward children and education appear quite familiar to us, though others seem bizarre, if not inhuman.

Hebrew culture was not different from other cultures in its imperialism and the unification of life around religion. The Hebrew religion was unusual—after all, it was the only ancient Near Eastern religion that has survived to our own day. Although there may be theological reasons for the continuation of Judaism,

1

its penetration of every aspect of life certainly contributed to its longevity. Slavery, childrearing, and diet all bore the imprint of Hebraic religion.

The following selections on the ancient Near East address fundamental topics in the social history of Western civilization. They identify common as well as dissimilar features among Near Eastern civilizations. At the same time, they provide comparisons with conditions of life in later cultures.

Formation of Western Attitudes Toward Women

VERN L. BULLOUGH

In order to understand later attitudes toward women in Western civilization, Vern L. Bullough investigates and compares the role of women in Mesopotamia and ancient Egypt.

The inhabitants of the Tigris-Euphrates river valley, whether Sumerians, Babylonians, or Assyrians, treated women as property rather than as persons. What implications did this have for marriage, the treatment of adultery, and the lives of female slaves? That we know the names of only a few Mesopotamian women suggests the tight grip of male dominance; women were rarely able to distinguish themselves as individuals. Law codes indicated the very real subordination of women, and religion, always a cultural phenomenon, likewise preached female inferiority.

Women fared better in Egypt, though certainly there was no pretence of equality. But at least Egyptian women had greater standing in law than their Mesopotamian counterparts. What legal rights did Egyptian women have? Do you agree with Bullough's reasons for the comparatively higher status of women in Egypt? The most famous Egyptian woman, besides Cleopatra, was Hatshepsut, who reigned for approximately twenty years. How did her gender affect her rule? Her experience shows clearly an ingrained and negative attitude toward women that would continue through Western civilization. Societies did not permit women to be warriors, for the military was a means to power. The only power attributed to women, other than that of mother, was the ability—or so men thought—to trap, delude, and steer men away from the right path.

The cradle of civilization, or at least of Western civilization, was the river valleys of the Near East (sometimes called the Middle East), particularly in the area extending from modern Egypt to modern Iraq. Attitudes formed in these areas were incorporated into Jewish, Greek, and later Western Roman and Christian attitudes. . . .

It has been said that man's vision of the gods reflects his own vision of himself and his activities. If there is any merit to this statement it seems clear that the inhabitants of the Tigris-Euphrates Valley quite early held man to be superior to woman, and in fact relegated her to

Vern L. Bullough, *The Subordinate Sex: A History of Attitudes toward Women* (Urbana, Chicago, & London: University of Illinois Press, 1973), 19–30, 32–40.

being a kind of property. There are hints that in the beginning of Sumerian society women had a much higher status than in the heyday of Sumerian culture, since in early Sumerian religious tradition goddesses occupy prominent roles in the Divine Assemblies.[1]. . . Nevertheless by the time the Babylonian theology was organized into the form in which it has come down to us the mother goddess was made clearly subordinate to male gods and monogamy had become the basic form of marriage.

The names and positions of the gods changed during different periods of Mesopotamian civilization as differing peoples achieved dominance. There were hundreds of deities but there were two major triads of gods: Anu, Enlil, and Ea; Sin, Shamash, and Ishtar. Over and above them was another god Marduk or Asshur. The only female in the group was Ishtar, or in Sumerian, Inanna, goddess of war and of love. Like humans, the gods had wives and families, court servants, soldiers, and other retainers. Ishtar, however, remained unmarried. Her lovers were legion but these unhappy men usually paid dearly for her sexual favors. She was identified with the planet Venus, the morning and evening star, and could arouse the amorous instinct in man, although she also had the power of causing brothers who were on good terms to quarrel among themselves and friends to forget friendship. If she perchance withdrew her influence "The bull refuses to cover the cow, the ass no longer approaches the she-ass, in the street the man no longer approaches the maidservant." Part of her difficulty was that she did not really know her place. In the poem translated as *Enki and World Order* the god Enki (whose powers are similar to Ea) assigned the gods various tasks. Ishtar, however, felt left out and complained to Enki. Her complaint applies to woman in general: "Me, the woman, why did you treat differently?/ Me, the holy Inanna, where are my powers?" She was given various tasks as a result, but as an unmarried and erotic figure it was no wonder that sacred prostitution formed part of her cult. When she descended to earth she was accompanied by courtesans and prostitutes. The implication might well be . . . that woman was either to be wife and mother, or an unmarried professional, a prostitute.

The mere presence of Ishtar, or Inanna, in the heavenly triad is probably striking evidence of the great strength of the forces of nature which had been so deeply rooted in primitive society. She represented the blending of several different characters into one, most obviously the lady of love and the lady of battles, although these different aspects of her powers were worshiped at different places. If Ishtar chose to favor a mere mortal he could gain fame and riches, and she was much sought after. Sargon, the Akkadian conquerer, who lived toward the end of

---

[1]The meetings of the gods and goddesses.

the third millenium B.C., felt himself to be under the protection of Ishtar and believed it was through her influence that he became king. . . .

If the place of women in official mythology was somewhat circumscribed, it was even more so in actual life. Our chief source of information about actual conditions is the various law codes. . . . [T]he first law code was that of the town of Eshnunna, dating from about 1800 B.C. The best known, however, was that of Hammurabi (c. 1700 B.C.), which contained about 250 laws. Later from the Assyrian scribes there exists another legal corpus dating from 1100 B.C., which has a long section on women and marriage.

Women basically were property. They were neither to be seen nor heard. Monogamy was the normal way of life but monogamy in practice meant something different for the man than for the woman. A wife who slept with another man was an adulteress but a man could not only visit prostitutes but in practice also took secondary wives as concubines. Rich men and royalty often had more than one legal wife. Women were always under the control of a male. Until the time of her marriage a girl remained under the protection of her father, who was free to settle her in marriage exactly as he thought fit. Once married she was under the control of her husband. During the marriage ceremony a free woman assumed the veil which she wore from then on outside her home. In fact the veil was the mark of a free woman, and anyone who met a slave or courtesan wearing a veil had the duty of denouncing her. A concubine could only wear a veil on those occasions when she accompanied the legal wife out of doors. It was an offence for a woman to have any dealings in business or to speak to a man who was not a near relation.

Some scholars have argued that the earliest form of marriage required the bridegroom to purchase his bride, emphasizing even further the woman as property. . . .

The economic dependence of the woman upon the male was demonstrated by the various provisions allowing her to remarry. In cases where a woman's husband was taken captive and he had not left enough for her to eat, she could live with another man as his wife, although if her husband returned she was to go back to him. Any children by the temporary husband remained with him. If, however, the absence of her husband was malicious, motivated by a "hatred of king and country," he had no further claim upon his wife if she took a second husband. Women could also hold property. An unmarried daughter, for example, could be given either a dowry, a share of her father's property, or the usufruct, the right to the profits from the land. She was free to dispose of her dowry as she wished, but in other cases her property rights upon her death reverted to her brothers, except under special conditions.

The purpose of marriage was procreation, not companionship. The wife's first duty was to raise her children and a sterile marriage was grounds for divorce. The wife who gave birth to children, particularly to sons, was accorded special protection. The man who divorced the mother of his sons or took another wife was committing a culpable act. Her childbearing responsibilites were emphasized by penalties to anyone injuring a woman sufficiently to cause a miscarriage, and also in the statutes against abortion.

Adultery was not a sin against morality but a trespass against the husband's property. A husband had freedom to fornicate, while a wife could be put to death for doing the same thing. Free women were inviolable and guarded; a man who gave employment to a married woman not closely related to him was in difficulty. A man caught fornicating with an adulterous woman could be castrated or put to death, while the woman could be executed or have her nose cut off. Offenses with unmarried free women were treated differently from those of married women because there was no husband. If the offender had a wife, she was taken from him and given to her father for prostitution and the offender was compelled to marry the girl who was his victim. If he had no wife he had to pay a sum of money to the girl's father as well as marry her, although the father might accept money and refuse to give him his daughter. In any case the payment was for damaging property, lessening the value of the girl. . . .

These laws applied to freewomen. There were other women, particularly slaves. A slave had no human personality but instead was real property. If he was injured it was his master and not he who was entitled to compensation. A female slave was under obligation to give her purchaser not only her labor but also herself, without any counter obligation on his part. He could in fact turn her over to prostitution. Even when she became the purchaser's concubine and had children by him she still remained a slave liable to be sold. At her owner's death, however, she and her children received liberty. If a female slave was bought by a married woman either as her servant or as a concubine for her husband (as in the case of a childless woman), she remained the property of the wife. A male slave could, with his master's consent, marry a freewoman, and even if she lacked a dowry she and her children would still remain free. If she brought a dowry she could keep it, but any increase from investment was split with her husband's master. There were also temple slaves who were not confined to the temple but worked in the towns and hired out to private employers. Their legal status was harsher than that of ordinary slaves since they had no hope of adoption, while their children, even if their mother was a freewoman, automatically became the property of the gods. Children and wives of freemen were different from slaves, but the father still had almost total control. He could deposit his children with creditors, and apparently also his wife, although she could not be kept for more than four years. . . .

Other than tavernkeepers, the only other occupations for women mentioned in the law codes were as priestesses and prostitutes. There were various kinds of both. At the head of the priestesses was the Entu, the wife of the gods, or the "lady [who is] a deity." They were of very high standing and the kings could make their daughters Entu of a god. They were expected to remain virgins, although they might eventually take husbands, perhaps after menopause. A second class of priestesses was the Naditu, who were lower in rank but who were also not expected to have children. The Hammurabic code had several provisions attempting to ensure the rights of a priestess to dowry and other shares of her father's goods. Apparently their conduct was rigidly circumscribed since any priestess who went to a tavern to drink could be put to death. Prostitutes seem to have been quite common and there was a considerable variety of harlots and hierodules[2]. . . .

With such a male-oriented society, few women emerged as real individuals in the history of the Mesopotamian civilizations. . . .

. . . It was only through their sons that women in the Mesopotamian civilizations seem to have had any influence at all. Even the wives of the king were not important enough to be regarded as queens since the use of the term was restricted to goddesses or to women who served in positions of power. The chief wife instead was usually called "she of the palace" and she lived along with the concubines and other wives in a harem guarded by eunuchs. Their way of life was carefully regulated by royal edicts, although in the last period of the Assyrian kingdom the influence of the king's wife and mother had somewhat greater power than before.

Other than a few exceptional royal wives, only a handful of women managed to break through into the pages of history. There is an isolated reference to a woman physician at the palace in an Old Babylonian text, and we can assume that women attended other women in childbirth, but there is no further reference. The professional physician was usually a male. Women were also generally illiterate if only because in this period reading and writing were restricted to a professional class of scribes who underwent long training. Poetry, however, is a preliterate form of literature, and one of the most remarkable poets, in fact one of the few we know by name, was a woman, Enheduanna. She was the daughter of Sargon, whose administration marked the fusion of Semitic and Sumerian culture. As part of this fusion the Sumerian Inanna and

[2]Temple slaves.

the Akkadian Ishtar came together and in this process Enheduanna played an important role, at least if her identification is correct. She was a high priestess of the moon god, the first of a long line of royal holders of this office, and in this capacity she wrote a poem usually entitled "The Exaltation of Inanna." Her poetry served as a model for much subsequent hymnography and her influence was so great that she later seems to have been regarded as a god herself. . . . Most of the cuneiform literature from the area is anonymous, or at best pseudonymous, so how many other women poets there were must remain unknown. . . .

In one of the great classics of Mesopotamian literature, the Gilgamesh epic, it seems obvious that woman's duty was to keep man calm and peaceful. In the beginning of the account Gilgamish was oppressing the city of Erech, taking the son from the father, the maiden from her lover. The people complained to the gods, who created a rival, Enkidu, from clay to deal with Gilgamish. Enkidu was a wild man whose whole body was covered with hair, who knew neither people nor country. When the existence of Enkidu was reported to Gilgamish he sent forth a temple harlot to ensnare the wild man: "Let her strip off her garment; let her lay open her comeliness;/ He will see her, he will draw nigh to her. . . . " Then with his innocence lost he could be more effectively handled by Gilgamish.

> The prostitute untied her loin-cloth and opened her legs, and he took possession
>   of her comeliness:
> She used no restraint but accepted his ardour,
> She put aside her robe and he lay upon her.
> She used on him, the savage, a woman's wiles,
> His passion responded to her.
> For six days and seven nights Enkidu approached and coupled with the prostitute.
> After he was sated with her charms,
> He set his face toward his game.
> [But] when the gazelles saw him, Enkidu, they ran away;
> The game of the steppe fled from his presence.
> Enkidu tried to hasten [after them, but] his body was [as if it were] bound.
> His knees failed him who tried to run after his game.
> Enkidu had become weak, his speed was not as before.
> But he had intelligence, wide was his understanding.

. . . The legend suggests that woman was designed to ensnare a man, to weaken him, to prevent him from realizing his full potentiality. In this forerunner of the stereotype of Eve, woman was both a source of pleasure and yet a delusion. . . .

Woman, nonetheless, was designed to be at the side of man, and as a proverb stated, "a house without an owner is like a woman without a husband." The ideal wife was both passionate and able to bear sons. . . . Obviously women were regarded as a mixed blessing, and it was best that they be kept in their place.

Life in Mesopotamia was harsh and unpredictable. There were floods, famine, scorching heat, and cloudbursts, and always the danger of invasions. It might well be that in such a society the strong man was admired while the weak woman was regarded as a liability, but necessary because of her childbearing abilities. Inevitably the male would be forced to assert himself, to man the armies, to do the fighting, to keep his womenfolk in subordination. Is this an adequate explanation for male dominance? The difficulty with such a thesis is quite simply that these same attitudes are found in other cultures where environmental conditions are quite different. Nonetheless environment might have had some influence, since the place of women in Egyptian society seems to be quite different from that of Mesopotamian society.

. . . Most recent studies would not regard Egypt as a matriarchal society but all would agree that the status of women was probably higher than in Mesopotamia and that women had the right to own and transmit property. . . .

Part of the difficulty with reconstructing the real status of women in Egypt is that we lack the kind of comprehensive law codes present in ancient Mesopotamian society. We do, however, have numerous legal documents, particularly from the time of the Persians and the Greeks who occupied Egypt in the last half of the first millenium B.C. From these it would appear that women had the right to own property, to buy, sell, and testify in court. . . . [I]t is apparent that women not only enjoyed full equality to own property but also could go about their transactions in the same manner as men. Moreover, they were allowed to regain the property they brought with them as dowry if their marriage broke up. If, however, the woman had committed adultery no such guarantee existed. Women were listed as taxpayers, and they could also sue. Apparently a woman did not need a guardian to be able to execute legal acts, nor did it matter whether she was married or not. A daughter, at least in the Ptolemaic period, was entitled to equal succession in the estate of her father. Women could acquire wealth or property through their parents, husbands, or purchase it. A wife was entitled to a third of her husband's possessions after his death, whereas the other two-thirds had to be divided among the children and sisters and brothers of the testator. If a husband desired his wife to receive more, he had the right to donate it to her before he died. . . .

Since goddesses were so important it would seem to follow that royal women would also be important if only because the pharaoh's first wife was the consort of a god. Inevitably, too, she became the "mother of the god" who would be the successor to her husband. At all periods in Egyptian society the queens were the first ladies of the land and originally the tombs of some were as big and as elaborate as those of the kings. . . .

. . . [I]t was not until the eighteenth dynasty (c. 1570–1305) that the Egyptian queen achieved her highest prestige. The most influential of all was Hatshepsut (c. 1486–1468), who stole the throne from her young nephew and stepson, Thutmose III, and wielded the scepter for about twenty years. Hatshepsut, however, ruled as a king and not as a queen, an indication of the difficulties women had in ruling. The reigning monarch of Egypt had to be male: the titles, laudatory inscriptions, and ceremonies were all designed for men and were so deeply rooted in tradition and dogma that it was easier for a woman to adapt herself to fit the titles than to change the titles to fit her sex. Inevitably her reign is somewhat confusing since she is shown both in a man's kilt (and body) wearing the king's crown and artificial beard, and as a woman with feminine dress and queen's crown. She also has two tombs, one in her capacity as queen and one as king, the latter being larger. When she died or was driven from the throne by her nephew, Thutmose III, he destroyed almost anything Hatshepsut had ever touched, and even tried to obliterate all inscriptions which referred to her. Though Hatshepsut must have been a strong-willed woman, one of her great difficulties seems to have been her inability to lead an army. She recorded no military conquests or campaigns; her great pride was in the internal development of Egypt. Though there was nothing in her biological makeup that would prevent a woman from being a soldier or general, in fact, many of them disguised themselves as males to serve in the American Civil War, women almost without exception were not trained as soldiers. In the past when kings had to lead their armies this discrimination might have prevented more women from being rulers. Hatshepsut obviously was supported by the bureaucracy of the state, but civil powers can be diffused. In a military crisis, however, power must be centralized into the hands of one person, and though a woman might appoint a male to act as commander, there is little to stop him from turning against her, particularly if he has the loyalty of the troops. It might well be that Thutmose III used his military ability to regain the throne, since he either deliberately introduced military imperialism or was forced to expand in order to defend his countries' borders.

Hatshepsut was not the only woman to sit on the throne. There were at least three others, although only as regents for their sons. . . . Women continued to exercise considerable influence down to the time of Cleopatra.[3] . . . Though Cleopatra was Greek rather

[3]69–30 B.C.

than Egyptian, her importance emphasizes the continuing influence of women in Egyptian affairs, whether foreign or native.

The relative importance of the queen mother was no indication that the king was restricted to one wife. Concubines and harems were common, but such women seldom appeared in public. The size of the harem probably varied and at times reached remarkable numbers. Ramses II (1290–1224 B.C.), for example, had at least seventy-nine sons and fifty-nine daughters. The members of the royal harem lived apart from the rest of the court. Employees of the harem were not eunuchs, as in Mesopotamia, but included normal men, many of them married, as well as numerous women. In general the harem women were chosen by the pharoah either for political reasons or for their great beauty. It was through this last procedure that many non-royal women gained admission and some became queens. There were also a number of women of foreign birth. Inevitably there were conspiracies in the harem as various wives tried to maneuver their sons into key positions. When women were not in the harem for political reasons, their chief purpose was to amuse their lord. They were instructed in dancing and singing and other arts designed to arouse and delight the male. Some of the richer Egyptians also had harems and concubines but as a general rule Egyptians practiced monogamy if only because economic factors worked against polygamy. The husband could dismiss his wife if he wished to remarry or if his wife ceased to please him but he had to return her dowry and give other forms of settlement. Women had no such freedom.

Like most societies, Egypt practiced a double standard. Concubinage existed but not polyandry. Maidservants belonged to their owner and adultery for the male was not considered a sin. Prostitution was widespread. . . . If a married woman committed adultery, however, she could be deprive of her property and be subject to punishment. We have two folktales from the Middle and New Kingdom of women committing adultery: in the first the woman was burned to death; in the second her husband killed her and threw her corpse to the hounds. In other folktales women appeared as very sexual creatures, willing to betray their husbands, use various kinds of tricks, and do other things in order to get the men who attracted them physically into bed. . . . Instead of female promiscuity, it seems possible that [these stories] might only indicate male wishful thinking. Before the late period of these tales the Egyptian woman was seldom pictured in any negative way in the literature. She was always the faithful caring wife, the princess with many suitors, or the mistress praised by songs and poems. Motherhood was her revered function. Not to have children was a terrible and lamentable situation, and mother and children were depicted at all times in Egyptian tombs and pictures. . . .

The extant literature seems to be from the hands of males, and it reflects the various attitudes of males toward women. Ptah Hotep, the semilegendary sage of the Old Kingdom who lived in the third millenium B.C., said: "If you are a man of note, found for yourself a household, and love your wife at home, as it beseems. Fill her belly, clothe her back; unguent is the remedy for her limbs. Gladden her heart, so long as she lives; she is a goodly field for her lord [that is, she will produce children if you cultivate her]. But hold her back from getting the mastery. [Remember that] her eye is her stormwind, and her vulva and mouth are her strength." Though wives were good if kept in their place, care should be exercised in their choice. . . . Women were also dangerous: "If you would prolong friendship in a house to which you have admittance, as master, or as brother, or as friend, into whatsoever place you enter, beware of approaching the women. It is not good in the place where this is done. Men are made fools by their gleaming limbs of carnelian. A trifle, a little, the likeness of a dream, and death comes as the end of knowing her." . . . Motherhood was especially revered. "Double the bread that thou givest to thy mother, and carry her as she carried [thee]. When thou wast born after thy months, she carried thee yet again about her neck, and for three years her breast was in thy mouth. She was not disgusted at thy dung, she was not disgusted and said not: 'What do I?' She put thee to school, when though hadst been taught to write, and daily she stood there [at the schoolhouse] . . . with bread and beer from her house. " When a man married he should keep the example of his mother in front of him. "When thou art a young man and takest to thee a wife and art settled in thine house, keep before thee how thy mother gave birth to thee, and how she brought thee up further in all manner of ways. May she not do thee harm nor lift up her hands to the Gods and may he not hear her cry." . . .

Women, in general, however, were a snare and a delusion. "Go not after a woman, in order that she may not steal thine heart away." In particular beware "of a strange woman, one that is not known in her city. Wink not at her . . . have no carnal knowledge of her. She is a deep water whose twisting men know not. . . . "

Yet a woman could also be a delight.

. . . .

Lovely are her eyes when she glances,
Sweet are her lips when she speaks,
   and her words are never too many!
Her neck is long, and her nipple is radiant,
   and her hair is deep sapphire.
Her arms surpass the brilliance of gold,
   and her fingers are like lotus blossoms.

Her buttocks curve down languidly from her trim belly,
   and her thighs are her beauties.
Her bearing is regal as she walks upon the earth—
   she causes every male neck to turn and look at her.
Yes, she has captivated my heart in her embrace!
In joy indeed is he who embraces all of her—
   he is the very prince of lusty youths!

. . . .

   In sum, the Egyptian woman had a relatively pleasant life and we do not need to resort to questionable generalizations like that of primitive matriarchy in order to explain it. Her somewhat higher status than the Mesopotamian woman still did not mean that she was considered equal to men. Women were clearly subordinate, and compared to men their lives were circumscribed. It might well be that the very passivity of living in Egypt due to the great fertility of the soil and to the regularity of life lent less emphasis to war and to the making of war. Women worked in the fields along with the men in ancient times, as they do now, although their assigned functions differed. Even the fact that women appeared as rulers does not mean that they had equality, since all apparently exercised their power in the name of their son or took a male name. It is also worthy of comment that most of the women rulers appeared at the end of a dynasty, apparently striving to keep the family in power either because their sons were young or their husbands enfeebled. Hatshepsut, of course, was an exception. Some Egyptian women worked outside of their homes, but the professions were not open to them nor were any of the crafts, except the traditionally feminine ones. They were not priests, nor were they carpenters, sculptors, or scribes. Woman's place was in the home, and it was as mothers that they had their greatest influence. If Egypt is the example of the power that women had under what some have called a matriarchy, their status in times past must never have been very high. . . .

Slavery in the Ancient Near East

ISAAC MENDELSOHN

For people in antiquity, a society without slaves was virtually inconceivable. The trade in slaves linked cultures in the ancient Near East, as did the shared belief in the necessity and virtue of slavery. That belief was as widespread then as the feeling today that slavery is morally wrong.

Mendelsohn first discusses various ways—war, sale, and indebtedness—in which one could become a slave in the ancient Near East. War was endemic in that period; individuals and entire populations could suddenly lose their freedom. Omnipresent poverty was the cause of the sale of minors and the sale of oneself as well as the reason for people falling into debt and hence into slavery. Such a precarious existence for ancient Near Eastern peoples! Terrorized by vengeful and sometimes fickle gods, they received no relief from the sociopolitical world. Invading armies routinely crisscrossed the countryside from present day Iraq to Israel. Enormous disparities in wealth, poor weather, and erratic harvests help explain the plunge into slavery for those whose life-long poverty became destitution. How did slavery affect family relationships in these conditions?

Second, Mendelsohn analyzes the legal status of slaves, how they were treated by various law codes, particularly that of Hammurabi in Babylonia and the Bible. Were there significant differences between the Old Testament and Hammurabi's Code concerning the regulation of slavery? Is there reason to believe that slaves were treated as the laws specified? How could a slave become free? Would slaves always desire liberty?

Third, in explaining the economic role of slavery, Mendelsohn shows that institution to be even more nuanced. Not only did slavery differ from culture to culture, but also according to the economic function of the slaves. Slaves worked for governments, temples, and private individuals, most often in agriculture or in industry. Historians of slavery are always drawn to the question of whether or not slavery was economically beneficial.

Finally, Mendelsohn looks at the attitude of religion toward slavery. Because religion is a product of culture, we should not be surprised to learn that Near Eastern religions accepted slavery as part of the natural order of things. But were there any seeds in religion that would later germinate to produce moral outrage against one person's owning another person?

Isaac Mendelsohn, "Slavery in the Ancient Near East," *The Biblical Archaeologist* IX (December 1946): 74–88.

The earliest Sumerian terms for male and female slaves are the composite signs *nita + kur* "male of a foreign country," and *nunus + kur* "female of a foreign country," indicating that the first humans to be enslaved in Ancient Babylonia were captive foreigners. That prisoners of war, spared on the battle field, were reduced to slavery is amply attested in the annals of the long history of the Ancient Near East. The Hammurabi Code[1] took this universal practice of the enslavement of war captives for granted and decreed that (1) a captive state official should be ransomed, in case he had no resources of his own, by his city temple or by the state, and (2) that a woman whose husband was taken prisoner may re-marry in case she had no means to support herself and her children. The Late Assyrian annals repeatedly mention large numbers of war captives "from the four corners of the world" who were dragged to Assyria and were compelled to perform forced labor. The small city-states of Syria in the middle of the second millennium B.C. employed the same procedure with regard to their war prisoners. In a war between the cities of Carchemish and Ugarit in which the former was victorious, many prisoners were taken. The king of Ugarit then requested the king of Carchemish to free one of the captives, offering him one hundred shekels as ransom. In answer to this request the king of Carchemish pointed out that he had already sold many prisoners for forty shekels a piece and that he could not be expected to free a high ranking captive for the small sum offered. The Tell el-Amarna letters (14th century B.C.)[2] tell us of war captives being sent as "gifts" by Syrian and Palestinian princes to their Egyptian overlords. The Old Testament tells us that in their conquest of Palestine the Israelites enslaved many of their Canaanite enemies.

No sooner was this practice of enslaving foreigners established than it was carried over and applied to natives themselves. Man became a commodity and the total exploitation of his physical strength served as a new source of profit. Although captives of war and imported foreign slaves made up a substantial part of the slave population of the Ancient Near East, the bulk of the Babylonian, Assyrian, Canaanite, and Hebrew slaves originally came from the ranks of the free-born native population. The native-born slaves were recruited from the following three sources: sale of minors by their parents, voluntary self-sale by adults, and enslavement of defaulting debtors.

Poor parents who were either unable to support their children or

---

[1]Main collection of law in Mesopotamia, named after the Babylonian king of the eighteenth century B.C.

[2]Correspondence uncovered at Tell Amarna in Egypt between Egyptian pharaohs and Syro-Palestinian rulers.

were in need of money sold their offspring in the market. These sales were transacted in two ways: (1) unconditional sale; that is, the parent(s) handed the child over to the buyer and in return received the purchase price "in full," and (2) conditional sale or sale-adoption; that is, the parent(s) received the price and the sold minor was adopted by the purchaser. We have documentary evidence showing that the practice of the sale of minors was in use throughout the history of Babylonia and Assyria. Our evidence from Syria and Palestine, however, is very inadequate. Still, there are enough references to prove that this practice was also prevalent there. The Tell el-Amarna letters tell us that some people were forced to sell their children in order to procure food. From the Old Testament we learn that parents sold their daughters into conditional slavery (Ex. 21:7-11); that creditors seized the children of their deceased debtors (II Kings 4:1); and that debt-ridden farmers were forced to hand over their sons and daughters as slaves (Nehemiah 5:5).

The evidence of the existence of the second method of sale, namely, the sale of young girls into conditional slavery, comes from Nuzi[3] and Palestine. Nuzian and Hebrew parents often sold their daughters with the condition that the purchaser give them into marriage when the girls will have reached puberty. In Nuzi this type of sale was drawn up in the form of a fictitious adoption. The general scheme of a Nuzian sale-adoption contract runs as follows: (1) Preamble: Contract of daughtership and daughter-in-lawship. A has given his daughter B "into daughtership and daughter-in-lawship" to C. (2) Conditions: After [B has] reached puberty C shall give B into marriage either to a free-born man or to a slave. (The free-born man may be the purchaser himself, one of his sons, or a stranger "in the gate." In case the girl is given into marriage to one of her purchaser's slaves, she must remain in her owner's house as long as she lives.) (3) Price: The sum paid by the purchaser to the girl's father. The condition that the girl be married was fundamental. Fathers took the precaution to safeguard for their daughters a continuous marital status by inserting in the sale document a special clause (in case the condition was that the girl be married to a slave) to the effect that should her first slave-husband die, her master would give her into marriage to another one of his slaves. In some documents provisions are made for four husbands and in one for as many as eleven: "If ten of her husbands have died, in that case to an eleventh into wife-hood she shall be given."

This Nuzian practice had its parallel in Palestine. A section of the earliest Old Testament slave legislation, that of Exodus 21:7-11 reads:

[3]Nuzi was a city in Assyria.

If a man sells his daughter to be an *amah* ("handmaid, female slave"), she shall not leave as the slaves do (i.e., in the seventh year). If her master dislikes her, although he had appointed her (as wife) for himself, then shall he let her be redeemed; to sell her (as a wife) to a stranger he shall have no power for he has dealt deceitfully with her. But if he has appointed her for his son, he shall treat her in the manner of daughters. If he takes to himself another (wife), he shall not diminish her food, her clothing, and her conjugal rights. If he does not do these three (things) to her, then she shall go out free without compensation.

In view of the Nuzian practice, this Biblical law represents a fragment of a series of enactments which originally dealt with all cases of conditional sales of young girls. The section before us deals, to use the Nuzian terminology, with a "daughtership and daughter-in-lawship" sale. The conditions as set forth in this case are: (1) that the master himself marry the girl (hence the prohibition of treating her like a slave woman or selling her into marriage to a stranger); (2) in case he refuses, after she had reached puberty, to abide by the stipulation in the contract on the ground that the girl now does not find favor in his eyes, he may take recourse to one of the following alternatives: (a) he may let her be redeemed, (b) he may give her as wife to one of his sons, or (c) he may retain her as his concubine. Should he refuse, however, to comply with any of these alternatives open to him; then, as a penalty for breach of contract, "she shall go out free without compensation. ". . .

Poverty or debt drove people to sell their children first and then themselves into slavery. In the absence of any state or community help for those driven from the soil by war, famine, or economic misfortune, a man or woman had only one recourse to save himself from starvation, and that was self-sale into slavery. Voluntary self-sale was a common phenomenon especially among strangers. From Nuzi we possess a number of documents relating to self-enslavement. These documents concern themselves mostly with the Habiru,[4] who not being able to find employment entered "of their own free will," singly or with their families, into the state of servitude. The term "servitude" is here used advisedly in preference to "slavery," because legally most of the Habiru self-sale cases in Nuzi differ fundamentally from the self-sale documents of Babylonia. In Babylonia the person who sold himself received his purchase price and as a result he became a slave, the property of another man. But in Nuzi no purchase price is paid to those who "sell themselves." The Habiru enter voluntarily into the state of servitude in exchange for food, clothing, and shelter. . . . These Habiru then, retain some kind of legal personality for in some documents it is

---

[4]Possible ancestors of the Hebrews.

expressly stated that only after desertion will they "be sold for a price," that is, be reduced to slavery.

Of all the ancient law codes, the Old Testament alone mentions the case of self-sale or voluntary slavery. Ex. 21:2-6 and Deut. 15:16-17 deal with the case of a Hebrew debtor-slave who refuses "to go out" after his six year term of service has been completed because he loves his master, his wife, and his children. The law provides that such a man (who prefers slavery with economic security to freedom with economic insecurity) shall have his ear bored through and shall remain a slave "forever." Leviticus 25:39-54 deals with a free Hebrew who, because of poverty, is forced to sell himself. In this case, the law provides that such a man, regardless of the fact that he had sold himself for ever, shall be freed in the year of the jubilee.

Although slaves were recruited from various indigenous and foreign sources, the basic source of supply for the ever mounting number of slaves in the Ancient Near East was the native defaulting debtor. Insolvency could be the result of many causes, such as drought, war, etc., against which the individual was powerless to act, but one of the chief factors leading to the foreclosure of property and man was unquestionably the exorbitant interest rate charged on loans. The average rate of interest in Ancient Babylonia was 20-25% on silver and 33 1/3% on grain. Assyria had no fixed or average rate. In Late Assyria the usurer had a free hand in determining the rate of interest. Interest on money varied from 20% to as high as 80% per annum. In addition to this general type there were two other kinds of loans current in Babylonia and Assyria. These were loans granted without interest by the temples and the landlords to their tenant-farmer and loans on which interest was charged only after the date of maturity. In the latter case the interest was enormous. In Babylonia the double of the principal, that is, 100% was charged; in Neo-Babylonia[5] we find 40% and also 100%; and in Late Assyria 100% and even 141% was charged. In Nuzi the average interest rate seems to have been 50% "till after the harvest." There is no information in the Old Testament as to the rate of interest charged in Palestine. From the injunction against the taking of interest from a fellow Hebrew we may infer that a higher interest rate was charged and that Palestine was no exception to the rule.

The fate of the defaulting debtor was slavery. The creditor had the right to seize him and sell him into slavery. It was at this unlimited power of the creditor, which tended to reduce large numbers of free-born people into slavery, that ... laws ... of the Hammurabi Code

---

[5]Period of the eleventh dynasty (626–539 B.C.), when Babylonia achieved its greatest power.

were aimed. These laws demand that the defaulting debtor or his free-born pledge shall be released after three years of compulsory service. The right of seizure of the defaulting debtor by his creditor was in like manner exercised in Palestine. In II Kings 4:1-2 the creditor seized the children of a deceased debtor and the widow appealed to Elisha for help: "The creditor has come to take unto him my children as slaves." This practice of seizure and the subsequent sale into slavery of the unsolvent debtor is reflected in the prophetic literature: "Because they have sold the righteous for a pair of sandals" (Amos 2:6), and "Which of my creditors is it to whom I have sold you?" (Isaiah 50:1). Nehemiah 5:1 ff. shows that creditors foreclosed the land of their defaulting debtors and reduced pledged children to slavery. Like the Hammurabi Code, the Old Testament codes (Ex. 21:2-3 and Dt. 15:12-18) sought to arrest the power of the creditor by demanding that the Hebrew defaulting debtor should be released after six years of compulsory labor.

Legally the slave was considered a chattel. He was a commodity that could be sold, bought, leased, or exchanged. In sharp contrast to the free man, his father's name was almost never mentioned; he had no genealogy, being a man without a name. . . . Family ties were disregarded in the disposal of slaves. Husbands were separated from their wives, wives were sold without their husbands, and even young children were not spared. The only exception made was in the case of infants "at the breast" who were sold with their mothers.

Babylonia had a class legislation but it was not a caste state. The inequality and discrimination before the law, displayed in the Hammurabi Code in regard to the three main classes which constituted Babylonian society, were based not on race or birth but primarily on wealth. To be sold or to sell oneself into slavery, because of poverty or indebtness, was a misfortune that could befall any man. This new status, however, was not irrevocable. The fact that the slave could, theoretically at least, be freed, made him a member of a low, dependent class, but not a member of a caste. However, as long as he remained a slave, he was subject to the wearing of a visible property mark. . . . It may have been an incised mark upon the forehead, a tattooed sign upon some visible part of the body, or a small tablet of clay or metal hung on a chain around the neck, wrist, or ankle. In the Neo-Babylonian period the prevailing custom of marking slaves was to tattoo the name of the owner (and in case of a temple slave the symbol of the god) on the wrist of the slave. There is no evidence that the Assyrian slave was marked. . . .

The Biblical law prescribes that he who voluntarily submits to perpetual slavery shall have his ear pierced with an awl (Ex. 21:6; Dt. 15:17). . . . We may, therefore, conclude that just as in Babylonia, the

Palestinian slaves were marked with a property sign either in the form of a suspended tag attached to the ear, or with a tattoo mark bearing the owner's name on the wrist.

While, legally, the slave was a mere chattel, classed with movable property, both law and society were forced to take into consideration the constantly self-asserting humanity of the slave. We thus have the highly contradictory situation in which on the one hand, the slave was considered as possessing the qualities of a human being while on the other hand, he was recognized as being void of the same and regarded as a mere "thing." The slave's status as a chattel, deprived of any human rights, was clearly and unmistakably emphasized in his relation to a third party. If injured, maimed, or killed by a third party, his owner was compensated for the loss, not the slave. The Biblical legislation mentions only the case of a slave who was killed by a goring ox and provides that the owner shall be compensated for his loss (Ex. 21:32).

. . . The slave's fate was in fact in his master's hand. Beatings and maltreatment of slaves seem to have been . . . common. . . . The Biblical legislation does not prohibit the maltreatment of a Hebrew slave by his master "for he is his money." It is only when the slave dies immediately (within three days) as a result of the beating that the master becomes liable to punishment (Ex. 21:20-21). In Ancient Babylonia a runaway slave was put in chains and had the words "A runaway, seize!" incised upon his face. The Hammurabi Code decrees the death penalty for those who entice a slave to flee from his master and also for those who harbor a fugitive slave. Furthermore, a reward of two shekels is promised to anyone who captures a fugitive slave and brings him back to his master.

The Old Testament slave legislations (Ex. 21, Dt. 15, Lev. 25) do not mention the case of the fugitive slave although the tendency to run away was prevalent in Palestine as it was in the adjacent countries. . . . Fugitive slaves were extradited when they fled into foreign countries (I Kings 2:39 f.). In view of these facts how should the Deuteronomic ordinance (chap. 23:16) "You shall not deliver a slave unto his master who escapes to you from his master" be interpreted? It is a most extraordinary law for its application in life would have spelled the end of slavery in Palestine. Perhaps this ordinance should be explained from a national-economic point of view. It was most probably drawn up in favor of Hebrew slaves who had fled from foreign countries. If this interpretation be correct, then the Deuteronomic law would have its parallel in . . . the Hammurabi Code according to which a native Babylonian slave who had been sold into a foreign country and fled from there was set free by the state. . . .

The slave enjoyed certain privileges which neither law nor society could deny him. According to the Hammurabi Code a slave could marry a free-born woman and a female slave could become her master's concubine. In both cases the children born of such unions were free. The slave could amass a peculium[6] and enjoy it during his life-time, though legally it belonged to his master. And finally the slave could be manumitted. The Hammurabi Code recognizes four legal ways by which a slave received his freedom ipso facto: (1) wives and children sold, or handed over as pledges, are to be freed after three years of service . . . ; (2) a slave concubine and her children become free after the death of the master . . . ; (3) children born of a marriage between a slave and a free woman are free . . . ; and (4) a native Babylonian slave bought in a foreign country and brought back to Babylonia is unconditionally freed. . . . In addition to these laws which applied only to certain classes and to specific cases of slaves, there were two other ways of manumission: release by adoption and by purchase. Release by adoption was, like that by purchase, a business transaction. . . . The manumitted slave entered into a sonship (or daughtership) relation to his former master and took upon himself the obligation to support him as long as he lived. After the death of the manumitter, the fictitious relationship and the very real material support were terminated and the "son" became completely free. If the adopted slave failed to live up to his promise of support, that is, repudiated his "parents" by saying "you are not my father" or/and "you are not my mother," the adoption was annulled and the "son" reverted to his former slave status. The difference between release by adoption with the condition to support the manumitter (or release with the condition of support without adoption) and that of release by purchase is that in the former case the released slave still remains in a state of dependency to his former master and becomes completely free only after the death of his former master, while in the second case, the slave severs all connections with his master and becomes immediately and irrevocably free.

According to the Biblical law there were five ways by which a Hebrew slave obtained his freedom. These were: (1) a debtor-slave is freed after six years of service (Ex. 21:2, Dt. 15:12); (2) he who sold himself into slavery is to be freed in the year of the jubilee (Lev. 25); (3) a free-born girl who was sold by her father with the condition that her master or his son marry her, is to be freed if the master refuses to abide by the conditions of the sale (Ex. 21:7-11); (4) by injury (Ex. 21:26-27); and (5) by purchase (Lev. 25:47 ff.). The six-years service limit of the defaulting debtor has its parallel in the Hammurabi Code . . . which demands the release of a debtor-slave in the fourth year. We have no evidence to prove that the Hammurabi law was ever enforced in Ancient

[6]Small savings.

Babylonia. We have hundreds of documents showing that this law was not enforced in Neo-Babylonia. Debtors were foreclosed and sold into slavery if the loans were not paid on the date of maturity. In view of the fact that we have no private documents from the Biblical period we cannot say whether the law of release of the debtor-slave was enforced in Palestine. . . . The law of the release of the Hebrew slave in the year of the jubilee is part of a great land reform utopia according to which all land, whether sold or given as security, must revert to its original owners in the year of the jubilee. . . . Was the law of the jubilee ever enforced in life? The sages of the Talmud[7] were very much in doubt about it. The law of release by injury presents considerable difficulties. The meaning of the law is, of course, quite clear. The loss of limb, as a result of beatings administered by the master, is considered sufficient ground for meriting release. . . . It seems . . . that the only plausible interpretation . . . would be to assume that the law . . . applies to the Hebrew defaulting debtor. From the point of view of the law, the Hebrew defaulting debtor is not a slave at all but merely a debtor temporarily in the service of his creditor. When such a debtor is permanently injured by his creditor, the loss of limb is considered to be the equivalent of the amount of the debt and hence he is to be released.

There were three main classes of slaves in the Ancient Near East, viz., state slaves, temple slaves, and privately owned slaves. Of these, the first group, recruited from war prisoners, was economically the most important. In Babylonia and Assyria the state slaves, with the assistance of corvee[8] gangs and hired laborers, constructed roads, dug canals, erected fortresses, built temples, tilled the crown lands, and worked in the royal factories connected with the palace. The small city-states of Syria and Palestine also had their state slaves. In the El-Amarna period (c. 1400 B.C.) Syrian and Palestinian "kings" sent large numbers of slaves and war captives . . . as gifts to their Egyptian overlords. . . . That this institution existed in Palestine from the days of David down to the period of Nehemiah and Ezra is attested by the numerous references to the state slaves in the Old Testament. Since this class of slaves (recruited from war captives and from the tribute paying Canaanites) was officially created by Solomon, they were appropriately called *abde Shelomo* ("Solomon's slaves"). Once formed, this class of state slaves remained in existence until the end of the Judaean kingdom.[9] . . . The end of independent statehood marked also the end of the institution of slavery.

[7]The books of Jewish law.
[8]Forced labor.
[9]586 B.C.

Already at the dawn of history the Babylonian temple with its vast wealth constituted the richest agricultural, industrial, and commercial single unit within the community. It was a well organized and efficiently run corporation controlling extensive tracts of land, enormous quantities of raw material, large flocks of cattle and sheep, sizeable amounts of precious metal, and a large number of slaves. This was also true, though to a lesser degree, of the Assyrinan, Syrian, and Palestinian temples. . . .

Temple slaves were recruited from two sources: prisoners of war who were presented to the temples by victorious kings, and dedications of slaves by private individuals. The sanctuaries in Palestine recruited their slaves from the same sources. After the successful campaign against the Midianites,[10] Moses is reported to have taken one of every five hundred, or one of every fifty, prisoners, and presented them as a gift to Yahweh (Num. 31:25ff.). Joshua made the Gibeonites[11] "hewers of wood and drawers of water in the sanctuary" (chap. 9:21ff.). . . . We have no evidence to prove that privately owned slaves were dedicated to temples in Palestine. The case of young Samuel who was dedicated to the sanctuary of Shiloh, however, shows that this practice was known in Palestine. While the number of state and temple slaves was very large, their economic role must not be overestimated. The state . . . employed them in non-competitive enterprises and the temple used them primarily for menial work. In its two main branches of activity, agriculture and industry, the temple employed mostly free-born people and not slaves. The land was cultivated by free-born tenant-farmers, and free-born artisans worked in the shops.

Unlike Egypt, where the land belonged to the crown, private ownership of land was the rule in the Sumero-Semitic countries. The case of the Israelite farmer Naboth who chose death in preference to selling his ancestral plot to king Ahab was characteristic of the attitude of all peasantry in the Ancient Near East. With the exception of the large holdings of the crown and the temples, the land was owned by two classes of people: small farmers and large landowners. Since the land property of the average farmer was small and his family large there was no great need for outside help either in the form of hired laborers or of slaves. The labor situation was, of course, different in the second group. These large estates had to be worked with hired help. This help, however, was only to a very small degree drawn from the ranks of hired laborers and slaves. It was drawn primarily and overwhelmingly from the ranks of the dispossessed peasantry croppers. . . . Instead of

[10]Semitic people who invaded southern Palestine after 1200 B.C.

[11]Palestinian people who derived their name from the city, Gibeon.

buying, maintaining, and guarding considerable numbers of unwilling slaves, the large landowners (and to a degree even the kings and the temples) preferred to lease parcels of their land to free-born tenant-farmers. . . . Like the upper class in the cities, well-to-do farmers owned slaves and employed them on the land, but slave labor was not a decisive factor in the agricultural life of the Ancient Near East.

The counterpart of the free-born tenant-farmer in agriculture was the free-born "hired laborer" in industry. There was, of course, great competition between free laborers and slaves in the field of unskilled labor, but the skilled fields were dominated by the free artisans. The reasons for this phenomenon, that is, the small number of slave artisans in the Ancient Near East, were: (1) the apprenticeship period lasted from two to six years, a period during which the slave not only did not bring in any profit, but the owner had to spend money for his upkeep; (2) the number of slaves in well-to-do families averaged from one to three and therefore only a few of them could be spared to be used as an investment with a view to future returns; and finally (3) the general unwillingness of the employer to hire slaves because they could not be trusted to operate with expensive tools even when they possessed the skill to handle them. We thus come to the conclusion that the role played by slaves in the skilled industries was very insignificant indeed. Ancient Near Eastern craftsmanship was the product of free labor.

We have seen that economically the Ancient Near Eastern civilization was not based on slave labor. We have also seen that society was unable to maintain consistently the legal fiction that the slave was a mere chattel, and hence some freedom was accorded to him. There remains one more aspect to be considered and that is the attitude of religion toward slavery, the ownership of man by man. Nowhere in the vast religious literature of the Sumero-Accadian world is a protest raised against the institution of slavery, nor is there anywhere an expression of sympathy for the victims of this system. The Old Testament justifies perpetual slavery of the Canaanites, but demands the release of the Hebrew defaulting debtor in the seventh year and of those who sold themselves in the year of the jubilee. The first case—the release of the debtor-slave after a limited term of service—has a parallel in the earlier Hammurabi Code which also demands the release of the defaulting debtor. But in the second case where the release is demanded of even those who had sold themselves voluntarily into slavery, we have for the first time an open denial of the right of man to own man in perpetuity. This denial of the right of possession of man by man is as yet restricted to Hebrews only (cf. Nehemiah 5:8), but it is a step which no other religion had taken before. The first man in the Ancient Near East who raised his voice in a sweeping condemnation of slavery as a cruel and inhuman institution, irrespective of nationality and race, was the philosopher Job. His was a condemnation based on the moral concept of the inherent brotherhood of man, for

> "Did not He that made me in the womb make him (the slave) also? And did not One fashion us in the womb?" (31:15)

The Roots of Restriction: Women in Early Israel

CAROL MEYERS

The Israelites were only one of many Semitic cultures in the ancient Near East. Although of minor contemporary importance in the ancient world, their contribution to the development of Western civilization bulks large. Their Holy Books, incorporated into the Christian scriptures as the Old Testament, had a great influence on the evolution of Christianity. Thus, for some purposes, historians must pay more attention to them than to cultures of greater contemporary significance (such as the Hittites, for example). One such purpose is to understand the position of females in Western civilization, which has often had a religious basis. Whether the Judeo-Christian god should be referred to as "he" or "she" (or "it," for that matter); whether women should be priests, ministers, or rabbis; and whether the Bible gives its authority to a male-dominated society—these are issues that evoke passionate responses all across the ideological spectrum, from feminist firebrands at one end to Protestant fundamentalists and orthodox Roman Catholics on the other.

Carol Meyers argues persuasively that those wishing to examine current issues in light of the Bible must study the Bible in its social context, not quote scriptural passages in a historical vacuum. In this selection, she examines the condition of women during the formative period of Israelite society and discovers changes there that are of great importance for the history of women.

Meyers finds Palestine in the Late Bronze Age (approximately 1500–1200 B.C.) to have been an agrarian peasant society experiencing a population crisis set off by war, famine, and, especially, plague. What evidence does she use to determine the existence and effects of widespread disease? According to Meyers, the recurring epidemics and the resultant rise in mortality made an increase in the birth rate essential to maintain the population level and bring unoccupied land in Palestine into cultivation. Women thus had an elevated status: they assumed public roles and were sought after as brides. Fertility had to be encouraged. What happened to prostitution in such an atmosphere? And, when the demographic crisis passed, why was the Israelite priesthood reserved exclusively for males? Why were women subjected to a male domination that would largely prevail for the next three thousand years, down to and including the present-day Western world? Did other Near Eastern societies influence the transformation of women's roles in Hebrew culture?

Meyers interprets several biblical texts in many ways that might outrage certain people today. How does she view, for example, the creation myth in

Carol Meyers, "The Roots of Restriction: Women in Early Israel," *The Biblical Archeologist* 41(1978): 91–103.

Genesis? Does Meyers' feminism lead her to use the Bible to serve her own personal beliefs, or, conversely, does the idea of a more egalitarian social role for women properly emerge from the evidence she has studied?

Perhaps the most significant advances in biblical studies in recent years have come about through scholarly efforts to understand the emergence of earliest Israel in terms of its social dynamics. These studies of the origins of Israel, which benefit from anthropological analyses of group behavior and social change, have made it no longer possible to contemplate the beginnings of biblical tradition as theological history or as a kind of history of holiness. To do so, however pious the motives, becomes instead an ultimately irrelevant and perhaps irreverent exercise because it precludes full understanding. Rather, attempts at reconstructing any period in antiquity must involve a sensitivity to and consideration of the entire historico-cultural spectrum which affects human development, individually or in groups.

In a sense, the archeological investigation of the Near Eastern past has fostered and facilitated such a contextual approach to scriptural study by making available the nonbiblical materials essential for understanding . . . Israelite life. Ironically, however, the very archeological revolution which brought about this new approach also became a serious stumbling block for reaping all its benefits. Archeology, enamored of and elated by its intimate contact with objects of the past, felt itself in possession of the key to that past.

For a long time, the exclusive preoccupation with material relics and political history (with little or no attention given to the social dynamics of the people who left these relics) limited the analysis of the archeological data. But now, aided by the insights of modern social science, archeologists are in a better position to understand how ancient societies operated and what social and ideological changes occurred in the ancient world. Such investigation of the process of social change has been particularly important in the study of ancient Israel's early formation and development.

If the emerging interest in reconstructing all dimensions of a crucial era in human history is to be expressed in thorough and balanced investigation, then it cannot do what so much of social history in the past has done, systematically omit or slight roughly half of humanity. In the natural and social history of any groupings of people, that slighted half—women—controls certain unique and critical functions within society. As the Harvard social historian David Herlihy puts it . . . , women "carry the new generation to term, sustain children in early life, and usually introduce the young to the society and culture of which they will be a part. [In other words,] women begin the processes through which human cultures strive to achieve what their individual members cannot—indefinite life, immortality. "

Moreover, an examination of women's social position, while eminently cogent and important for historical studies of any period of our past, becomes extraordinarily pertinent and imperative in consideration of biblical society, especially in its formative and idealistic period. That specific period is the one in which the biblical community was formed, a community bound in covenant with God through the leadership of Moses and developing its characteristic and radical new way of looking at the world and living in that world in the few centuries after Moses and before the Davidic monarchy. Archeologically, this formative period coincides with the closing decades of the Late Bronze Age[1] and the beginning centuries of the Iron Age in Palestine.[2]

Concern for the evaluation of the social history of women during the early Israelite experience arises from the fact that this is precisely the period in which one of the major—if not *the* major—transitions occurred in the history of the position and role of women in the world. Some three thousand years of male dominance in western civilization, and in particular in religious institutions, have clouded our vision of the prebiblical past and have led to the belief that the exclusion of females from regular leadership, at least in public and/or religious life, has been the norm in human history. Further, it is difficult, psychologically and emotionally, to deal with the fact that the liberating principles of Mosaic Israel and the egalitarian society which it set about to establish turned out to be the very force which caused a dramatic turnabout in the history of women. Yet, as more and more material from the ancient world becomes available to us, the realities of the status of women in ancient societies, including their role in religious life, are becoming invisible behind the double veils of time and misapprehension. It is being discovered that the position and role of women in society were very different in some crucial areas than what they became subsequent to the beginnings of Israel.

For this reason, historical investigation of women in the formative period is crucial—otherwise, it is too easy to fall prey to the same process which has led to the gradual later misogynistic interpretations of early biblical tradition. It is needed to correct anachronistic interpretations as well as statements taken out of context and used dogmatically and authoritatively. Moreover, this investigation is necessary to iden-

---

[1]1500–1200 B.C.

[2]After 1200 B.C.

tify long-ignored functional aspects within a particular setting of what appears in the finished scriptural product as God-given sanctions.

Perhaps this point should be illustrated before proceeding. The story of the Garden of Eden provides a parade example. The creation and early activity of male and female in the stories of the glorious garden of Genesis 2 and 3 present no evidence for any theory of subordination or inferiority of women. . . . If anything, the opposite is true. Read on its *own terms*, the story shows a primordial male who appears passive and submissive. This ancient tale must have been understood this way for centuries as part of Hebraic literature.

Yet somewhere and gradually along the line, complicated socio-historical processes which cannot be traced here turned the edenic paradigm upside down. By the late biblical period, a rash of religious literature, produced by Jewish groups and nascent Christianity, took considerable pains to demonstrate that Eve was significant not as the source of life but rather as the source of death and evil . . . ; and, therefore, women needed to be controlled and dominated by their male relatives.

Centuries of such distortions resulting from later interpretations of biblical traditions involving women can come to an end, it seems, only by going back to the very beginnings of Israelite life, where it all began, for it was then that there occurred a shift in sexual roles and meanings that was to have a profound and longlasting impact.

In order to appreciate this shift, it is important to consider the Near Eastern cultures from which Israel emerged. The Bronze Age religious ideology against which early Israel rebelled was the product of a millennia-old pattern. The pantheons of divine beings exalted in Near Eastern antiquity represented those forces in nature upon which humanity was dependent but which humanity could not bring under its control. Fertility was an underlying concern. Fertility cults in which mankind could create mechanisms for exerting control of or at least influence over the capricious natural world helped resolve humanity's helplessness and anxiety in the face of rainfall or lack of it, sunshine or lack of it, blight or lack of it. The great goddesses and great gods mated, producing a union of earth and sun/rain necessary for productivity. Cultic rehearsals of this union, while tantalizingly vague and distant in the face of our modern inquiries, seem to have taken place within the context of what is described by the suitably ill-defined phrase "fertility cult."

The particular Canaanite manifestations of such religous ideologies are generally described in terms of their relationship to the impoverished—in comparison to Egypt or Mesopotamia—resources of Syria-Palestine. Thus, the emphasis tends to focus on fertility of the soil. Yet, concerns with human fertility should not be excluded from the parameters of pagan religion. Particularly in the land bridge of Syria-Palestine, and in contrast to the relative stability and tendency toward over-population in the Nile and Tigris-Euphrates Valleys . . . , frequent outbreaks of violence added to the natural insecurity of continuity of human life. The repeated prophetic warning in the Bible about the triple threat of death through famine, pestilence, and the sword bears with it an urgent concern for the continued existence of any socio-political group. Warfare, famine, and disease were inseparable forces posing continuing threats to human existence. At certain times of upheaval, population losses far exceeded natural increment. Depopulation—i.e., decline in population—was a recurrent fact, archeologically demonstrable. . . . Population growth, or the replenishing of the population, was a societal aim, expressed in Israel's national literature . . . , in the face of considerable environmental odds at various points in ancient Palestinian history.

The biological experiences of women in Bronze Age society were undoubtedly keyed to this fact. The fertility cults, however crucial for a concept of agrarian productivity, were no less crucial for notions of human reproduction. In this respect, the Near Eastern high goddesses are featured in the role of the Great Mother . . . who some believe was the Supreme Deity in the ancient world until the 3rd millennium. She was revered and worshipped as the creator of all life, as the female principle which was the source of life. The mystery of birth and of all creation and thus of human existence itself rested in the female power. From as early as the Old Stone Age onward (ca. 30,000 B.C.E.), material expressions of religious convictions by which mankind sought to establish links to that divine creative power have been found. . . . In the various places of Stone Age habitation, the naked female figurines with exaggerated sexual features are found, attesting to the cult of the Great Goddess. By the time of the great Bronze Age cultures of the Near East, the supreme Mother Goddesses were joined by or in some cases superseded by male deities. The societal changes connected with this transition have yet to be explored fully, since they are difficult to retrieve from the limited documents of antiquity.

Though it seems that a patriarchal system replaced the primary role of women in primitive agricultural-village economies, reflected in and by the Great Mother Goddess, the primacy of the female role nonetheless persisted in a limited way. The documents of Mesopotamian and Egyptian cities show women involved in a variety of public positions and occupations, exercising economic and legal rights, which varied from place to place and from time to time. . . .

Perhaps the most important arena within which women functioned was the temple precincts. Priestesses served the gods and goddesses.

The elaborate temple organizations within the royal bureaucracy included female public servants. Some women functioned sexually in such occupations, as references to cultic sexuality attest. Others, it seems, refrained from sexuality and marriage by entering a sort of convent existence. . . . It is hard to reconstruct the social motivations for such a choice. Indeed, certain kinds of temple service for women may have represented an escape from the high risks and rigors of childbirth, and/or a way to provide economically for unmarried women. At least certain ancient mythographers saw a relationship between those cultic roles for women involving chastity and celibacy and the social necessity for population control by the limiting of child bearing. . . .

Whatever the social dynamics of the situation in the Late Bronze Age urban life may have been, certain facts about female roles emerge, dimly perhaps, but nonetheless apparent. The persistent strengths and appeals of Anat and Asherah[3] (cf. Judg 3:7; 1 Kgs 15:13; 2 Chr 15:16; 1 Kgs 18:19; Jer 44:15ff.) in the Bible itself are evidence of the active participation of women in cultic, and therefore public life. Women served female deities and the female deities served women in return, affirming their ultimate creative worth. . . .

Early Israel . . . constituted a radical break with the city-state feudalism and nation-state imperialism of Late Bronze Age Palestine. The description of the motivation for that break (and the implementation through the Yahwistic covenant of a liberating replacement for city-state oppression) involves an understanding of the life of the peasantry. . . . The natural resources of Palestine could no longer support an inflated urban bureaucracy and thus Late Bronze Age peasant society was at the subsistence level. The so-called Israelite "Conquest" represents a return of a full share of the products of the land to the people, a cessation of the continuous draining contributions to urban bureaucracies. . . . The fact that nearly half of the Book of Joshua is concerned with tribal allotments points to the early Israelite recovery of land so that the people, according to their several tribes, would derive the benefit therefrom.

Claims to land ownership, once the domination of the city-based power structures had broken down, depended to a great extent on populating that land. . . . In addition to establishing local tribal control over certain territories formerly administered by oppressive city-states, the Israelite federation was about to embark upon the settlement of previously uninhabited territories, namely, the core of Palestine, the central hill country.

This territory was largely empty throughout the Bronze Age . . . ,

---

[3]Anat was the Canaanite goddess of war; Asherah was a Canaanite goddess of fertility.

except for occasional, usually minor sites near springs and in valleys. Generally poor soil and scarce water supplies precluded significant habitation, particularly if Bronze Age urban centers siphoned off a portion of the meager productivity. If anything, the Late Bronze Age had even fewer settlements in the hill country proper than the preceding Middle Bronze Age centuries.

The ensuing Iron Age, in sharp contrast, brought an extensive settlement of this region. . . . Technically, the storage of water in lined cisterns, the introduction of iron in the manufacture of farm tools, and the development of methods of agricultural terracing resolved the environmental difficulties and made this demographic shift possible. An enormous amount of human energy was required, however, to clear land that had never before been tilled, to build homes and villages where none had existed, and to cut back forests and undergrowth that had covered the landscape since time immemorial.

This understanding of early Israel as an agrarian peasantry is dispelling the romantic attachment to the notion of a biblical bias in favor of some sort of bedouin or seminomadic ideal. This understanding likewise affords an appreciation of a biblical undercurrent protesting—understandably so considering the ills and evils of Late Bronze Age Canaanite cities—against urban life. The first city, for example, is built according to biblical tradition by the first murderer (Gen 4:17). The concluding exhortation of the Holiness Code (Lev 26:25-26) links city life—"if you gather within your cities"—with famine, disease, and violence. The negative experience underlying such a bias is clear. The orientation of the period of the judges rejected the urban centers. In this process there arose social sanctions, ultimately translated into law, which strengthened and favored land-based village life.

Against this background, what was life like for roughly half the population? How were women to do their share in espousing and furthering the Yahwistic ideals of a free peasantry? Thus far, two major issues emerge in the attempt to answer these questions. Both of these had dramatic effects upon women and, while seemingly independent of each other, may prove ultimately to be interrelated.

The first issue concerns the biological need for productivity, the need to effect a population increase. Israel was obsessed both with having descendants to inherit its portion and with keeping its landholdings within its kinship-based groups. In investigating this issue, anthropological and paleo-osteological[4] studies which seek to describe fluctuations in ancient populations are extremely valuable. Such studies inevitably lead to descriptions of mortality rates—or life expectancies—in the premodern world. In particular, the analysis of skeletal remains

---

[4]Scientific study of bones that archeologists have found.

from various periods of Palestinian history . . . provides information about life expectancies. Excavations in Palestine have included—and in a sense began with—the investigation of tomb groups. Ironically, the skeletal remains of human beings from these tombs have so far received relatively slight attention; tomb studies have tended to focus on typologies of grave goods or of the tomb chambers themselves. However, although osteological studies have been carried out on relatively small numbers of the actual skeletal remains, the results present valid evidence for general demographic conditions and fluctuations in ancient Palestine, since the results of those studies correspond exceedingly well to the results of similar studies on all premodern populations. . . .

To begin with, the death rate was clearly highest among the preadult population. In one tomb group, 35% of the individuals died before the age of five, and nearly half of the individuals did not survive the age of eighteen. . . . For those who did survive to adulthood, another clear pattern existed: the mortality rate of females in the child-bearing years greatly exceeded that of the males. . . . In a population in which the life expectancy for men would be 40, women would have a life expectancy closer to 30. Consequently, it should not be surprising that the elders of any ancient tribal system were males, since a greater proportion of males would have survived into the chronological seniority which was at the basis of political seniority and leadership. It is no wonder that ancient biologists, Aristotle among them, proclaimed that the males of all species live longer than the females. It is a relatively modern phenomenon that the converse is true for humans. Women in antiquity were a class of humanity in short supply.

Paleo-pathologists have established that the cause of half, if not more, of all deaths, whatever the age of the individual at the time of death, was the presence of endemic parasitic disease, that is, infections which occur in a community more or less all the time without much alteration in their effects from year to year or even century to century. . . . The biblical term "pestilence" . . . seems to be used in reference to such endemic disease. Very young children and old people, being the most susceptible to such infections, were the most likely to succumb. This fact is archeologically evident in the high infant mortality rate as well as in the scarcity of people past forty. To put it bluntly, in normal times, families would have had to produce twice the number of children desired in order to achieve optimal family size.

The outbreak of epidemics, or the *abnormal* occurrence of acute infectious disease, reduced the usual low life expectancy even further. Epidemiological statistics, for historic periods in which records were kept, show the devastating effects of plague upon mortality rates. For example, in the plague-free early medieval years in Europe, life expectancy has been estimated as being between 35 and 40 years.

For the generations during and immediately following the Black Death (1348-49), which introduced an epoch of recurring plagues, the average life expectancy was as low as 17 or 18 years. It took nearly 100 years or more thereafter for life spans to creep back up to around 30. . . .

The Bible has a word that seems to describe such abnormal outbreaks of disease. This word, *maggephah*, normally translated "plague" (as opposed to "pestilence"), appears in several biblical accounts, chiefly in certain nonpriestly narratives of Numbers, and also once in Exodus. Despite the layers of later explanations, these passages have preserved certain critical incidents of Israel's formative period and thus provide important information about public health and population density.

One such episode is Korah's rebellion in Numbers 16. The nature of the violent power struggle within the Israelite camp depicted here is peripheral to the present discussion. What does attract attention is the devastating plague associated with this rebellion in the mind of the biblical writer. The 250 leaders of the Korahites were consumed in a fire coming forth from the Lord. But God's wrath did not stop there; before Moses could carry out his efficacious atoning acts, 14,700 more deaths were recorded. There can be little doubt that this devastating plague, however that large and symbolic-sounding figure is to be interpreted, decimated the nascent community.

Num 21:6 recounts another population loss. In this instance, the actual word *maggephah* is not used. Nonetheless, the description seems to reflect a plague situation: "Then the Lord sent fiery serpents among the people, so that many people of Israel died."

Another passage, Num 11:1-3, while not mentioning plague or pestilence specifically, describes in similar language the effects of the wrath of God at a place called Taberah, which in itself means "Burning.". . . At this particular place God's anger—attributed to the complaining of the people—was kindled and the "fire of the Lord burned among them, and consumed some outlying parts of the camp." The destructive fever of plague, an outbreak of some kind of epidemic disease, seems to be the life situation, theologically interpreted, which gives rise to the association between divine anger and punitive, consuming heat/fire. The text does not give the number of casualties, but the losses in the Israelite camp must have been severe.

Num 14:11 is another relevant text: except for Joshua (who brings back a good report), the spies who had gone into Canaan are said to have died from the plague.

Another incident, the unfortunate sequence of events at Beth Baal Peor . . . , stems from the Mosaic period and is recounted in Numbers 25. In some sort of orgiastic rite, various Israelite men participated in sacrifice to the Baal of Peor (Peor seems to be related to a Hittite word for "fire," which underlies that English word) and in relationships with the local unmarried Midianite girls. God's anger was kindled and turned upon Israel. No fewer than 24,000 people died in that epidemic which broke out among the people.

Exodus 32 provides one additional text dealing with death by plague. In the story of the Golden Calf, a plague caused the loss of an unspecified portion of the population (v 35: "And the Lord sent a plague upon the people, because they made the calf which Aaron made").

Epidemic disease was clearly rampant. This clustering of biblical texts dealing with the age of Moses and using the word "plague" or *maggephah* reflects a public health crisis. Furthermore, nearly every extrabiblical source from the Late Bronze Age indicates the devastation wrought by epidemic infections. . . . A similar situation did not occur again in Palestine until 200-250 years later in the period of the Philistine wars, for which there is another clustering of biblical texts reflecting a plague situation.

The biblical passages cited above as well as the extrabiblical sources mentioned can be associated with what has been identified archeologically as a massive disruption of the urbanized life of the petty kingdoms—or kinglets—in Palestine at the end of the Late Bronze Age. City after city suffered violent destruction. In many cases, if not all, the termination of Bronze Age culture in these cities is marked archeologically by a thick layer of ashes, indicating a conflagration of major proportions.

These burnings of cities, it seems, are an aftermath of military conquest or overthrow rather than a part of it. If anything, military conflicts or guerilla warfare took place outside the city walls, so well constructed were the fortifications of the Late Bronze cities. It is quite possible that the widespread burnings were not so much related to military actions as they were to a kind of primitive and desperate public health measure. The fiery destruction of plagues needed to be fought with fire. Immediately following the recollection of the destructive plague of Baal Peor in Num 31:21-23, the instructions to the Israelite warriors stipulate that "only the gold, the silver, the bronze, the iron, the tin, and the lead, everything that can stand the fire, you shall pass through the fire, and it shall be clean. Nevertheless, it shall also be purified with the water of impurity; and whatever cannot stand the fire you shall pass through the water." Thus, the unconscionable *herem*, or utter destruction of cities as presented in the book of Joshua, perhaps can be seen as a kind of plague control. It is difficult in the western world today, with relatively little experience of such epidemics, to grasp the enormity of the plagues and the staggering death tolls which devastated the premodern world. Yet, the effort must be made to comprehend the drastic measures taken to stop epidemics in light of the ancient context.

Recognition of the existence of a period of widespread plague and death at the end of the Late Bronze Age is crucial, because that factor even more than famine and warfare (or at least in combination with those other two evils) created a life situation—or rather a death situation—of monumental proportions. The measures taken within the emergent Israelite community to deal with this situation are the ones that profoundly affected the lives of the female segment of the population.

Plague severely reduced the population of the peasantry at the time when sheer numbers counted most. The normal difficulties in maintaining rural population in Palestine were compounded dramatically during this period. The biological creativity of females, a matter of vital concern even in normal times because of high infant mortality rates and the often fatal complications of childbearing, was most sorely needed in the aftermath of plagues. The devastation of plague had caused a demographic crisis. The repeated biblical exhortation, "Be fruitful and multiply," is singularly appropriate to this situation.

The strength and solidarity of the family were the basis for the vitality of the restored peasantry in early Israel and its ability to occupy the hill country of Palestine. At the most basic level, Israelite society urgently required a replenishment and even a surge in population to combat the effect of the famine, war, and disease at the end of the Late Bronze Age and to provide the human factor necessary for normal agricultural efforts. Moreover, this need for population increase was intensified as settlement of virgin areas proceeded. In addition to their specifically biological contribution, the full participation of women in the chores of a land-based economy was essential. . . . Further, since males were called away for occasional military duty in the absence of a standing army, the woman's role in managing all aspects of a household would increase.

From all perspectives, then, female creativity and labor were highly valued in early Israel. This female worth was not biological exploitation but rather part of the full cooperation of all elements in society in pursuing the goals of the Israelite people. Further, the early Iron Age experience of Israel was within the liberating matrix of the covenant with Yahweh, which emphasized ethical concerns and sought to maintain all human dignity. The precepts of the Decalogue and the Covenant Code are dedicated passionately against the exploitation of any groups of human beings or even animals. The Fifth Commandment (Exod 20:12) bears this out. Both parents are to be honored, for on the two together depends the existence of Israel. The second part of this commandment is not a vague generality but rather an intrinsic complement of the familiar first half of that commandment ("Honor your father and your mother"). It expresses a hope for continued life and a restoration of public well-being: "that your days may be long in the land which the Lord your God gives you" (i.e., that life expectancies will stabilize above the low level characteristic of plague epochs).

The Bible generally reflects the fact that there were relatively fewer women of child-bearing age than men of the same age, a condition which Israel shared with the rest of the ancient world. Perhaps the existence of the *mohar*, translated variously as "bride price" or "marriage present," illustrates one way in which the community dealt with a shortage of marriageable women. The *mohar* may be a compensation to the bride's family . . . , since a daughter contributed through her work to a parent's household. This bride-gift, a kind of reverse dowry, indicates that grooms had to compete for relatively few brides. Likewise, the financial burden of setting up a new household lay with the male, another indication of the socio-economic dimensions of the shortage of brides. The dowry was rarely if ever bestowed in biblical times. . . . Fathers did not need to entice husbands. (Compare European history: it is perhaps not until the central Middle Ages that a combination of relative peace and a new urban economy brought about a relative increase in female population and led to the reversal of the terms of marriage. Girls became excess economic burdens and fathers gave dowries and paid for weddings to entice young men to take these girls off their hands. . . .)

Beyond this, however, the intensified need for female participation in working out the Mosaic revolution in the early Israelite period can be seen in the Bible. Looking again at Numbers 31, an exception to the total purge of the Midianite population is to be noted. In addition to the metal objects which were exempt from utter destruction, so too were the "young girls who have not known man by lying with him" (Num 31:18). These captives, however, were not immediately brought into the Israelite camp. Instead, they and their captors were kept outside the camp for seven days in a kind of quarantine period. (Note that the usual incubation period for the kinds of infectious diseases which could conceivably have existed in this situation is two or three to six days. . . .) Afterward, they thoroughly washed themselves and all their clothing before they entered the camp. This incident is hardly an expression of lascivious male behavior; rather, it reflects the desperate need for women of childbearing age, a need so extreme that the utter destruction of the Midianite foes—and the prevention of death by plague—as required by the law of the *herem* could be waived in the interest of sparing the young women. The Israelites weighed the life-death balance, and the need for females of child-bearing age took precedence.

Such a source of female population, however, was not to be regularized. Instead, the extraordinary needs for female reproductive power in the tribal period precipitated strong sanctions against the expending of sexual energy in ways that either detracted from the primary reproductive channels or interfered with the strengths of nuclear family life or the transmission of family-based land ownership. The whole array of sexual customs and rules which exist in the Bible and which had the ultimate effect of relegating women to a narrowed and eventually subordinate position in later biblical times are in many cases radical changes from what had existed previously in the ancient world. These changes, which limited human sexual contacts and options, must be reconsidered in light of the demographic crisis of early Israel. Sanctions that eventually became expressed in biblical laws dealing with incest, rape, adultery, virginity, bestiality, exogamy, homosexuality, and prostitution require reexamination and reevaluation within the dynamics of the socio-economic situation . . . and human crisis of the earliest days of Israel. The dimension of purity and polemic in sexual sanctions is not to be ignored; but the role of the concern for repopulation and the need for human resources must also enter the picture.

. . . [P]rogress can tentatively begin by looking at one expression of sexuality and the way the societal pressures of ancient Israel transformed it. Harlotry is a good example, since it leads directly to considering the second major issue which effected the turnabout in the status of women in ancient society.

Until the period of the Judges, the existence of harlotry was an accepted, if not condoned, fact. . . . Courtesans and prostitutes have existed at least since the dawn of recorded history without accompanying moral judgment or moral condemnation of harlotry *per se*. It was a legitimate though not necessarily desirable occupation for some women. In the Genesis story of Judah and Tamar, Tamar is not condemned for her temporary identification as a prostitute nor is Judah condemned for lying with her, except insofar as it signaled an evasion of his responsibilities toward his sons' widow (Genesis 38). Similarly, Rahab the harlot of Jericho is actually a heroine who helped the Israelite spies, in return for which they spared the destruction of her family (Joshua 2 and 6).

By the time that biblical legislation records attitudes toward harlotry, a considerable change had occurred. Lev 19:29 is explicit: "Do not profane your daughter by making her a harlot, lest the land fall into harlotry and the land fall into wickedness." A father was responsible in the patriarchal system for his daughters. He was to limit their choice of occupation. Prostitution was not a possibility. The priorities and values of early Israelite existence had made family-centered life the chief, if not the only, course of action for a young woman.

There was another reason for closing out the option of harlotry in early Israel beside the need to have all available women of child-bearing years integrated into self-sufficient families. Harlotry was closely associated with the special use of sexual energy involved in ritual or cultic prostitution in the nature religions of the ruling urban elites. The efforts to secure productivity in the Israelite village and rural settings were to be separated from the rituals of the fertility cults. . . .

In biblical law, the particular emphasis on the dissociation of the priests from harlotry can only be understood in this context. In Lev 21:7, 14-15, priests are commanded to marry virgins. They are forbidden to marry any of four categories of women (widows, divorcees, "defiled" women, and harlots) whose sexual energies may already have been somewhat dissipated and whose fitness for child-bearing may have been reduced. Harlots in this law are not singled out as detestable or illegal members of society at large. However, in the same passage, the daughters of priests are condemned to burning by fire should they play the harlot (v 9). This extraordinarily strong penalty for prostitution is aimed specifically at women who lived near or in the Israelite sanctuary area, the daughters of priests. It indicates the danger of pagan cultic expression that existed when men and women were together in cultic contexts, a danger that to some extent necessitated the removal of one of the two sexes from cultic services.

In the Bible, it is apparent which sex was barred from cultic leadership, but the reasons for such a limitation have not been properly explored. The priesthood of the Old Testament represents a radical break with the nature of priesthoods in the history of the ancient world; the priesthood of biblical religion is, from the outset, portrayed as a strictly and absolutely male profession.

The traditional answer to the query as to why the priesthood is male no doubt would have invoked the notion that the anthropomorphizing tendencies in the Bible made God out to be a male deity, some sort of macho warrior at one end or loving father at the other end. Male deities would naturally require a male priesthood. This response, however, does not account for the nonsexuality and non-humanity of Yahweh's unity. Gender-oriented language for Yahweh is metaphoric. Furthermore, in addition to the all-too-familiar andromorphic images of Yahweh, there are a multitude of gynomorphic images, once one is open to reading them as such. . . .

Still, the establishment of an exclusively male priesthood was in a sense a natural development at the end of the 2nd millennium. While a few millennia earlier a female priesthood in service of the Great Mother might have been the paradigm, the urban social systems of the Bronze Age were male dominated. Male deities outnumbered the goddesses.

Thus, the kings, priest-kings, and priests were the dominant figures and provided the models for early Israel.

The priesthood before the monarchy was no doubt a decentralized and purposefully limited factor in Israelite life. . . . The egalitarian economy of the reestablished peasantry of the period of the Judges rejected the bureaucratic concentration of wealth that an elaborate priesthood requires. Circumscribed as it may have been, a priesthood nevertheless was established and thus siphoned off some portion of manpower as well as some economic surplus. The possibility of female service within any sort of cultic context could be eliminated purely on the basis of the felt priorities of early Israel in its allocation of human energies. Female energies were desperately needed in the family setting.

Partially as a rejection of the mythological and cultic sexuality of prebiblical religion and its integral connection with the urban power centers, and partly under pressures to concentrate female energies within the home and family, the Israelite priesthood emerged as a male occupation. In ancient Israel, thousands and thousands of years of female participation in this most crucial of all public institutions, an organized cultus, were terminated. One might speculate as to whether or not women might have entered priestly roles once the demographic crisis had been alleviated were it not for the continued attraction of the nature religions, particularly after the establishment of the monarchy and the return to urbanized life as the dominant mode in Israel. Thereafter, the social sanctions against such occupations as harlotry achieved the status of divine laws governing a priesthood distinct from that of pagan religion. From that situation, the moral judgment upon this kind of female sexual activity outside the family was only a step away.

Two major factors, then, appear to be primary causes of the profound change that occurred in the status and role of women during premonarchic Israel. The first was the drastic need to concentrate human energy, male and female, into family life and into intensive cultivation of the land, including considerable new territory. This meant a sex ethic, the primary societal function of which was to make childbirth and sexuality within the family crucial societal goals. Reversing the devastating depopulation of the Late Bronze Age was an enormous task. Likewise, setting about to reemphasize an agricultural economy and even to settle new lands was a highly ambitious goal which called for the labor of women alongside men. The second factor was the rejection of pagan deities in favor of a covenant with a unified Yahweh. In cultic terms, this translated into a male priesthood. Neither of these two factors *within their contemporary settings* was particularly exploitive of male or female. On the contrary, strong female involvement in an agricultural economy and in the birth of new generations of Israelites who would literally inherit the land meant that women and men worked together to achieve the covenant ideals.

It is indeed an irony of history, then, that this very tight channeling of female (and male) energies into domestic affairs, which was a liberating event in its own time, became, ultimately, the *raison d'etre* for continued and exclusive confinement of female energies to that sphere. A functional restriction to meet a demographic crisis of critical proportions became so deeply engrained that with the passing of the crisis the restrictions remained and ultimately became the basis for ideologies of female inferiority and subordination. Once the pattern of female nonparticipation in other spheres of life—the priesthood in particular— became established, society adhered to it in ways that became limiting and oppressive to women.

This was particularly true with the establishment of the monarchy and a gradual movement toward urbanization. Women became less important as participants in economic survival and therefore diminished in social importance. They were also the first to suffer when urban centers drained off the productivity of the land to support the monarchy and the military. Hard work under conditions of increased population and reduced nutrition meant even greater risks of death in childbirth. The introduction of slave wives under the phenomenal growth of the Davidic empire no doubt also contributed to the reduced importance of women. Thus, it was likely during the monarchy that the functional restriction of women in society became transformed gradually into an ideological restriction.

By this time opportunities for women to assume important roles outside the family, possibilities which had previously existed in ancient Near Eastern societies, especially in aristocratic settings, had been more or less systematically cut off in order to meet the needs of the emerging tribal groups. Yet, the exceptional leadership of women such as Miriam, Deborah, and the wise women of Tekoa and Abel are not so much "dynamic remnants" . . . of a time when women could hold natural positions of leadership within a community, positions which would have been based in inherited power structures (as queens or nobelwomen); rather, their existence gives testimony to an epoch of liberation in which stratified hereditary leadership was abolished and anyone, women included, could rise to irregular positions of authority. They thus testify to the notion that God's spirit or wisdom could rest upon any individual, male or female, and grant that person a certain role in the community based on personal gifts rather than on social status. However, the patriarchal structuring of egalitarian tribal life with males as heads of families and of clans, with the elders of Israel becoming leaders, meant that women did not participate regularly in any sort of public political life, just as they did not perform priestly duties. The famous biblical women just enumerated occupy a kind of exceptional position, a nonrecurring charismatic participation. It is important to recognize that, however limited in proportion to males such leadership may have been, it was thoroughly accepted and acceptable. No notion of female inferiority intruded.

The reality for most women in the biblical world during the monarchy was one in which the vigorous equal-participation momentum of the formative period had been transformed gradually into a kind of masculine domination and female subordination. However, various biblical texts . . . which depict a kind of harmonious ideal or balance between the sexes preserve the premonarchic situation. The Creation chapters of Genesis are one such text. Both the Priestly account in Genesis 1 ("So God created mankind in his image, . . . male and female he created them. And God blessed them and said to them, 'Be fruitful and multiply and fill the earth and subdue it' [i.e., till it together]"; Gen 1:27–28) and the Yahwistic narrative in Genesis 2 affirm the existence of two sexes as the necessary and equal balance in human life.

In addition to the creation stories, the Song of Songs presents a beautiful picture of human love. The maiden and lad share in their desire and love for the other and in their expression of that love. Ideas of subordination or inferiority of one or the other are absent.

Also, the very anthropomorphism of Yahweh, when it is expressed in feminine terms, reaffirms and encourages the female in society. God, the warrior, is only half of the Exodus event. God, the provider of food and water, sustains the refugees from Egypt until they reach arable land. The redemptive acts of Yahweh, to be sure, are neither masculine nor feminine, but the working out of those actions involved the might that masculine imagery expresses and also the love and caring—and even the giving birth—that feminine imagery conveys.

These latter, then, are the biblical ideals which can provide the balance in the endeavor to sort out the realities of life for women in ancient Israel amidst the social changes through which it passed. . . .

The Semiotics[1]
of Food in the Bible

JEAN SOLER

At one time nearly all Jews kept kosher, that is, lived according to very specific dietary laws. Many Jews, though certainly not a majority, maintain kosher house-holds today. Yet the reasons for these customs and laws have remained somewhat of a puzzle. In this bold piece, Jean Soler attempts first to provide a coherent explanation for the dietary prohibitions in the Old Testament and second to use this evidence about cooking to understand the collective way of thinking of the ancient Hebrews.

Soler begins at the beginning, in Paradise. What type of food was available there, according to the Old Testament? How did food mark the difference between man and god? What historical turning point constituted the rupture between the eating habits in Paradise and those after the expulsion? What other historical developments occurred to refine the Hebrews' conception of proper food?

After describing the major changes in the evolution of the dietary prohibitions, Soler organizes the totality of customs around the themes of cleanness, purity, and order. How does Soler use these concepts to describe what meats could be eaten, why some animals are forbidden, or what fish and birds are edible? Are these explanations satisfactory? Is Soler justified in expanding the discussion to the Hebrews' notion of the priesthood, homosexuality, incest, and even to what clothes one is permitted to wear? Finally, what do the dietary laws of the Hebrews tell us about the nature of their god? Why was Mosaic logic bound to reject the god-man, Jesus?

How can we explain the dietary prohibitions of the Hebrews? To this day these rules—with variations, but always guided by the Mosaic laws—are followed by many orthodox Jews. Once a number of false leads, such as the explanation that they were hygienic measures, have been dismissed, the structural approach appears to be enlightening.

Lévi-Strauss[2] has shown the importance of cooking, which is pecu-

[1]The science of signs, which holds that all cultural artifacts have meaning.

[2]Twentieth-century anthropologist. He is the leading exponent of structuralism, which maintains that cultural elements have meaning only as part of an entire system of relationships.

Jean Soler, "The Semiotics of Food in the Bible," in *Food and Drink in History*, edited by Robert Forster and Orest Ranum (Baltimore and London: The Johns Hopkins University Press, 1979), 126–138.

liar to man in the same manner as language. Better yet, cooking is a language through which a society expresses itself. For man knows that the food he ingests in order to live will become assimilated into his being, will become himself. There must be, therefore, a relationship between the idea he has formed of specific items of food and the image he has of himself and his place in the universe. There is a link between a people's dietary habits and its perception of the world.

Moreover, language and dietary habits also show an analogy of form. For just as the phonetic system of a language retains only a few of the sounds a human being is capable of producing, so a community adopts a dietary regime by making a choice among all the possible foods. By no means does any given individual eat everything; the mere fact that a thing is edible does not mean that it will be eaten. By bringing to light the logic that informs these choices and the interrelation among its constituent parts—in this case the various foods—we can outline the specific characteristics of a society, just as we can define those of a language.

. . . [T]he dietary laws of the Hebrews have been laid down in a book, the Book, and more precisely in the first five books of the Bible, which are known as the Torah to the Jews and the Pentateuch to the Christians. This set of writings is composed of texts from various eras over a wide span of time. But to the extent that they have been sewn together, have coexisted and still do coexist in the consciousness of a people, it is advisable to study them together. I shall therefore leave aside the historical dimension in order to search for the rules that give cohesion to the different laws constituting the Law. . . .

Man's food is mentioned in the very first chapter of the first book. It has its place in the plan of the Creation: "Behold, I have given you every plant yielding seed which is upon the face of all the earth, and every tree with seed in its fruit; you shall have them for your food" (Gen. 1:29), says Elohim. Paradise is vegetarian.

In order to understand why meat eating is implicitly but unequivocally excluded, it must be shown how both God and man are defined in the myth by their relationship to each other. Man has been made "in the image" of God (Gen. 1:26–67), but he is not, nor can he be, God. This concept is illustrated by the dietary tabu concerning the fruit of two trees. After Adam and Eve have broken this prohibition by eating the fruit of one of these trees, Elohim says: "Behold, the man has become like one of us, knowing good and evil; and now, lest he put forth his hand and take also of the tree of life, and eat, and live forever" (Gen. 3:22). This clearly marked distance between man and God, this fundamental difference, is implicitly understood in a threefold manner.

First, the immortality of the soul is unthinkable. All life belongs to

God, and to him alone. God is Life, and man temporarily holds only a small part of it. We know that the notion of the immortality of the soul did not appear in Judaism until the second century B.C. and that it was not an indigenous notion.

Secondly, killing is the major prohibition of the Bible. Only the God who gives life can take it away. If man freely uses it for his own ends, he encroaches upon God's domain and oversteps his limits. From this it follows that meat eating is impossible. For in order to eat an animal, one must first kill it. But animals, like man, belong to the category of beings that have within them "a living soul." To consume a living being, moreover, would be tantamount to absorbing the principle that would make man God's equal.

The fundamental difference between man and God is thus expressed by the difference in their foods. God's are the living beings, which in the form of sacrifices (either human victims, of which Abraham's sacrifice represents a relic, or sacrificial animals) serve as his "nourishment" according to the Bible; man's are the edible plants (for plants are not included among the "living things"). Given these fundamental assumptions, the origins of meat eating constitute a problem. Did men, then, at one point find a way to kill animals and eat them without prompting a cataclysm?

This cataclysm did indeed take place, and the Bible does speak of it. It was the Flood, which marks a breaking point in human history. God decided at first to do away with his Creation, and then he spared one family, Noah's, and one pair of each species of animal. A new era thus began after the Flood, a new Creation, which coincided with the appearance of a new dietary regime. "Every moving thing that lives shall be food for you; as I gave you the green plants, I give you everything" (Gen. 9:3).

Thus, it is not man who has taken it upon himself to eat meat; it is God who has given him the right to do so. And the cataclysm does not come after, but before the change, an inversion that is frequently found in myths. Nevertheless, it must be understood that meat eating is not presented as a reward granted to Noah. If God has wanted "to destroy all flesh in which is the breath of life from under heaven" (Gen. 6:17), it is because man has "corrupted" the entire earth: "and the earth was filled with violence" (Gen. 6:17), in other words, with murder. And while it is true that he spares Noah because Noah is "just" and even "perfect" (Gen. 6:9), the human race that will come from him will not escape the evil that had characterized the human race from which he issued. The Lord says, after the Flood: "I will never again curse the ground because of man, for the imagination of man's heart is evil from his youth; neither will I ever again destroy every living creature as I have done" (Gen. 8:21). In short, God takes note of the evil that is in man. A few verses later, he gives Noah permission to eat animals. Meat eating is given a negative connotation.

Yet even so, it is possible only at the price of a new distinction; for God adds the injunction: "Only you shall not eat flesh with its life, that is, its blood" (Gen. 9:4). Blood becomes the signifier of the vital principle, so that it becomes possible to maintain the distance between man and God by expressing it in a different way with respect to food. Instead of the initial opposition between the eating of meat and the eating of plants, a distinction is henceforth made between flesh and blood. Once the blood (which is God's) is set apart, meat becomes desacralized—and permissible. The structure remains the same, only the signifying elements have changed.

At this stage the distinction between clean and unclean animals is not yet present, even though three verses in the account of the Flood refer to it. Nothing is said that would permit Noah to recognize these two categories of animals, and this distinction is out of place here, since the power to eat animals he is given includes all of them: "Every moving thing that lives shall be food for you."

It is not until Moses appears that a third dietary regime comes into being, one that is based on the prohibition of certain animals. Here we find a second breaking point in human history. For the covenant God had concluded with Noah included all men to be born from the sole survivor of the Flood (the absence of differentiation among men corresponded to the absence of differentiation among the animals they could consume), and the sign of that covenant was a cosmic and hence universal sign, the rainbow (Gen. 9:12–17). The covenant concluded with Moses, however, concerns only one people, the Hebrews; to the new distinction between men corresponds the distinction of the animals they may eat: "I am the Lord your God, who have separated you from the peoples. You shall therefore make a distinction between the clean beasts and the unclean; and between the unclean bird and the clean; you shall not make yourselves abominable by beast or by bird or by anything with which the ground teems, which I have set apart for you to hold unclean" (Lev. 20:24-25). The signs of this new covenant can only be individual, since they will have to become the distinctive traits of the Hebrew people. In this manner the Mosaic dietary code fulfills the same function as circumcision or the institution of the Sabbath. These three signs all involve a cut (a cut on the male sex organ: a partial castration analogous to an offering, which in return will bring God's blessing upon the organ that ensures the transmission of life and thereby the survival of the Hebrew people; a cut in the regular course of the days: one day of every seven is set apart, so that the sacrificed day will desacralize the others and bring God's blessing on their work;

a cut in the *continuum* of the created animals—added to the already accomplished cut, applying to every animal, between flesh and blood, and later to be strengthened by an additional cut within each species decreed to be clean between the first-born, which are God's, and the others which are thereby made more licit). The cut is at the origin of differentiation, and differentiation is the prerequisite of signification.

Dietary prohibitions are indeed a means of cutting a people off from others, as the Hebrews learned at their own expense. When Joseph's brothers journeyed to Egypt in order to buy wheat, he had a meal containing meat served to them: "They served him by himself, and them by themselves, for the Egyptians might not eat bread with the Hebrews, for that is an abomination to the Egyptians" (Gen. 43:32). It is likely that the nomadic Hebrews already had dietary prohibitions but, according to Biblical history, they began to include their dietary habits among the defining characteristics of their people only after the exodus, as if they were taking their model from the Egyptian civilization.

Dietary habits, in order to play their role, must be different; but different from what? From those, unquestionably, of the peoples with whom the Hebrews were in contact. Proof of this is the famous injunction: "You shall not boil a kid in its mother's milk," for here a custom practiced among the people of that region was forbidden. Yet the dietary regime of the Hebrews was not contrary to the regimes of other peoples in every point; had this been the case they would have had very few things to eat! Why, then, did they strictly condemn some food items and not others? The answer must not be sought in the nature of the food item. . . . A social sign—in this case a dietary prohibition— cannot be understood in isolation. It must be placed into the context of the signs in the same area of life, together with which it constitutes a system; and this system in turn must be seen in relation to the systems in other areas, for the interaction of all these systems constitutes the sociocultural system of a people. The constant features of this system should yield the fundamental structures of the Hebrew civilization or— and this may be the same thing—the underlying thought patterns of the Hebrew people.

One first constant feature naturally comes to mind in the notion of "cleanness," which is used to characterize the permissible foods. In order to shed light on this notion, it must first of all be seen as a conscious harking back to the Origins. To the extent that the exodus from Egypt and the revelation of Sinai represent a new departure in the history of the World, it can be assumed that Moses—or the authors of the system that bears his name—felt very strongly that this third Creation, lest it too fall into degradation, would have to be patterned after the myth of Genesis. . . . Man's food would therefore be purest of all if it were patterned as closely as possible upon the Creator's intentions. Now the myth tells us that the food originally given to man was purely vegetarian. Has there been, historically, an attempt to impose a vegetarian regime on the Hebrews? There is no evidence to support this hypothesis, but the Bible does contain traces of such an attempt or, at any rate, of such an ideal. One prime trace is the fact that manna, the only daily nourishment of the Hebrews during the exodus, is shown as a vegetable substance. . . . Moreover, the Hebrews had large flocks, which they did not touch. Twice, however, the men rebelled against Moses because they wanted to eat meat. The first time, this happened in the wilderness of Sin: "Would that we had died by the hand of the Lord in the land of Egypt, when we sat by the flesh-pots" (Exod. 16:3). God thereupon granted them the miracle of the quails. The second rebellion is reported in Numbers (11:4): "O that we had meat to eat," wail the Hebrews. God agrees to repeat the miracle of the quails, but does so only unwillingly and even in great wrath. . . . And a great number of the Hebrews who fall upon the quails and gorge themselves die on the spot. Here, as in the myth of the Flood, meat is given a negative connotation. It is a concession God makes to man's imperfection.

Meat eating, then, will be tolerated by Moses, but with two restrictions. The tabu against blood will be reinforced, and certain animals will be forbidden. The setting apart of the blood henceforth becomes the occasion of a ritual. Before the meat can be eaten, the animal must be presented to the priest, who will perform the "peace offering," in which he pours the blood upon the altar. This is not only a matter of separating god's share from man's share; it also means that the murder of the animal that is to be eaten is redeemed by an offering. Under the elementary logic of retribution, any murder requires in compensation the murder of the murderer; only thus can the balance be restored. Since animals, like men, are "living souls," the man who kills an animal should himself be killed. Under this basic assumption, meat eating is altogether impossible. The solution lies in performing a ritual in which the blood of the sacrificial animal takes the place of the man who makes the offering. "For the life of the flesh is in the blood, and I have given it for you upon the altar to make atonement for your souls; for it is the blood that makes atonement, by reason of the life" (Lev. 17:11). But if a man kills an animal himself in order to eat it, "bloodguilt shall be imputed to that man; he has shed blood; and that man shall be cut off from among his people" (Lev. 17:4); that is, he shall be killed. The importance of the blood tabu thus becomes very clear. It is not simply one prohibition among others; it is the *conditio sine qua non*[3] that makes meat eating possible. . . .

[3]Essential condition.

As for the prohibition of certain animals, we must now analyze two chapters (Lev. 11 and Deut. 14) devoted to the distinction between clean and unclean species. Neither of these texts, which are essentially identical, provides any explanation. The Bible only indicates the particular traits the clean animals must possess—though not always; for when dealing with the birds, it simply enumerates the unclean species.

The text first speaks of the animals living on land. They are "clean" if they have a "hoofed foot," a "cloven hoof," and if they "chew the cud." The first of those criteria is clearly meant to single out the herbivorous animals. The Hebrews had established a relationship between the foot of an animal and its feeding habits. . . .

But why are herbivorous animals clean and carnivorous animals unclean? Once again, the key to the answer must be sought in Genesis, if indeed the Mosaic laws intended to conform as much as possible to the original intentions of the Creator. And in fact, Paradise was vegetarian for the animals as well. The verse dealing with human food, "I have given you every plant yielding seed which is upon the face of all the earth, and every tree with seed in its fruit; you shall have them for your food," is followed by a verse about the animals (and here, incidentally, we note a secondary differentiation, serving to mark the distance between humankind and the various species of animals): "And to every beast of the earth, and to every bird of the air, and to everything that has the breath of life, I have given every green plant for food" (Gen. 1:29-30). Thus, carnivorous animals are not included in the plan of the Creation. Man's problem with meat eating is compounded when it involves eating an animal that has itself consumed meat and killed other animals in order to do so. Carnivorous animals are unclean. If man were to eat them, he would be doubly unclean. The "hoofed foot" is thus the distinctive trait that contrasts with the claws of carnivorous animals—dog, cat, felines, etc.—for these claws permit them to seize their prey. Once this point is made, the prohibition against eating most of the birds that are cited as unclean becomes comprehensible: they are carnivorous, especially such birds of prey as "the eagle," which is cited at the head of the list.

But to return to the beasts of the earth. Why is the criterion "hoofed foot" complemented by two other criteria? The reason is that it is not sufficient to classify the true herbivores, since it omits pigs. Pigs and boars have hoofed feet, and while it is true that they are herbivores, they are also carnivorous. In order to isolate the true herbivores it is therefore necessary to add a second criterion, "chewing the cud." One can be sure that ruminants eat grass; in fact, they eat it twice. In theory, this characteristic should be sufficient to distinguish true herbivores. But in practice, it is difficult to ascertain, especially in wild animals, which can properly be studied only after they are dead. Proof

of this is the fact that the hare is considered to be a ruminant by the Bible
(Lev. 11:6 and Deut. 14:7), which is false; but the error arose from mis-
taking the mastication of the rodents for rumination. This physiological
characteristic therefore had to be reinforced by an anatomical criterion,
the hoof, which in turn was strengthened by using as a model the hoof
of the ruminants known to everyone: cows and sheep. (In the myth
of Creation, livestock constitutes a separate category, distinct from the
category of wild animals. There is no trace of the domestication of animals; livestock was created tame). This is why clean wild animals must
conform to the domestic animals that may be consumed; as it happens,
cows and sheep tread the ground on two toes, each encased in a layer
of horn. This explains the third criterion listed in the Bible: the "cloven
hoof."

One important point must be made here: The presence of the criterion "cloven hoof" eliminates a certain number of animals, even though
they are purely herbivorous (the horse, the ass, and especially the three
animals expressly cited in the Bible as "unclean": the camel, the hare,
and the rock badger). A purely herbivorous animal is therefore not automatically clean. This is a necessary, though not a sufficient condition.
In addition, it must also have a foot analogous to the foot that sets the
norm: that of domestic animals. Any foot shape deviating from this
model is conceived as a blemish, and the animal is unclean.

This notion of the "blemish" and the value attributed to it is eluci-
dated in several passages of the Bible. Leviticus prohibits the sacrificing
of animals, even of a clean species, if the individual animal exhibits
any anomaly in relation to the normal type of the species: "And when
any one offers a sacrifice of peace offerings to the Lord, to fulfill a
vow or as a freewill offering, from the herd or from the flock, to be
accepted it must be perfect; there shall be no blemish in it. Animals
blind or disabled or mutilated or having a discharge or an itch or scabs,
you shall not offer to the Lord or make of them an offering by fire
upon the altar to the Lord" (Lev. 22:21). This prohibition is repeated in
Deuteronomy. . . . The equation is stated explicitly: the blemish is an
evil. A fundamental trait of the Hebrews' mental structures is uncovered here. There are societies in which impaired creatures are considered divine.

What is true for the animal is also true for man. The priest must be
a wholesome man and must not have any physical defects. The Lord
says to Aaron (Lev. 21:17-18): "None of your descendants throughout
their generations who has a blemish may approach to offer the bread of
his God. For no one who has a blemish shall draw near, a man blind or
lame, or one who has a mutilated face or a limb too long, or one who
has an injured foot or an injured hand, or a hunchback, or a dwarf, or
a man with a defect in his sight or an itching disease or scabs or crushed

testicles. . . . " The men who participate in cultic acts must be true men: "He whose testicles are crushed or whose male member is cut off shall not enter the assembly of the Lord" (Deut. 23:1). To be whole is one of the components of "cleanness"; eunuchs and castrated animals are unclean.

To the blemish must be added alteration, which is a temporary blemish. Periodic losses of substance are unclean, whether they be a man's emission of semen or a woman's menstruation (Lev. 15). The most unclean thing of all will therefore be death, which is the definitive loss of the breath of life and the irreversible alteration of the organism. And indeed, death is the major uncleanness for the Hebrews. It is so strong that a high priest (Lev. 21:11) or a Nazirite[4] (Num. 6:6-7) may not go near a dead body, even if it is that of his father or his mother, notwithstanding the fact that the Ten Commandments order him to "honor" them.

The logical scheme that ties cleanness to the absence of blemish or alteration applies to things as well as to men or animals. It allows us to understand the status of ferments and fermented substances. I shall begin with the prohibition of leavened bread during the Passover. The explanation given in the Bible does not hold; it says that it is a matter of commemorating the exodus from Egypt when the Hebrews, in their haste, did not have time to let the dough rise (Exod. 12:34). If this were the reason, they would have been obliged to eat poorly leavened or half-baked bread; but why bread without leavening? In reality, even if the Passover is a celebration whose meaning may have changed in the course of the ages . . . it functions as a commemoration of the Origins, a celebration not only of the exodus from Egypt and the birth of a nation but also of the beginning of the religious year at the first full moon after the vernal equinox. The Passover feast is a sacrifice of renewal, in which the participants consume the food of the Origins. This ritual meal must include "bitter herbs," "roasted meat," and "unleavened bread" (Exod. 12:8). The bitter herbs must be understood, it would seem, as the opposite of vegetables, which are produced by agriculture. Roast meat is the opposite of boiled meat, which is explicitly proscribed in the text (Exod. 12:9): the boiling of meat, which implies the use of receptacles obtained by an industry, albeit a rudimentary form of it, is a late stage in the preparation of food. As for the unleavened bread, it is the bread of the Patriarchs. Abraham served cakes made of fine meal to the three messengers of God on their way to Sodom (Gen. 18:6). . . . But unleavened bread is clean not only because it is the bread of the Origins. It is clean also and above all because the flour of which it is made is not changed by the ferment of the leavening: it is true

---

[4]An ancient Hebrew who took certain religious vows.

to its natural state. This interpretation allows us to understand why fermented foods cannot be used as offerings by fire: "No cereal offering which you shall bring to the Lord shall be made with leaven; for you shall burn no leaven nor any honey as an offering by fire to the Lord" (Lev. 2:11). A fermented substance is an altered substance, one that has become other. Fermentation is the equivalent of a blemish. Proof *a contrario* is the fact that just as fermentation is forbidden, so salt is mandatory in all offerings (Lev. 2:13). Thus, there is a clear-cut opposition between fermentation, which alters a substance's being, and salt, which preserves it in its natural state. Leavened bread, honey, and wine all have the status of secondary food items; only the primary foods that have come from the hands of the Creator in their present form can be used in the sacred cuisine of the offering. It is true, of course, that wine is used in cultic libations. But the priest does not consume it; indeed he must abstain from all fermented liquids before officiating in order to "distinguish between the holy and the common, and between the clean and the unclean" (Lev. 10:10). Fermented liquids alter man's judgment because they are themselves altered substances. The libation of wine must be seen as the parallel of the libation of blood, which it accompanies in burnt offerings. Wine is poured upon the alter exactly like blood, for it is its equivalent in the plant; wine is the "blood of the grapes" (Gen. 49:11, etc.).

To return to my argument, then, the clean animals of the earth must conform to the plan of the Creation, that is, be vegetarian; they must also conform to their ideal models, that is, be without blemish. In order to explain the distinction between clean and unclean fish, we must once again refer to the first chapter of Genesis. In the beginning God created the three elements, the firmament, the water, and the earth; then he created three kinds of animals out of each of these elements: "Let the waters bring forth swarms of living creatures, and let birds fly above the earth across the firmament of the heavens" (Gen. 1:20); "Let the earth bring forth living creatures according to their kinds, cattle and creeping things and beasts of the earth according to their kinds" (Gen. 1:24). Each animal is thus tied to one element, and one only. It has issued from that element and must live there. Chapter 11 of Leviticus and Chapter 14 of Deuteronomy reiterate this classification into three groups: creatures of the earth, the water, and the air. Concerning the animals of the water, the two texts only say: "Everything in the waters that has fins and scales . . . you may eat." All other creatures are unclean. It must be understood that the fin is the proper organ of locomotion for animals living in the water. It is the equivalent of the leg in the animal living on land and of the wing in the animal that lives in the air. . . . [T]he animals of the earth must walk, fish must swim, and birds must fly. Those creatures of the sea that lack fins and do not move about (mullusks) are unclean. So are those that have legs and can walk (shellfish), for they live in the water yet have the organs of a beast of the earth and are thus at home in two elements.

In the same manner, scales are contrasted with the skin of the beasts of the land and with the feathers of the birds. As far as the latter are concerned, the Biblical expression "birds of the air" must be taken quite literally; it is not a poetic image but a definition. In the formulation "the likeness of any winged bird that flies in the air" (Deut. 4:17), the three distinctive traits of the clean bird are brought together: "winged," "which flies," and "in the air." If a bird has wings but does not fly, (the ostrich, for instance, that is cited in the text), it is unclean. If it has wings and can fly but spends most of its time in the water instead of living in the air, it is unclean (and the Bible mentions the swan, the pelican, the heron, and all the stilted birds). Insects pose a problem. "All winged animals that go upon all fours are an abomination to you," says Leviticus (11:20). This is not a discussion of four-legged insects, for the simple reason that all insects have six. The key expression is "go upon" [walk]. The insects that are meant here are those that "go upon all fours," like the normal beasts of the earth, the quadrupeds. Their uncleanness comes from the fact that they walk rather than fly, even though they are "winged." The exception mentioned in Leviticus (11:21) only confirms the rule: no uncleanness is imputed to insects that have "legs above their feet, with which to leap on the earth." Leaping is a mode of locomotion midway between walking and flying. Leviticus feels that it is closer to flying and therefore absolves these winged grasshoppers. Deuteronomy, however, is not convinced and prohibits all winged insects (14:19).

Leviticus also mentions, toward the end, some unclean species that cannot be fitted into the classification of three groups, and it is for this reason, no doubt, that Deuteronomy does not deal with them. The first of these are the reptiles. They belong to the earth, or so it seems, but have no legs to walk on. "Upon your belly you shall go," God had said to the serpent (Gen. 3:14). This is a curse. Everything that creeps and goes on its belly is condemned. These animals live more under the earth than on it. They were not really "brought forth" by the earth, according to the expression of Genesis 1:24. They are not altogether created. And like the serpent, the centipede is condemned (Lev. 11:30) in the expression "whatever has many feet" (Lev. 11:42). Having too many feet or none at all falls within the same category; the clean beast of the earth has four feet, and not just any kind of feet either, as we have seen.

All these unclean animals are marked with a blemish; they show an anomaly in their relation to the element that has "brought them forth" or to the organs characteristic of life, and especially locomotion, in that element. If they do not fit into any class, or if they fit into two classes at once, they are unclean. They are unclean because they are unthinkable. At this point, instead of stating once again that they do not fit into the plan of the Creation, I should like to advance the hypothesis that the dietary regime of the Hebrews, as well as their myth of the Creation, is based upon a taxonomy in which man, God, the animals, and the plants are strictly defined through their relationships with one another in a series of opposites. The Hebrews conceived of the order of the world as the order underlying the creation of the world. Uncleanness, then, is simply disorder, wherever it may occur.

Concerning the raising of livestock and agriculture, Leviticus 19:19 mentions the following prohibition: "You shall not let your cattle breed with a different kind." A variant is found in Deuteronomy 22:10: "You shall not plow with an ox and an ass together." The reason is that the animals have been created (or classified) "each according to its kind," an expression that is a very leitmotif of the Bible. Just as a clean animal must not belong to two different species (be a hybrid), so man is not allowed to unite two animals of different species. He must not mix that which God (or man) has separated, whether the union take place in a sexual act or only under the yoke. Consider what is said about cultivated plants: "You shall not sow your field with two kinds of seeds" (Lev. 19:19), an injunction that appears in Deuteronomy as: "You shall not sow your vineyard with two kinds of seed." The same prohibition applies to things: "nor shall there come upon you a garment of cloth made of two kinds of stuff" (Lev. 19:19). In Deuteronomy 22:11, this becomes: "You shall not wear a mingled stuff, wool and linen together." Here the part plant, part animal origin of the material further reinforces the distinction. In human terms, the same schema is found in the prohibition of mixed marriages—between Hebrews and foreigners— (Deut. 7:3), and also in the fact that a man of mixed blood (offspring of a mixed marriage) or, according to a different interpretation, a bastard (offspring of adultery) may not enter the assembly of the Lord (Deut. 23:3). This would seem to make it very understandable that the Hebrews did not accept the divine nature of Jesus. A God-man, or a God become man, was bound to offend their logic more than anything else. Christ is the absolute hybrid.

A man is a man, or he is God. He cannot be both at the same time. In the same manner, a human being is either a man or a woman, not both: homosexuality is outlawed (Lev. 18:22). The prohibition is extended even to clothes: "A woman shall not wear anything that pertains to a man, nor shall a man put on a woman's garment" (Deut. 22:4). Bestiality is also condemned (Lev. 18:20) and, above all, incest (Lev. 18:6 ff.): "She is your mother, you shall not uncover her nakedness." This tautological formulation shows the principle involved here: once a woman is defined as "mother" in relation to a boy, she cannot also be something else to him. The incest prohibition is a logical one. It thus becomes evident that the sexual and the dietary prohibitions of the Bible are coordinated. This no doubt explains the Bible's most mysterious prohibition: "You shall not boil a kid in its mother's milk" (Exod. 23:19 and 34:26; Deut. 14:21). These words must be taken quite literally. They concern a mother and her young. They can be translated as: you shall not put a mother and her son into the same pot, any more than into the same bed. Here as elsewhere, it is a matter of upholding the separation between two classes or two types of relationships. To abolish distinction by means of a sexual or culinary act is to subvert the order of the world. Everyone belongs to one species only, one people, one sex, one category. And in the same manner, everyone has only one God: "See now that I, even I, am he, and there is no God beside me" (Deut. 32:39). The keystone of this order is the principle of identity, instituted as the law of every being.

The Mosaic logic is remarkable for its rigor, indeed its rigidity. It is a "stiff-necked" logic, to use the expression applied by Yahveh to his people. It is self-evident that the very inflexibility of this order was a powerful factor for unification and conservation in a people that wanted to "dwell alone." On the other hand, however, the Mosaic religion, inseparable as it is from the sociocultural system of the Hebrews, could only lose in power of diffusion what it gained in power of concentration. Christianity could only be born by breaking with the structures that separated the Hebrews from the other peoples. It is not surprising that one of the decisive ruptures concerned the dietary prescriptions. Matthew quotes Jesus as saying: "Not what goes into the mouth defiles a man, but what comes out of the mouth, this defiles a man" (15:11). Similar words are reported by Mark, who comments: "Thus he declared all foods clean" (7:19). The meaning of this rejection becomes strikingly clear in the episode of Peter's vision at Jaffa (Acts 10): a great sheet descends from heaven with all kinds of clean and unclean animals in it, and God's voice speaks: "Rise, Peter; kill and eat." Peter resists the order twice, asserting that he is a good Jew and has never eaten anything unclean. But God repeats his order a third time. Peter's perplexity is dispelled by the arrival of three men sent by the Roman centurion Cornelius, who is garrisoned in Caesarea. Cornelius wants to hear Peter expound the new doctrine he is propagating. And Peter, who had hitherto been persuaded that Jesus' reform was meant only for the Jews, now understands that it is valid for the Gentiles as well. He goes to Caesarea, shares the meal of a non-Jew, speaks to Cornelius, and baptizes him. Cornelius becomes the first non-Jew to be converted to Christianity. The vision in which the distinction between clean and unclean foods was abolished had thus implied the abolition of the distinction between Jews and non-Jews.

From this starting point, Christianity could begin its expansion, grafting itself onto the Greco-Roman civilization, which, unlike the Hebrew civilization, was ready to welcome all blends, and most notably a God-man. A new system was to come into being, based on new structures. This is why the materials it took from the older system assumed a different value. Blood, for instance, is consumed by the priest in the sacrifice of the Mass in the form of its signifier: "the blood of the grape." This is because the fusion between man and God is henceforth possible, thanks to the intermediate term, which is Christ. Blood, which had acted as an isolator between two poles, now becomes a conductor. In this manner, everything that Christianity has borrowed from Judaism . . . , must in some way be "tinkered with," to use Lévi-Strauss's comparison.

By contrast, whatever variations the Mosaic system may have undergone in the course of history, they do not seem to have shaken its fundamental structures. This logic, which sets up its terms in contrasting pairs and lives by the rule of refusing all that is hybrid, mixed, or arrived at by synthesis and compromise, can be seen in action to this day in Israel, and not only in its cuisine.

II

CLASSICAL GREECE AND ROME

In the eighteenth century, Voltaire, the French intellectual, wrote that true glory belonged only to "four happy ages" in the history of the world. The first was ancient Greece, specifically the fifth and fourth centuries B.C., and the second the Rome of Julius Caesar and Augustus, the first emperor. (The other two were Renaissance Italy and Louis XIV's France.) Voltaire praised classical Greece and Rome because he believed them civilized, holding the arts, literature, and refined living in high regard. The social historian, aware of the underside of classical civilization, can not share Voltaire's optimism.

There is much to admire in Greek civilization. The political competition of its many independent city-states promoted some freedom of experimentation, evidenced in art, in literature, and in the diversities of philosophical schools. Greek social life too was more heterogeneous than that of other cultures, such as Egypt. Yet Greek civilization was rooted in slavery and oppression; life was difficult for most Greeks, and warfare among the city-states was constant. The Olympics and other games show that the Greeks admired brawn as well as brains. In Athens, the cradle of democracy and the center of classical Greek civilization, well-to-do males virtually locked up for life their wives and daughters. The family in Athens is as distinguishable historically as its philosophy and art are distinguished. Greek sexuality is also rather notorious and the subject of much speculation, if not myths.

Law, engineering, architecture, and literature bear witness to the glories of Rome; gladiatorial combats, mass murders in the Colosseum, and the persecution of Christians remind us of the streak of cruelty that was as Roman as an aqueduct. The Roman historian Tacitus remarked about imperial conquest: "Where they make a desert, they call it peace." Slavery, infanticide, and other brutalities were basic features of life in Roman civilization, as they had been in Greece and in the Near East. Women in Rome, however, seem to have fared better than their counterparts in Athens.

Certainly much has been written about the legacy of Greece and Rome to Western civilization. One of the great developments in classical Rome was the rise of Christianity, which has had a tremendous impact on Europe until the present day. Historians have documented the classical heritage in the Middle Ages, in seventeenth-century France, eighteenth-century Germany, Victorian Britain, and in American universities. When the term renaissance is applied to a culture such as twelfth-century France or fifteenth-century Italy, it refers to a rebirth of classical art, literature, style. But social structures, people's attitudes, and lifestyles are as significant and as rich as the cultural developments more commonly studied.

Organized Greek Games

WILLIAM J. BAKER

The history of sports, like women's history and the history of children, is a relatively new area of interest for scholars. A culture's games and its perception of sports and athletes tell us much about that society's priorities, values, and beliefs. No longer do historians view sports and leisure activities as unimportant.

Virtually everyone knows that the modern Olympics are patterned on the Olympic Games of ancient Greece, yet few people have more than a hazy understanding of the original Olympics. This selection describes the Greek games and points out their differences from the modern games (which date only from 1896).

One should bear in mind that, while the ancient Olympics were the most famous athletic contests in Greece, there were other games, including some limited to women. Baker is careful to use Greek athletics as a means to raise larger questions about Greek culture. Why were women excluded from the Olympic Games? What was the relationship between religion and athletics in Greece? How did Greek philosophers perceive the role of athletics? Answers to such questions lead one to conclude that sports were not a mere sideshow but a basic component of Greek civilization.

If that is so, then the Greeks were violent, for wrestling, boxing, and the pancration were more brutal than any modern Olympic contest (of course, such current professional sports as boxing, ice hockey, and rugby are violent). On the other hand, some events, such as footraces, appear almost identical to those staged today. The professionalism of the athletes and the honor they derived from their victories resemble the culture of sports in our society. On balance, were the ancient games vastly different from our Olympics? What does the role of games in ancient civilization suggest about the significance of sports in any society?

The story of organized athletics in the ancient world is primarily the story of Greece. A land of sunshine, mild climate, and rugged mountains rimmed by sparkling seas, Greece spawned philosophers and civic leaders who placed equal value on physical activity and mental cultivation. A vast array of gymnasiums and palaestras (wrestling schools) served as training centers for athletes to prepare themselves to compete in stadiums situated in every major city-state.

For more than a thousand years athletic festivals were an important part of Greek life. Originally mixtures of religious ceremony and athletic competition, hundreds of local festivals were held each year throughout

William J. Baker, *Sports in the Western World* (Totowa, NJ: Rowman and Littlefield, 1982), 14–23, 25–6.

the country and in Greek colonies in Egypt, Sicily, and on the banks of the Bosporus. By the fifth century B.C. four major festivals dominated the scene, forming a kind of circuit for ambitious athletes. The Pythian Games, held every fourth year at the sacred site of Apollo in Delphi, crowned victory with a laurel wreath. The Isthmian Games at Corinth in honor of Poseidon, the god of the sea, were conducted every other year, providing a victor's wreath of pine from a nearby sacred grove. The Nemean Games at Nemea, honoring Zeus every second year, awarded a sacred wreath of celery. The oldest and most prestigious of all the festivals, the Olympic Games, bestowed the olive wreath every four years in honor of Zeus.

The Olympics were the Super Bowl, the World Cup, the Heavyweight Championship of Greek athletics. By Olympic standards were the other festivals judged; at Olympia the sweet "nectar of victory" filled athletes with self-esteem and accorded them public acclaim. . . .

The Olympic Games originated in a most unlikely place. Far removed from Athens, Corinth, and Sparta, the teeming centers of Greek culture and power, Olympia was a little wooded valley in the remote district of Elis on the northwestern tip of Peloponnesus (the peninsula that makes up the southern half of Greece). . . . Mount Olympus, a site readily associated with the gods, lay far to the northeast. Yet according to ancient lore, little Olympia was the place where gods and heroes mingled to accomplish feats worthy of immortal praise.

The origins of the Olympic Games are shrouded in mystery and legend. According to one yarn, Hercules founded the games in celebration of his matchless feats. Some Greeks insisted that their two mightiest gods, Zeus and Cronus, contested for dominance on the hills above Olympia, and that the games and religious ceremonies held later in the valley were begun in commemoration of Zeus's victory. Others clung to the legend of Pelops, who won his bride in a daring chariot escape. The girl's father was an expert with the spear, and according to tradition, thirteen suitors had met death while attempting to steal the daughter away. But Pelops was shrewd. He loosened the axle of his adversary's chariot, took off with his prize, and breathed a sigh of relief when his lover's father broke his neck in the ensuing crash. . . . [S]upposedly on that hallowed ground Pelops instituted the games and religious sacrifices in celebration of his god-given victory.

Significantly, all these tales involve competition, physical aggressiveness, and triumph. . . . [L]ike most sporting activities in the ancient world, the competitive games associated with Olympia grew out of religious ceremonies and cultic practices. With all their emphasis on man and his achievements, the Greeks were extremely religious. Polytheists, they looked to particular gods for assistance and blessing in every sphere of life. . . . Most of all they feared the wrath and sought the favor of Zeus, the mightiest of the gods.

In prayers, processions, and sacrifices, the ancient Greeks sought diligently to appease their gods. Religious festivals, accompanied by feasts, music, dancing, and athletic contests, were scattered throughout the Greek world. About 1000 B.C. Olympia became a shrine to Zeus. In addition to their religious ceremonies, young Greeks competed athletically in honor of Zeus, himself reckoned to be a vigorous warrior god who cast his javelinlike thunderbolts from on high. Competitors at Olympia swore by Zeus that they would play fair and obey all the rules. When they broke their oaths, they were required to pay fines, which in turn were spent to erect statues to Zeus.

The actual date of the first competitive games at Olympia is unknown. But the year 776 B.C. stands as a milestone, for in that year the Greeks first recorded the name of the victor in a simple footrace. For a time the footrace—a sprint of about 200 meters—was the only event associated with the religious festival at Olympia. In 724 B.C., however, a "double race" (400 meters) was added, and in 720 B.C. a long-distance race of 4,800 meters became a fixture. Within the next hundred years other events were established: wrestling and the pentathlon in 708 B.C., boxing in 688 B.C., chariot races in 680 B.C., and boys" footraces, wrestling, and boxing between 632 and 616 B.C. Finally in 520 B.C. the Olympic program was completed with the introduction of a footrace in armor. For almost a thousand years the list of events remained essentially intact. Every four years, strong, young Greeks gathered to compete, to strive for the victory wreath of olive branches.

In the beginning, however, Olympia was a simple site unadorned with buildings. A few scattered stone altars to Zeus stood in the *altis*, the sacred grove. . . . Competitive events were held in randomly selected open spaces, as near to the *altis* as possible. Not until about 550 B.C. were buildings constructed. . . . Finally a hippodrome and stadium were constructed, the latter . . . providing space for about 40,000 spectators. A gymnasium and palaestra completed the athletic complex.

In the spring of every fourth year three heralds departed from Olympia to traverse the Greek world, announcing the forthcoming games and declaring a "sacred truce." By the authority of Zeus, competitors and spectators making their way to Olympia were allowed to pass safely through the countryside, even in times of war. The athletes and their trainers arrived in Olympia a month before the games. First they had to prove their eligibility—that they were Greek, freeborn (not slaves), and without criminal records. Then they had to swear by Zeus that they had been in training for the previous ten months. Participation in the Olympic Games was no lighthearted matter. Strict judges supervised a grueling month-long training program in order to ensure the fitness of prospective competitors, and they arranged elimination heats for those events that had attracted an unusually large number of athletes. . . .

While the athletes sweated and grunted through their preparatory exercises, little Olympia and the surrounding countryside took on a carnival atmosphere. Spectators came from all directions, and official delegations from Greek city-states arrived with gifts for Zeus. Food and drink vendors did a brisk business, as did hawkers of souvenirs and pimps with their prostitutes. Jugglers, musicians, dancers, and magicians displayed their talents, and soothsayers dispensed their wisdom. Deafening noise and stifling dust added to the midsummer heat, making attendance at the Olympic Games something of an ordeal.

Until late in the history of the games, tiny Olympia was ill-prepared to cope with the crowds. A few springs and the nearby rivers provided water for drinking and bathing, but sanitation and planned water facilities were not available until the second century A.D. Flies were everywhere. As one first-century visitor complained, life at the Olympics would have been unbearably crude and unpleasant were it not for the excitement of the games themselves: "Do you not swelter? Are you not cramped and crowded? Do you not bathe badly? Are you not drenched whenever it rains? Do you not have your fill of tumult and shouting and other annoyances? But I fancy that you bear and endure it all by balancing it off against the memorable character of the spectacle."

The athletes fared little better. Although they ate well during their month's training, they, too, received scant provision for physical comfort. Housing, or the lack of it, was a main problem. Servants of wealthy spectators and official delegations pitched richly embroidered tents on the hillsides, but most athletes simply wrapped themselves in blankets, slept under the stars, and hoped it would not rain. Not until about 350 B.C. was housing provided for the athletes, and even then it was too spartan for comfort. Certainly nothing approximating a modern Olympic village was ever constructed. . . .

For three centuries after the first recorded Olympic victor in 776 B.C., the sequence and duration of the games fluctuated from Olympiad to Olympiad according to the whims of the judges. In 472 B.C., however, the games were reorganized and fixed into a pattern that remained virtually unchanged for the next eight hundred years. The duration of the entire festival was set at five days, with only two and a half days devoted to the games themselves. The first day was given to religious ceremony: oaths, prayers, sacrifices, and the singing of hymns. Some athletes presented gifts and offered prayers to the statues of past victors who had been deified, at the shrines of various patron gods, and especially to the several statues of Zeus.

On the second day the sports competition began. Spectators gathered at the hippodrome, a level, narrow field about 500 meters long, to witness the chariot race. Amid great fanfare, splendid two-wheeled chariots pulled by four horses lined up in staggered starting places. Here was the most costly and colorful of all the Olympic events, a signal to the world that the owners were men of great wealth. Their drivers, decked out in finely embroidered tunics, tensely awaited the start. They could scarcely afford to relax. Their course was not a rounded oval but rather around posts set at each end of the hippodrome about 400 meters apart, requiring 180-degree turns for twelve laps. Rules forbade swerving in front of an opponent, but bumps and crashes and even head-on collisions around the posts were inevitable. In one race only one of forty chariots finished intact.

As soon as the dust settled and battered chariots were removed from the hippodrome, single horses and their jockeys moved into starting positions. Riding without saddles or stirrups, the jockeys were nude. Even more than the charioteers, jockeys got little credit if they won. They were the hirelings of wealthy owners, whose names were recorded as the winners of the race. Even the olive crown was placed on the owner's head, not the jockey's.

The morning having been given to these equestrian events, the afternoon was devoted to an altogether different contest, the pentathlon. Spectators crowded onto the grassy slopes of the stadium. Except for a few marble slabs provided for the Olympic officials, no seats were ever built. Through a narrow passageway at one end of the stadium the competitors entered. Naked and bronzed by the sun, they more than any of the other contestants at Olympia represented the Greek ideal of physical beauty. Pentathletes had to be fast as well as strong, with muscles well-proportioned and supple but not overdeveloped. . . .

Like the modern decathlon, the pentathlon rewarded the versatile athlete. First he had to throw the discus, a round, flat object originally made of stone and later of bronze. Five throws were allowed, and only the longest counted. Next came the javelin throw. About six feet long, the javelin had a small leather loop attached near the center of gravity. The athlete inserted one or two fingers in the loop, wound the thong around the javelin, and thus obtained leverage to make the javelin spin in flight. In the third event, the standing broad jump, the athlete carried weights in his hands, swung them forward to shoulder height, and then down as he leaped. Made of stone or metal in the shape of small dumbbells, the weights both increased the distance and helped the jumper to keep his balance when landing. A 200-meter sprint and a wrestling contest were the last two events in the pentathlon, but they were often not held: The athlete who first won three of the five events was declared the victor without further contest.

As the sun set on that second day of the Olympic festival, attention turned from athletic competition to religious ceremony. In honor of the hero-god Pelops, a black ram was slain and offered as a burnt sacrifice — always as the midsummer full moon appeared above the *altis*. On the following morning were religious rites, followed by a magnificent procession of priests, Olympic judges, representatives from the Greek city-states, the athletes and their kinsmen, and trainers. All finally arrived at the altar of Zeus, where one hundred oxen were slain and their legs burned in homage to Zeus. The carcasses were cooked and eaten at the concluding banquet on the final day of the festival.

On the afternoon of the third day, the footraces were held: 200-meter sprints the length of the stadium, 400-meter dashes around a post and back, and long-distance runs of 4800 meters (twelve laps). Marble slabs provided leverage for quick starts, and a trumpet blast served as the starting signal. . . .

The fourth day of the festival brought on the "heavy" events: wrestling, boxing, the pancration, and armored footraces. The first three were especially violent, brutal contests of strength and will. There were few rules, no time limit, and no ring. More important, there were no weight limits, thus restricting top-level competitors to the largest, best-muscled, and toughest men to be found throughout Greece. In the wrestling contests biting and gouging were prohibited, but not much else. A wrestler won when he scored three falls, making his opponent touch the ground with his knees. Wrestlers therefore concentrated on holds on the upper part of the body and tripped their opponents when possible. . . .

Yet wrestling was mild exercise compared to boxing. Boxers wound heavy strips of leather around their hands and wrists, leaving the fingers free. They aimed primarily for the opponent's head or neck, rather than the body. Slapping with the open hand was permissible, and it was often done to divert the attention, cut the face, or close the eyes of the opposition. The fight went on without a break until one of the competitors was either exhausted or knocked out, or until one raised his right hand as a sign of defeat. Blood flowed freely. Scarcely an Olympic boxer finished his career without broken teeth, cauliflower ears, a scarred face, and a smashed nose. He was lucky if he did not have more serious eye, ear, and skull injuries.

As if boxing and wrestling were not brutal enough, the Greeks threw them together, added some judo, and came up with the contest most favored by spectators at Olympia — the pancration. Pancratiasts wore no leather thongs on the fists, but they could use their heads, elbows, and knees in addition to hands and feet. They could trip, hack, break fingers, pull noses and ears, and even apply a stranglehold until tapped on the back, the sign that the opponent had given up. In 564 B.C. a pancratiast who had won in two previous Olympics found himself in both a leg scissors grip and a strangle-hold. Literally in the process of being choked to death, he frantically reached for one of his opponent's toes and broke it. As he gasped his final breath, his opponent, suffering excruciating pain, gave the signal of capitulation. So the strangled pancratiast was posthumously awarded the crown of victory, and in the central square of his native village a statue was erected in his honor.

After the deadly serious business of wrestling, boxing, and the pancration, the final Olympic contest added a farcical touch to the festival. The 400-meter footrace in armor pitted naked men clad only in helmets, shin guards, and shields, a fitting though ludicrous reminder of the military origins of most of the games. Although the armored footrace remained on the Olympic program from its introduction in 520 B.C. until the end, it was never a prestigious event. Apparently it provided comic relief at the end of a gory day.

The fifth and final day of the festival was devoted to a prize-giving ceremony, a service of thanksgiving to Zeus, and a sumptuous banquet at which the sacrificial animals were consumed. . . .

. . . [S]ome of the limited features of the Olympic Games should be noted. In the first place, the athletic program was narrowly confined to two equestrian contests, six track-and-field events, three physical-contact sports, and the armored footrace. From a modern point of view, conspicuously absent were relay races, hurdles, pole vaults, high jumps, running broad jumps, weight lifting, and shot puts. Nothing approximating a modern marathon ever appeared on the ancient Olympic program. . . .

Given the fact that Greece is a peninsula and half of it virtually an island, it is surprising to find no water sports such as swimming, diving, sailing, or rowing in the ancient Olympic program. . . . Less apparent was the reason for the lack of competitive ball games. In fact, the Greeks played a number of individual and team games of ball. At Sparta "ball player" and "youth" were synonymous. . . . Without doubt the Greeks played a kind of field hockey game. . . . Most common of all competitive ball play in Greece, however, was the game of *episkyros*, a team sport in which opposing sides threw a ball back and forth "until one side drives the other back over their goal line."

Why, then, were no ball games ever played in the ancient Olympics? When the Olympics began in the eighth century B.C., most ball play was still mere exercise, keep-away games at most. . . . [T]hey were played by women, children, and old men, but not by serious athletes. Not yet rough mock forms of combat, ball games were considered child's play compared to the warrior sports of chariot racing, javelin throwing, wrestling, and the like. By the time competitive ball play became respectable for adult males, the Olympic program was already set on its traditional course. . . .

Another limitation of the Olympics that more tellingly reflected the mentality of ancient Greek society was the exclusion of women from the games. In that patriarchal world, matters of business, government, and warfare were reserved for men. A woman might attend the theater if accompanied by a man, but even in the home she lived in separate quarters. Except for the honorary presence of the priestess of Demeter, women were altogether excluded from the Olympic Games, as spectators as well as competitors. Apparently only one woman ever broke the taboo, and her ploy provoked a rule change. In 404 B.C. a mother who wanted to see her son box slipped into the stadium disguised as a trainer. But when the boy won his match, she leaped over the barrier to congratulate him and in so doing gave herself away. Horrified Olympic officials immediately laid down a new rule: trainers henceforward must appear in the stadium stark naked, like the athletes.

Barred from the Olympic Games, women held their own competitive contests at Olympia in honor of Hera, the sister-wife of Zeus. Their competition was largely in the form of footraces, wrestling, and chariot races. Apparently these Heraean Games even predated the Olympic Games as fertility rites representing an early matriarchal society. During the history of the Olympic Games, however, Olympic officials proved to be a highly conservative group of men committed primarily to maintaining a successful formula, thus inadvertently protecting traditional male interests. Their conservatism is best seen by comparison with the other major Panhellenic games. As Greek women increasingly became emancipated (primarily in the cities) toward the end of the pre-Christian era, short-distance races for girls were introduced as an integral part of the program in the Pythian, Isthmian, and Nemean Games.

Olympia's relation to the other festivals on the athletic "circuit" calls to mind another myth long entertained about athletes in the ancient world: Olympic victors received no cash prizes or other material rewards with their olive crowns; thus it would appear that they were purely amateur, competing for the honor of victory. The appearance was a mere shadow of reality. Throughout the history of the Olympics, only aristocrats could afford the horses and chariots for the equestrian events. For the first 300 years or so, the games were dominated by athletes from wealthy families who could afford trainers and coaches, a proper diet (plenty of meat), full-time training, and travel. Around 450 B.C., however, lower-class athletes began participating in the track-and-field and physical-contact sports. Financed by local patrons and public funds drawn from taxes on wealthy citizens, they ran and fought to bring honor to their city-states as well as to themselves. Their city-states, in turn, rewarded them with cash prizes, free food, and lodging. Therefore, although the Olympic Games paid no direct material rewards, they existed in a maze of commercial enterprise. A victory at Olympia dramatically raised an athlete's value as he went off to sell his talents and brawn for further competition at the Pythian, Isthmian, and Nemean Games. Whether or not he received money for his Olympic exploits is beside the point. Well paid for his full-time efforts, he was a professional athlete.

A sure sign of this professionalism was the emergence of athletic guilds in the second century B.C. Like today's unions or players' associations, the guilds originated on the principle of collective bargaining. And bargain they did: for the athletes' rights to have a say in the scheduling of games, travel arrangements, personal amenities, pensions, and old-age security in the form of serving as trainers and managers.

When Greek poets, philosophers, and playwrights turned a critical eye on the athletes of their day, they seldom attacked professionalism. . . . Yet athletics were scarcely beyond criticism. For well-born, highly cultured Greeks, athletics appeared to be a lamentably easy way for lower-class citizens to rise quickly to affluence, then to fall back into poverty once the strength of youth waned. . . .

Worse still, the successful athlete had to specialize to such an extent that he made a poor soldier. . . .

Yet of all the barbs directed against Greek athletics, the most common had to do with the glorification of physical strength to the detriment of mental and spiritual values. To the philosopher and satirist Xenophanes, it was "not right to honor strength above excellent wisdom." . . . Milo of Croton was the butt of numerous jokes and slurs on the mindlessness of the muscle-bound athlete. "What surpassing witlessness," declared a moralist when he heard that Milo carried the entire carcass of a bull around the stadium at Olympia before cutting it up and devouring it. Before it was slaughtered, the bull carried its own body with much less exertion than did Milo. "Yet the bull's mind was not worth anything—just about like Milo's." The image of the "dumb jock" is as old as athletics.

. . . "How very unlike an athlete you are in frame," Socrates once chided a young Athenian weakling. "But I am not an athlete," retorted the literal-minded youth. "You are not less of an athlete," shot back the wise Socrates, "than those who are going to contend at the Olympic Games. Does the struggle for life with the enemy, which the Athenians will demand of you when circumstances require, seem to you to be a trifling contest?" For Socrates, the key words were *contend, struggle,* and *contest*. Moreover, for Socrates the athlete provided the model for the principle that "the body must bear its part in whatever men do; and in all the services required from the body, it is of the utmost importance to have it in the best possible condition."

Socrates' prize pupil, Plato, agreed fully with his master. Plato, in fact, trained under the best wrestling teacher in Athens and reportedly competed in the Isthmian games. Originally his name was Aristocles, but his wrestling teacher changed it to Plato, meaning "broad shouldered." In *The Republic*, Plato set up a dialogue with Socrates to argue logically that gymnastic exercise was the "twin sister" of the arts for the "improvement of the soul." His ideal was the body and mind "duly harmonized."

This sense of balance between the physical and the mental prompted the third of the great Greek philosophers, Aristotle, to devote several sections of his *Politics* to the training of children to be good Greek citizens. "What is wanted," he insisted, "is not the bodily condition of an athlete nor on the other hand a weak and invalid condition, but one that lies between the two." Coming to manhood a hundred years or so after Socrates, Aristotle was more critical of "the brutal element" involved in organized athletics. Yet he, too, held the Olympic victors in awe. . . .

Critical as they were of overspecialized athletes, the great philosophers still did not reject athletics. For them, the association of body and mind was literally intimate: gymnasiums were places where men not only exercised, but gathered to hear the lectures of philosophers and itinerant orators. Plato's Academy and Aristotle's Lyceum in Athens were, in fact, gymnasiums, centers of training "for the body and the soul." Ironically, the terms "academy" and "lyceum" have come to refer solely to intellectual pursuits, wholly divorced from physical training. . . .

Marriage and the Family in Athens

W.K. LACEY

In the last two decades, historians of the family have demolished any lingering notion that families have not changed appreciably over time. Recent studies demonstrate that husbands, wives, and children, and their relationship with one another and with society at large, possess a complex past. In the long history of the family, that of classical Athens stands out because of its rigidity and connection to the politics of the city.

For example, one would be hard-pressed to think of another society that kept women of wealthy families hidden. Athenian men felt their betrothed had to be virgins and their wives chaste. Why were Athenian males so uncompromising in these matters? How did the laws of the state serve to maintain the virtue of citizens' wives? Citizenship was the key, and the concept of citizenship affected marriage and children. Attitudes toward adultery also related to worries about citizenship.

Athens may have been the "cradle of democracy," but it was a very limited democracy. In what ways did Athenian legislation concerning the family discriminate against those groups, such as foreigners or slaves, excluded from the democratic system? What kind of "democratic" values could be nurtured in such families?

Finally, how did Athenian males treat their wives, children, and parents? What explains their behavior and attitudes toward those groups? Is there evidence of love in these relations?

... In 451 Pericles[1] persuaded the assembly[2] to modify the rules for entitlement to citizenship by a law which decreed that a man's parents must both be citizens for him to be a citizen. ... The motives for Pericles' law have been much discussed; selfishness—*i.e.* not wanting to share the profits of empire; race-consciousness—*i.e.* fear of diluting the Athenian autochthonous stock; ... but, from the point of view of the

---

[1]Dominant Athenian statesman, 495–429 B.C.

[2]Popular assembly made up of all male citizens 18 and older; only legislative body in Athens.

W.K. Lacey, *The Family in Classical Greece* (Ithaca, NY: Cornell University Press, 1968), 100,103–118.

family, much the most convincing reason was the desire of Athenian fathers to secure husbands for their daughters. . . .

Prior to the law Athenians had always been able to contract legal marriages with non-Athenian women. . . .

That is not to say that there were no such people as illegitimate children before Pericles' day; bastards are known in the Homeric poems, mostly the children of slave girls or concubines begotten by the great heroes . . . ; but their status and rights depended upon the decision of their father about them while he lived, or of their kinsmen when he had died. When a man had no son by his recognized wife he might adopt a bastard as his heir. . . .

Slave girls' children, and the children of common prostitutes, must always have been classed as bastards, and so, presumably, were the offspring of parents who did not live together, such as the children of the victims of rape or seduction. . . .

Pericles' law, however, added a new class of persons to the illegitimate, by declaring the offspring of unions with non-citizen mothers non-citizens . . . however formal the marriage agreement had been, and thus the procreation of legitimate children became impossible except from the legitimate daughter of an Athenian. . . .

The law required that an Athenian's marriage should be preceded by either a betrothal agreement . . . or a court judgment. . . . This latter was the legal process whereby a man's claim to be the legitimate husband of an *epikleros*[3] was established. Otherwise the normal process . . . was for a girl's *kyrios*[4] to pledge her to a prospective bridegroom. The pledge was a formal one, and witnesses were present on both sides; it also stated what her dowry was to be as one of its conditions. It is uncertain at what age this agreement was normally made for girls. . . . But it is quite certain that betrothal, though obligatory, did not itself make a marriage. . . . This was because, if a child's mother was not properly married, the child was a bastard, and suffered severe disabilities in respect of the capacity to succeed to property, and exclusion from civic privileges as a citizen.

Marriages within the *anchisteia* or wider family were extremely common; they were prescribed by the law for *epikleroi*,[5] we hear of half-brothers marrying their half-sisters, and uncles often married their nieces; . . .

The normal age for men to marry seems to have been about thirty,

[3]A woman to whom property was attached. She was thus an attractive bride.

[4]The male guardian of a woman. An Athenian woman was an eternal minor; she always had a guardian.

[5]Plural of *epikleros*.

an age approved by the philosophers as suitable, but there were sound family reasons as well as those of imaginary eugenics. These lay in the Athenian custom of old men retiring from the headship of (or at least from economic responsibility for) their families in favour of their sons, and the son's marriage was an appropriate moment for this to occur. . . . A man who married at about thirty would be about sixty when his son reached thirty; fifty-nine was the age at which a man's military service ended and he was therefore considered an old man.

Girls were married much younger; philosophers and other writers recommended about eighteen or nineteen as suitable. . . . In Athens, girls were presented to the phratry[6] on . . . the third day of the Apatouria,[7] when a sacrifice was made by their (new) husband; this is associated with the boys' sacrifice on the same day, made on the occasion of their cutting their hair as indicating the end of their childhood. Therefore it will have been not later than about sixteen, and the Greeks' fanatical emphasis on premarital virginity will have made it tend to be earlier than this rather than later.

A few instances are known in which a woman is said to have chosen her own husband, but in every case it is clear that it was most unusual. . . . It is important to stress that all these women belonged to the highest social class, in which the women have always had markedly more independence than among the bulk of the population.

Society demanded that a man procure marriages for his daughters, and, if necessary, sisters; it was regarded as a slight on his excellence if he did not do so. Nature, however, ordained . . . that more girl-babies than boys should survive infancy, and battle casualties were at least as numerous as deaths in childbirth; the excess of brides seeking husbands therefore created a competitive situation for the fathers of girls, which ensured that a dowry was an invariable accompaniment (though by no means a legal requirement) of a marriage. Girls who had no dowry could not get married, and therefore to marry a girl without a dowry, or with only a very small one, was to do her a very great honour, and was a matter for self-congratulation by orators, especially when the girl was an *epikleros*. Unmarried girls had either to remain at home, or enter the world of the demimondaines[8] if they were destitute orphans. After marriage, however, a girl seems to have had more ability to determine her lot. . . . [For] most married couples divorce was easy, and widows were often remarried.

In the choice of their second husband widows were certainly some-

---

[6]Tribe or clan.

[7]An annual festival.

[8]Women who lost social standing owing to their sexual promiscuity.

times able to exercise some element of choice. . . . There can be little doubt, however, that young widows, even if they had children, were expected to remarry.

Moreover, Athenian women had as much right to divorce their husbands as their husbands had to divorce them, and we even hear of a father taking his daughter away when he quarrelled with his son-in-law; divorce by consent was also possible, especially in connection with a suit for an *epikleros*. In all cases, however, the woman's dowry had to be repaid to her *kyrios*, and a large dowry is said to be something which protects a woman and prevents her being divorced. It is therefore alleged that a woman whose citizenship was doubtful would necessarily have a large dowry so that her husband would not easily get rid of her.

The dowry was a field in which it is accepted that a man would express his self-esteem. . . . Nobody failed to give a dowry if he could help it; an uncle, it is said, guardian to four nieces and one nephew, would be sure to see that the girls were given dowries; friends gave dowries to the daughters of the poor; the daughters of *thetes*, the lowest financial class, who lacked brothers had by law to be given dowries by their relatives in accordance with their means; even the state stepped in very occasionally (in return for outstanding public services) to dower a man's daughters. . . . Dowries consisted of cash, or real-estate valued in cash. . . . Widows on their remarriage received dowries in exactly the same way as unmarried girls, and this is only natural since a woman's dowry was deemed to be her share of her paternal estate, a share set apart for her maintenance, and it is an unfailing principle of Athenian law that the head of the family who had a woman's dowry in his possession had to maintain her. . . .

. . . [A] dowry was intended primarily for a woman's maintenance. It remained in her husband's control while he lived; if he predeceased her and there were no children, it returned with her to her own family; if there were children, it was part of the children's inheritance provided that they supported their mother if adult, or their guardian did if they were infants. . . .

After the betrothal . . . came the wedding . . . , at which the bride was brought to the bridegroom's house and the marriage really began . . . , so that the various songs of the wedding were then appropriate. It was living together which made a marriage a marriage; its existence was therefore essentially a question of fact. Living together . . . is the Greek for being married, and the procreation of children was its explicit object. Xenophon's[9] Socrates says: 'Surely you do not suppose that it is for sexual satisfaction that men and women

---

[9]A student of Socrates who, like Plato, wrote an *Apology* (a work purporting to be what Socrates said on his own behalf at his trial).

breed children, since the streets are full of people who will satisfy that appetite, as are the brothels? No, it is clear that we enquire into which women we may beget the best children from, and we come together with them and breed children'. . . .

The Athenians were even a bit sentimental about children, if about anything; weeping children were a stock-in-trade of the defendant at a trial. . . .

Formal marriage and the birth of children from it also had a public side; this was due to the importance of asserting the child's legitimacy. With this in view a marriage was registered with the *phrateres*,[10] the husband's *phrateres* in most cases, but also, when the girl was an *epikleros*, with her family's. Similarly, when a child was born, it was exhibited at least to relatives on the tenth day festival, at what seems to have been a big celebration; and on this occasion the father named him. . . . [T]he father swore 'that he knew that the child had citizen-status, being born to him from a citizen mother, properly (*i.e.* formally) married'.

Children who could not substantiate their claim to legitimacy were bastards; they not only lacked rights of succession after 403 . . . they were also excluded from the family religious observances, and they did not enjoy citizen-rights. This did not mean that they had no rights. . . . Bastards resembled outsiders . . . in that they lacked the right to claim citizens' estates, but they must have had rights at law. . . .

. . . Apollodorus[11] cites a law forbidding a foreigner to live with a citizen woman as his wife . . . and a foreign woman to live with a citizen, on pain of enslavement or a heavy fine; clearly this did not mean a prohibition of sexual intercourse across these boundaries, nor a prohibition on keeping a concubine, or, in the case of a woman, a lover, but it prohibited such people from pretending that they were formally married, and from claiming to breed citizen children. . . .

During the Peloponnesian War, after the Sicilian disaster in 413, we are told that the Athenians temporarily abandoned their rules about requiring a child's father and mother to be formally married because of the shortage of men, and citizens were allowed to marry one wife, and breed children (that is, legitimate children) from another. This has shocked commentators, . . . but it accords fully with the Athenian view of marriage—as an arrangement for maintaining the *oikoi*,[12] and (in the case of the city) for replenishing the supply of citizen-soldiers. . . .

The importance of being able to prove legitimacy had two principal results; it made adultery a public as well as a private offense, and it made the Athenians excessively preoccupied with the chastity of

[10]Tribe or clan (phraty).

[11]Important only because of his involvement with a famous legal case.

[12]Households or families.

their womenfolk, with the result that they were guarded in a manner nowadays thought to be intolerable.

Adultery in Athens (it is sometimes said) meant 'the sins of a wife'. The evidence is not quite so unequivocal; in the first place, the punishment of death is prescribed for the adulterer and not the adulteress— she was punished, naturally, but it is odd that, if the offense was only hers, her lover should be put to death, not she.

Secondly, . . . it is stated that a man may with impunity kill an adulterer caught in the act with any of the women in his *kyrieia*[13]—his mother, sister and daughter are mentioned as well as his wife. . . .

. . . Plato's laws on sexual matters are revealing. They were intended to be as severe for men as for women, but, as he admitted, he had to compromise; though he wished to brand all sexual intercourse with anyone other than a wife as adultery, and claimed that the law of nature was to preserve virginity until the age of procreation, then to remain faithful to one's mate, he admitted that most men, both Greeks and non-Greeks, did not do this; he therefore fell back on 'the possible', which was to prohibit all sexual intercourse with freeborn or citizen women other than a man's wedded wife, to forbid sodomy, and impose secrecy on intercourse with any other (*i.e.* non-free) woman on pain of disfranchisement. Obviously Plato was reacting against contemporary attitudes, which did allow men extra-marital sexual relations provided that they were not with women in the *kyrieia* of other citizens. This is to say that adultery was not *solely* an offense by a female; a man was punishable as an adulterer if he seduced a woman he was forbidden to seduce, and his punishment was apt to be more severe, as his liberty of action was greater.

Athenian women had no sexual liberty, but the explanation of the Athenians' attitude was primarily civic, not moral. Euphiletus[14] says that 'the lawgiver prescribed death for adultery' (though not for rape) ' . . . because he who achieves his ends by persuasion thereby corrupts the mind as well as the body of the woman . . . gains access to all a man's possessions, and casts doubt on his children's parentage'. This was the point; if an Athenian had an affair with a citizen-woman not his wife, a baby would not have any claim on his property or family or religious associations, nor impose on them a bogus claim for citizenship; but the woman would be compelled to claim that her husband was the father, and his kinship-group and its cult was therefore deeply implicated, since it would be having a non-member foisted upon it, and if she were detected, all her husband's children would have difficulty in

[13]Headship of a family.
[14]An aggrieved husband in a famous Athenian law case dealing with adultery.

proving their rights to citizenship if they were challenged. An unmarried Athenian girl who had been seduced could be sold into slavery according to Solon's laws; Hypereides[15] implies that it was more usual 250 years later merely to keep her at home unmarried—when he hints that neither she nor a widow who had been seduced would be able to get a husband.

Death for an adulterer, even if caught in the act, was quite certainly not always demanded; comedy speaks of payment, depilation and other humiliating, vulgar but comical indignities being inflicted on an adulterer, which would prevent him appearing in public, certainly from appearing in the wrestling-school, for some time. Divorce for a woman taken in adultery was compulsory, but we may be pretty certain that the demand was not always complied with; a woman with a large dowry would have to have it repaid, and this might be impossible for her husband, or be something he was unwilling to do. . . .

Non-citizens could contract legally valid marriages and dower their daughters to non-citizens, and the Athenian law upheld their contracts; what the Athenian law was concerned to prevent was non-citizens claiming to be citizens, and making claims on the property of citizens. . . .

The attitude of the Athenians to old age was somewhat unusual. On the one hand they hated old age with its loss of the youthful beauty which they so much admired, and they dreaded the time when they would no longer have the strength to earn their daily bread. Senility moreover was one of the causes which made an Athenian's acts invalid at law in that it was deemed that he was out if his mind if senile. . . . On the other hand the city laid it on children as a legal obligation, not merely a moral duty, to ensure that their parents were looked after when they were old. Maltreatment of parents ranks with maltreatment of orphans and *epikleroi* as a prosecution in which a prosecutor ran no risk of punishment. . . . [E]xpectations did not stop at refraining from maltreatment; positive services were required, especially the provision of food-supplies. . . . Hence getting children in order to have someone to tend their old age is a frequently mentioned motive for parenthood, and equally for adoption.

The state also made provision for looking after old women; here the law was explicit; the person who had charge of her dowry had the obligation to maintain her. . . . The class of people most obviously concerned are widows, whose situation at the death of their husbands was possibly that they could remain in their husband's *oikos* and be maintained by its new *kyrios*, who was sometimes a son, sometimes the

[15]Mid-fourth-century speech writer and orator.

guardian of an infant, or (if she were childless) a relative; alternatively the widow could return to her own family, if she had no children, and get her dowry back, or interest on it at a prescribed rate, or, if she were young enough, she could be remarried with an appropriate dowry . . . , or she could be adjudicated as *epikleros* if her situation warranted it. But whatever happened, the person who was *kyrios* of her dowry had to support her.

On the other hand, one effect of the law about senility was that fathers of adult sons often handed over the management of their *oikos* to their sons, and virtually stepped down from the management of the house. . . .

Throughout his life an Athenian was essentially a part of his *oikos*; as a baby his birth had to be accepted by the *kyrios* of his *oikos* (his father) and registered by the *phrateres* of the phratry to which his *oikos* belonged—the city was not interested in him directly until he was ready to be trained to serve it in war; as a man he married usually at an age at which his father was ready to retire from economic responsibility for the *oikos*, and his *phrateres* took note of his marriage, so that his son in turn would readily be accepted as a member of the *oikos*; when he retired in his turn, his *oikos* continued to support him under its new *kyrios*, his son. An Athenian woman was equally a part of her *oikos* until she married, at which time she removed into her husband's *oikos* taking with her a portion out of the possessions of her own *oikos*; this was designated for her support until her dying day whether she was wife or mother or widow or even divorcée. All the Athenian law was framed with this membership of the *oikos* in view; a man's *oikos* provided both his place in the citizen body and what measure of social security there was, and this helps to account for that passionate determination to defend the *oikoi* alike against foreigners and against grasping individual Athenians which is characteristic of the democratic period.

Classical Greek Attitudes to Sexual Behavior

K.J. DOVER

In this article, K.J. Dover analyzes Greek standards of sexual morality. Male citizens had numerous opportunities for sexual activity, yet there were restrictions. Why? How were Greek adolescents supposed to behave sexually? How did the city and family influence the adolescents' sexual activity? At an early age, males learned responsibility and moral values. What were those values? How did the Greeks view love and love-making?

Homosexuality (more properly, bisexuality) is a frequently noted feature of ancient Greece. Dover offers a nuanced interpretation of the sexual relationship between men, or between men and boys. How do you account for the Greeks' tolerance of homosexuality? Why were men so attracted to other men? What qualities did the Greeks praise in men?

What did Greek males think of women as sexual beings? Did they believe that women had different sexual appetites? Dover discusses the sexual roles that daughters, wives, slaves, and prostitutes played in ancient Greece. Why was there a double standard?

Dover's sources for this essay include public speeches, the theatre, art, and the works of philosophers. Do these sources present different views of Greek attitudes toward sex? Dover notes that the reality of sexual activity may have been different from attitudes expressed in speech and in writing.

The Greeks regarded sexual enjoyment as the area of life in which the goddess Aphrodite[1] was interested, as Ares was interested in war and other deities in other activities. Sexual intercourse was *aphrodisia*, 'the things of Aphrodite.' Sexual desire could be denoted by general words for 'desire,' but the obsessive desire for a particular person was *eros*, 'love' in the sense which it has in our expressions 'be in love with . . . ' . . . and 'fall in love with . . . '. . . . Eros, like all powerful emotional forces, but more consistently than most, was personified and deified. . . .

[1]Goddess of love and beauty.

Arethusa 6(1973):59–70.

Eros generates *philia*, 'love'; the same word can denote milder degrees of affection, just as 'my *philoi*' can mean my friends or my innermost family circle, according to context. For the important question 'Do you love me?' the verb used is *philein*, whether the question is put by a youth to a girl as their kissing becomes more passionate or by a father to his son as an anxious preliminary to a test of filial obedience.

Our own culture has its myths about the remote past, and one myth that dies hard is that the 'invention' of sexual guilt, shame and fear by the Christians destroyed a golden age of free, fearless, pagan sexuality. That most pagans were in many ways less inhibited than most Christians is undeniable. Not only had they a goddess specially concerned with sexual pleasure; their other deities were portrayed in legend as enjoying fornication, adultery and sodomy. A pillar surmounted by the head of Hermes[2] and adorned with an erect penis stood at every Athenian front-door; great models of the erect penis were borne in procession at festivals of Dionysus,[3] and it too was personified as the tirelessly lascivious Phales.[4] The vase-painters often depicted sexual intercourse, sometimes masturbation (male or female) and fellatio, and in respect of any kind of sexual behaviour Aristophanic[5] comedy appears to have had total license of word and act. . . .

There is, however, another side of the coin. Sexual intercourse was not permitted in the temples or sanctuaries of deities (not even of deities whose sexual enthusiasm was conspicuous in mythology), and regulations prescribing chastity or formal purification after intercourse played a part in many Greek cults. Homeric epic, for all its unquestioning acceptance of fornication as one of the good things of life, is circumspect in vocabulary, and more than once denotes the male genitals by *aidos*, 'shame,' 'disgrace.' . . . Poets (notably Homer) sometimes describe interesting and agreeable activities—cooking, mixing wine, stabbing an enemy through a chink in his armour—in meticulous detail, but nowhere is there a comparable description of the mechanisms of sexual activity. Prose literature, even on medical subjects, is euphemistic ('be with . . . ' is a common way of saying 'have sexual intercourse with . . . '). . . .

Linguistic inhibition, then, was observably strengthened in the course of the classical period; and at least in some art-forms, inhibition extended also to content. These are data which do not fit the popular concept of a guilt-free or shame-free sexual morality, and require

---

[2]Messenger of the gods.

[3]God of wine and fertility.

[4]Personification of the phallus, often said to accompany Dionysus.

[5]Aristophanes (c.448–c.380 B.C.) was an Athenian writer of comedy.

explanation. Why so many human cultures use derogatory words as synonyms of 'sexual' and reproach sexual prowess while praising prowess in (e.g.) swimming and riding, is a question which would take us to a remote level of speculation. Why the Greeks did so is a question which can at least be related intelligibly to the structure of Greek society and to Greek moral schemata which have no special bearing on sex.

As far as was practicable . . . , Greek girls were segregated from boys and brought up at home in ignorance of the world outside the home; one speaker in court seeks to impress the jury with the respectability of his family by saying that his sister and nieces are 'so well brought up that they are embarrassed in the presence even of a man who is a member of the family.' Married young, perhaps at four- teen (and perhaps to a man twenty-years or more her senior), a girl exchanged confinement in her father's house for confinement in her husband's. When he was invited out, his children might be invited with him, but not his wife; and when he had friends in, she did not join the company. Shopping seems to have been a man's job, to judge from references in comedy, and slaves could be sent on other errands outside the house. Upholders of the proprieties pronounced the front door to be the boundaries of a good woman's territory.

Consider now the situation of an adolescent boy growing up in such a society. Every obstacle is put in the way of his speaking to the girl next door; it may not be easy for him even to get a glimpse of her. Festivals, sacrifices and funerals, for which women and girls did come out in public, provided the occasion for seeing and being seen. They could hardly afford more than that, for there were too many people about, but from such an occasion (both in real life and in fiction) an intrigue could be set on foot, with a female slave of respectable age as the indispensable go-between.

In a society which practices segregation of the sexes, it is likely that boys and girls should devote a good deal of time and ingenu- ity to defeating society, and many slaves may have co-operated with enthusiasm. But Greek laws were not lenient towards adultery, and *moikheia*, for which we have no suitable translation except 'adultery,' denoted not only the seduction of another man's wife, but also the seduction of his widowed mother, unmarried daughter, sister, niece, or any other woman whose legal guardian he was. The adulterer could be prosecuted by the offended father, husband or guardian; alternatively, if caught in the act, he could be killed, maltreated, or imprisoned by force until he purchased his freedom by paying heavy compensation. A certain tendency to regard women as irresponsible and ever ready to yield to sexual temptation . . . relieved a cuckolded husband of a sense of shame or inadequacy and made him willing to seek the co-operation of his friends in apprehending an adulterer, just as he would seek their co-operation to defend himself against fraud, encroachment, breach of contract, or any other threat to his property. The adulterer was open to reproach in the same way, and to the same extent, as any other violator of the laws protecting the individual citizen against arbitrary treatment by other citizens. To seduce a woman of citizen status was more culpable than to rape her, not only because rape was presumed to be unpremeditated but because seduction involved the capture of her affection and loyalty; it was the degree of offense against the man to whom she belonged, not her own feelings, which mattered.

It naturally follows from the state of the law and from the attitudes and values implied by segregation that an adolescent boy who showed an exceptional enthusiasm for the opposite sex could be regarded as a potential adulterer and his propensity discouraged just as one would discourage theft, lies and trickery, while an adolescent boy who blushed at the mere idea of proximity to a woman was praised as *sophron*, 'right-minded,' i.e. unlikely to do anything without reflecting first whether it might incur punishment, disapproval, dishonour or other undesirable consequences.

Greek society was a slave-owning society, and a female slave was not in a position to refuse the sexual demands of her owner or of anyone else to whom he granted the temporary use of her. Large cities, notably Athens, also had a big population of resident aliens, and these included women who made a living as prostitutes, on short-term relations with a succession of clients, or as *hetairai*, who endeavoured to establish long-term relations with wealthy and agreeable men. Both aliens and citizens could own brothels and stock them with slave-prostitutes. Slave-girls and alien girls who took part in men's parties as dancers or musicians could also be mauled and importuned in a manner which might cost a man his life if he attempted it with a woman of citizen status. . . .

It was therefore easy enough to purchase sexual satisfaction, and the richer a man was the better provision he could make for himself. But money spent on sex was money not spent on other things, and there seems to have been substantial agreement on what were proper or improper items of expenditure. Throughout the work of the Attic orators,[6] who offer us by far the best evidence on the moral standards which it was prudent to uphold in addressing large juries composed of ordinary citizens, it is regarded as virtuous to impoverish oneself by gifts and loans to friends in misfortune (for their daughters' dowries, their fathers' funerals, and the like), by ransoming Athenian citizens taken prisoner in war, and by paying out more than the required minimum in the perfomance of public duties (the upkeep of a warship, for

---

[6]Athenians who wrote or gave speeches in law courts or in the assembly.

example, or the dressing and training of a chorus at a festival). This kind of expenditure was boasted about and treated as a claim on the gratitude of the community. On the other hand, to 'devour an inheritance' by expenditure on one's own consumption was treated as disgraceful. Hence gluttony, drunkenness and purchased sexual relations were classified together as 'shameful pleasures.'. . . When a young man fell in love, he might well fall in love with a hetaira or a slave, since his chances of falling in love with a girl of citizen status were so restricted, and to secure the object of his love he would need to purchase or ransom her. A close association between eros and extravagance therefore tends to be assumed, especially in comedy; a character in Menander[7] says, 'No one is so parsimonious as not to make some sacrifice of his property to Eros.' More than three centuries earlier, Archilochus[8] put the matter in characteristically violent form when he spoke of wealth accumulated by long labour 'pouring down into a whore's guts.' A fourth-century litigant venomously asserts that his adversary, whose tastes were predominantly homosexual, has 'buggered away all his estate.'

We have here another reason for the discouragement and disapproval of sexual enthusiasm in the adolescent; it was seen as presenting a threat that the family's wealth would be dissipated in ways other than those which earned honour and respect from the community. The idea that one has a right to spend one's own money as one wishes (or a right to do anything which detracts from one's health and physical fitness) is not Greek, and would have seemed absurd to a Greek. He had only the rights which the law of his city explicitly gave him; no right was inalienable, and no claim superior to the city's.

Living in a fragmented and predatory world, the inhabitants of a Greek city-state, who could never afford to take the survival of their community completely for granted, attached a great importance to the qualities required of a soldier: not only to strength and speed, in which men are normally superior to women, but also to the endurance of hunger, thirst, pain, fatigue, discomfort and disagreeably hot or cold weather. The ability to resist and master the body's demands for nourishment and rest was normally regarded as belonging to the same moral category as the ability to resist sexual desire. Xenophon[9] describes the chastity of King Agesilaus[10] together with his physical toughness, and elsewhere summarises 'lack of self-control' as the inability to hold out against 'hunger, thirst, sexual desire and long hours without sleep.'

[7]Greek writer of comedy, 342?–291? B.C.

[8]Greek poet of the mid-seventh century B.C.

[9]Greek general and historian, 430?–355? B.C.

[10]Spartan king (444–360 B.C.) who began his reign in 399.

The reasons for this association are manifold: the treatment of sex—a treatment virtually inevitable in a slave-owning society—as a commodity, and therefore as something which the toughest and most frugal men will be able to cut down to a minimum; the need for a soldier to resist the blandishments of comfort (for if he does not resist, the enemy who does will win), to sacrifice himself as an individual entirely, to accept pain and death as the price to be paid for the attainment of a goal which is not easily quantified, the honour of victory; and the inveterate Greek tendency to conceive of strong desires and emotional states as forces which assail the soul from the outside. To resist is manly and 'free'; to be distracted by immediate pleasure from the pursuit of honour through toil and suffering is to be a 'slave' to the forces which 'defeat' and 'worst' one's own personality.

Here is a third reason for praise of chastity in the young, the encouragement of the capacity to resist, to go without, to become the sort of man on whom the community depends for its defence. If the segregation and legal and administrative subordination of women received their original impetus from the fragmentation of the early Greek world into small, continuously warring states, they also gave an impetus to the formation of certain beliefs about women which served as a rationalization of segregation and no doubt affected behavior to the extent that people tend to behave in the ways expected of them. Just as it was thought masculine to resist and endure, it was thought feminine to yield to fear, desire and impulse. 'Now you must be a *man*;' says Demeas[11] to himself as he tries to make up his mind to get rid of his concubine, 'Forget your desire, fall out of love;' Women in comedy are notoriously unable to keep off the bottle, and in tragedy women are regarded as naturally more prone than men to panic, uncontrollable grief, jealousy and spite. It seems to have been believed not only that women enjoyed sexual intercourse more intensely than men, but also that experience of intercourse put the woman more under the man's power than it put him under hers, and that if not segregated and guarded women would be insatiably promiscuous.

It was taken for granted in the Classical period that a man was sexually attracted by a good-looking younger male, and no Greek who said that he was 'in love' would have taken it amiss if his hearers assumed without further enquiry that he was in love with a boy and that he desired more than anything to ejaculate in or on the boy's body. I put the matter in these coarse and clinical terms to preclude any misapprehension arising from modern application of the expression 'Platonic love' or from Greek euphemism (see below). . . . Aphrodite,

[11]Character in a play of Menander.

despite her femininity, is not hostile to homosexual desire, and homosexual intercourse is denoted by the same term, *aphrodisia*, as heterosexual intercourse. Vase-painting was noticeably affected by the homosexual ethos; painters sometimes depicted a naked woman with a male waist and hips, as if a woman's body was nothing but a young man's body plus breasts and minus external genitals, and in many of their pictures of heterosexual intercourse from the rear position the penis appears (whatever the painter's intention) to be penetrating the anus, not the vagina.

Why homosexuality—or, to speak more precisely, 'pseudo-homosexuality,' since the Greeks saw nothing surprising in the co-existence of desire for boys and desire for girls in the same person—obtained so firm and widespread a hold on Greek society, is a difficult and speculative question. Segregation alone cannot be the answer, for comparable segregation has failed to engender a comparable degree of homosexuality in other cultures. Why the Greeks of the Classical period accepted homosexual desire as natural and normal is a much easier question: they did so because previous generations had accepted it, and segregation of the sexes in adolescence fortified and sustained the acceptance and the practice.

Money may have enabled the adolescent boy to have plenty of sexual intercourse with girls of alien or servile status, but it could not give him the satisfaction which can be pursued by his counterpart in a society which does not own slaves: the satisfaction of being welcomed *for his own sake* by a sexual partner of equal status. This is what the Greek boy was offered by homosexual relations. He was probably accustomed (as often happens with boys who do not have the company of girls) to a good deal of homosexual play at the time of puberty, and he never heard from his elders the suggestion that one was destined to become *either* 'a homosexual' *or* 'a heterosexual.' As he grew older, he could seek among his juniors a partner of citizen status, who could certainly not be forced and who might be totally resistant to even the most disguised kind of purchase. If he was to succeed in seducing this boy (or if later, as a mature man, he was to seduce a youth), he could do so only by *earning* hero-worship.

This is why, when Greek writers 'idealize' eros and treat the physical act as the 'lowest' ingredient in a rich and complex relationship which comprises mutual devotion, reciprocal sacrifice, emulation, and the awakening of sensibility, imagination and intellect, they look not to what most of us understand by sexual love but to the desire of an older for a younger male and the admiration felt by the younger for the older. It is noticeable also that in art and literature inhibitions operate in much the same way as in the romantic treatment of heterosexual love in our own tradition. When physical gratification is directly referred to, the younger partner is said to 'grant favours' or 'render services'; but a great deal is written about homosexual eros from which the innocent reader would not easily gather that any physical contact at all was involved. Aeschines,[12] who follows Aeschylus[13] and Classical sentiment generally in treating the relation between Achilles and Patroclus in the *Iliad*[14] as homoerotic, commends Homer for leaving it to 'the educated among his hearers' to perceive the nature of the relation from the extravagant grief expressed by Achilles at the death of Patroclus. The vase-painters very frequently depict the giving of presents by men to boys and the 'courting' of boys (a mild term for an approach which includes putting a hand on the boy's genitals), but their pursuit of the subject to the stage of erection, let alone penetration, is very rare, whereas depiction of heterosexual intercourse, in a variety of positions, is commonplace.

We also observe in the field of homosexual relations the operation of the 'dual standard of morality' which so often characterizes societies in which segregation of the sexes is minimal. If a Greek admitted that he was in love with a boy, he could expect sympathy and encouragement from his friends, and if it was known that he had attained his goal, envy and admiration. The boy, on the other hand, was praised if he retained his chastity, and he could expect strong disapproval if he was thought in any way to have taken the initiative in attracting a lover. The probable implication is that neither partner would actually say anything about the physical aspect of their relationship to anyone else, nor would they expect any question about it to be put to them or any allusion to it made in their presence.

Once we have accepted the universality of homosexual relations in Greek society as a fact, it surprises us to learn that if a man had at any time in his life prostituted himself to another man for money he was debarred from exercising his political rights. If he was an alien, he had no political rights to exercise, and was in no way penalized for living as a male prostitute, so long as he paid the prostitution tax levied upon males and females alike. It was therefore not the physical act *per se* which incurred penalty, but the incorporation of the act in a certain deliberately chosen role which could only be fully defined with reference to the nationality and status of the participants.

This datum illustrates an attitude which was fundamental to Greek society. They tended to believe that one's moral character is formed in the main by the circumstances in which one lives: the wealthy man

[12]Athenian orator 397?– 322? B.C..

[13]Athenian tragic poet, 525–456 B.C..

[14]Achilles was the great hero and Patroclus his friend in the *Iliad*, Homer's epic poem.

is tempted to arrogance and oppression, the poor man to robbery and fraud, the slave to cowardice and petty greed. A citizen compelled by great and sudden economic misfortune to do work of a kind normally done by slaves was shamed because his assumption of a role which so closely resembled a slave's role altered his relationship to his fellow-citizens. Since prostitutes were usually slaves or aliens, to play the role of a prostitute was, as it were, to remove oneself from the citizen-body, and the formal exclusion of a male prostitute from the rights of a citizen was a penalty for disloyalty to the community in his choice of role.

Prostitution is not easily defined—submission in gratitude for gifts, services or help is not so different in kind from submission in return for an agreed fee—nor was it easily proved in a Greek city, unless people were willing (as they were not) to come forward and testify that they had helped to cause a citizen's son to incur the penalty of disenfranchisement. A boy involved in a homosexual relationship absolutely untainted by mercenary considerations could still be called a prostitute by his family's enemies, just as the term can be recklessly applied today by unfriendly neighbours or indignant parents to a girl who sleeps with a lover. He could also be called effeminate; not always rightly, since athletic success seems to have been a powerful stimulus to his potential lovers, but it is possible (and the visual arts do not help us much here) that positively feminine characteristics in the appearance, movements and manner of boys and youths played a larger part in the ordinary run of homosexual activity than the idealization and roman-ticisation of the subject in literature indicate. There were certainly circumstances in which homosexuality could be treated as a substitute for heterosexuality; a comic poet says of the Greeks who besieged Troy for ten years, 'they never saw a hetaira . . . and ended up with arseholes wider than the gates of Troy.' . . . A sixth-century vase in which all of a group of men except one are penetrating women shows the odd man out grasping his erect penis and approaching, with a gesture of entreaty, a youth—who starts to run away. In so far as the 'passive partner' in a homosexual act takes on himself the role of a woman, he was open to the suspicion, like the male prostitute, that he abjured his prescribed role as a future soldier and defender of the community.

The comic poets, like the orators, ridicule individuals for effeminacy, for participation in homosexual activity, or for both together; at the same time, the sturdy, wilful, roguish characters whom we meet in Aristophanes are not averse to handling and penetrating good-looking boys when the opportunity presents itself, as a supplement to their busy and enjoyable heterosexual programmes. . . . [T]here is one obvious factor which we should expect to determine different sexual attitudes in different classes. The thorough-going segregation of women of citizen status was possible only in households which owned enough slaves and could afford to confine its womenfolk to a leisure enlivened only by the exercise of domestic crafts such as weaving and spinning. This degree of segregation was simply not possible in poorer families; the women who sold bread and vegetables in the market— Athenian women, not resident aliens—were not segregated, and there must have been plenty of women . . . who took a hand in work on the land and drove animals to market. No doubt convention required that they should protect each other's virtue by staying in pairs or groups as much as they could, but clearly . . . the obstacles to love-affairs between citizens' sons and citizens' daughters lose their validity as one goes down the social scale. Where there are love-affairs, both boys and girls can have decided views . . . on whom they wish to marry. The girl in Aristophanes' *Ecclesiazusae* who waits impatiently for her young man's arrival while her mother is out may be much nearer the norm of Athenian life than those cloistered ladies who were 'embarrassed by the presence even of a male relative.' It would not be discordant with modern experience to believe that speakers in an Athenian law-court professed, and were careful to attribute to the jury, standards of propriety higher than the average member of the jury actually set himself.

Much Classical Greek philosophy is characterized by contempt for sexual intercourse. . . . Xenophon's Socrates, although disposed to think it a gift of beneficent providence that humans, unlike other mammals, can enjoy sex all the year round, is wary of troubling the soul over what he regards as the minimum needs of the body. . . . One logical outcome of this attitude to sex is exemplified by Diogenes the Cynic, who was alleged to have masturbated in public when his penis erected itself, as if he were scratching a mosquito-bite. Another outcome was the doctrine (influential in Christianity, but not of Christian origin) that a wise and virtuous man will not have intercourse except for the purpose of procreating legitimate offspring, a doctrine which necessarily proscribes much heterosexual and all homosexual activity.

Although philosophical preoccupation with the contrast between 'body' and 'soul' had much to do with these developments, we can discern, as the ground from which these philosophical plants sprouted, Greek admiration for invulnerability, hostility towards the diversion of resources to the pursuit of pleasure, and disbelief in the possibility that dissimilar ways of feeling and behaving can be synthesised in the same person without detracting from his attainment of the virtues expected of a selfless defender of his city. It is also clear that the refusal of Greek law and society to treat a woman as a responsible person, while on the one hand it encouraged a complacent acceptance of prostitution and concubinage, on the other hand led to the classification of sexual activity as a male indulgence which could be reduced to a minimum by those who were not self-indulgent. . . .

Roman Women

GILLIAN CLARK

*Although historians lack good evidence about Roman women, there is enough
to illuminate many aspects of their lives. In this article, Gillian Clark explores
their standing in law, customs relating to child-bearing and child-raising, female
education, and the nature of marriage.*

*Clark seeks to know if women were oppressed in this society. Information
about female mortality provides one part of the answer. Why were women more
likely to be killed at birth and to die young? Today, women outnumber men, but
Roman society had more males than females. How did this fact affect arrangements
for marriage? What was married life like? Did well-born Roman husbands treat
their wives differently than did Athenian husbands? What options were available to
women who were not free or who did not marry in a society that reserved education
and political activity, save in rare instances, exclusively for men? What can the
family life of Romans tell us about their success in conquering and maintaining
an extensive empire?*

*Clark often cites the opinions of Roman literary figures and physicians. How
did they regard women and women's lives? Some of the beliefs are timeless, hardly
peculiar to ancient Rome. The medical ideas often appear bizarre, but they do help
explain the condition of women in Roman society.*

*From the very beginning of their lives, women had great disadvantages,
though Clark argues that many of them probably were reasonably content with
their situations in life. Perhaps only in upper-class marriages did women find
some measure of happiness. That happiness, as Clark concludes, can be measured
in relation to how the women fulfilled men's expectations of them as ideal mothers
and wives. The women who were not slaves, prostitutes, poor, or the victims of
infanticide, may have achieved success—insofar as that could be achieved—in an
uneventful marriage, occupied with a loving husband and several children (but
probably only one daughter!). In the ancient world, a solvent security attached to
an enduring boredom may have been the most for which women could strive.*

. . . What did Roman women do all day, besides getting dressed? How
did they feel about it? What else could they have done? Were they
oppressed, and did they notice? Why do we know so little about half
the human race?

. . . We are still working with evidence strongly biassed towards the
upper classes and the city of Rome. The lives of women not in, or in

Gillian Clark, *"Roman Women"*, Greece and Rome, 28(1981): 193–207, 208–210.

contact with, the senatorial class, can only be guessed at from inscriptions, if someone troubled to put one up. And even within the senatorial class, it was not the women who wrote. . . . [T]he only extended work of literature to survive from the period I shall concentrate on, that of the late Republic and early Empire, is the elegies of Sulpicia.[1] . . . Moreover, there is little Roman literature which is concerned with the daily life and experience of particular people: the lives of women tend to be incidental to oratory or history or philosophy or agriculture, or to the emotions of an elegiac poet.

What then can be said? . . . To begin at the beginning: a girl's chances of being reared were less than her brother's. *Patria Potestas*[2] . . . was uniquely strong in Rome, and if a father decided that his new-born child was not to be reared there was no law (before the time of the Severi)[3] to prevent him. . . . Cicero[4] . . . and Seneca[5] . . . reveal that deformed babies were exposed . . . , and it was part of a midwife's training to decide which babies were worth rearing. Healthy but inconvenient babies might also be left to die. Musonius Rufus . . . in the mid-first century A.D. devoted one of his lectures on ethics to the question whether one should rear all one's children. The rich do not, he says, so that there shall be fewer children to share the family property. . . . Since the law required property to be shared among *sui heredes*,[6] it must have been a temptation. Among the poor, there was no question of splitting up an estate. Pliny[7] . . . praises Trajan's[8] extension of the grain-dole to children:

'There are great rewards to encourage the rich to rear their children, and great penalties if they do not. The only way the poor *can* rear their children is through the goodness of the *princeps*.'[9]

If a family did, from greed or necessity, expose a child, it would probably be a girl. Dionysius of Halicarnassus, writing his *Antiquities of Rome* . . . under Augustus, included a 'constitution of Romulus' which has strong links with first-century thought. It provides that citizens must rear all male children (except those who are acknowledged by five neighbours to be deformed)—and the first girl. Apuleius[10] . . . has

[1]Roman poet, late first century B.C.

[2]The father's power.

[3]Line of emperors, 193–235 A.D.

[4]Roman orator and politician, 106–43 B.C.

[5]Roman statesman and philosopher, 3 B.C.–65 A.D.

[6]His heirs.

[7]Pliny (the Younger)—statesman and civil servant, 61/2–113 A.D.

[8]Emperor, 98–117 A.D.

[9]Official title, meaning "first citizen," what we refer to as emperor.

[10]Rhetorician and writer, mid-second century A.D.

a prospective father instruct his wife: 'si sexus sequioris edidisset fetum, protinus quod esset editum necaretur.'[11] (This father, like those who speak now of 'the product of conception', is not prepared to acknowledge the child's humanity.) Some odd facts about sex-ratios make it likely that Dionysius and Apuleius reflect a general tendency. We simply do not hear of spinsters, except the Vestals[12]—and Augustus found it difficult enough to recruit them. (Even they could marry at the end of their term of office, aged 36–40, though they tended not to.) There is not even a normal word for a spinster. . . . Unmarried women were young *virgines*—and there were no nunneries for the women who did not marry.

Some families did, of course, raise more than one daughter. The daughter of L. Aemilius Paullus Macedonicus had three daughters and three sons; Appius Claudius Pulcher, cos. 79 B.C., also had three daughters. . . . But tombstones in general record many more men than women, and this again suggests that either more males were reared or they mattered more to their families. Sometimes there is information about a specific group. A list of aqueduct maintenance men and their families . . . includes two families with two daughters each, but shows a very low proportion of daughters to sons overall. Trajan's alimentary scheme at Veleia supported only 36 girls out of 300 places: this cannot be used straightforwardly as evidence for sex-ratios, since girls got a smaller food-allowance and a family would obviously claim for a boy if it could, but does suggest that there were few families satisfied with daughters alone. Most impressive . . . is Augustus' concession that 'well-born men, other than senators and senators' sons, might marry *libertinae*.[13] Dio[14] . . . says there were just not enough women of good family to go round—and if this is true, after several decades of bloody civil war, then people must have been choosing not to rear daughters. But is Dio guessing? The senate, according to him, said that young men were not marrying because of . . . their failure to settle down, not because they could not find wives.

There are, of course, other causes than selective infanticide for a relative shortage of women. Many must have died in childbirth, from infection or difficult births, or because they were just too young. Soranus . . . , the second-century A.D. physician whose work was the basis of gynaecology until well on in the nineteenth century, thought

[11]"If she bears a foetus of the inferior sex, that which she bore is to be killed immediately."

[12]Priestesses dedicated to the goddess of the hearth, Vesta, and sworn to remain virgins for thirty years.

[13]Freed women.

[14]Dio Cassius, statesman and historian, late second-early third century A.D.

fifteen was the earliest suitable age for conception: most gynaecologists now would add three years to that. Child mortality too was alarmingly high, as it has been at all times and places except for some privileged Western countries in the twentieth century. . . . Girls are usually tougher than boys, but some societies undernourish them, either because they value girls less or because they think (wrongly) that girls need less. Roman governmental schemes like that at Veleia, and several private schemes, gave girls a smaller food-allowance. But these factors have affected other societies which do not show the same apparent shortage of women: so perhaps we do have to come back to parents not rearing girls.

How could they bear it? Even abortion, in this society, is tolerable only so far as we can avoid seeing the foetus as a baby: once the child is born, even for some time before birth, her rights are protected. But the father's right to decide the fate of his own infant probably seemed as obvious as, now, a woman's right to decide about her own body: so infanticide was not made criminal, even though low birth-rate was a persistent anxiety. Besides, Roman parents could not plan their families with much success. Contraceptives varied from quite effective spermicides and pessaries . . . to decoctions of herbs (and worse), faith in douches and wriggling, and entirely magical beliefs. The ovum was undiscovered and the relation between menstruation and fertile periods was misunderstood; this is less surprising in that conception can occur before the first menstruation if a girl marries before she reaches puberty. Observers may also have been confused by amenorrhea (failure to menstruate), which is a common reaction to stress and poor diet and which gets a lot of space in ancient medical text-books. Soranus . . . held that the best time for conception was at the end of a menstrual period, when (he says) a women's desire is strongest, and suggested a rhythm method based on this belief. No wonder Augustus' daughter played safe, and never took a lover unless she was legitimately pregnant. . . . And no wonder abortion was also practiced. Doctors used herbal baths, suppositories, and potions first; then purges, diuretics, massage, violent exercise, and hot baths after drinking wine. If these ancient equivalents of gin, hot baths, and jumping off the kitchen table failed, there seem to have been back-street abortionists using the knitting-needle technique.

Abortion, like infanticide, was not a crime before the time of the Severi, and then the crime was not against the foetus, who was not a person in law, but against the defrauded husband. Why was it not made illegal before? There was strong feeling against abortion, which was taken to be proof of vanity . . . or, worse, of adultery . . . on the part of the mother. Perhaps it was simply too difficult to prove deliberate as against spontaneous abortion: Soranus' . . . list of causes for the latter make one wonder how anyone ever managed to have a baby.

An unwanted pregnancy may yet produce a wanted child, but there were some practices which may have prevented, at least among the upper classes, the emotional bonding of mother and baby. Many mothers did not breast-feed, because it is tiring, but expected to use a wet-nurse. The wet-nurse's own baby had perhaps died, or been exposed, or was expected to manage on some substitute for breast-milk — which last was a major cause of child mortality in the nineteenth century. If Soranus' instructions . . . reflect general practice, the new-born was washed, swaddled, and then put somewhere to be quiet, and to be fed, if at all, the equivalent of glucose (boiled honey and water): Soranus advocated breast-feeding but thought colostrum was bad for babies. So the mother might scarcely have seen the child before the decision to expose it. Poorer people could not afford luxuries of feeling. It may have seemed better to expose the child and hope for the fairy-story to come true and the child to be rescued by some wealthy childless couple. Just occasionally it did. Slavery or a brothel . . . were more likely fates, but even that may have seemed more like putting a child to be raised 'in service', where the chances were better and at least there was food.

If, then, a Roman girl survived her parents' possible indifference, or resignation, to her death, and if she did not despite their best efforts die anyway, what would her life be like?

If she were a slave, she might have little time with her parents: she, or they, could be sold at any time, and there are epitaphs of very young children who had been freed by someone other than the master who freed either parent. But it may have been a relative who bought out the child, since at least the family was united enough for the epitaph to be made. Some slave families did manage gradually to buy the freedom of spouses and children. What a slave girl did depended on the size and type of household to which she belonged. She was most likely to be an *ancilla*, which may mean anything from a maid-of-all-work to a lady's maid — obviously the second was a better chance, since she could collect tips and win her mistress' (or master's) favour. She might have special skills: some slave-girls were dressers, hairdressers, dressmakers, woolworkers, and some perhaps worked in small factories rather than for the household stores. Some were childminders . . . , which was a job not regarded as needing skill, or, if they were lactating, wet-nurses.

Some households were brothels, and so in effect were some eating- and drinking-places. . . . A few slave-girls, who had other abilities for entertaining, were trained to dance, sing, and act. . . .

If a slave-girl were freed, it did not much enlarge the possibilities:

she might be a prostitute, a *mima*, or, if she were lucky, a housewife, doing much the same work as an *ancilla* did but in her own home. If she had caught the fancy of someone of high social status, she would be his *concubina* not his wife: it was not respectable to marry a *libertina*, though it had been known to happen even before Augustus allowed it for non-senators. Housework was hard: there was spinning and weaving and sewing and mending, cooking and cleaning, and water-carrying and baby-minding. Doubtless one reason for child mortality was the impossibility of keeping a swaddled baby clean on the fourth floor of a tenement with the water-supply at the end of the street. Soranus . . . said babies should be bathed and massaged once a day; the undersheets should often be aired and changed and one should watch for insect bites and ulceration. It sounds optimistic. If the housewife had learnt a trade before she married—baking, brickmaking, selling vegetables—she would probably go on with it, often working with her husband. The nearest approach to a professional woman would be a woman doctor, or the midwife who was called in for female complaints, though their social status was not high.

Rich girls had to learn to run a household rather than doing its work, but they too had spinning and weaving. By the first century B.C. there were ready-made fabrics for those who could afford them . . . , but *lanificium*[15] was part of traditional devotion to the home and was still, for most women, an essential part of household economy. A bride carried a spindle and distaff . . . : this is one marriage custom with an obvious relevance. Whether *lanificium* was an enjoyable craft skill or an exhausting chore depended on how much one had to do. Livy's[16] picture . . . of the virtuous Lucretia, sitting up with her maids doing wool-work by lamplight, needs to be supplemented by Tibullus'[17] . . . of the weary slave falling asleep over her work, and the neglected old woman who has no other resource. Too much woolwork, despite the lanolin in the wool, hardened the hands—a point to bear in mind when choosing a midwife. . . . But the custom was kept up by ladies of old-fashioned virtue. There were looms in the *atrium* of M. Aemilius Lepidus when thugs broke in on his admirable wife; Augustus' women-folk kept him in homespun, though Livia[18] had a large staff of skilled workers. *Lanificium*, for ladies, perhaps took the place of the 'accomplishments'—music, drawing, fine sewing—which young ladies of the nineteenth century learnt before marriage and used to fill idle hours after. . . .

[15]The making of wool.

[16]Titus Livy, Roman historian, 59 B.C.–17 A.D.

[17]Roman poet, 48–19 B.C.

[18](58 B.C.–29 A.D.), wife to the first Roman emperor, Augustus.

Little is heard of more intellectual pursuits. There was a chance of picking up some education from parents, brothers, even a sympathetic husband. The younger Pliny and his friend Pompeius Saturninus, who were civilized people, both continued the literary education of their wives. . . . Pompeius' wife wrote letters which sounded like prose Plautus or Terence, so pure was their Latin (Pliny was inclined to give Pompeius the credit). Pliny's wife set his verses to music with no tutor but Love, which sounds less promising. . . .

Some girls may have gone to school, at least for primary schooling, and some had private tutors. Pompeius' wife Cornelia had been taught literature, music, and geometry, and had 'listened with profit' to lectures on philosophy—which may mean ethics or physics. . . . Pompeius' daughter had a tutor for Greek. . . . Pliny's friend Fundanius had *praeceptores*[19] for his daughter, but he was a progressive: a philosopher, a friend of Plutarch[20] who wrote on the education of women, a pupil of Musonius[21] who argued for equal education for girls. These people may be exceptions. . . .

Some girls learnt music and singing, and the dramatic recitations which rose to a form of ballet and could be very strenuous, but it was not proper for them to aim at a professional standard. Scipio Aemilianus[22] had been shocked, as early as 129 B.C., to find well-born boys and girls at a dancing class; . . . Horace[23] thought it was part of the rot that grown girls should learn *Ionicos motus*.[24]

Some women, then, were reasonably well-educated: Quintilian[25] . . . cites as shining examples Cornelia (mother of the Gracchi),[26] and Hortensia and Laelia who were daughters of orators. . . . But at the age when a boy was going on to the secondary education which trained him in the use of language and prepared him for public life, a girl was entering her first marriage. . . .

Fourteen was evidently a proper age for marriage. It was assumed to be the age of menarche, though if a girl had not reached puberty the marriage might well be arranged anyway, and menstruation encouraged by massage, gentle exercise, good food, and diversion. The legal

---

[19]Tutors.

[20]Greek moralist and biographer, c.46–120 A.D.

[21]Roman philosopher, c.30–c.101 A.D.

[22](185–129 B.C.), often known as Scipio the Younger, Roman statesman and general responsible for the final destruction of Carthage.

[23]Roman poet, 65–8 B.C.

[24]Ionic dance (a type of Greek dancing).

[25]Roman teacher and rhetorician, 35–95 A.D.

[26]Tiberius Gracchus (163–133 B.C.) and Gaius Gracchus (153–121 B.C.), brothers who were Roman statesmen and reformers.

minimum age of marriage, as fixed by Augustan legislation which followed Republican precedent, was 12: earlier marriage was not penalized, but was not valid until the girl reached 12. (It followed that
she could not be prosecuted for adultery.) Some marriages were certainly pre-pubertal. Augustus' own first wife was *vixdum nubilis*,[27] and
Suetonius[28] . . . found it worth recording that he sent her back *intacta*.[29]
One girl . . . was 'taken to her husband's bosom' at 7: perhaps the marriage was not consummated, though Petronius[30] . . . relates (in order to
shock?) the defloration of a seven-year-old. . . .

Plutarch, not surprisingly, thought that Roman girls married too
young, and the Lycurgus[31] was right in ensuring that brides should
be ready for childbearing. Romans, he says, were more concerned to
ensure an undefiled body and mind. . . . Evidently they thought they
had to catch the girls young to be sure. Doctors supposed that sexual
desires began at puberty, especially in girls who ate a lot and did
not have to work; society made provision for such desires instead of
trying to sublimate them. Epictetus[32] remarks sadly that when girls are
fourteen they begin to be called *kuria*,[33] the address of a grown woman:
then they see that there is nothing for it but to go to bed with men,
and begin to make themselves pretty in hopes. (His solution is for
them to learn that men really admire them for modesty and chastity—
and then, one supposes, they may go to bed with philosophers.)
So marriage at fourteen was, in one sense, practical. But were girls
in any sense ready for it? Physically, no: teenage pregnancies were
known to be dangerous, and Soranus . . . stoutly disagrees with the
school of thought which held that conception is good for you. . . . [O]ne
striking contrast between Roman and Greek *mores*: the *materfamilias*[34]
was at the centre of the household's social life. Visitors found her in the
atrium (maybe even doing her wool work) and conversed with her; she
went out shopping, to visit friends, to temples, theatres, and games.
Decorum might require her to be suitably dressed and chaperoned,
and restrained to the point of discourtesy in returning a greeting, but
decorum is not always observed. Probably she had her daughters with
her on some of these occasions; she may even have taken them

---

[27]Scarcely nubile.

[28]Roman biographer and civil servant, c.69–c.140 A.D.

[29]Intact, that is, still a virgin.

[30]Roman satirist, mid-first century A.D.

[31]Legendary founder of the Spartan constitution.

[32]Stoic philosopher, c.55–135 A.D.

[33]Term for a mature woman.

[34]Mother of the family.

to dinner-parties, though some people thought that girls learnt rather too much when out to dinner. A society which did not segregate women, and which praised wives for being pleasant company, gave married life a far better chance than did the conventions of classical Athens. A fourteen-year-old who had grown up in it, expecting to be grown up at fourteen, might well be reasonably mature. And where the expectation of life was nearer 30 + than 70 +, there was no use in delaying recognized adulthood to 16 or 18.

The pressure of mortality was the underlying reason for early marriage. Tullia, Cicero's cherished daughter, was engaged at 12, and married at 16, to an excellent young man. She was widowed at 22, remarried at 23, divorced at 28; married again at 29, divorced at 33—and dead, soon after childbirth, at 34. The evidence of inscriptions shows that she was not untypical. So the fathers who arranged the marriages had good reason to start making alliances, and getting grandchildren, fast.

Fathers arranged marriages: but that was not all there was to it. A father's consent was necessary to the marriage of a daughter in his *potestas*,[35] though he was presumed to have given it unless he explicitly refused. The mother's consent was not relevant. The daughter's consent was necessary, but could be refused only if her father's choice were morally unfit—and, in practice, if she could get relatives and neighbours to back her up. . . . But, in practice, mothers and daughters might well have a say in the matter. Cicero, admittedly an indulgent father, wondered whether Tullia would accept the suitor suggested by Atticus . . . ; Tullia and Terentia presented him with a *fait accompli* and her engagement to Dolabella, though indeed Cicero was out of Italy at the time, and Tullia was a woman entering her third marriage, not a girl of twelve. . . . Anyone who reads Victorian novels will have a picture in mind of the complexities of family feeling and economic necessity which affect the choice of a husband—and of how much can be achieved by helpless young ladies and wives without civil rights. But it seems fair to ask whether the character of a *jeune fille*[36] got much consideration. Pliny . . . was delighted to find the ideal husband for the niece of Junius Mauricus. . . . Minicius, he says, is of a most respectable family, worthy of that into which he will marry. He has already held office, so they will not have the bother of canvassing for him. He is good-looking: Pliny thinks this deserves a mention (other people evidently would not) as a sort of reward for the bride's virginity. He is also rather well off. A very proper display of feeling, which makes no mention of the girl: she had

[35]Legal power.
[36]Young girl.

not met her future husband. Another letter . . . congratulates a friend on his choice of son-in-law and his future grandchildren, but says nothing about the expected happiness of the friend's daughter. It may be relevant that nowhere in the *Aeneid*[37] are Lavinia's[38] views on her future husband considered: she does, once, blush. . . . A suitable connection for the family is what mattered: in the absence of social mobility and Social Security, a family is too much affected by the marriages of its members to leave them to romance.

An arranged marriage, with goodwill and similar expectations on both sides, may have as good a chance of happiness as a romantic marriage. . . . Roman marriages were expected to be happy. Musonius . . . rates the mutual affection of husband and wife above all other ties. . . . In the proscription,[39] . . . wives showed greater loyalty than sons or slaves. The husband of the lady known as Turia recorded . . . his acute distress when she offered him a divorce (they were childless), though he said that marriages as happy and long-lasting as theirs, uninterrupted by death or divorce, were a rarity. Augustus and Livia had one. . . . The ideal was long-lived, harmonious, fertile marriage. But the death rate was not the only impediment. . . .

A woman who married *cum manu*[40] did indeed pass out of her father's *potestas* and into her husband's, on a par with his daughter—with two major exceptions. A daughter could not compel her father to anything, but a wife could compel her husband to divorce; and although a husband with *manus*[41] over his wife controlled all that she possessed and inherited, and need surrender only her dowry if they divorced, wives do seem to have kept control over some property (perhaps by sheer force of character or connections). A woman married *sine manu*,[42] as seems to have been the norm by the mid-first century B.C., remained in her father's *potestas*, needed his consent to any major financial transaction, and might have her marriage ended by him even against her wish. . . .

Divorce could in fact end the commitment of wife to husband very easily. There was no need to prove breakdown of marriage; guilty par-

[37]Roman epic poem, late first century B.C., composed by Virgil.

[38]Character in the *Aeneid* who marries Aeneas, the mythical founder of the Roman people.

[39]During the period of the civil wars in the first century B.C., the proscription was a list proclaiming certain people public enemies.

[40]Literally, "with legal control." A woman who marries *cum manu* passed from the legal control of her father to her husband.

[41]Legal control.

[42]Without legal control.

ties needed to be established only in so far as there might be a financial penalty in the divorce settlement (apparently for an adulterous wife or for the spouse who took the initiative in divorcing). There would, of course, be financial tangles over the repayment of dowry and in sorting out the assets which the couple had managed in common, and these might well be enough to ensure that, among poorer people, marriage contracts would be respected: it is difficult to find clear evidence of divorce at that economic level. But legal tangles and massive debts seldom discouraged upper-class Romans, and the financial patterns of marriage *sine manu* suggest that . . . they were prepared for a break-up.

It is often suggested that the move from marriage *cum manu* to marriage *sine manu* was prompted by the demands of late Republican women for greater freedom. . . . The marriage law of the late Republic is said to have given women exceptional freedom and dignity: 'for the first time in human civilization . . . a law founded on a purely humanistic idea of marriage, as being a free and freely dissoluble union of two equal partners for life.' Now marriage either *cum manu* or *sine manu* gave women more hope of release, if the marriage was unhappy, than indissoluble marriage, which was believed to have been the rule in the early Republic. (As always, there were those who thought it was still the best solution to marital problems—especially the problem of how to stop women causing trouble.) And if one's object was to be *sui iuris*,[43] independent but for the nominal control of a guardian, one's father was likely to release one from his *potestas* by dying sooner than one's husband was, so marriage *sine manu* was a better bet. But it does not appear that women were in a position to make a free choice. A *filiafamilias*[44] could not choose her husband unless she could get round her father; could not divorce him without her father's economic support; and could not prevent herself from being divorced at the instigation of her husband, her father, or his father. She was, indeed, almost her husband's equal in this: he too was subject, at least in theory, to his father's financial control, required his consent to marry (but could refuse his own) and perhaps to divorce, and could be made to divorce: but sons had, in practice, more scope. A woman *sui iuris*, like a man, could make independent decisions, allowing for family and financial constraints. But she had one major disadvantage. If she decided for divorce, she would lose her children, for they belonged to the father's family. Women cannot adopt, say the jurist Gaius . . . , for not even the children of their own bodies are in their *potestas*.

---

[43]Literally, "under your own law." \
[44]Daughter of a family.

The father presumably decided who actually looked after the children of broken marriages. . . .

Women did not vote, did not serve as *iudices*,[45] were not senators or magistrates or holders of major priesthoods. They did not, as a rule, speak in the courts. . . . As a rule, women took no part in public life, except on the rare occasions when they were angry enough to demonstrate, which was startling and shocking. . . .

Women might, then, have considerable influence and interests outside their homes and families, but they were acting from within their families to affect a social system managed by men: their influence was not to be publicly acknowledged. Why were women excluded from public life? The division between arms-bearers and child-bearers was doubtless one historical cause, but the reasons publicly given were different. Women were alleged to be fragile and fickle, and therefore in need of protection; if they were not kept in their proper place they would (fragility and fickleness notwithstanding) take over. As the elder Cato[46] . . . said in defense of the *lex Oppia*:[47]

'Our ancestors decided that women should not handle anything, even a private matter, without the advice of a guardian; that they should always be in the power of fathers, brothers, husbands. . . . Call to mind all those laws on women by which your ancestors restrained their license and made them subject to men: you can only just keep them under by using the whole range of laws. If you let them niggle away at one law after another until they have worked it out of your grasp, until at last you let them make themselves equal to men, do you suppose that you'll be able to stand them? If once they get equality, they'll be on top.' . . .

A social system which restricted women to domestic life, and prevailing attitudes which assumed their inferiority, must seem to us oppressive. I know of no evidence that it seemed so at the time. The legal and social constraints detailed above may have frustrated the abilities of many women and caused much ordinary human unhappiness. But there evidently were, also, many ordinarily happy families where knowledge of real live women took precedence over the theories, and women themselves enjoyed home, children, and friends. There were some women who enjoyed the political game, and who found an emotional life outside their necessary marriages. And there were certainly women who found satisfaction in living up to the standards of the time.

[45]Judges.

[46]Cato the Elder (234–149 B.C.), a statesman of the Roman Republic.

[47]A wartime law, lasting from 215–195 B.C., limiting the freedom and luxuries of Roman women.

They were, as they should be, chaste, dutiful, submissive, and domestic; they took pride in the family of their birth and the family they had produced; and probably their resolution to maintain these standards gave them the support which women in all ages have found in religious faith. But the religious feelings of Roman women, as opposed to the acts of worship in which they might take part, are something of which we know very little. . . .

The son of Murdia,[48] in the age of Augustus, made her a public eulogy. Some of what he said has happened to survive . . . , and, since we should not otherwise know of her existence, may make the best epitaph for the women who did not make the history books.

'What is said in praise of all good women is the same, and straightforward. There is no need of elaborate phrases to tell of natural good qualities and of trust maintained. It is enough that all alike have the same reward: a good reputation. It is hard to find new things to praise in a woman, for their lives lack incident. We must look for what they have in common, lest something be left out to spoil the example they offer us. My beloved mother, then, deserves all the more praise, for in modesty, integrity, chastity, submission, woolwork, industry, and trustworthiness she was just like other women.'

---

[48]Roman woman distinguished only by the fact that her son made a eulogy of her.

Gladiatorial Combat in
Ancient Rome

JÉRÔME CARCOPINO

In the first century A.D., *the population of the city of Rome may have approached one million. The city faced many problems, but the major one for the emperors was the potential for revolt in the hundreds of thousands of Romans who were poor and unemployed. In order to keep the masses contented, the government distributed free food, mainly grain, but other products as well. In addition, the population could look forward to lavish spectacles, which might keep their minds off the wretched and filthy living conditions in the Roman metropolis. Thus did the government follow the policy of "bread and circuses."*

Jérôme Carcopino is awestruck at the sheer horror of the spectacles that pandered to the bloodlust of the populace. Why were the Romans not horrified? Why did the Romans prefer above all else the sport of men killing one another? But perhaps sport is not always the proper term, for Carcopino outlines practices that simply slaughtered people, often in grotesque and gruesome ways.

The appeal of the combats was evident, as the Roman Colosseum filled up with 50,000 frenzied spectators. What sorts of combat did they witness? Who appeared in the arena? If it is difficult to appreciate the cruelty of the crowd, it is likewise perplexing why many men chose to become gladiators. Who became gladiators? What were their lives like? What rewards went to the victors?

Most Romans, of course, accepted gladiatorial contests and public killings as justifiable. What arguments did Romans offer in support of the fights? Was the Roman fondness for such cruelty unique historically?

Revisiting the arenas of Rome after nearly two thousand years of Christianity, we feel as if we were descending into the Hades of antiquity. The amphitheatre demands more than reproach. It is beyond our understanding that the Roman people should have made the human sacrifice, the *munus*, a festival joyously celebrated by the whole city, or come to prefer above all other entertainment the slaughter of men armed to kill and be killed for their amusement. . . . By the first century B.C. the populace had grown so greedy for these sights that candidates sought to win votes by inviting the people to witness spectacular scenes of carnage. In

Jérôme Carcopino, *Daily Life in Ancient Rome. The People and the City at the Height of the Empire* (New Haven: Yale University Press, 1940), 231–247.

order to put an end to corrupt practices the Senate in 63 B.C. passed a law disqualifying for election any magistrate who had financed such shows for the two years preceding the voting. It was natural that aspirants for the imperial throne should play on the people's passion to promote their own ambitious aims. Pompey[1] even sated his fellow-citizens with combats; Caesar freshened their attraction by the luxury with which he surrounded them. Finally the emperors, deliberately pandering to the murderous lust of the crowds, found in gladiatorial games the most sure, if also the most sinister, of their instruments of power.

Augustus was the first. Outside the city itself, he adhered to the posthumous laws of Julius Caesar and continued to limit the municipal magistrates to offering one annual *munus*. Within the city, he ordered the praetors[2] to give annually two *munera* limited to 120 gladiators. In 27 A.D., Tiberius[3] forbade any private person with a fortune less than an "equestrian capital" of 400,000 sesterces[4] to give a *munus*. Claudius[5] transferred the duty of providing the public gladiatorial shows from the praetors to the more numerous quaestors,[6] at the same time again limiting them to 120 gladiators per spectacle.

This restriction aimed less at curbing the passion of his subjects than at enhancing the prestige of their sovereign. For while thus regulating the giving of the public *munera*, Augustus recognized no limit save his own caprice to the number of "extraordinary" *munera*, which he offered the people three times in his own name and five times in the names of his sons and grandsons. By the incomparable splendour of these private gladiatorial spectacles, he practically monopolized the right to provide "extraordinary" *munera*, which was accomplished later by the formal prohibitions of the Flavians.[7] Thus the decrees of Augustus made the *munera* the imperial show par excellence, as official and obligatory as . . . the theatre and the circus. At the same time the empire provided grandiose buildings specially suited to their purpose. The design of these buildings, improvised more or less by chance, and repeated in hundreds of examples, seems to us today a new and mighty creation of Roman architecture—the amphitheatre. . . .

The first permanent amphitheatre was that built in 29 B.C. at Rome . . . and was destroyed in the great fire of 64 A.D. The Flavians decided almost at once to replace it by a larger one of the same

[1]Roman general, rival of Julius Caesar.

[2]Judges.

[3]Emperor, 14–37 A.D.

[4]The fortune needed to qualify for membership in the equestrian social order.

[5]Emperor, 41–54 A.D.

[6]Financial agents of the government.

[7]Emperors from 69–96 A.D.

design. It was started by Vespasian,[8] completed by Titus,[9] and decorated by Diocletian.[10] Since 80 A.D. neither earthquakes nor the Renaissance plunderers who carried off its blocks of stone . . . have seriously damaged it. . . . This is the Flavian amphitheatre, better known since the Middle Ages as the Colosseum. By the year 2 B.C. Augustus, after much costly labour on the right bank of the Tiber, had supplemented the amphitheatre of Taurus, which had been built only for land combats, by a *naumachia*[11] intended for the representation of naval battles. Its exterior ellipse . . . enclosed not an arena of beaten earth covered with sand, but a sheet of water cut by an artificial island and curving through thickets and gardens. Though the *naumachia* of Augustus covered an area almost treble that of the Colosseum, . . . the public soon became dissatisfied, and Trajan[12] was forced to build first the supplementary Amphitheatrum Castrense, . . . and then the supplementary Naumachia Vaticana. . . . Of the two *naumachiae* and of the Amphitheatrum Castrense almost nothing but the memory remains. But the ruins of the Colosseum suffice to show the typical arrangement of the Roman amphitheatre in its most perfect form.

The Colosseum was built of blocks of hard travertine[13] stone extracted from the quarries of Albulae near Tibur (the modern Tivoli) and brought to Rome by a wide road specially constructed for the purpose. The building forms an oval, 527 metres in circumference, with diameters of 188 and 156 metres, and rears its four-storied walls to a height of 57 metres. . . . The seats began four metres above the arena with a terrace or *podium* protected by a bronze balustrade. On the *podium* were ranged the marble seats of the privileged, whose names have been handed down to us. Above these were the tiers for the ordinary public. . . .

✳   . . . [I]t is calculated that the number of sitting places was 45,000 and of standing places 5,000. . . .

The arena, 86 by 54 metres in diameter, enclosed an area of 3,500 square metres. It was surrounded by a metal grating, 4 metres in front of the base of the *podium*, which protected the public from the wild beasts which were loosed into the arena. Before the gladiators entered through one of the arcades of the longer axis, the animals were already imprisoned in the underground chambers of the arena. This basement

[8]Emperor, 69–79 A.D.

[9]Emperor, 79–81 A.D.

[10]Emperor, 284–305 A.D.

[11]Building designed to hold simulated sea battles.

[12]Emperor, 98–117 A.D.

[13]A light-colored limestone.

was originally fitted with a water system which in 80 A.D. could flood the arena in a twinkling and transform in into a *naumachia*. Later—no doubt at the time when Trajan built his *Naumachia Vaticana*—it was provided with cages of masonry, in which the animals could be confined, and also with a system of ramps and hoists, so that they could either be quickly driven up or instantaneously launched into the arena. . . . Every detail of its internal arrangement is a triumph of technical ingenuity. Its solidity has defied the centuries and it still inspires the beholder with the sense of utter satisfaction that one feels in gazing on the Church of Saint Peter—the sense of a power so great as to be overwhelming, an art so sure that the infallible proportions blend into perfect harmony. But if its charm is to hold us, we must forget the inhuman ends for which this monument was raised, the spectacles of unpardonable cruelty for which the imperial architects of old created it.

At the period which we are studying, the organisation of these bloody games left no room for improvement. In the Italian *municipia*[14] and in the provincial towns, the local magistrates whose duty it was annually to provide the *munera* called in the expert advice of specialist contractors, the *lanistae*. These contractors, whose trade shares in Roman law and literature the same infamy that attaches to that of the pander or procurer . . . , were in sober fact Death's middlemen. The *lanista* would hire out his troupe of gladiators . . . , at the best figure he could command, . . . for combats in which about half were bound to lose their lives. He maintained his "family" at his own expense, under a system of convict discipline which made no distinction between the slaves he had purchased, starving wretches whom he had recruited, and ruined sons of good family. These young ne'er-do-wells were lured by the rewards and fortune they would win from the victories he would ensure them, and by the certainty of being well and amply fed in his "training school.". . . They discounted the premium which he was to pay them if they survived the term of their contract, and hired themselves out to him body and soul, abandoning all their human rights . . . and steeling themselves to march at his command to the butchery.

At Rome on the other hand there were no longer any *lanistae*. Their functions were performed exclusively by the *procuratores*[15] of the princeps. These agents had special official buildings . . . at their disposal. . . . They were also in charge of the wild and exotic animals which subject provinces and client kings, even to the potentates of India, sent to fill the emperor's menagerie. . . . Their gladiators, con-

[14]Municipalities.
[15]Deputies.

stantly recruited from men condemned to death and from prisoners taken in war, formed an effective army of fighters.

The body of gladiators was divided into pupils and instructors, who were assigned according to their physical aptitudes to the different "arms": the Samnites carried the shield . . . and sword . . . ; the Thracians protected themselves with a round buckler . . . and handled the dagger . . . ; the *murmillones* wore a helmet crowned with a sea fish; the *retiarii*, who were usually pitted against the *murmillones*, carried a net and a trident.

Like the games, the *munera* usually lasted from dawn to dusk, although sometimes . . . they were prolonged into the night. It was, therefore, all important to vary the fighting, and the gladiators were trained to fight on water in a *naumachia* as readily as on the firm arena of the amphitheatre. They were not, however, pitted against wild animals; such contests were reserved for the *bestiarii*.[16]

Writers and inscriptions on monuments tell of several types of animal contests or hunts *(venationes)*. There were some relatively innocent ones to break the monotony of massacre—tame animals doing incredible circus turns . . . : teams of panthers obediently drawing chariots; lions releasing from their jaws a live hare they had caught; tigers coming to lick the hand of the tamer who had just been lashing them; elephants gravely kneeling before the imperial box or tracing Latin phrases in the sand with their trunks. There were terrible spectacles, in which ferocious beasts fought duels to the death: bear against buffalo, buffalo against elephant, elephant against rhinoceros. There were disgusting ones in which the men, from the safe shelter of iron bars or from the height of the imperial box . . . let fly their arrows at animals roaring with baffled rage, and flooded the arena with the blood of butchery. Some were given a touch of beauty by living greenery planted in the arena which ennobled the courage and the skill of the fighters. They risked their lives, it is true, in battle with bulls, panthers and lions, leopards and tigers; but they were always armed with hunting spears and glowing firebrands, with bows, lances and daggers, and often accompanied by a pack of Scotch hounds, so that they were exposing themselves no more than the emperor himself in the hunts, which were in those days a kind of minor war. They made it a point of honour to redouble the danger by their daring, stunning the bear with their fists instead of their weapons, or blinding the lion by flinging over his head the folds of their cloak; or they would quicken the spectators' pleasure by waving a red cloth in front of the bull, as the Spanish toreadors still do, or by eluding his charge with deft feints and skilful ruses. Sometimes to escape the beast's attack they would scale a wall or leap onto a pole, slip into

[16]Fighters of wild beasts.

one of the partitioned turnstiles . . . which had been prepared before-hand in the arena, or hastily disappear into a spherical basket fitted with spikes which gave it the forbidding appearance of a porcupine. . . .

Such *venationes*, however, usually provided an added attraction to the main spectacle of gladiators. They were but a slight exaggeration of the stern reality of ancient hunting, and can hardly be held a reproach to the amphitheatre, for the Praetorian[17] cavalry sometimes took part in them as in military manoeuvres. What revolts us is the quantity of victims, the bath of animal blood: 5,000 beasts were killed in one day of the *munera* with which Titus inaugurated the Colosseum in 80 A.D.; 2,246 and 443 in two *munera* of Trajan. The extent of this carnage nauseates us today, but it served at least one practical purpose. Thanks to this large-scale slaughter the Caesars purged their states of wild beasts; the hippopotamus was driven out of Nubia, the lion out of Mesopotamia, the tiger from Hyrcania, and the elephant from North Africa. . . .

But the Roman Empire also dishonoured civilisation with all the forms of *hoplomachia* and with a variety of *venatio* as cowardly as it was cruel.

Hoplomachia was the gladiatorial combat proper. Sometimes the bat-tle was a mimic one, fought with muffled weapons, as our fencing matches are staged with buttons on the foils. . . . These mock battles were only a foretaste of the *munus*, a sequence or simultaneous perfor-mance of serious duels in which the weapons were not padded nor the blows softened, and in which each gladiator could hope to escape death only by dealing it to his opponent. The night before, a lavish banquet, which was destined to be the last meal of many, united the combatants of the morrow. The public was admitted to view this *cena libera*,[18] and the curious circulated round the tables with unwholesome joy. Some of the guests brutalised or fatalistic, abandoned themselves to the plea-sures of the moment and ate gluttonously. Others, anxious to increase their chances by taking thought for their health, resisted the tempta-tions of the generous fare and ate with moderation. The most wretched, haunted by a presentiment of approaching death, their throats and bel-lies already paralysed by fear, gave way to lamentation, commended their families to the passers-by, and made their last will and testament.

On the following day the *munus* began with a parade. The gladia-tors, driven in carriages . . . to the Colosseum, alighted in front of the amphitheatre and marched round the arena in military array, dressed in chlamys[19] dyed purple and embroidered in gold. They walked non-chalantly, their hands swinging freely, followed by valets carrying

[17]The Praetorians constituted the emperor's guard.

[18]Free meal.

[19]A short mantle clasped at the shoulder.

their arms; and . . . they turned toward the emperor, their right hands extended in sign of homage, and addressed to him the justifiably melancholy saluation: "Hail, Emperor, those who are about to die salute thee! . . . " When the parade was over, the arms were examined . . . and blunt swords weeded out, so that the fatal business might be expedited. Then the weapons were distributed, and the duellists paired off by lot. Sometimes it was decided to pit against each other only gladiators of the same category, while at other times gladiators were to oppose each other with different arms: a Samnite against a Thracian; a *murmillo* against a *retiarius*; or, to add spice to the spectacle, such freak combinations as negro against negro, as in the *munus* with which Nero[20] honoured Tiridates, king of Armenia; dwarf against woman, as in Domitian's[21] *munus* in 90 A.D.

Then at the order of the president the series of duels opened, to the cacophonies of an orchestra, or rather a band, which combined flutes with strident trumpets, and horns with a hydraulic organ. The first pair of gladiators had scarcely come to grips before a fever, like that which reigned at the races, seized the amphitheatre. As at the Circus Maximus[22] the spectators panted with anxiety or hope, some for the Blues, others for the Greens, the spectators of the *munus* divided their prayers between the *parmularii* (men armed with small shields) . . . or the *scutarri* (men armed with large shields). . . . Bets . . . were exchanged . . . ; and lest the result be somehow prearranged between the fighters, an instructor stood beside them ready to . . . excite their homicidal passion by crying "Strike! . . . "; "Slay! . . . "; "Burn him! . . . "; and, if necessary, to stimulate them by thrashing them with leather straps *(lora)* till the blood flowed. At every wound which the gladiators inflicted on each other, the public—trembling for its stakes—reacted with increasing excitement. If the opponent of their champion happened to totter, the gamblers could not restrain their delight and savagely counted the blows: "That's got him! . . . "; "Now he's got it! . . . "; and they thrilled with barbaric joy when he crumpled under a mortal thrust.

At once the attendants, disguised either as Charon[23] or as Hermes Psychopompos,[24] approached the prostrate form, assured themselves that he was dead by striking his forehead with a mallet, and waved to

[20]Emperor, 54–68 A.D.

[21]Emperor, 81–96 A.D.

[22]The major race track in Rome.

[23]The ferryman in Greek mythology responsible for taking the dead across the river Styx.

[24]Hermes the messenger-god who leads souls to the underworld.

their assistants . . . to carry him out of the arena on a stretcher, while they themselves hastily turned over the blood-stained sand. Sometimes it happened that the combatants were so well matched that there was no decisive result; either the two duellists, equally skilful, equally robust, fell simultaneously or both remained standing. . . . The match was then declared a draw and the next pair was called. More often the loser, stunned or wounded, had not been mortally hit, but feeling unequal to continuing the struggle, laid down his arms, stretched himself on his back and raised his left arm in a mute appeal for quarter. In principle the right of granting this rested with the victor, and we can read the epitaph of a gladiator slain by an adversary whose life he had once spared in an earlier encounter. It professes to convey from the other world this fiercely practical advice to his successors: "Take warning by my fate. No quarter for the fallen, be he who he may! . . . " But the victor renounced his claim in the presence of the emperor, who often consulted the crowd before exercising the right thus ceded to him. When the conquered man was thought to have defended himself bravely, the spectators waved their handkerchiefs, raised their thumbs, and cried: ". . . Let him go!" If the emperor sympathised with their wishes and like them lifted his thumb, the loser was pardoned and sent living from the arena. . . . If, on the other hand, the witnesses decided that the victim had by his weakness deserved defeat, they turned their thumbs down, crying: " . . . Slay him!" And the emperor calmly passed the death sentence with inverted thumb. . . .

The victor had, this time, escaped and he was rewarded on the spot. He received silver dishes laden with gold pieces and costly gifts, and taking these presents in his hands he ran across the arena amid the acclamations of the crowd. Of a sudden he tasted both wealth and glory. In popularity and riches this slave, this decadent citizen, this convicted criminal, now equalled the fashionable pantomimes and charioteers. At Rome as at Pompeii, where the *graffiti* retail his conquests, the butcher of the arena became the breaker of hearts: "decus puellarum, suspirium puellarum."[25] But neither his wealth nor his luck could save him. He usually had to risk his own life again and sacrifice other lives in new victories before he could win, not the palms which symbolised success, but the more coveted wooden sword, the *rudis*, which signified his liberation and was granted as a title of honour.

At the period which we have reached, the emperors inclined to cut short the period of service which delayed the liberation of the best duellists. Martial[26] praises the magnanimity of the invincible

---

[25]"The women's prize, the one who makes them breathe heavily."

[26]Roman poet, c.40–104 A.D.

Domitian . . . because he had cried a halt to a fight between two gladiators who had reached a deadlock, and handed to both the *rudis* of
liberty along with the palm of victory. . . .

There are therefore occasional gleams of humanity in this business of wholesale butchery. At first the gladiator often begged leave
to decline the emperor's clemency; he had fallen so low morally that he
preferred to resume his trade of slayer rather than renounce the luxu-
rious life of his barracks, the thrill of danger, and the intoxication of
victory. We possess the epitaph of such a one, Flamma by name, who,
after bearing off the palm twenty-one times, had four times received the
rudis and each time "signed on again." Later the *munera* developed to
astounding proportions. I shall quote only the figures . . . which cover
the period extending from the end of March, 108 A.D., through April,
113 A.D. There we find mention of two minor shows, one of 350 pairs
of gladiators, the other of 202, while the major event was a *munus*
lasting 117 days in which 4,941 pairs of gladiators took part. Even the
assumption that Trajan granted the survivors their liberty *en bloc* does
little to assuage the memory of a field strewn with corpses. Cicero[27]
indeed assures us that although there may be other methods of teaching contempt for pain and death, there is assuredly none which speaks
more eloquently to the eye than a *munus*; and later Pliny the Younger[28]
contended that these massacres were essentially calculated to engender courage by showing how the love of glory and the desire to conquer could lodge even in the breast of criminals and slaves. These are
specious excuses. The thousands of Romans who day after day, from
morning until night, could take pleasure in this slaughter and not spare
a tear for those whose sacrifice multiplied their stakes, were learning
nothing but contempt for human life and dignity.

These feigned combats, moreover, were often made the cloak
of sordid murders and ruthless executions. Rome and even the
municipia retained until the end of the third century the practice of
proclaiming . . . gladiatorial combats from which none might escape
alive. No sooner had one of the duellists fallen than a substitute . . . was
produced to fight the conqueror, until the entire body of combatants
was exterminated. Then, too, there were moments in the normal full-
day program at Rome when exceptional atrocities were committed. The
gladiatores meridiani, whose account was squared at the noon pause,
were recruited exclusively from robbers, murderers, and incendiaries,
whose crimes had earned them the death of the amphitheatre. . . . The
pitiable contingent of the doomed was driven into the arena. The first

---

[27]Roman philosopher and republican statesman of the first century B.C.
[28]Statesman and civil servant, 61/2–113 A.D.

pair were brought forth, one man armed and one dressed simply in a tunic. The business of the first was to kill the second, which he never failed to do. After this feat he was disarmed and led out to confront a newcomer armed to the teeth, and so the inexorable butchery continued until the last head had rolled in the dust.

The morning massacre was even more hideous. Perhaps it was Augustus who unintentionally invented this spectacular punishment when he erected in the Forum a pillory which collapsed and dropped the victim, the bandit Selurus, into a cage of wild beasts. Later the idea was taken up and made general. Criminals of both sexes and all ages, who by reason of their villainy—real or supposed—and their humble status had been condemned *ad bestias*,[29] were dragged at dawn into the arena to be mauled by the wild animals loosed from the basement below. . . .

This was the kind of torture heroically undergone by the virgin Blandina in the amphitheatre at Lyons, by Perpetua and Felicita[30] in Carthage, and in the Eternal City itself by so many Christians, anonymous or canonised, of the Roman Church. In memory of these martyrs a cross now rises in the Colosseum in silent protest against the barbarism which cost so many of them their lives before the spirit of Christianity succeeded in abolishing it. . . .

. . . [T]he Roman people remain guilty of deriving a public joy from their capital executions by turning the Colosseum into a torture-chamber and a human-slaughter house.

We must, however, credit the flower of Rome with terror at the progress of this dread disease and more than one attempt to reduce its virulence.

⟩ Augustus . . . tried to acclimatise Greek games at Rome. These contests strengthened the body instead of destroying it, and included artistic as well as physical competitions. Both to commemorate his victory over Anthony and Cleopatra and to give thanks for it to Apollo, Augustus founded the Actiaca, which were to be celebrated every fourth year both at Actium[31] and Rome. But by 16 A.D. the Actiaca are no longer recorded. Nero wished to revive them in his Neronia, which were to be periodic festivals comprising tests of physical endurance and competitions of poetry and song. The senators deigned to take part in the former; but in the latter none dared to dispute the crown with the emperor, who believed himself an unrivalled artist. Despite their august

[29]To the wild beasts.

[30]Christian martyrs.

[31]Battle in 31 B.C. in which Augustus (then known as Octavian) defeated Anthony and Cleopatra.

patronage, however, the Neronia fell quickly into abeyance, and it was Domitian who at length succeeded in endowing Rome with a lasting cycle of games in the Greek style. In 86 A.D. he instituted the *Agon Capitolinus*, whose prizes the emperor awarded alternately for foot races and for eloquence, for boxing and Latin poetry, for discus-throwing and Greek poetry, for javelin-casting and for music. He built the Circus Agonalis . . . especially for his sports; and for the more "spiritual" contests erected the Odeum. . . . In his reign the Greek games which his bounty maintained enjoyed an ephemeral popularity. . . . The games survived their founder, but though we have proof that they were celebrated in the fourth century and that the jurists never ceased to emphasise the high honour they deserved, they never seriously rivalled the *munera* in favour. For one thing the *Agon Capitolinus* recurred only once in four years. Furthermore, Domitian designed them to appeal to a select and limited public, for his Odeum provided only 10,600 *loca*[32] and his Circus Agonalis only 30,088—say 5,000 and 15,000 seats respectively—so that the two together were less than half the size of the Amphitheatrum Flavium alone.

There is no denying the fact that the Greek games were never very popular. The crowd, addicted to the thrills of the Colosseum, looked on them as colourless and tame; and they enjoyed no greater favour among the upper classes, who professed to detect an exotic degeneracy and immorality in their nudism.

Pliny the Younger applauds the Senate's decision under Trajan to forbid the scandal of the gymnastic games at Vienne in Gallia Narbonensis and complacently quotes his colleague Junius Mauricus, . . . as saying, "and I would that they could be abolished in Rome, too!" for "these games have greatly infected the manners of the people of Vienne, as they have universally had the same effect among us." The incompatibility between the . . . Greek games and the brutality of gladiatorial combats was bound to be irreconcilable. It is significant that while the majority of provincial towns imitated Rome by building amphitheatres, whose ruins have been found in South Algeria and on the banks of the Euphrates, Greece herself fought tooth and nail against the contagion, and in Attica, at least, apparently succeeded. This one exception is a poor make-weight to the general infatuation. . . .

It seemed indeed that the *munus* was not to be eradicated. Good emperors, therefore, sought to humanise it. While Hadrian[33] forbade impressment of slaves into gladiatorial troupes, Trajan and Marcus Aurelius[34] exerted themselves to the utmost to extend the part played

[32]Places.

[33]Emperor, 117–138 A.D.

[34]Philosopher and emperor, 161–180 A.D.

in their festivals by the mimic combats *(lusiones)*, at the expense of the *munus* proper. On March 30, 108, Trajan finished a *lusio* which had lasted thirty days and involved 350 pairs of gladiators. Marcus Aurelius, obeying the dictates of his Stoic philosophy, exhausted his ingenuity in reducing the regulations and budgets of the *munera* and in this way lessening their importance, and whenever it fell to him to offer entertainment to the Roman plebs he substituted simple *lusiones*. But philosophy lost the round in this struggle against spectacles where, as Seneca phrased it, man drank the blood of man. . . .

After Marcus Aurelius, whose son Commodus[35] himself aspired to gladiatorial fame, the Romans, not contented with the discontinuation of *lusiones*, inclined to desert the theatre for the amphitheatre. From the second century on we find the theatre architects in the provinces, notably in Gaul and Macedonia, modifying their building plans to accommodate gladiatorial duels and *venationes*. At Rome the representation of sinister drama was transferred to the arena, and it became usual to play the most terrifying mimes at the Colosseum— *Laureolus*, who was crucified alive for the amusement of the public, *Mucius Scaevola*, who plunged his right hand into the burning coals of a brazier, and the *Death of Hercules*, whose hero in the last act writhed in the flames of his pyre. As the amphitheatre henceforth sufficed for the more lurid dramatic representations, no attempt was made to repair the ruined theatres. . . .

It might have been predicted that the *munera* would be everlasting and that nothing henceforward could stop their invading growth. But where Stoicism had failed the new religion was to succeed. The conquering Gospel taught the Romans no longer to tolerate the inveterate shame. Racing continued as long as the races of the circus were maintained, but the butcheries of the arena were stopped at the command of Christian emperors. On October 1, 326, Constantine decreed that condemnation *ad bestias* must be commuted to forced labour . . . , and dried up at one blow the principal source of recruitment for the gladiatorial schools. By the end of the fourth century gladiatorial shows had disappeared from the East. In 404 an edict of Honorius suppressed gladiatorial combats in the West. Roman Christianity thus blotted out the crime against humanity which under the pagan Caesars had disgraced the amphitheatre of the empire.

[35]Emperor, 180–192 A.D.

Why Were the Early Christians Persecuted?

G.E.M. DE STE. CROIX

Advocates of brotherly love, humility, moral uprightness, and religious righteous-ness, Christians were nevertheless persecuted, albeit sporadically, from the end of the first to the fourth century. G.E.M. de Ste. Croix attempts to explain why. He looks at the Roman government's attitudes toward Christians, the legal proce-dures under which Christians could be tried and punished, the reasons why the pagan populace abhorred Christians, and the views that educated Romans held of Christianity.

What was the government's role in persecuting Christians? To what extent did emperors influence persecution? What leeway did provincial governors have in determining whether or not to try Christians? Did the legal process encourage persecution or did it function to prevent maltreatment of Christians? The role of private as opposed to state prosecutors surely made persecution more difficult, for the accuser himself could be liable if the court determined his charge to be without foundation.

Many of the charges against Christians, such as cannibalism and incest, had no basis in fact. Most often, Christians were simply charged with being Christians. Some Christians renounced their faith, often only temporarily, yet others courageously maintained it. Many publicly acknowledged their Christianity and thus committed religious suicide. Why were numerous Christians anxious to become martyrs? It is important to remember that, unlike others charged with capital offences, Christians did not usually have to die; they could deny their religion and live. Thus we can not lay all the blame for persecution on the Romans; Christians bore much responsibility for their fate. In addition, different Christian groups leveled charges against one another that could only convince Romans that the evil things they had heard about Christians must have been true. It must not be forgotten, too, that, when the Roman Empire officially became Christian in the fourth century, Christians began to persecute pagans.

. . . The question I have taken as a title needs to be broken down in two quite different ways. One is to distinguish between the general population of the Graeco-Roman world and what I am going to call for convenience "the government": I mean of course the emperor, the senate, the central officials and the provincial governors, the key fig-

G.E.M. de Ste. Croix, "Why Were The Early Christians Persecuted?" *Past and Present* 26 (1963): 6–17, 18–31.

ures for our purpose being the emperor and even more the provincial governors. In this case we ask first, "For what reasons did ordinary pagans demand persecution?", and secondly, "Why did the government persecute?" The second way of dividing up our general question is to distinguish the reasons which brought about persecution from the purely legal basis of persecution—the juridical principles and institutions invoked by those who had already made up their minds to take action.

But let us not look at the persecutions entirely from the top, so to speak—from the point of view of the persecutors. Scholars who have dealt with this subject . . . have with few exceptions paid too little attention to . . . persecution as seen by the Christians—in a word, martyrdom, a concept which played a vitally important part in the life of the early Church.

It is convenient to divide the persecutions into three distinct phases. The first ends just before the great fire at Rome in 64; the second begins with the persecution which followed the fire and continues until 250; and the third opens with the persecution under Decius[1] in 250-1 and lasts until 313—or, if we take account of the anti-Christian activities of Licinius[2] in his later years, until the defeat of Licinius by Constantine[3] in 324. We know of no persecution by the Roman government until 64, and there was no general persecution until that of Decius. Between 64 and 250 there were only isolated, local persecutions; and even if the total number of victims was quite considerable (as I think it probably was), most individual outbreaks must usually have been quite brief. Even the general persecution of Decius lasted little more than a year, and the second general persecution, that of Valerian[4] in 257-9, less than three years. The third and last general persecution, by Diocletian[5] and his colleagues from 303 onwards (the so-called "Great Persecution"), continued for only about two years in the West, although it went on a good deal longer in the East. In the intervals between these general persecutions the situation . . . remained very much what it had been earlier, except that on the whole the position of the Church was distinctly better: there were several local persecutions, but there were also quite long periods during which the Christians enjoyed something like complete peace over most of the empire; and in addition the

[1]Emperor, 249–251.

[2]Coemperor in 308, then emperor of the East, 313–324.

[3]Emperor, 310–337.

[4]Emperor, 253–259.

[5]Emperor, 284–305.

capacity of the Christian churches to own property was recognized, at least under some emperors. . . . [C]omplete toleration of Christianity was never officially proclaimed before the edict of Galerius[6] in 311.

The subject is a large one, and I cannot afford to spend time on the first phase of persecution (before 64), during which, in so far as it took place at all, persecution was on a small scale and came about mainly as a result of Jewish hostility, which tended to lead to disturbances. After the execution of Jesus, the organs of government come quite well out of it all: their general attitude is one of impartiality or indifference towards the religious squabbles between Jews and Christians. In consequence of riots provoked by Christian missionary preaching, action was sometimes taken by the officials of local communities. But any Christians who were martyred . . . were victims of purely Jewish enmity, which would count for little outside Judaea itself. . . .

I do not intend to give a narrative, even in outline, of the second and third phases of persecution, which I shall mainly deal with together. The earliest stages of intervention on the part of the government, before about 112, are particularly obscure to us. We cannot be certain how and when the government began to take action; but . . . I believe it was in the persecution by Nero at Rome which followed the great fire in 64. . . . In order to kill the widely believed rumour that he himself was responsible for starting the fire, Nero falsely accused and savagely punished the Christians. First, those who admitted being Christians were prosecuted, and then, on information provided by them (doubtless under torture), a great multitude were convicted, not so much (according to Tacitus)[7] of the crime of incendiarism as because of their hatred of the human race. . . . The Christians were picked on as scapegoats, then, because they were already believed by the populace to be capable of horrid crimes, *flagitia*: that is worth noticing. (Had not the Empress Poppaea Sabina[8] been particularly sympathetic towards the Jews, they might well have been chosen as the most appropriate scapegoats.) And once the first batch of Nero's Christian victims had been condemned, whether on a charge of organised incendiarism or for a wider "complex of guilt", there would be nothing to prevent the magistrate conducting the trials . . . from condemning the rest of the charge familiar to us in the second century, of simply "being a Christian" — a status which now necessarily involved, by definition, membership of an anti-social and potentially criminal conspiracy.

I now want to begin examining the attitude of the government

[6]Emperor, 305–311.

[7]Roman historian, c.55–c.117.

[8]Wife of the Emperor Nero, d.65.

towards the persecution of the Christians. I propose to consider mainly the legal problems first, . . . and we shall then be in a very much better position to understand the reasons which prompted the government to persecute; although before we can finally clarify these, we shall have to consider the other side of our problem: the reasons for the hatred felt towards Christianity by the mass of pagans.

The legal problems, from which a certain number of non-legal issues can hardly be separated, may be grouped under three heads. First, what was the nature of the official charge or charges? Secondly, before whom, and according to what form of legal process, if any, were Christians tried? And thirdly, what was the legal foundation for the charges? . . .

I will deal with the first question now, and then the other two together.

First, then, the nature of the charges against the Christians. . . . [F]rom at least 112 onwards (perhaps, as we have seen, from 64) the normal charge against Christians was simply "being Christians": they are punished, that is to say, "for the Name". . . . Pliny[9] speaks of the Christians he had executed as "those who were charged before me *with being Christians*" . . . , and the only question he says he asked these confessors was whether they admitted this charge . . . , and Trajan[10] in his reply speaks of "those who had been charged before you *as Christians*" . . . , and goes on to say that anyone "who *denies he is a Christian*" . . . and proves it "by offering prayers to our gods" can go free. With the other evidence, that settles the matter. Now the *delatores*[11] who first accused the Christians as such before Pliny could not be sure . . . that Pliny would consent to take cognizance of the matter at all, let alone inflict the death penalty. Since they thought it was worth "trying it on", they evidently knew that in the past other officials had been prepared to punish Christians as such. And in fact Pliny now did so, although later on he had second thoughts and consulted the emperor, saying he was doubtful on what charge and to what extent he should investigate and punish, and in particular whether he should take the age of the accused into account, whether he should grant pardon to anyone who was prepared to apostatize, and whether he should punish for the Name alone or for the abominable crimes associated with being a Christian. . . . Trajan explicity refused to lay down any general or definite rules and was very selective in his answers to Pliny's questions. In two passages which do him great credit he instructs Pliny that Chris-

---

[9]Pliny (the Younger), statesman and civil servant, 61/2–113.

[10]Emperor, 98–117.

[11]Private prosecutors. Private prosecution was the norm in Rome; today, state prosecution is.

tians must not be sought out . . . , and that anonymous denunciations are to be ignored, "for they create the worst sort of precedent and are quite out of keeping with the spirit of our age". Christians who are accused as such, in due form . . . , and are convicted must be punished, but anyone who denies he is a Christian, and proves it "by offering prayers to our gods", is to receive "pardon on the score of his repentance" and be set free. . . . Pliny could justifiably take this to mean that punishment was to be for the Name alone.

. . . One often hears it said that the Christians were martyred "for refusing to worship the emperor". In fact, emperor-worship is a factor of almost no independent importance in the persecution of the Christians. It is true that among our records of martyrdoms emperor-worship does crop up occasionally, but far more often it is a matter of sacrificing *to the gods*—as a rule, not even specifically to "the gods *of the Romans*". And when the cult act involved does concern the emperor, it is usually an oath by his Genius . . . or a sacrifice to the gods on his behalf. Very characteristic is the statement of Vigellius Saturninus, proconsul of Africa in 180, to the Scillitan martyrs:[12] "We too are religious, and our religion is simple, and we swear by the Genius óf our lord the emperor, and we pray for his welfare, as you also ought to do.". . . And there is ample evidence to show that the situation remained substantially the same right through the third and early fourth centuries, even during the general persecutions.

I now turn to the nature of the judicial process against the Christians. . . .

The procedure against Christians was in every case that used for the vast majority of criminal trials under the Principate: *cognitio extra ordinem* (or *extraordinaria*),[13] which I shall discuss in a moment. Capital trials under this process in the provinces took place before the provincial governor and no one else. In Rome . . . none of the known cases was important enough to come directly before the emperor himself, or the senate, although in the early Principate appeals by Roman citizens first accused elsewhere may have gone to the emperor's court.

Now Roman law was surely the most impressive intellectual achievement of Roman civilization. But what Roman lawyers of today mean when they speak of Roman law is essentially private law, a large part of which is concerned with property rights, their definition and protection. . . . Large areas of Roman criminal and public law, however, were by contrast very unsatisfactory, and one of the worst of these blemishes was precisely *cognitio extra ordinem*, the procedure by

---

[12]Twelve Christian martyrs from Scillium in North Africa.
[13]Extraordinary criminal procedure or jurisdiction.

which the large deficiencies of the *quaestio*[14] system (the *ordo iudiciorum publicorum*,[15] regulating the punishment of what may be called "statutory crimes"), which at least was subject to fairly strict rules, were supplemented by direct governmental intervention. . . . [T]he rather few offences dealt with by the *quaestio* system were essentially those of "high society and the governing personnel"; the "crimes of the common man"—theft and so forth—had largely to be dealt with *extra ordinem*, even at Rome. In making use of *cognitio extra ordinem* the magistrate concerned had a very wide discretion—even more so, of course, in criminal trials than in civil actions, just because of the relative vagueness of the criminal law. This discretion extended not only to fixing penalties, but even to deciding which cases the magistrate would recognize as criminal and which . . . he would refuse even to consider. The right of judicial *cognitio* (*iurisdictio*)[16] belonged to all provincial governors as part of their *imperium*.[17] In the criminal sphere it was almost unlimited, save in so far as the rights of Roman citizens . . . had to be respected, and in so far as a prosecution might be brought against the governor at Rome after his term of office was over. . . .

In a sense, the power to conduct a criminal *cognitio* was part of the power of *coercitio*[18] inherent in *imperium*; but it is quite wrong to conceive the Christians as being punished by pure *coercitio* in the narrower sense, summarily and without the exercise of proper *iurisdictio*: *coercitio* in that sense, exercised . . . in an informal manner, was limited to minor offences. I cannot help feeling that some of those who have persisted in speaking of the proceedings against the Christians as "police measures" have not fully realized that the trials in question were in no way summary proceedings by pure *coercitio* but proper legal trials, involving the exercise of *iurisdictio* in the fullest sense. . . .

Since our information comes almost entirely from Christian sources, interested in recording martyrdoms, the great majority of the trials of Christians we know about in detail end in conviction and a death sentence. But the very wide discretion exercised by the provincial governor might on occasion work in favour of accused Christians. The most significant evidence comes from Tertullian's[19] *Ad Scapulam*,[20] written probably in 212, where we hear that the very first proconsul to

---

[14]The ordinary criminal procedure.

[15]System of public judgments.

[16]Jurisdiction.

[17]Right to command, or full executive power.

[18]Coercion.

[19]Christian theologian, c.160–c.230.

[20]*To Scapula.*

shed Christian blood in Africa was Vigellius Saturninus, who was in office as late as 180; and that a whole series of African proconsuls (after Saturninus, it seems) had gone out of their way to be friendly to accused Christians: one of them helped the Christians to conduct their case in such a way as to secure an acquittal . . . ; another acquitted an accused Christian outright, apparently on the ground that to convict him would cause a riot; yet another, reluctant at having to deal with such a case, released an accused Christian who consented under torture to apostatize, without actually making him sacrifice; and a fourth tore up the vexatious indictment of a Christian when his accuser failed to appear.

That shows how things might work in practice. A governor exercising *cognitio extraordinaria* in a criminal case was bound (for all practical purposes) only by those imperial *constitutiones*[21] and *mandata*[22] which were relevant in his particular area and were still in force. Unfortunately, official publication of imperial *constitutiones* seems to have been an extremely inefficient and haphazard process, and a conscientious governor might often find himself in great perplexity as to what the law was. . . .

Once Pliny's correspondence with Trajan had been "published" (no doubt by his friends, soon after 117, when he and Trajan were both dead), every educated Roman would be likely to know what instructions Trajan had given regarding the Christians; and thereafter any provincial governor might well feel that until official policy towards the Christians changed he had better follow the same procedure. But other governors, at any rate in other provinces, were not absolutely bound by this precedent. . . .

It is important to remember that the standard procedure in punishing Christians was "accusatory" and not "inquisitorial": a governor would not normally take action until a formal denunciation (*delatio nominis*) was issued by a *delator*, a man who was prepared not merely to inform but actually to conduct the prosecution in person, and to take the risk of being himself arraigned on a charge of *calumnia*, malicious prosecution, if he failed to make out a sufficient case. Trajan . . . forbade the seeking out of Christians. This principle, however, could be and sometimes was disregarded. The best attested example comes from the savage persecution at Lyons and Vienne in 177, when the governor did order a search to be made for Christians. . . . It is wrong to say the governor here was acting "illegally", because of course he was not absolutely bound to follow Trajan's rescript to Pliny; but it looks as if the great majority of gov-

---

[21]Constitutions.
[22]Instructions.

ernors did follow it. On this occasion the governor actually condemned to the beasts, as a favour to the enraged populace, a Christian named Attalus, who was a Roman citizen, although the emperor had just given specific instructions to the governor that Christians who were Roman citizens should be beheaded. He was exceeding his instructions, certainly; but he could plead political necessity, and there is no reason to think he was taken to task by the emperor. . . .

This raises another point: the attitude of the emperor. Christian propaganda from at least the middle of the second century onwards tried to make out that it was only the "bad emperors" who persecuted, and that the "good emperors" protected the Christians; but there is no truth in this at all. . . . In reality, persecution went on automatically, if sporadically, whoever the emperor might be; and until the third century at any rate it is better not to think of persecutions primarily in terms of emperors. It was the provincial governor in each case who played the more significant role—and even his attitude might be less important than what I must call "public opinion". If the state of local feeling was such that no one particularly wanted to take upon himself the onus of prosecuting Christians, very few governors would have any desire to instigate a persecution. If, on the other hand, public opinion was inflamed against the Christians . . . , then delators would not be lacking, and Christians would be put on trial; and few governors would have any motive for resisting strong local feeling demonstrated in this perfectly permissible way, especially if some of the more influential men in the area were leading the agitation, as they often would be. Imperial instructions . . . given to provincial governors bade them take care to rid their provinces of "bad men" (*mali homines*). . . . Probably the main reason why some martyrdoms—perhaps many martyrdoms—took place was that they were thought to be necessary if the province were to be kept "pacata atque quieta".[23] Most governors were doubtless only too willing to take action against men who were strongly disapproved of by "all right-thinking people", and who tended to become the centre of disturbances. Everyone will remember how Pilate yielded to the vociferous demands of the local notables and their followers for the crucifixion of Jesus. If a governor, indeed, refused to do what was expected of him in this way, not only would he become unpopular: the general indignation against the Christians would be only too likely to vent itself in riots and lynching, as we have evidence that it did on occasion; and once violence began, anything might happen.

Christians might also be suspect, as *mali homines*, in the eyes of some governors, because they worshipped a man who had admittedly

---

[23]Settled and orderly.

been crucified by a governor of Judaea, as a political criminal, who thought of himself as "king of the Jews". Their loyalty to the state, whatever they might say, could well appear doubtful, if only because they refused even to swear an oath by the emperor's Genius. They were always talking about the imminent end of the world; and one of their books[24] spoke with bitter hatred of Rome, thinly disguised under the name of Babylon, and prophesied its utter ruin. And furthermore the secrecy of their rites might well seem a cover for political conspiracy, or at any rate anti-social behaviour. A governor who had such considerations in mind when trying Christians might even decide to find them guilty of *maiestas* (treason). . . . In any event, the factors I have just been mentioning would have less and less weight as time went on, and it became clear that Christians had no political objectives whatever and few particularly anti-social habits.

Sometimes a Christian who was in danger of being put on trial might be able to escape altogether by bribing the intending delator or the authorities. There is evidence that this was happening in Africa by the early third century at the latest: not merely individuals but whole churches had purchased immunity, to the disgust of Tertullian, who believed that during persecution Christians must stand their ground and neither take to flight nor buy themselves off. This rigorist attitude was only partly shared by the churches of the West, and in the East it seems to have been generally repudiated: flight or concealment during persecution was officially approved everywhere (except in so far as leading clergy might incur disapproval for deserting their flocks); but in the West, though apparently not in the East, the purchase of immunity, at any rate in a form which might give the impression of apostasy, was regarded as a sin, if not a particularly grave one. Our evidence comes mainly from Africa, Spain and Rome during the Decian persecution, when certificates of compliance with the imperial order to sacrifice to the gods were purchased wholesale by the less steadfast members of the Christian community.

Although we have not yet disposed of all the legal issues, we have at least reached a point from which we can see that the last of my three questions of a legal nature, "What was the legal foundation for the charges against the Christians?", has answered itself, because under the *cognitio* process no foundation was necessary, other than a prosecutor, a charge of Christianity, and a governor willing to punish on that charge. . . .

On the face of Pliny's letter the "obstinacy" of the Christians consisted merely in their threefold confession of Christianity, in face of a warning (after the first confession) that they would be punished for

[24]Revelation.

it. Further light is shed upon this "obstinacy" by some of the Passions of the martyrs, many of whom either repeat the standard formula, "Christianus sum",[25] in reply to all questions, or make legally irrelevant replies.

> *If you will give me a quiet hearing, I will tell you the mystery of simplicity. . . . I do not recognize the empire of this world, but rather I serve that God whom no man sees or can see with these eyes. I have committed no theft; but if I buy anything, I pay the tax, because I recognize my Lord, the King of kings and Emperor of all peoples. . . . It is evil to advocate murder or the bearing of false witness.*

These are the answers given to the proconsul of Africa by Speratus the Scillitan[26]—edifying, no doubt, but irritating to a judge and certainly giving an impression of other-worldly "pertinacity and inflexible obstinacy".

My next point concerns what I call "the sacrifice test", used by Pliny in order to give those who denied being Christians a chance to prove their sincerity. . . . The character of the sacrifice test changed when judicial torture, which until the second century had been used (except in very special circumstances) only on slaves, came to be regularly applied to all those members of the lower classes (the vast majority of the population of the empire) who became involved in criminal trials, whether they were Roman citizens or not. Once judicial torture had become a standard practice, the sacrifice test naturally tended to lose its original character as a privilege, and to become something which was enforced, usually with the aid of torture. But the essential aim was to make apostates, not martyrs. One could say without exaggeration that a governor who really wanted to execute Christians would be careful to avoid torturing them, lest they should apostatize and go free. For there is no doubt that with few exceptions an accused who was prepared to perform the prescribed cult acts was immediately released without punishment. Tertullian, of course, . . . makes much of this as evidence that the authorities did not really regard the Christians as criminals at all. "Others, who plead not guilty", he cries, "you torture to make them confess, the Christians alone to make them deny". This was perfectly true, and it must surely count as a lonely anomaly in the Roman legal system. The explanation is that the only punishable offense was *being* a Christian, up to the very moment sentence was pronounced, not *having been* one. I certainly know of no parallel to this in Roman criminal law. Tertullian ridicules the situation. What is the use of a forced and insincere denial, he asks scornfully. What is to prevent a Christian who

---

[25]"I am a Christian."

[26]One of the twelve from Scillium in North Africa martyred in 180.

has given such a denial and been acquitted from "laughing at your efforts, a Christian once more?".

I need not spend much time on the question of the supposed abominations (*flagitia*) with which the Christians were charged— ... cannibalism and incest. It is hard to say how seriously these charges were taken by the government. The Christian Apologists of the second and early third centuries devote a good deal of attention to rebutting such accusations, which were evidently believed by the populace in both the eastern and the western part of the empire. After the first half of the third century, however, they seem to have died out. ... The reproaches of *flagitia* seem to have been essentially appendages of some more real complaint. Unfortunately, these charges were given some colour by the fact that orthodox Christians and heretics tended to fling them at each other. ...

... I want to take a brief glance at a long series of events which may have given pagans rather more ground for their active antagonism to Christianity than we tend to suppose: I refer to what I have called "voluntary martyrdom". Examination of it will require us to look at persecution, for once, mainly from the receiving end.

It is a significant fact ... that a very large number of sources ... show intrepid Christians going far beyond what their churches officially required of them, often indeed offering themselves up to the authorities of their own accord, and occasionally acting in a provocative manner, smashing images and so forth. After making a detailed study of the evidence for these "voluntary martyrs", I would claim that the part they played in the history of the persecutions was much more important than has yet been realized. It seems to me impossible to doubt that the prevalence of voluntary martyrdom was a factor which, for obvious reasons, both contributed to the outbreak of persecution and tended to intensify it when already in being. ... The heads of the churches, sensibly enough, forbade voluntary martyrdom again and again, and were inclined to refuse to these zealots the very name of martyr. ... Nevertheless, we do hear of an astonishingly large number of volunteers, most of whom, whatever the bishops might say, were given full honour as martyrs, the general body of the faithful apparently regarding them with great respect.

One of the most fascinating of the Passions of the Great Persecution is that of Euplus, who suffered at Catana in Sicily. It begins

> ... [I]n 304, in the most famous city of Catana, in the court room, in front of the curtain, Euplus shouted out, "I wish to die, for I am a Christian". His excellency Calvisianus ... said, "Come in, whoever shouted". And the Blessed Euplus entered the court room, bearing the immaculate Gospels—

and he achieved the end he had sought.

In the next year, 305, while a festival was being celebrated at Caesarea in Palestine, a false rumour began to spread that certain Christians would be given to the beasts as part of the joyful celebrations. While the governor was on his way to the amphitheatre, six young men suddenly presented themselves before him with their hands bound behind them, crying out that they were Christians and demanding to be thrown to the beasts with their brethren. . . . [T]he governor and his entire suite were reduced to a condition of no ordinary amazement. The young men were arrested and imprisoned, but instead of giving them to the beasts as they had demanded, the merciless pagan condemned them to a speedy death by decapitation.

These are but two of a large number of similar examples. Sometimes the fact that certain martyrs were volunteers, and were not sought out by the authorities, may alter our whole picture of a persecution. . . . The seeking out of Christians . . . , therefore, need not have been nearly as vigorous as we might otherwise have assumed from the evidently large number of victims.

The positive evidence for voluntary martyrdom begins . . . about 150. . . . But I should like to suggest . . . that in fact it is likely to have begun much earlier, and that the reason why we do not hear of it before the middle of the second century is simply that we have too little specific evidence of any sort about persecution or martyrdom before that time. Here the Jewish background of Christianity, above all the Jewish martyr-literature, is a very material factor. . . . We have examples of voluntary martyrdom on the part of Jews even before the Christian era, notably the incident in 4 B.C., . . . when two pious rabbis instigated their followers to cut down the golden eagle set up by Herod[27] over the great gate of the Temple: about forty men were executed, the rabbis and the actual perpetrators of the deed being burnt alive. Now the two most fervent works of Jewish martyr-literature, the Second and Fourth Books of Maccabees,[28] with their unrestrained sensationalism and gruesome descriptions of tortures, both formed part of the Septuagint, and must therefore have been well known to the early Church. . . .

We are in a position at last to attempt to answer the question confronting us, which, it will be remembered, is twofold: "Why did the government persecute?", and "Why did the mass of pagans often demand and initiate persecution?". I propose to take the second question first.

---

[27]Herod the Great, King of Judea, 40–4 B.C.

[28]Two books in the Old Testament in the Christian, but not in the Hebrew Bible, named after a family that led Jewish resistance to Syrian rule in the second and first centuries B.C.

. . . It was not so much the positive beliefs and practices of the Christians which aroused pagan hostility, but above all the negative element in their religion: their total refusal to worship any god but their own. The monotheistic exclusiveness of the Christians was believed to alienate the goodwill of the gods, to endanger what the Romans called the *pax deorum* (the right harmonious relationship between gods and men), and to be responsible for disasters which overtook the community. I shall call this exclusiveness, for convenience, by the name the Greeks gave to it, "atheism" . . . ; characteristically, the Latin writers refer to the same phenomenon by more concrete expressions having no philosophical overtones, such as "deos non colere" (not paying cult to the gods). . . .

Whatever view we may hold about the mentality of educated, upper-class intellectuals, we must admit that the great mass of the population of the Roman empire, in both East and West, were at least what we should call deeply superstitious; and I see not the least reason why we should deny them genuine religious feeling, provided we remember the essential differences between their kind of religion and that with which we are familiar. By far the most important of these was that pagan religion was a matter of performing cult acts rather than of belief, or ethics. No positive and publicly enforceable obligation, however, rested upon any private individual, whether a Roman citizen or not, or upon a common soldier, to participate in any particular acts of cult, although magistrates and senators of Rome itself, and magistrates (and perhaps senators) of individual Greek and Roman towns, might be legally obliged to do so; and of course great social pressure might be brought to bear upon individuals who refused (on adopting Christianity or Judaism, for instance) to take part in family or other observances. No compulsion was necessary, because until the advent of Christianity no one ever had any reason for refusing to take part in the ceremonies which others observed—except of course the Jews, and they were a special case, a unique exception. Much as the Jews were detested by the bulk of the Roman governing class, as well as by many humbler Romans and Greeks, it was admitted (by the educated, at any rate) that their religious rites were ancestral, and very ancient. All men were expected piously to preserve the religious customs of their ancestors. And so even Tacitus, who strongly disliked Judaism, could say that the religious rites of the Jews "have the recommendation of being ancient". The gods would forgive the inexplicable monotheism of the Jews, who were, so to speak, licensed atheists. The Jews of course would not sacrifice to the emperor or his gods, but they were quite willing, while the Temple still stood, to sacrifice to their own god for the well-being of the emperor. . . . Matters were very different with the Christians, who had . . . abandoned their ancestral religions. Gibbon[29] expressed the contrast perfectly when he wrote, "The Jews were people which followed, the Christians a sect which deserted, the religion of their fathers".

The Christians asserted openly either that the pagan gods did not exist at all or that they were malevolent demons. Not only did they themselves refuse to take part in pagan religious rites: they would not even recognize that others ought to do so. As a result, because a large part of Greek religion and the whole of the Roman state religion was very much a community affair, the mass of pagans were naturally apprehensive that the gods would vent their wrath at this dishonour not upon the Christians alone but upon the whole community; and when disasters did occur, they were only too likely to fasten the blame on to the Christians. That the Christians were indeed hated for precisely this reason above all others appears from many passages in the sources, from the mid-second century right down to the fifth. Tertullian sums it all up in a brilliant and famous sentence . . . : the pagans, he says, "suppose that the Christians are the cause of every public disaster, every misfortune that happens to the people. If the Tiber overflows or the Nile doesn't, if there is a drought or an earthquake, a famine or a pestilence, at once the cry goes up, 'The Christians to the lion'."

The essential point I want to make is that this superstitious feeling on the part of the pagans was due above all to the Christians' "atheism", their refusal to acknowledge the gods and give them their due by paying them cult. . . .

We must not confuse the kind of atheism charged against the Christians with philosophical scepticism. Tertullian pretends to be very indignant because philosophers are permitted openly to attack pagan superstitions, while Christians are not. "They openly demolish your gods and also attack your superstitions in their writings, and you applaud them for it", he exclaims. The vital difference was, of course, that the philosophers, whatever they might believe, and even write down for circulation among educated folk, would have been perfectly willing to perform any cult act required of them—and that was what mattered.

That the religious misbehaviour of certain individuals should be thought of by pagans as likely to bring unselective divine punishment may seem less strange to us when we remember that similar views were held by Jews and Christians. Orthodox Christians felt towards heretics much as pagans felt toward them. The martyred bishop Polycarp,[30] who

---

[29]Edward Gibbon, (1737-1794), English historian, author of *The History of the Decline and Fall of the Roman Empire*.

[30]Saint, c.69–c.155.

(it was said) had actually known the Apostles personally, used to tell how the Apostle John,[31] entering the baths at Ephesus, rushed out again when he saw the heresiarch Cerinthus[32] inside, crying, "Away, lest the very baths collapse, for within is Cerinthus the enemy of the truth".

About the middle of the third century, however, the attitude of the general run of pagans towards the Christians begins to undergo a distinct change. Whereas until then the initiative in persecution seems to have come from below, from 250 onwards persecution comes from above, from the government, and is initiated by imperial edict, with little or no sign of persecuting zeal among the mass of pagans. The beginning of the change seems to me to come with the Decian persecution. . . . The change has gone quite far by the time of the Great Persecution, when the majority of pagans . . . seem to be at least indifferent, some even sympathetic to the Christians, and few provincial governors display any enthusiasm for the task. . . . The reason for the change . . . is that Christianity had by now spread widely and lost its secretive character, and pagans had come to realize that Christians were not so different from themselves, and just as religious.

I have ignored minor reasons for popular dislike of the Christians; but no doubt some people might feel a grudge against them on simple economic grounds. . . .

Finally, we can try to analyse the attitude of the government. . . . [T]he great problem posed by Christianity, its exclusiveness, was something Rome had never encountered before—except under very different conditions, in the Jewish national religion.

I do not myself believe that there is a single solution to our problem. I believe that different members of the governing class may have been actuated by different motives, and I think that each one of us must decide for himself how much weight he would attach to each. I have already mentioned some minor factors, which may in some cases have played an important and even a decisive part: the need to pacify public opinion; and suspicion of the Christians as a conspiratorial body, or at least as undesirables, *mali homines*. . . . I believe that the main motives of the government, in the long run, were essentially religious in character, according to the ancient conception of religion. These religious motives appear in two rather different forms, which some people might prefer to call "superstitious" and "political" respectively, thereby avoiding the term "religious" altogether. Some of the governing class, in the third century at any rate (and I believe from the first), were undoubtedly inspired by the very motives I have described as characteristic of their

[31]Saint and author of the fourth Gospel.
[32]Gnostic, flourished c.100.

subjects. Among the persecuting emperors, we must certainly place Galerius in this category, . . . and also Diocletian, who seems to have been a thoroughly religious man. . . . [E]ven in the third century, and to a far greater extent in the second, especially the early second, there may have been a significant number of members of the governing class who did not share the superstitious horror felt for the Christians by the masses. But even such people, I believe, were impelled to persecute—perhaps as vigorously as their less emancipated brethren—by motives I think we are justified in calling religious, in that their aim also was always primarily to break down the Christian refusal to worship the pagan gods, even if the basis from which they proceeded was different.

I want to stress two vital pieces of evidence which I do not see how we can explain away. First, there is the fact that except to a limited extent in the time of Valerian, and more seriously under Diocletian, what I have called the positive side of Christianity is never officially attacked: persecution did not extend to any aspect of the Christian religion other than its refusal to acknowledge other gods. No attempt was ever made, even in the general persecutions, to prohibit Christians from worshipping their own god in private, although Valerian and Diocletian (but not Decius) forbade them to assemble for common worship, and Diocletian also ordered the destruction of churches and the confiscation of sacred books and church property. As the deputy perfect of Egypt said to Bishop Dionysius of Alexandria in 257, "Who prevents you from worshipping your own god also, if he is a god, along with the natural gods?". And of course the sacrifice test continues to be used, and if the Christian complies with it he goes free, even in the general persecutions.

Secondly, there is what I believe to have been the complete immunity from persecution of most of the Gnostic sects. Some of these professed doctrines of a recognizably Christian character (heretical in varying degrees as they were) and called themselves Christians. Yet in Roman eyes there was evidently a fundamental difference between Gnostics and orthodox Christians, if Gnostics were not persecuted. Why? The reason can only be that the Gnostics did not think it necessary to be exclusive, like the orthodox, and refuse to pay outward respect to the pagan gods when the necessity arose. We are told by orthodox Christian sources that Basilides,[33] perhaps the most important of all the Gnostic heresiarchs, permitted his followers to eat meat which had been offered to idols, and in time of persecution "casually to deny the faith", doubtless by accepting the sacrifice test. It appears, then, that although the tenets of the Gnostics must have appeared to the Roman

---

[33]Gnostic theologian at Alexandria, second century.

governing class to be very similar to those of the orthodox, the Gnostics escaped persecution precisely because they consented to take part in pagan religious ceremonies on demand, when the orthodox refused to do so.

What then was the attitude of the more enlightened pagans among the governing class? Why did they too persecute? . . .

. . . Religion, for such Romans, was above all the *ius divinum*, the body of state law relating to sacred matters, which preserved the *pax deorum*[34] by means of the appropriate ceremonial. It derived its great value . . . mainly from the fact that it rested upon the . . . force of ancestral tradition. . . . The Roman state religion contained nothing that was personal to the individual. And as for *rational* belief (or disbelief) in the gods—did it ever figure in the thoughts of Cicero[35] and his kind except when they were playing the Greek game of philosophical disputation? . . . These people had a deep emotional feeling for Roman religion, as the *ius divinum*, the "foundation of our state", an essential part of the whole Roman way of life. One can still hold this to be true, even if, taking perhaps an uncharitable view (as I would myself), one holds that quite a large part of that religion was above all an instrument by which the governing class hoped to keep the reins of power in its own hands. . . .

. . . For Cicero's spiritual descendants of the early Principate,[36] Roman religion was part of the very stuff of Roman life and Roman greatness; and they were prepared to extend their protection also to the cults of the peoples of their empire, whose devotion to their ancestral religions seemed to their rulers only right and proper. Can we imagine that such men, however intellectually emancipated from the superstitions of the vulgar, would have had any compunction about executing the devotees of a new-fangled sect which threatened almost every element of Roman religion, and indeed of all the traditional cults conducted by the inhabitants of the Roman world? I would be prepared to speak of persecution so motivated as being conducted for religious reasons, though I realize that other people might prefer to use another word—political, perhaps.

I shall end by quoting what seems to me the most illuminating single text in all the ancient sources, for the understanding of the persecutions. Paternus, proconsul of Africa, is speaking to Cyprian[37] at his first trial in 257, and telling him what the emperors have just

---

[34]Peace of the gods.
[35]Roman orator and politician, 106–43 B.C.
[36]The Early Empire, 27 B.C.–180 A.D.
[37]Saint and martyr, c.200–258.

decreed. This, it is true, is a special edict, making it incumbent upon the Christian clergy, on pain of exile, to perform certain acts which ordinary folk would not normally be obliged to carry out; but what is enjoined is something any accused Christian might be ordered to perform, and this gives the text general significance. The decree is: . . . "Those who do not profess the Roman religion"—it is admitted that there are such people—"must not refuse to take part in Roman religious ceremonies".

III

THE MIDDLE AGES

Covering the years roughly from 500 to 1500, the Middle Ages included a number of cultures and territories. Western civilization during this epoch was increasingly confined to Western Europe, leaving the eastern Mediterranean to the expanding Islamic world. Opening with Germanic invasions of the Western Roman Empire, the Middle Ages concluded with European invasions of exotic and distant lands as men crossed the oceans in the guise of explorers, soldiers, and missionaries in the fifteenth and sixteenth centuries to discover, fight, and convert the indigenous peoples.

Some historians further subdivide the medieval epoch into the early (500–1000), high (1000–1300), and late Middle Ages. The early Middle Ages, often misnamed the Dark Ages, witnessed Germanic invasions, political fragmentation, a rural economy, small population, little international trade, and a decline in education, urbanization, and commercialization. Christianity spread throughout Western Europe so completely that the entire Middle Ages is sometimes branded the Age of Faith or the Christian centuries. Following Charlemagne's reign (768–814), which saw administrative innovations and a small cultural flowering, invasions by the Vikings, Hungarians, and Saracens plunged Europe back into the chaotic conditions that recalled the collapse of Roman rule in the fifth and sixth centuries. But the ninth and tenth centuries also provided the final elements that defined rural life and the method of governance, feudalism.

The high Middle Ages was an era of relative prosperity that saw medieval civilization approach its zenith, marked perhaps by the prodigiously tall cathedrals built according to a new architectural and artistic style, the Gothic. The population expanded as a result of the surplus provided by improved agricultural techniques; towns and commerce grew; education (though highly limited in social scope) blossomed, first in cathedral schools and later in universities; and the slow accumulation of power in fewer hands offered a greater measure of political stability. Religion infused the economy, social order, politics, art,

131

and mentality of the Middle Ages. The crusades exemplified the brash exuberance and confidence of this period. It took the unprecedented disasters of the fourteenth and fifteenth centuries to end this vibrant civilization, though there was certainly much continuity with succeeding centuries. A worsening climate, famines, economic depression, international warfare, peasant revolts, and the worst scourge in history—the Plague—made the later Middle Ages a bleak era in many ways. But this was also, in Italy, the age of the Renaissance, a cultural flowering that coincided with economic depression and severe population loss. Humanism (the major intellectual movement of the Renaissance), artistic innovation, and political experimentation made Italy arguably the most dynamic area in Europe at the end of the Middle Ages.

The selections that follow describe basic subjects in the social history of the Middle Ages: the nobility, the family, marriage, children, peasants, pollution, religion, social behavior, women, and death. They show medieval societies to have been violent, intense, severe, patriarchal, and devoted to professed values and traditional modes of conduct from which nonetheless they often enthusiastically broke away. This was an energetic culture, difficult to categorize because of the substantial gap between people's ideals and the harsh reality of their daily life and behavior.

Rural Economy
and Country Life in
the Medieval West

GEORGES DUBY

Europe of the ninth and tenth centuries was a rural civilization, in which seasonal rhythms and patterns of cultivation determined the lifestyles of all, even the few who lived in small towns. In contrast, today less than twenty percent of the population in the Western world live in rural areas, large-scale mechanized agriculture is the norm, and farmers are linked to the outside world by television, automobiles, and package tours.

Georges Duby begins his study of medieval agricultural communities by describing peasant settlements. What did a village comprise? Beyond the living area and the fields were forests. How did medieval people use the forests? What type of food did peasants consume? How effectively did the agricultural technology of the time exploit the land? Put another way, what factors limited the production of more food?

For most of history, people have stood rather helpless before the inadequacies of their land, the unpredictability of the weather, and their own inability to influence their environment in a stable, effective way. Medieval peasants proved no exception. Their constant battle against the soil and climate, not to mention the parasitic aristocracy and clergy, gave them little food and much insecurity. In theory at least, the lords and clergy provided certain forms of security, but the reality was that the peasantry faced an epic struggle, with few material rewards.

One fact is outstanding: in the civilization of the ninth and tenth centuries the rural way of life was universal. Entire countries, like England and almost all the Germanic lands, were absolutely without towns. Elsewhere some towns existed: such as the few ancient Roman cities in the south which had not suffered complete dilapidation, or the new townships on trade routes which were making their appearance along the rivers leading to the northern seas. But except for some in Lombardy, these 'towns' appear as minute centres of population, each numbering at most a few hundred permanent inhabitants and deeply immersed in the life of the surrounding countryside. Indeed they

Georges Duby, *Rural Economy and Country Life in the Medieval West* (Columbia, S.C.: University of South Carolina Press, 1968), 5–11, 15, 21–25, 27.

could hardly be distinguished from it. Vineyards encircled them; fields penetrated their walls; they were full of cattle, barns and farm labourers. All their inhabitants from the very richest, bishops and even the king himself, to the few specialists, Jewish or Christian, who conducted long-distance trade, remained first and foremost countrymen whose whole life was dominated by the rhythm of the agricultural seasons, who depended for their existence on the produce of the soil, and who drew directly from it their entire worldly wealth. . . .

Another thing is also certain. It was a countryside created by man around a few fixed points of settlement. Western Europe was peopled by a stable peasantry rooted in its environment. Not that we should picture it as totally immobile. There was still room in rural life for nomadic movements. In high summer cartage and pastoral activities took many peasants to distant places, while others were occupied in gathering the wild products of the woodland, in hunting, in raiding their neighbours, and in some other activities that were necessary to acquire vital food supplies for survival. Other members of the rural population regularly participated in warlike adventures. However, most of these were only seasonal or part-time nomads. They spent most of their days on land which housed their families and formed part of organized village territories. They give the impression of belonging to villages.

Indeed the countryman's life was very rarely conducted in solitude. Dwelling houses appear to have been close together and very seldom isolated. Clusters of houses were usual. . . . [T]he village, whatever its size or shape, provided the normal background of human existence. In Saxon England, for instance, the village served as the basis for the levying and collection of taxes. Around these fixed points was laid out the pattern of the cultivated land, and particularly the network of trackways and paths, which appear in the landscape of today as the most tenacious relic of our ancient heritage, the reality which provides the starting point for archeological study of the village territory.

In western Europe, pioneer excavations are under way which will one day help us to know better what medieval rural dwellings were like. Already evidence exists which leads us to believe that, except in the Mediterranean coastal lands where building was in stone, men's habitations in the early, and even the not-so-early, Middle Ages were huts of wattle and daub, short-lived and destructible; even at the beginning of the thirteenth century an English peasant was found guilty of having destroyed the house of his neighbour by merely sawing through the central beam.

. . . [T]he land on which the village stood was subject to a particular legal status, different from that of the surrounding land, and enjoying customary privileges which made its boundaries unalterable. Legal historians have shown that the village was made up of contiguous parcels of land which most Carolingian documents describe by the word *mansus*, and which the peasant dialects of the earliest Middle Age called variously *meix, Hof, masure, toft.* . . . We understand by this an enclosure, solidly rooted to its site by a permanent barrier such as a palisade or a living hedge, carefully maintained, a protected asylum to which the entry was forbidden and the violation of which was punished by severe penalties: an island of refuge where the occupant was assumed to be the master and at whose threshold communal servitude and the demands of chiefs and lords stopped short. These enclosures provided a haven for possessions, cattle, stocks of food, and sleeping men, protected them against natural and supernatural dangers, and taken together, constituted the kernel of the village, and expressed in terms of land and territory the essence of a society of which the family was the nucleus. Furthermore, it is probable that occupation of such a *manse* carried with it a place in the village community with collective rights over the surrounding fields. By the same token newcomers remained dwellers in a secondary zone of habitations outside the enclosures. . . .

. . . The soil which lay nearest to the house and to the stable was especially rich and fertile. By proximity alone the site of peasant settlement fertilized itself: household waste and the domestic animals were sufficient to establish around the dwelling, precisely because it was immovable, a permanent condition of fertility. Moreover, this land, because it was so conveniently placed, could be repeatedly dug over. In no other spot could the natural state of the earth be so profoundly modified to meet the needs of man; the constant manuring and digging created there an artificial soil and raised on it a specialized and particular plant life. Thus each domestic fence enclosed and protected a vegetable garden, . . . in other words a continually cultivated plot, where the ground was never left to rest, and where in carefully protected conditions grew tender plants, the herbs and roots of the daily diet, hemp and the vine. These plots were undoubtedly most productive and the atmosphere of garden care which they cast over their surroundings did much to anchor the village to its site.

Beyond the encircling hedges, nature was also subject to a certain, even if a not very rigorous, discipline. Without the need to tame her, men could win from nature a large part of their subsistence. River, marsh, forest and thicket offered to whoever could take advantage of them, fish, game, honey and many other edible substances in generous measure. . . . We are encouraged to believe that [the countryman] was as skilled in the use of the hunting spear, the net and the warrener's stick as he was with the plough. In 1180 when Alexander Neckham, an English teacher in the schools of Paris, wrote his treatise *Du Nom des Outils*,[1] he listed nets, lines, and snares for trapping hares and deer amongst the ordinary tools of the peasant household. It is certain that the thinly growing forest of the early Middle Ages, with its numerous clearings, and its varied vegetation ranging from thick woodland to grassy glades, formed an essential background to the domestic economy. Apart from the livelihood that it bestowed generously on foodgatherer and hunter, it furnished the larger domestic animals with their chief sources of nourishment. Sheep and cows grazed there and war- and farm-horses were let loose in it. But above all else the woods were the domain of pigs. . . . Indeed over vast stretches of northern Europe in the ninth century bacon was an essential ingredient in the household economy. Herds of swine yielding both meat and lard formed everywhere the mainstay of every farming system, large and small. . . . In fact agrarian archeology leads us to suppose that many villages and especially those in the north-west and north-east, in England, Frisia and Saxony, possessed no cultivated lands, apart from the 'tofts'. And in the eleventh century we know of communities in the English fenlands, on the Wash and in the flooded valley of the Saône which lived solely by fishing.

However, because of man's customary eating habits the cultivation of the small plots around the dwelling houses and the quest for the gifts of nature were nearly everywhere allied to the efforts to farm more extensively. We know very little about the food of early medieval man in western Europe outside the monastic communities. . . . It is clear that at this period not only were men unable to feed themselves on what they found by chance, but they were driven to grow what custom decreed they should consume. . . . [T]he expansion of winegrowing in Gaul was a direct consequence of the social habits of the nobles, with whom it was a point of honour to drink and to offer their guests none but the best wine. But on a much humbler level also the whole system of agricultural production was organized to fulfil the social requirements which determined eating habits.

References in documents . . . reveal the universal acceptance of bread as a basic foodstuff, even in the least civilized regions of the Christian world. . . . Indeed, all the documents indicate that peas, vetches, beans—the leguminous plants—together with 'herbs' and 'roots', the ancestors of our garden vegetables (the hermits were praised for restricting their diet to these) and of course meat, a most desirable item of consumption from which the clergy ostentatiously abstained, comprised only the *companaticum*, the accompaniment to bread. It was the latter that was the mainstay of existence.

[1]*The Names of Tools.*

It is reasonably clear that bread was not baked solely from wheat, rye or spelt, but also from other, lesser, cereals, such as barley and even oats, which was eaten as much by humans as by animals. What is less easy to distinguish is in what measure these food grains were consumed in the form of porridge . . . or brewed into ale, the commonest beverage throughout north-western Europe. Ale had often the consistency of thick soup and so could be counted perhaps more as a food than a drink. Eleventh-century peasants had to grow cereals even when climatic conditions were not favourable. As arable fields had to be laid out around the villages, the least exposed and most easily worked sites had to be cleared for the purpose, in close proximity to habitations and in the midst of woods and pastures.

Here and there, in places where the climate allowed grapes to ripen, a few vines were planted for the masters on the most suitable and permanently enclosed plots. Meadows were confined to damper ground, and the hay, together with the grass and rushes which could be gathered in the marshes, provided winter fodder for the cattle. Nevertheless neither vines nor meadows covered more than a very limited part of the cultivated area since the cereal crop was the really important one, and almost the whole of the area given over to agricultural activity was reserved for its culture. These fields had also to be protected against the depredations of animals, both domestic and wild. They can thus be visualized as separated from the uncultivated lands, which were open to pasture, by enclosures which in the country of the Franks seemed generally to have been temporary. In spring as soon as the new grass began to push up and the corn to sprout these mobile barriers made of wooden stakes . . . were erected and signs were put up forbidding shepherds to let their animals stray there. For a season therefore these strips seemed, like the cultivated 'tofts' of the village, to be the territory of individual owners. But after the harvest, signs and fences were removed, and the strips returned for a time to pastoral use, and were reincorporated into the larger areas where access to animals was free. To a greater or lesser extent then, according to the quantity of bread men were used to eating, the arable appeared as a limited and temporary extension of the cultivated 'toft' area and thus private property, at the expense of the wild area which was left to collective use.

Can we ever hope, even in the best documented regions, to plot the portion of village lands occupied by the arable fields? . . . What we know now suggests that this area was small everywhere and that a large space was being left to natural vegetation, the forest and pasture, whose presence 'had helped to form this combination of agriculture and animal husbandry which was the principal feature' of rural economy in the west. . . . This union indeed appears constant and fundamental throughout the Middle Ages. What we might describe as three concentric zones formed the picture . . . —the village enclosures, the *coûtures*, that is the arable, and finally surrounding all, a broad uncultivated belt. These were the three zones in which the effects of man's labour became less and less visible as the distance from the inhabited centre grew greater, but which were of equal importance to him as a means of subsistence.

Village communities thus found themselves hemmed in with no way of absorbing the increase in their birth rate. Periodic waves of mortality, such as those caused by military activity and, increasingly in the second half of the ninth and in the tenth centuries, raids of invaders, rather than any systematic clearing of the wastes and the resulting hiving off of colonists, relieved demographic pressure at intervals. Such a situation suggests a peasantry poorly equipped with efficient tools and incapable for this reason of taming the encircling wilderness.

Was the undoubted technical progress to which the diffusion of the water mill bears witness accompanied in Europe of the ninth and tenth centuries by the spread of ploughs with wheeled foreparts, by improvements in harness, and by the adoption of a more efficient ploughshare? This important problem of technique cannot be resolved, but it is reasonable to assume that even in the most favoured sectors of rural life, those of the great farming complexes described by inventories, men used feeble wooden implements. They found themselves ill-equipped to come to grips with nature and worked with their bare hands for a great part of the time. The primitive technical equipment obviously restricted narrowly the individual's productive capacity. And this observation agrees completely with the impression gained from land settlement. Villages teemed with people whose efforts were needed to work the soil on the home fields, but they were situated in clearings separated by stretches of wild country because agricultural tools were not robust enough to overcome the obstacles of heavy, wet and thickly wooded land. Areas of natural vegetation adjoining the villages were of course actually necessary because the cultivation of cereals was so demanding of manpower that each rural community had to supplement its means of livelihood by making the most of the products of the wastelands— animal husbandry, hunting and foodgathering.

These limited portions of the village lands suitable for grain growing and therefore providing the village's main food supply . . . , or 'furlongs' to use the English term, were not given over wholly to food production every year. Unlike the cultivated 'tofts' whose soil, manured by the household waste and stable dung, could be cultivated without interruption, the fields demanded a periodic rest if fertility was not to be lost. Every spring a section of the arable was not sown; it remained open, unenclosed, available for pasture, in the same way as the wild area of wastes and commons. For an understanding of the productivity of the land and the manner in which it was able to support human life, we need to know the rhythm of the resting periods. What was the place of the fallow and what the place of spring-sown corn, oats and leguminous crops? How much land was devoted to autumn-sown corn, that is the bread grains—wheat, rye and spelt (the most widely grown grain in the Rhineland and north-west France), and lastly barley, which was in those days often a winter-sown crop? . . .

1.   The description of harvest and sowing and, more often, that of dues in the form of grain exacted from peasant tenants proved that the fields of peasants as well as lords very frequently produced spring as well as winter corn and especially oats.

2.   The arrangement of the ploughing services exacted from manorial dependants in the agricultural calendar shows that the cycle of ploughing was often divided into two sowing 'seasons', one in the winter . . . , and the other in the summer or the spring. . . .

3.   Ploughing units on the great properties appear often in groups of three. . . . This arrangement leads us to think that cultivation was organized on a ternary rhythm. . . . By this arrangement, a third portion was prepared in May by a preliminary ploughing, and was turned over again by the plough in November before sowing; the following year after harvest the same fields were left throughout autumn and winter for the animals to graze on, and were then ploughed in Lent and sown with spring grain, after which they rested for a year. Thus at least a third of the agricultural area produced nothing, while another third produced bread grains and the last third the ingredients of porridge and soup.

I do not consider, however, that these indications are sufficient for us to conclude without further consideration that a regular three-year rotation was general, or even widespread. What argues against any such conclusion is that none of our examples is in southern Europe where climatic conditions, and above all early spring droughts, made March sowings somewhat hazardous, and also that our documents describe none but the great monastic or royal farms which were run in an unusually rational and even scientific manner. . . .

. . . It is therefore safest to conjecture that there was considerable variation in the crop rotation in use. Man was forced to bow to the natural capacity of the soil because he was poorly prepared to alter it. We can imagine an infinite variety of systems in use ranging all the way from the strict three-course rotation to temporary cultivation based on burning where bits and pieces of land on the outer fringes of the village enclave would be tilled after the undergrowth had been burned, and continued to be cropped for years until fertility was exhausted. It is also probable that oats and other spring grains were often a supplementary crop taken from the fallow, and that such a system, even when the regular ploughings in winter and early spring . . . were adhered to, frequently lasted more than one year on the largest part of the available arable. It must be added that seed corn was sown very thinly. . . . The agricultural practice of those early days demanded not only plentiful manpower, but wide open spaces.

The insistent demands for long fallow periods, and the need to scatter the seed thinly arose at least partly because of mediocre ploughing implements which could not turn the ground over properly, but they were also due to the virtual absence of manure. It is true that animal husbandry was always complementary to agriculture and the draught oxen whose task was to plough the fields could also fertilize them with their dung. In reality the combination of arable with pasture was not close enough to enable animal manure to make much impression. Men who were so inadequately equipped with tools were forced to devote all their energies to producing their own food, and cattle had to take second place. A little fodder was harvested, but barely enough to keep those few beasts which had not been slaughtered in the autumn alive during the lean winter months when nature's offerings failed. But for the rest of the year the herds grazed alone in the open air on the land which was not enclosed. They must also have ranged over the fallow fields and in doing so deposited their manure on them; but the deposit was quite insufficient to maintain fertility. Scarce fodder meant restricted periods of stall-feeding, and the limited quantities of stable manure thus available were almost wholly devoured by the cultivated 'tofts' in the inner fertile belt of the village territory. No wonder areas of fallow had to be huge. And we can appreciate afresh the need of each family to dispose of as large a space for subsistence as possible which had to cover, besides pasture, an arable area much more extensive than the portion actually in use each year. Even so, despite the long resting periods, output remained extremely low.

. . . These elusive details allow at any rate one firm conclusion. Carried out with rudimentary equipment and in a generally unfavourable climate, the cultivation of cereal crops was at the mercy of the caprices of the weather. Even on the best equipped farms an excessively wet spring or summer could render the heavy toil in the fields totally unproductive. Despite an enormous expenditure of manpower and the disproportionate size of the village lands country folk could be racked with hunger. Obviously their main preoccupation was to survive through spring and early summer, that period of backbreaking toil. When the scraps of food remaining to them after the demands of their masters had been exhausted, the yearly nightmare of hand-to-mouth existence began, and the pangs of hunger had to be stilled by devouring garden herbs and forest berries and by begging bread at the gates of the rich. At such moments the threat of starvation overshadowed the whole village world.

The Life
of the Nobility

MARC BLOCH

The nobility of twelfth-century Europe were rough, cruel, physical beings. In describing the life of medieval noblemen, Marc Bloch stresses their ferocity. The aristocracy loved war and fought for economic and political reasons. How did economic and political pressures subvert the culture of Christianity? Nobles killed with abandon other knights, the defenseless, and even prisoners; they robbed and mutilated. Why did the nobility so love war? Why did Christian virtues not dominate their lives? What were the qualities of the ideal knight? Even during periods of peace, knights fought in hunts and tournaments. How did those activities prepare knights for war?

If not yet well-behaved gentlemen, the nobility did at least subscribe to certain rules of courtesy that tempered their violence. How did courtly love influence the behavior of knights? By what processes did high-born ladies affect the nobility? From reading this selection, one can easily understand why churchmen and townspeople feared the nobility, unruly pests that they were.

'I love the gay Eastertide, which brings forth leaves and flowers; and I love the joyous songs of the birds, re-echoing through the copse. But also I love to see, amidst the meadows, tents and pavilions spread; and it gives me great joy to see, drawn up on the field, knights and horses in battle array; and it delights me when the scouts scatter people and herds in their path; and I love to see them followed by a great body of men-at-arms; and my heart is filled with gladness when I see strong castles besieged, and the stockades broken and overwhelmed, and the warriors on the bank, girt about by fosses, with a line of strong stakes, interlaced. . . . Maces, swords, helms of different hues, shields that will be riven and shattered as soon as the fight begins; and many vassals struck down together; and the horses of the dead and the wounded roving at random. And when battle is joined, let all men of good lineage think of naught but the breaking of heads and arms; for it is better to die than to be vanquished and live. I tell you, I find no such savour in food, or in wine, or in sleep, as in hearing the shout "On! On!"

Marc Bloch, *Feudal Society* (Chicago: The University of Chicago Press, 1961), pp. 293–301, 303–305, 307–311.

from both sides, and the neighing of steeds that have lost their riders, and the cries of "Help! Help!"; in seeing men great and small go down on the grass beyond the fosses; in seeing at last the dead, with the pennoned stumps of lances still in their sides.'

Thus sang, in the second half of the twelfth century, a troubadour who is probably to be identified with the petty nobleman from Périgord, Bertrand de Born. The accurate observation and the fine verve, in contrast with the insipidity of what is usually a more conventional type of poetry, are the marks of an uncommon talent. The sentiment, on the other hand, is in no way extraordinary; as is shown in many another piece from the same social world, in which it is expressed, no doubt with less gusto, but with equal spontaneity. In war . . . the noble loved first and foremost the display of physical strength, the strength of a splendid animal, deliberately maintained by constant exercises, begun in childhood. 'He who has stayed at school till the age of twelve,' says a German poet, repeating the old Carolingian[1] proverb, 'and never ridden a horse, is only fit to be a priest.' The interminable accounts of single combats which fill the epics are eloquent psychological documents. The reader of today, bored by their monotony, finds it difficult to believe that they could have afforded so much pleasure—as they clearly did— to those who listened to them in days of old; theirs was the attitude of the sedentary enthusiast to reports of sporting events. In works of imagination as well as in the chronicles, the portrait of the good knight emphasizes above all his athletic build: he is 'big-boned', 'large of limb', the body 'well-proportioned' and pitted with honourable scars; the shoulders are broad, and so is the 'fork'—as becomes a horseman. And since this strength must be sustained, the valiant knight is known for his mighty appetite. In the old *Chanson de Guillaume*,[2] so barbarous in its tone, listen to Dame Guibourc who, after having served at the great table of the castle of the young Girart, her husband's nephew, remarks to her spouse:

. . . .

> By God! fair sire! he's of your line indeed,
> Who thus devours a mighty haunch of boar
> And drinks of wine a gallon at two gulps;
> Pity the man on whom he wages war!

A supple and muscular body, however, it is almost superfluous to say, was not enough to make the ideal knight. To these qualities he

[1]From the period named after the Carolingian dynasty, which began in 751.
[2]*Song of William.*

must add courage as well. And it was also because it gave scope for the exercise of this virtue that war created such joy in the hearts of men for whom daring and the contempt for death were, in a sense, professional assets. It is true that this valour did not always prevent mad panics (we have seen examples of them in face of the Vikings), nor was it above resorting to crude stratagems. Nevertheless the knightly class knew how to fight—on this point, history agrees with legend. Its unquestionable heroism was nurtured by many elements: the simple physical reaction of a healthy human being; the rage of despair—it is when he feels himself 'wounded unto death' that the 'cautious' Oliver[3] strikes such terrible blows, in order 'to avenge himself all he could'; the devotion to a chief or, in the case of the holy war, to a cause; the passionate desire for glory, personal or collective; the fatalistic acquiescence in face of ineluctable destiny . . . finally, the hope of reward in another world, promised not only to him who died for his God, but also to him who died for his master.

Accustomed to danger, the knight found in war yet another attraction: it offered a remedy for boredom. For these men whose culture long remained rudimentary and who—apart from a few great barons and their counsellors—were seldom occupied by very heavy administrative cares, everyday life easily slipped into a grey monotony. Thus was born an appetite for diversions which, when one's native soil failed to afford the means to gratify it, sought satisfaction in distant lands. William the Conqueror, bent on exacting due service from his vassals, said of one of them, whose fiefs he had just confiscated as a punishment for his having dared to depart for the crusade in Spain without permission: 'I do not believe it would be possible to find a better knight in arms; but he is unstable and extravagant, and he spends his time gadding about from place to place.' . . . The roving disposition was especially widespread among the French. The fact was that their own country did not offer them, as did half-Moslem Spain, or, to a less degree, Germany with its Slav frontier, an arena for conquests or swift forays; nor, like Germany again, the hardships and the pleasures of the great imperial expeditions. It is also probable that the knightly class was more numerous there than elsewhere, and therefore cramped for room. In France itself it has often been observed that Normandy was of all the provinces the richest in bold adventurers. Already the German Otto of Freising spoke of the 'very restless race of the Normans'. Could it have been the legacy of Viking blood? Possibly. But it was above all the effect of the state of relative peace which, in that remarkably centralized principality,

---

[3]In medieval romances, Oliver was one of the twelve peers of Charlemagne and the friend of Roland, hero of the *Song of Roland*.

the dukes established at an early date; so that those who craved the opportunity for fighting had to seek it abroad. Flanders, where political conditions were not very different, furnished an almost equally large contingent of roving warriors.

These knights-errant[4] helped the native Christians in Spain to reconquer the northern part of the peninsula from Islam; they set up the Norman states in southern Italy; even before the First Crusade they enlisted as mercenaries in the service of Byzantium and fought against its eastern foes; finally, they found in the conquest and defence of the Tomb of Christ their chosen field of action. Whether in Spain or in Syria, the holy war offered the dual attraction of an adventure and a work of piety. 'No need is there now to endure the monk's hard life in the strictest of the orders . . . ' sang one of the troubadours; 'to accomplish honourable deeds and thereby at the same time to save oneself from hell—what more could one wish?' These migrations helped to maintain relations between societies separated from each other by great distances and sharp contrasts; they disseminated Western and especially French culture beyond its own frontiers. . . . At the same time the bloodletting thus practised abroad by the most turbulent groups in the West saved its civilization from being extinguished by guerilla warfare. The chroniclers were well aware that at the start of a crusade the people at home in the old countries always breathed more freely, because now they could once more enjoy a little peace.

Fighting, which was sometimes a legal obligation and frequently a pleasure, might also be required of the knight as a matter of honour: in the twelfth century, Périgord ran with blood because a certain lord thought that one of his noble neighbours looked like a blacksmith and had the bad taste to say so. But fighting was also, and perhaps above all, a source of profit—in fact, the nobleman's chief industry.

The lyrical effusions of Bertrand de Born have been mentioned above. He himself made no secret of the less creditable reasons which above all disposed him 'to find no pleasure in peace'. 'Why', he asks, 'do I want rich men to hate each other?' 'Because a rich man is much more noble, generous and affable in war than in peace.' And more crudely: 'We are going to have some fun. For the barons will make much of us . . . and if they want us to remain with them, they will give us *barbarins*' (i.e. coin of Limoges). And again: 'Trumpet, drums, flags and pennons, standards and horses white and black—that is what we shall shortly see. And it will be a happy day; for we shall seize the usurers' goods, and no more shall beasts of burden pass along

[4]Knights traveling in search of adventures.

the highways by day in complete safety; nor shall the burgess journey without fear, nor the merchant on his way to France; but the man who is full of courage shall be rich.' The poet belonged to that class of petty holders of fiefs, the 'vavasours'—he so described himself—for whom life in the ancestral manor-house lacked both gaiety and comforts. War made up for these deficiencies by stimulating the liberality of the great and providing prizes worth having.

The baron, of course, out of regard for his prestige as well as his interest, could not afford to be niggardly in the matter of presents, even towards vassals summoned to his side by the strictest conventions of feudal duty. If it was desired to retain them beyond the stipulated time, to take them farther or call on them more often than an increasingly rigorous custom appeared to permit, it was necessary to give them more. Finally, in face of the growing inadequacy of the vassal contingents, there was soon no army which could dispense with the assistance of that wandering body of warriors to whom adventure made so strong an appeal, provided that there was a prospect of gain as well as of mighty combats. Thus cynically, our Bertrand offered his services to the count of Poitiers: 'I can help you. I have already a shield at my neck and a helm on my head. . . . Nevertheless, how can I put myself in the field without money?'

But it was undoubtedly considered that the finest gift the chief could bestow was the right to a share of the plunder. This was also the principal profit which the knight who fought on his own account in little local wars expected from his efforts. It was a double prize, moreover: men and things. It is true that the Christian code no longer allowed captives to be reduced to slavery and at most permitted a few peasants or artisans to be forcibly removed from one place to another. But the ransoming of prisoners was a general practice. A ruler as firm and prudent as William the Conqueror might indeed never release alive the enemies who fell into his hands; but most warriors were not so far-sighted. The ransoming of prisoners occasionally had more dreadful consequences than the ancient practice of enslavement. The author of the *chanson*[5] of Girart de Roussillon, who certainly wrote from personal observation, tells us that in the evening after a battle Girart and his followers put to the sword all the humble prisoners and wounded, sparing only the 'owners of castles', who alone were in a position to buy their freedom with hard cash. As to plunder, it was traditionally so regular a source of profit that in the ages accustomed to written documents the legal texts treat it as a matter of course— on this point, the barbarian codes, at the beginning of the Middle

[5]Song.

Ages, and the thirteenth-century contracts of enlistment at the end, speak with the same voice. Heavy wagons followed the armies, for the purpose of collecting the spoils of war. Most serious of all, by a series of transitions almost unnoticed by the rather simple minds of the time, forms of violent action which were sometimes legitimate—requisitions indispensable to armies without commissariat, reprisals exacted against the enemy or his subjects—degenerated into pure brigandage, brutal and mean. Merchants were robbed on the highway; sheep, cheeses, chickens were stolen from pens and farmsteads. . . . The best of men contracted strange habits. William Marshal[6] was certainly a valiant knight. Nevertheless when, as a young and landless man travelling through France from tourney to tourney, he encountered on the road a monk who was running away with a girl of noble family and who candidly avowed his intention of putting out to usury the money he was carrying, William did not scruple to rob the poor devil of his cash, under the pretext of punishing him for his evil designs. One of his companions even reproached him for not having seized the horse as well.

Such practices reveal a signal indifference to human life and suffering. War in the feudal age was in no sense war in kid gloves. It was accompanied by actions which seem to us today anything but chivalrous; as for instance—a frequent occurrence, sometimes even in disregard of a solemn oath—the massacre or mutilation of garrisons which had held out 'too long'. It involved, as a natural concomitant, the devastation of the enemy's estates. Here and there a poet, like the author of *Huon of Bordeaux*, and later a pious king like St. Louis protested in vain against this 'wasting' of the countryside which brought such appalling miseries upon the innocent. The epics, the German as well as the French, are faithful interpreters of real life, and they show us a whole succession of 'smoking' villages. 'There can be no real war without fire and blood,' said the plain-spoken Bertrand de Born.

In two passages exhibiting striking parallels, the poet of *Girart de Roussillon* and the anonymous biographer of the Emperor Henry IV[7] show us what the return of peace meant for the 'poor knights': the disdainful indifference of the great, who would have no more need of them; the importunities of money-lenders; the heavy plough-horse instead of the mettlesome charger; iron spurs instead of gold—in short an economic crisis as well as a disastrous loss of prestige. For the merchant and the peasant, on the contrary, peace meant that it was possible once again to work, to gain a livelihood—in short,

---

[6]Earl of Pembroke and regent of England in the early thirteenth century.

[7]Holy Roman Emperor, 1056–1105.

to live. . . . [T]he knight, proud of his courage and skill, despised the unwarlike *(imbellis)* people—the villeins who in face of the armies scampered away 'like deer', and later on the townsmen, whose economic power seemed to him so much the more hateful in that it was obtained by means which were at once mysterious and directly opposed to his own activities. If the propensity to bloody deeds was prevalent everywhere—more than one abbot indeed met his death as the victim of a cloister feud—it was the conception of the necessity of war, as a source of honour and as a means of livelihood, that set apart the little group of 'noble' folk from the rest of society.

Favourite sport though it was, war had its dead seasons; but at these times the knightly class was distinguished from its neighbours by a manner of life which was essentially that of a nobility.

We should not think of this mode of existence as having invariably a rural setting. . . . It was only gradually and in consequence of a more pronounced differentiation of classes that knightly society, outside Italy and southern France, became almost entirely divorced from the urban populations properly so called. Although the noble certainly did not cease altogether to visit the town, he henceforth went there only occasionally, in pursuit of pleasure or for the exercise of certain functions. . . .

The manor-house usually stood in the midst of a cluster of dwellings, or nearby; sometimes there were several in the same village. The manor-house was sharply distinguished from the surrounding cottages . . . —not only because it was better built, but above all because it was almost invariably designed for defence. . . .

These edifices were generally of a very simple type. For a long time the most common, at least outside the Mediterranean regions, was the wooden tower. . . . Normally, a ditch was dug at the foot. Sometimes, at a little distance from the tower, there was a stockade or a rampart of beaten earth, surrounded in its turn by another ditch. . . . Tower and stockade frequently stood on a mound *(motte)*, sometimes natural, sometimes—at least in part—man-made. Its purpose was twofold: to confront the attackers with the obstacle of the slope and to gain a better view of the surrounding country. . . . It was the great men who first had recourse to stone as a building-material. . . . Before the completion of the great clearings, the forests seem to have been easier and less expensive to exploit than the quarries; and while masonry called for specialist workers, the tenants, a permanent source of compulsory labour, were almost all to some extent carpenters as well as wood-cutters. . . .

The favourite amusements of the nobility bore the imprint of a warlike temper.

First, there was hunting. . . . [I]t was more than a sport. The people of western Europe were not yet living in surroundings from which the menace of wild beasts had been finally removed. Moreover, at a time when the flesh of cattle, inadequately fed and of poor stock, furnished only indifferent meat, much venison was eaten, especially in the homes of the rich. . . .

Then there were the tournaments. . . . [T]he practice of these make-believe combats undoubtedly dates back to the remotest times. . . . The distinctive contribution of the feudal age was to evolve from these contests, whether military or popular, a type of mock battle at which prizes were generally offered, confined to mounted combatants equipped with knightly arms; and hence to create a distinctive class amusement, which the nobility found more exciting than any other.

Since these meetings, which could not be organized without considerable expense, usually took place on the occasion of the great 'courts' held from time to time by kings or barons, enthusiasts roamed the world from tournament to tournament. . . .

. . . Since the victor frequently took possession of the equipment and horses of the vanquished and sometimes even of his person, releasing him only on payment of a ransom, skill and strength were profitable assets. More than one jousting knight made a profession, and a very lucrative one, out of his skill in combat. Thus the love of arms inextricably combined the ingredients of 'joy' and the appetite for gain.

. . . The term which, from about the year 1100, commonly served to describe the sum of noble qualities was the characteristic word 'courtesy' (*courtoisie*). . . .

'We shall yet talk of this day in ladies' chambers,' said the count of Soissons, at the battle of Mansurah.[8] This remark . . . is characteristic of a society in which sophistication has made its appearance and, with it, the influence of women. The noblewoman had never been confined within her own secluded quarters. Surrounded with servants, she ruled her household, and she might also rule the fief—perhaps with a rod of iron. It was nevertheless reserved for the twelfth century to create the type of the cultivated great lady who holds a salon. This marks a profound change, when we consider the extraordinary coarseness of the attitude usually ascribed by the old epic poets to their heroes in their relations with women, even with queens—not stopping at the grossest insults, which the lady requites with blows. One can hear the guffaws of the audience. The courtly public had not lost their taste for this heavy humour; but they now allowed it only . . . at the expense of the peasants or the bourgeoisie. For courtesy was essentially an affair of class. The boudoir of the high-born lady and, more generally, the court, was henceforth the place where the knight sought to outshine and to

---

[8]Battle in Egypt in 1249 where the Saracens defeated the French and captured their king, Louis IX.

eclipse his rivals not only by his reputation for great deeds of valour, but also by his regard for good manners and by his literary talents. . . .

Towards the pleasures of the flesh the attitude of the knightly class appears to have been frankly realistic. It was the attitude of the age as a whole. . . .

. . . The noble's marriage . . . was often an ordinary business transaction, and the houses of the nobility swarmed with bastards. . . .

The characteristic features of courtly love can be summarized fairly simply. It had nothing to do with marriage, or rather it was directly opposed to the legal state of marriage, since the beloved was as a rule a married woman and the lover was never her husband. This love was often bestowed upon a lady of higher rank, but in any case it always involved a strong emphasis on the man's adoration of the woman. It professed to be an all-engrossing passion, constantly frustrated, easily jealous, and nourished by its own difficulties; but its stereotyped development early acquired something of a ritual character. . . . Finally, . . . it was, ideally, a 'distant' love. It did not indeed reject carnal intercourse on principle, nor according to Andrew the Chaplain,[9] who discoursed on the subject, did it despise minor physical gratifications if obliged to renounce 'the ultimate solace'. But absence or obstacles, instead of destroying it, only enriched it with a poetic melancholy. If possession, always to be desired, was seen to be quite out of the question, the sentiment none the less endured as an exciting emotion and a poignant joy. . . .

Still less, in spite of what has sometimes been said, was this code dependent on religious ideas. . . . [W]e must in fact recognize that it was directly opposed to them, although its adherents had no clear consciousness of this antithesis. It made the love of man and woman almost one of the cardinal virtues, and certainly the supreme form of pleasure. Above all, even when it renounced physical satisfaction, it sublimated—to the point of making it the be-all and end-all of existence—an emotional impulse derived essentially from those carnal appetites whose legitimacy Christianity only admits in order to curb them by marriage (profoundly despised by courtly love), in order to justify them by the propagation of the species (to which courtly love gave but little thought), and in order, finally, to confine them to a secondary plane of moral experience. It is not in the knightly lyrics that we can hope to find the authentic echo of the attitude of contemporary Christianity towards sexual relations. This is expressed, quite uncompromisingly, in that passage of the pious and clerical *Queste du Saint-Graal*[10] where

---

[9]Andreas Capellanus, author of the twelfth-century treatise, *The Art of Courtly Love.*
[10]*Quest for the Holy Grail.*

Adam and Eve, before they lie together under the Tree to beget 'Abel the Just', beg the Lord to bring down upon them a great darkness to 'comfort' their shame. . . .

Thus set apart by its power, by the nature of its wealth and its mode of life, by its very morals, the social class of nobles was toward the middle of the twelfth century quite ready to solidify into a legal and hereditary class. The ever more frequent use which from that time onwards seems to have been made of the word *gentilhomme*—man of good *gent* or lineage—to describe the members of this class is an indication of the growing importance attributed to qualities of birth. With the wide adoption of the ceremony of 'dubbing' or formal arming of the knight the legal class of nobility took definite shape.

Environment and Pollution

JEAN GIMPEL

Medieval people believed that God had made the world for man, who could therefore exploit nature as he wished. They viewed nature as spiritually instructive, as the "Book of God's Works" to complement the "Book of God's Words," but they had little appreciation for the beauties of nature. Our medieval ancestors viewed forests, waters, and animals as objects, good only to meet people's needs, though they did not countenance mindless destruction. Given these attitudes, waste and pollution developed. How did industrialization cause pollution in its varying forms? Jean Gimpel cites people who worried about the destruction of the environment, but they lamented only the increasing lack of materials to be exploited—they did not criticize the God-given right, for example, to clear forests. Their objections were purely practical. Did medieval civilization find any successful means to combat pollution?

Gimpel argues against those who date the industrialization of Europe from the late eighteenth and nineteenth centuries. He believes there was an industrial revolution in the Middle Ages. Also, he reminds us that concerns we have today— such as those relating to pollution and the environment—have a long history; those worries are not especially new. Does he succeed in making the Middle Ages seem a bit modern (or modern times relatively medieval)? In the same way, he dispels any notion that care for personal hygiene is a recent development. The profusion of public and private baths speaks for a medieval sense of cleanliness. Why did those baths disappear in the late Middle Ages?

The industrialization of the Middle Ages played havoc with the environment of western Europe. Millions of acres of forests were destroyed to increase the area of arable and grazing land and to satisfy the ever greater demand for timber, the main raw material of the time. Not only was timber used as fuel for the hearths of private homes and for ovens, it was also in one way or another essential to practically every medieval industry. In the building industry wood was used to build timber-framed houses, water mills and windmills, bridges, and military installations such as fortresses and palisades. In the wine industry wood was used for making casks and vats. Ships were made of wood, as was all medieval machinery such as weavers' looms. Tanners needed the bark of the trees and so did the rope makers. The glass industry

Jean Gimpel, *The Medieval Machine. The Industrial Revolution of the Middle Ages* (NY: Holt, Rinehart and Winston, 1976), 75–87, 91–92.

demolished the woods for fuel for its furnaces, and the iron industry needed charcoal for its forges. By 1300, forests in France covered only about 32 million acres—2 million acres less than they do today.

There is a remarkable document from 1140 which provides evidence of this onslaught on the medieval forests. Suger,[1] France's first great nationalist prime minister . . . wrote in one of his books of his difficulty in finding the 35-foot beams that he desperately needed as tie beams for the roof of the central nave of the Abbey of Saint-Denis, which he was having rebuilt. He had been told by all his master carpenters that it was absolutely impossible to find such large beams any longer in the area around Paris and that he would have to go far afield for that sort of timber. But Suger was not a man to take no for an answer:

> On a certain night, when I had returned from celebrating Matins, I began to think in bed that I myself should go through all the forests of these parts. . . . Quickly disposing of other duties and hurrying up in the early morning, we hastened with our carpenters, and with the measurements of the beams, to the forest called Iveline. When we traversed our possession in the Valley of Chevreuse we summoned . . . the keepers of our own forests as well as men who knew about the other woods, and questioned them under oath whether we would find there, no matter with how much trouble, any timbers of that measure. At this they smiled, or rather would have laughed at us if they had dared; they wondered whether we were quite ignorant of the fact that nothing of the kind could be found in the entire region. . . . We however—scorning whatever they might say—began, with the courage of our faith as it were, to search through the woods; and towards the first hour we found one timber adequate to the measure. Why say more? By the ninth hour or sooner, we had, through the thickets, the depths of the forest and the dense, thorny tangles, marked down twelve timbers (for so many were necessary) to the astonishment of all. . . .

The Forest of Yvelines toward which he had "hastened" had once covered an immense area to the southwest of Paris. It now covers only 15,500 hectares (38,750 acres).

Suger must have ridden well over 50 kilometers that morning to reach his final destination. . . .

. . . Richard Fitz Nigel, treasurer to the King of England, writing in the 1170s (a period when there seems to have been extensive clearing), shows clearly the concern felt at the time for forests cleared without the ground being prepared properly for agriculture. "If," he says, "woods are so severely cut that a man standing on the half-buried stump of an oak or other tree can see five other trees cut down about him, that is

[1](1081–1151) Abbot of Saint-Denis as well as advisor to the king.

regarded as waste. Such an offense," he goes on to say, "even in a man's own woods, is regarded as so serious that even these men who are free of taxation because they sit at the king's exchequer must pay a money penalty all the heavier for their position."

Whatever Fitz Nigel's concerns, the fact remains that medieval man brought about the destruction of Europe's natural environment. He wasted its natural resources, and very soon felt the consequences of his destructive activities, the first of which was the considerable rise in the price of timber as a result of its increasing scarcity. At Douai, in northern France, in the thirteenth century wood had already become so scarce and expensive that families from the lower income groups could not afford to buy a wooden coffin for their dead. They had to rent one, and when the ceremony at the cemetery was over, the undertaker would open the coffin, throw the corpse into the earth, and bring back the coffin to use again.

Owing to the difficulty of finding suitable large timber, men looked for new technical solutions to building and construction problems. For example, in the famous sketchbook of Villard de Honnecourt, the thirteenth-century architect and engineer, who was working in the north of France not very far from Douai, there is a design for a bridge. The author of the drawing states proudly that it is built with short timber only twenty feet long: "How to make a bridge over water with twenty-foot timber." On another page is a drawing of a floor, under which is written: "How to work on a house or tower even if the timbers are too short." The lack of long beams had a considerable influence on the techniques of timber-framed building, and carpenters created a revolutionary timber-framed house with many shorter timbers.

A few figures from building accounts serve to show how quickly medieval man could destroy his environment. An average house built of wood needed some twelve oaks. In the middle of the fourteenth century, for the building operation at Windsor Castle, a whole wood was bought and all the trees felled—3,004 oaks. This was still not sufficient, for some ten years later 820 oaks were cut in Combe Park and 120 in Pamber Forest, bringing the total for this one castle up to 3,994 oaks. . . .

The building of thousands of furnaces in hundreds of medieval forests to satisfy the extensive demand for iron was a major cause of deforestation. Iron ore, unlike gold ore, is practically never found in its natural state except in meteorites, and it requires a special fuel to smelt and reduce it. From the very beginning, the fuel used was charcoal, the black porous residue of burned wood. This absolute reliance on charcoal made it essential for iron smelters up to the late eighteenth century to build their furnaces in the forests, where wood for the making of charcoal was directly at hand.

The extent of the damage caused by iron smelters to forests can be appreciated when one realizes that to obtain 50 kilograms of iron it was necessary at that time to reduce approximately 200 kilograms of iron ore with as much as 25 steres (25 cubic meters) of wood. It has been estimated that in forty days, one furnace could level the forest for a radius of 1 kilometer.

It is not surprising to hear that certain authorities took measures to halt or at least slow down the massacre of the forests. It was in their financial interest. . . . In the Dauphiné in 1315 the representatives of the Dauphin[2] were greatly alarmed at the widespread destruction of the woods of that region. They formally accused the iron-producing factories of being directly responsible for this disaster and recommended that forcible measures should be taken to arrest the situation.

There were objections in 1255 when two limekilns in the Forest of Wellington consumed five hundred oaks in one year, and on the territory of Colmars in the Basses-Alpes water-powered saws were forbidden at the end of the thirteenth century. In 1205 exploitation of the woods belonging to the monks of Chelles in France was regulated, and in the same year the commune of Montaguloto in Italy required every citizen to plant ten trees annually.

In England, the royal forest, which covered quite an extensive area of the kingdom, was protected by the much-hated forest law (laid down to protect the hunting grounds of the Norman conquerors rather than for any ecological reasons). Nevertheless, encroachments were made regularly on the woodlands in the royal forests, and kings in financial difficulties had to accept vast disforestations. In 1190, the first year of Richard I's reign, the knights of Surrey offered him 200 marks that "they might be quit of all things that belong to the forest from the water of Wey to Kent and from the street of Guildford southwards as far as Surrey stretches." In 1204 the men of Essex offered King John 500 marks and 5 palfreys for the disforestation of "the forest of Essex which is beyond the causeway between Colchester and Bishops Stortford." . . .

The decreasing availability of timber and the progressive rise in the price of wood led England to import timber from Scandinavia. The first fleet of ships loaded with Norwegian fir trees sailed into Grimsby harbor, on the east coast of England, in 1230. And in 1274, the master carpenter of Norwich Cathedral went to Hamburg to buy timber and boards. During this same period a substitute fuel for wood was found—coal.

Some of the great European coalfields of the nineteenth and twentieth centuries were first mined in the thirteenth century. . . .

[2]Eldest son of the French king.

As early as 1226, we find in London a Sea Coal Lane, also known as Lime Burners Lane. The lime-burning industry was one of the first to convert to the use of coal, along with the iron industry. Brewers, dyers, and others followed. In 1243 the first recorded victim of coal mining, Ralph, son of Roger Ulger, drowned in an open pit. At first coal was mined in shallow pits, usually 6 to 15 meters (20 to 50 feet) deep, but sometimes, as in the French coal mines of Boussagues in the Languedoc, there were already underground galleries. In Newcastle there were such extensive diggings around the city that it was danger-ous to approach it by night, lest one fall and break one's neck in the open trenches. Here and in many other places, the medieval environ-ment was already an industrial environment. . . .

With the burning of coal, western Europe began to face atmospheric pollution. The first person recorded to have suffered from medieval pollution was a Queen of England, Eleanor, who was driven from Nottingham Castle in 1257 by the unpleasant fumes of the sea coal burned in the industrial city below. Coal smoke was considered to be very detrimental to one's health, and up to the sixteenth century coal was generally used as a domestic fuel only by the poorer members of society, who could not afford to buy wood. Medieval coal extracted from the surface was of inferior quality, with more bitumen in it than the coal mined today. As it burned, it gave off a continuous cloud of choking, foul-smelling, noxious smoke. The only good domestic coal was that extracted from the coalfields bordering the Firth of Forth, which was burned by the Scottish kings, and the coal extracted at Aachen in Germany, which was used to make fires in the town hall and in the mayor's chambers.

By the last decades of the thirteenth century, London had the sad privilege of becoming the first city in the world to suffer man-made atmospheric pollution. In 1285 and 1288 complaints were recorded concerning the infection and corruption of the city's air by coal fumes from the limekilns. Commissioners of Inquiry were appointed, and in 1307 a royal proclamation was made in Southwark, Wapping, and East Smithfield forbidding the use of sea coal in kilns under pain of heavy forfeiture. . . .

The bad reputation of sea coal continued throughout the ages. In the fifteenth century Enea Sylvio Piccolomini, who later became Pope Pius II, wrote when visiting Scotland, "this kind of stone being impreg-nated with sulfur or some fatty matter is burned instead of wood, of which the country is destitute." Sea coal was still unpopular in the sixteenth century when the Venetian envoy Soranzo wrote an account of England in which he says: "In the north towards Scotland they find a certain sort of earth, almost mineral, which burns like charcoal and is extensively used by blacksmiths, and but for a bad odour which it leaves would be yet more employed as it gives great heat and costs but little." The London Company of Brewers offered in 1578 to burn wood instead of sea coal in the brew-houses nearest to the Palace of Westminster because its members understood that the Queen "findeth hersealfe greately greved and anoyed with the taste and smoke of the sea-cooles." . . .

While Londoners were choked with noisome fumes, tens of thousands of villagers throughout Europe were deafened by the din of the village forges. . . .

In the towns people suffered also from industrial water pollution. Two industries in particular were held responsible in the Middle Ages for polluting the rivers: the slaughtering and the tanning industries, especially tanning. Municipalities were always trying to move the butchers and the tanners downstream, outside the precincts of the town.

The slaughtering and quartering of livestock in the Middle Ages was generally done on the butcher's premises. A French parliamentary decree of September 7, 1366, compelled Paris butchers to do their slaughtering and cleaning alongside a running stream beyond the city. This decree was certainly necessary, as some 250,000 head of livestock were slaughtered each year in Paris. The author of the *Menagier de Paris*[3] worked out that 269,256 animals had been slaughtered in 1293: 188,522 sheep, 30,346 oxen, 19,604 calves, and 30,784 pigs. Quite enough to pollute the Seine.

The Paris authorities tried to limit the degree of this pollution not only by restricting the slaughtering of animals within the precincts of the city but also by imposing restrictions on the tanners, who dressed ox, cow, and calf hides, and the tawers, who dressed the skins of deer, sheep, and horses. "In 1395 the king's representative at the *Châtelet*[4] wanted to compel the tawers who were dressing their leather on the banks of the Seine, between the Grand-Pont and the Hôtel du duc de Bourbon to move downstream, because industry corrupted the water of the riverside dwellers, both those lodging in the Louvre and those lodging in the Hôtel du duc de Bourbon."

Tanning polluted the river because it subjected the hides to a whole series of chemical operations requiring tannic acids or lime. Tawing used alum and oil. Dried blood, fat, surplus tissues, flesh impurities, and hair were continually washed away with the acids and the lime into the streams running through the cities. The water flowing from

[3]*The Parisian Household.*
[4]Royal court and prison in Paris.

the tanneries was certainly unpalatable, and there were tanneries in every medieval city. . . .

Many local authorities took measures to combat the pollution of their cities, but in 1388 the English Parliament sitting in Cambridge passed the first nationwide antipollution act. It concerned not only the pollution of the air but also of the waters. It forbade throwing garbage into rivers or leaving it uncared for in the city. All garbage had to be carried away out of town. Otherwise, the law proclaimed, "the air . . . is greatly corrupt and infect and many Maladies and other intolerable Diseases do daily happen. . . . "

However effective these various antipollution measures were, medieval people usually preferred to rely on wells for drinking water. Sometimes they repaired the Roman aqueducts, which were often in a half-ruined state, and occasionally they built new ones. Sometimes they brought water considerable distances in underground conduits. Just about a century after the Norman Conquest, in 1167, the monks of the Cathedral Priory of Canterbury, who had obtained a grant of land containing the springs, installed a very elaborate and complete system of water supply. . . . The water was carried by an underground pipe and, after entering the city walls, flowed into a whole series of pipes. One pipe fed water to the infirmary hall; another went to the refectory, the scullery, and the kitchen; another carried water to the baker's house, the brewer's house, the guest hall, and the bathhouse; and a pipe ran into a tank beside the prior's chambers and fed his water tub. Waste from the water tub and from the bathroom flowed into the main drain, flushing the rere-dorter or *necessarium*.[5]

Numerous documents of the period mention the existence of private and public baths as well as private and public toilets. If there was medieval pollution, there was also medieval hygiene. But the medieval pollution must have increased still more with the breaking down of medieval hygiene. The standards of hygiene in the twelfth and thirteenth centuries were relatively high, but progressively the authorities worried about the "permissiveness" they discovered in the many public baths, and the incidence of the Black Death certainly hardened this attitude. . . .

In the thirteenth century there were no less than thirty-two public baths in Paris, for men and women. According to the professional statutes . . . recorded in 1268 by the provost of Paris, Etienne Boileau, the owners of the bathhouses were allowed to ask two prices at the entrance: 2d. for a steam bath and 4d. for a bath in a tub. In the linen inventories of private houses, mention is sometimes made of a piece

[5]Toilet.

of linen to be laid on the bottom of the wooden tub as a protection against splinters. In the statutes, the owners of the bathhouses made a reservation for the future: if the price of wood or coal (another example of the use of coal in the Middle Ages) should go up, the prices of the steam and hot baths would be raised accordingly. The owners were to protect their establishments materially and morally by making sure that men such as lepers could not enter and that men with a bad reputation would be kept out. The bathhouse was not to be used as a house of prostitution or as a *bordel.* . . . (Interestingly, the medieval word in English for bathhouse was *stew*, which has come down to the English today as a synonym for brothel.) Miniatures of the period show that the bath was indeed a place where people gossiped, ate, and soaked socially, often with a companion of the opposite sex. . . . One entertained one's friends in one's *baignerie*,[6] generally situated near one's bedroom.

On the manuscript page where the provost of Paris had had transcribed the statutes of the bathhouse owners . . . a few lines were added at a later date which show that the authorities were getting increasingly worried about hygiene, or the way hygiene was put to use by lovers. From then on a bathhouse proprietor had to decide if he wanted to run a bathhouse for women or for men. He was not allowed to accommodate both sexes in the same establishment. The author of these lines went on to relate what happens when the bathhouses are mixed. "Shameful things. Men make a point of staying all night in the public baths and women at the break of day come in and through 'ignorance' find themselves in the men's rooms." This prudish attitude toward the growing permissiveness brought the bathhouses into financial difficulties, and they finally had to close one after another. . . . Hygiene thus disappeared from Western society, not to reappear for half a millennium.

[6]Bath.

Medieval Children

DAVID HERLIHY

In this survey of children in the Middle Ages, David Herlihy emphasizes the complexity of the subject. There is first the problem of documentation. Children did not write about themselves and adults usually did not specifically detail their attitudes and behavior toward children. Herlihy thus has had recourse to many different types of source materials. What sources does he rely on in his discussion of children in classical society, among the barbarians, and, finally, in the Middle Ages? Second, Herlihy notes that the information available about medieval children can lead the historian to quite opposite conclusions, that the Middle Ages either maltreated offspring or took pleasure in their spirituality and goodness. Which conclusion does Herlihy adopt? Does the evidence support his interpretation?

What explains the different treatment of children in classical, barbarian, and medieval cultures? Instead of looking within the family for the causes of these changes, Herlihy usually points to outside influences, such as Christianity, and socioeconomic developments. Christian theologians disagreed on the basic nature of children, stressing their ties to original sin or their holy innocence. According to Herlihy, changing attitudes toward the baby Jesus reflected the way in which society viewed all children. Of course, the impact of theology and Christian art on the family is impossible to measure exactly—one wonders, for example, about peasant children, a subject Herlihy neglects in favor of urban social groups. Increasing commercialization and urbanization in the eleventh and twelfth centuries led to a new concern for children, one that was both practical and psychological. The establishment of schools and orphanages suggests that children received more attention and care. Pedagogues, both religious and lay, worried about children's education, health, and spiritual well-being. The result, says Herlihy, was an idealization of childhood in the Middle Ages, long before many historians place that development. Herlihy thus refutes those historians who argue that a concept of and an appreciation for childhood did not emerge until the sixteenth and seventeenth centuries.

. . . Many, perhaps most, children in most traditional societies did no more than come and go. And most never acquired, or were given, a voice which might have recorded and preserved their impressions concerning themselves, their parents, and the world they had recently

David Herlihy, "Medieval Children," in *Essays on Medieval Civilization*, edited by Bede Karl Lackner and Kenneth Roy Philp (Austin & London: University of Texas Press, 1978), 109–130.

discovered. Of all social groups which formed the societies of the past, children, seldom seen and rarely heard in the documents, remain for historians the most elusive, the most obscure.

The difficulties of interviewing the mute have doubtlessly obstructed and delayed a systematic investigation of the history of childhood. But today, at least, historians are aware of the commonplace assumption of psychologists, that childhood plays a critical role in the formation of the adult personality. Perhaps they are awakening to an even older wisdom, the recognition that society, in the way it rears its children, shapes itself. . . .

Today, the literature devoted to the history of children in various places and epochs may be described, rather like children themselves, as small but growing daily. It remains, however, difficult to discern within that literature a clear consensus, an acceptable hypothesis, concerning the broad trends of children's history, even within Western societies. To be sure, there is frequent allusion within these recent publications to a particular interpretation which, for want of a better name, we shall call the "theory of discovered childhood." The principal formulator of this interpretation, at least in its most recent form, has been the French social historian Philippe Ariès. In a book published in 1960, called in its English translation *Centuries of Childhood*, Ariès entitled the second chapter "the discovery of childhood." In it he affirmed that the Middle Ages of Western history did not recognize childhood as a distinct phase in life. Medieval people allegedly viewed and treated their children as imperfectly formed adults. Once the infant was weaned, medieval parents supposedly made no concessions to its special and changing psychological needs and took little satisfaction in the distinctive traits of the young personality. The corollary to this assumption is that, at some point in the development of Western society and civilization, the young years of life were at last discovered: childhood needed a Columbus.

Proclamations of the alleged discovery of childhood have become commonplace in the growing literature, but wide differences in interpretation still separate the authors. When, for example, was childhood first recognized? On this important question, Ariès himself is indefinite, even evasive, and seems to place the discovery over three or four hundred years, from the fifteenth to the eighteenth centuries. . . .

If historians of the modern world do not agree concerning the date of childhood's discovery, their colleagues, working in more remote periods, show signs of restiveness with Ariès' postulate, that medieval people did not distinguish children from adults. A number of scholars . . . have noted among the pedagogues, humanists, and even artists of fifteenth-century Italy a new orientation toward children, a new awareness of their problems, and an appreciation of their qualities.

The fat and frolicksome babies, the *putti*, who cavort through many solemn paintings of the Italian Renaissance, leave little doubt that the artists of the epoch knew how to depict, and they or their patrons liked to contemplate, children. A still more radical departure from Ariès' views was proposed, in 1968, by the French medievalist Pierre Riché. Riché accepted Ariès' phrase, the "discovery of childhood," but radically changed his chronology. The initial explorers of childhood were, for Riché, the monastic pedagogues active in Western Europe between the sixth and eighth centuries. Their sensitivity toward the psychology of children allegedly transformed the harsh educational methods of classical antiquity and developed a new pedagogy which was finely attuned to the personality of the child-monk. Thus, over an extended period of time, from the early Middle Ages until the present, one or another author would have us believe that a consciousness of childhood was at last emerging.

The lessons that I would draw from this confusion of learned opinions are the following. Historians would be well advised to avoid such categoric and dubious claims, that people in certain periods failed to distinguish children from adults, that childhood really did lie beyond the pale of collective consciousness. Attitudes toward children have certainly shifted, as has the willingness on the part of society to invest substantially in their welfare or education. But to describe these changes, we need terms more refined than metaphors of ignorance and discovery. I would propose that we seek to evaluate, and on occasion even to measure, the psychological and economic investment which families and societies in the past were willing to make in their children. However, we ought also to recognize that alternative and even competitive sets of child-related values can coexist in the same society, perhaps even in the same household. Different social groups and classes expect different things from their children; so do different epochs, in accordance with prevailing economic, social, and demographic conditions. In examining the ways in which children were regarded and reared in the past, we should not expect either rigorous consistency across society or lineal progress over time.

In the current, lively efforts to reconstruct the history of children in Western civilization, the long period of the Middle Ages has a special importance. The medieval child represents a kind of primordial form, an "eo-pais," a "dawn child" as it were, against whom Western children of subsequent epochs must be measured if we are to appreciate the changes they have experienced. To be sure, the difficulties of observing medieval children cannot be discounted. Medieval documentation is usually sparse, often inconsistent, and always difficult. . . . We can hope to catch only fleeting glimpses of medieval children in their

rush through, or out of, life. On the other hand, even glimpses may
be enough to dispel some large misconceptions concerning medieval
children and to aid us toward a sound reconstruction of the history of
children in the Western world.

In surveying medieval children, it is first necessary to consider the
two prior traditions which largely shaped the medieval appraisal of
the very young—the classical and the barbarian. It is important also
to reflect upon the influence exerted upon child rearing by a special
component of the ancient Mediterranean heritage: the Christian church.

Classical society, or at least the elites within it, cultivated an impressive array of intellectual traditions, which were founded upon literacy
and preserved over time through intensive, and expensive, educational
methods. Classical civilization would be inconceivable in the absence
of professional teachers, formal instruction, and numerous schools and
academies. But as social historians of antiquity now emphasize, the
resources that supported ancient society were in truth scant. "The classical Mediterranean has always been a world on the edge of starvation," one historian has recently written, with much justice if perhaps
some exaggeration. Scarce resources and the high costs of rearing children helped form certain distinctive policies regarding the young. The
nations which comprised the Roman Empire, with the exception only
of the Jews, refused to support deformed, unpromising, or supernumerary babies. In Roman practice, for example, the newborn baby was
at once laid before the feet of him who held the *patria potestas*[1] over it,
usually the natural father. Through a ritual gesture called *susceptio*, the
holder of paternal authority might raise up the infant and receive it into
his family and household. But he could also reject the baby and order
its exposure. Infanticide, or the exposure of infants, was a common and
accepted social practice in classical society, shocking perhaps to modern
sensibilities but rational for these ancient peoples who were seeking to
achieve goals with limited means.

Here however is a paradox. Widespread infanticide in ancient society does not imply disinterest in or neglect of those children elected
for survival. On the contrary, to assure a good return on the precious
means invested in them, they were subject to close and often cruel
attention and to frequent beatings. St. Augustine[2] in his *Confessions*
tells how his father, Patricius, and even his pious mother, Monica,
urged him to high performance at school, "that I might get on in the
world and excel in the handling of words, to gain honor among men

[1]Paternal authority.
[2]Christian theologian, 354–430, and Bishop of Hippo in North Africa.

and deceitful riches." "If I proved idle in learning," he says of his teachers, "I was soundly beaten. For this procedure seemed wise to our ancestors; and many, passing the same way in the days past, had built a sorrowful road, by which we too must go, with multiplication of grief and toil upon the sons of Adam." The memories which the men of antiquity preserved of their childhood were understandably bleak. "Who would not shudder," Augustine exclaims in the *City of God*, "if he were given the choice of eternal death or life again as a child? Who would not choose to die?"

The barbarian child grew up under quite different circumstances. Moreover, barbarian practices of child rearing seem to have been particularly influential in the society of early medieval Europe, between the fifth and eleventh centuries. This is not surprising. Early in the Middle Ages, the cities which had dominated society and culture in antiquity lost importance, the literate social elites of classical society all but disappeared, and their educational institutions and ideals went down amid the debacle of the Western empire. On the other hand, barbarian practices were easily preserved within, and congenial to, the semibarbarized society of the early medieval West.

In a tract called *Germania*, written in A.D. 98, the Roman historian Tacitus has described for us the customs of the barbarian Germans, including their treatment of children. Tacitus, to be sure, likes to contrast barbarian virtues with Roman vices and doubtlessly exaggerates in his depictions of both, but his words are nonetheless worth our attention. The Germans, he claims, did not, like the Romans, kill their supernumerary children. Rather, the barbarians rejoiced in a numerous progeny. Moreover, the barbarian mother, unlike her Roman counterpart, nursed her own baby and did not hand it over for feeding to servants or a hired nurse. On the other hand, Tacitus notes, the barbarian parents paid little attention to their growing children. "In every household," he writes, "the children grow up naked and unkempt. . . . " "The lord and slave," he continues, "are in no way to be distinguished by the delicacy of their bringing up. They live among the same flocks, they lie on the same ground. . . . " Barbarian culture did not depend for its survival on the costly instruction of the young in complex skills and learned traditions; barbarian parents had no need to invest heavily in their children, either psychologically or materially. The cheap costs of child rearing precluded the adoption of infanticide as standard social policy but also reduced the attention which the growing child received from its parents. Only on the threshold of adulthood did the free German male re-establish close contacts with adult society. He typically joined the following of a mature warrior, accompanied him into battle, observed him, and gained some instruction in the arts of war, which, like the arts of rhetoric in the classical world, were the key to his social advance.

A casual attitude toward children seems embodied in the laws of the barbarian peoples—Franks, Lombards, Visigoths, Anglo-Saxons, and others—which were redacted into Latin largely between the sixth and the ninth centuries. The barbarian laws typically assigned to each member of society a sum of money—a fine, or wergeld—which would have to be paid to the relatives if he or she was injured or killed. The size of the wergeld thus provides a crude measure of social status or importance. One of the barbarian codes, the Visigothic, dating from the middle seventh century, gives a particularly detailed and instructive table of values which shows how the worth of a person varied according to age, sex, and status. A free male baby, in the first year of life, was assigned a wergeld of 60 solidi. Between age 1 and age 9, his social worth increased at an average rate of only 3.75 solidi per year, thus attaining the value of 90 solidi in the tenth year of life. Between ages 10 and 15, the rate of increase accelerated to 10 solidi per year; and between ages 15 and 20 it grew still more, to 30 solidi per year. In other words, the social worth of the free Visigothic male increased very slowly in the early years of childhood, accelerated in early adolescence, and grew most substantially in the years preceding full maturity. Considered mature at age 20, he enjoyed a wergeld of 300 solidi—five times the worth of the newborn male infant—and this he retained until age 50. In old age, his social worth declined, to 200 solidi between ages 50 and 65 and to 100 solidi from age 65 to death. The old man, beyond age 65, was worth the same as a child of ten years.

The contrast between the worth of the child and the worth of the adult is particularly striking in regard to women. Among the Visigoths, a female under age 15 was assigned only one-half the wergeld enjoyed by males—only 30 solidi during her first year of life. Her social worth, however, increased enormously when she entered the years of childbearing, between ages 15 and 40 in the Visigothic codes. Her wergeld then leaped to 250 solidi, nearly equal to the 300 solidi assigned to the male and eight times the value of the newborn baby girl. The sterile years of old age brought a reduction of the fine, first to 200 solidi, which she retained to age 60, and then to 100 solidi. In old age, she was assigned the same worth as the male. . . .

The low values assigned to children in these barbarian codes is puzzling. Did the lawgivers not realize that the supply of adults, including the especially valued childbearing women, was critically dependent on the protection of children? This obvious truth seemingly escaped the notice of the barbarian lawgivers; children, and their relation to society, did not loom large in their consciousness.

Apart from laws, one other source offers some insight into the treatment of children in the early Middle Ages: surveys of the population settled on particular estates and manors. These sporadic surveys have survived from the Carolingian period of medieval history, the late eighth and ninth centuries. The largest of them, redacted in the first quarter of the ninth century, lists nearly 2,000 families settled on the lands of the abbey of Saint-Germain-des-Prés near Paris. The survey gives no exact ages, but of 8,457 persons included in it, 3,327 are explicitly identified as *infantes*, or children. . . .

The proportion of known children within the population is very low—only 85 children for every 100 adults. Even if all those of uncertain age are considered *infantes*, the ratio then becomes 116 children for every 100 adults. This peasant population was either singularly barren or it was not bothering to report all its children. Moreover, the sexual composition of the population across these age categories is perplexing. Among the known adults, men and women appear in nearly equal numbers. But among the known children, there are 143 boys for every 100 girls—a male-to-female ratio of nearly three to two. Among those of uncertain age, the sex ratio is even higher. The high sex ratio among the known children may indicate widespread female infanticide, but if this were so, we should expect to find a similarly skewed ratio among the known adults. The death of numerous baby girls inevitably would affect over time the proportions of adult women in this presumably closed population. But the proportions of males and females among the known adults are reasonably balanced. The more likely explanation is that the monastic surveyors, or the peasants who reported to them, were negligent in counting children and were particularly deficient in reporting the presence of little girls in the households. As the barbarian legal codes suggest, children, and especially girls, became of substantial interest to society, and presumably to their families, only as they aged.

The low monetary worth assigned to the very young, and the shadowy presence of children in the statistical documents of the early Middle Ages, should not, however, imply that parents did not love their children. Tacitus notes that the barbarian mother usually nursed her own babies. Kinship ties were strongly emphasized in barbarian society, and these were surely cemented by affection. The German epic fragment the *Song of Hildebrand* takes as its principal theme the love which should unite father and son. The warrior Hildebrand flees into exile to live among the Huns, leaving "a babe at the breast in the bower of the bride." Then, after sixty years of wandering, he confronts his son as his enemy on the field of battle. He recognizes his offspring and tries to avoid combat; he offers the young warrior gold and, as the poet tells us, his love besides. . . . If classical methods of child rearing can be called cruel but closely attentive, the barbarian child grew up within an atmosphere of affectionate neglect.

The Christian church also powerfully influenced the treatment of children in many complex ways. Christianity, like Judaism before it, unequivocally condemned infanticide or the exposure of infants. To be sure, infanticide and exposure remained common social practices in Western Europe across the entire length of the Middle Ages. Church councils, penitentials, sermons, and secular legal codes yield abundant and repeated references to those crimes. As late as the fifteenth century, if we are to believe the great popular preachers of the period, the streams and cesspools of Europe echoed with the cries of abandoned babies. But medieval infanticide still shows one great difference from the comparable practice in the ancient world. Our sources consistently attribute the practice to two motivations: the shame of seduced and abandoned women, who wished to conceal illegitimate births, and poverty—the inability of the mother, and often of both parents, to support an additional mouth. The killing or abandonment of babies in medieval society was the characteristic resort of the fallen, the poor, the desperate. In the ancient world, infanticide had been accepted practice, even among the social elites.

Christian teachings also informed and softened attitudes toward children. Christian scriptures held out several examples of children who enjoyed or earned God's special favor: in the Old Testament, the young Samuel and the young Daniel; in the New, the Holy Innocents and the Christ child himself. According to the evangelists, Jesus himself welcomed the company of children, and he instructed his disciples in the famous words: "Unless you become as little children, you will never enter the Kingdom of Heaven."

This partiality toward children evoked many echoes among patristic[3] and medieval writers. In a poem attributed to St. Clement of Alexandria,[4] Christ is called the "king of children." Pope Leo the Great[5] writes . . . "Christ loves childhood, for it is the teacher of humility, the rule of innocence, the model of sweetness." . . .

A favorable appraisal of childhood is also apparent in the monastic culture of the early Middle Ages. Western monasteries, from the sixth century, accepted as oblates to the monastic life children who were hardly more than toddlers, and the leaders of the monastic movement gave much attention to the proper methods of rearing and instructing these miniature monks. In his famous rule, St. Benedict of Nursia

---

[3]Referring to the fathers, or theologians, of the early Christian Church.

[4]Greek Christian theologian, c.150–c.215.

[5]440–461.

insisted that the advice of the children be sought in important matters, "for often the Lord reveals to the young what should be done." St. Columban[6] in the seventh century, and the Venerable Bede[7] in the eighth, praised four qualities of the monastic child: he does not persist in anger; he does not bear a grudge; he takes no delight in the beauty of women; and he expresses what he truly believes.

But alongside this positive assessment of the very young, Christian tradition supported a much harsher appraisal of the nature of the child. In Christian belief, the dire results of Adam's fall were visited upon all his descendants. All persons, when they entered the world, bore the stain of original sin and with it concupiscence, an irrepressible appetite for evil. Moreover, if God had predestined some persons to salvation and some to damnation, his judgments touched even the very young, even those who died before they knew their eternal options. The father of the Church who most forcefully and effectively explored the implications of predestination for children was again St. Augustine. Voluminous in his writings, clear in his logic, and ruthless in his conclusions, Augustine finally decided, after some early doubts, that the baby who died without baptism was damned to eternal fires. There were heaven and hell and no place in-between. "If you admit that the little one cannot enter heaven," he argued, "then you concede that he will be in everlasting fire."

This cruel judgment of the great African theologian contrasts with the milder views of the Eastern fathers, who affirmed that unbaptized children suffer only the loss of the vision of God. The behavior of Augustine's God seems to mimic the posture of the Roman paterfamilias, who was similarly arbitrary and ruthless in the judgment of his own babies, who elected some for life and cast out others into the exterior darkness. And no one in his family dared question his decisions. . . .

Augustine was, moreover, impressed by the early dominion which evil establishes over the growing child. The suckling infant cries unreasonably for nourishment, wails and throws tantrums, and strikes with feeble but malicious blows those who care for him. "The innocence of children," Augustine concludes, "is in the helplessness of their bodies, rather than any quality of soul." . . .

The suppression of concupiscence thus becomes a central goal of Augustine's educational philosophy and justifies hard and frequent punishments inflicted on the child. While rejecting the values of pagan antiquity, he adheres to the classical methods of education. Augustine prepared the way for retaining under Christian auspices that "sorrowful road" of schooling which he, as a child at school, had so much hated.

[6]Irish monk and missionary, c.543–615.
[7]English monk, historian, and saint, c.673–735.

Medieval society thus inherited and sustained a mix of sometimes inconsistent attitudes toward children. The social historian, by playing upon one or another of these attitudes, by judiciously screening his sources, could easily color as he pleases the history of medieval children. He could compile a list of the atrocities committed against them, dwell upon their neglect, or celebrate medieval views of the child's innocence and holiness. One must, however, strive to paint a more balanced picture, and for this we obviously need some means of testing the experiences of the medieval child. The tests we shall use here are two: the social investment, the wealth and resources which medieval society was apparently willing to invest in children; and the psychological investment, the attention they claimed and received from their elders. The thesis of this essay, simply stated, is that both the social and psychological investments in children were growing substantially from approximately the eleventh and twelfth centuries, through to the end of the Middle Ages, and doubtlessly beyond.

The basic economic and social changes which affected medieval society during this period seem to have required a heightened investment in children. From about the year 1000, the medieval community was growing in numbers and complexity. Commercial exchange intensified, and a vigorous urban life was reborn in the West. Even the shocking reduction in population size, coming with the plagues, famines, and wars of the fourteenth century, did not undo the importance of the commercial economy or of the towns and the urban classes dependent upon it. Medieval society, once a simple association of warriors, priests, and peasants, came to include such numerous and varied social types as merchants, lawyers, notaries, accountants, clerks, and artisans. A new world was born, based on the cultivation and preservation of specialized, sophisticated skills.

The emergence of specialized roles within society required in turn a social commitment to the training of children in the corresponding skills. Earlier educational reforms—notably those achieved under Charlemagne[8] —had largely affected monks and, in less measure, clerics; they had little impact on the lay world. One novelty of the new medieval pedagogy, as it is developed from the twelfth century, is the attention now given to the training of laymen. Many writers now comment on the need and value of mastering a trade from early youth. Boys . . . should be taught a trade "as soon as possible." . . . "Men from childhood," Thomas Aquinas[9] observes, "apply themselves to those offices and skills in which they will spend

[8]Carolingian Emperor, 768–814.
[9]Saint and theologian, c.1225–1274.

their lives. . . . This is altogether necessary. To the extent that something is difficult, so much the more must a man grow accustomed to it from childhood."

Later in the thirteenth century, Raymond Lull,[10] one of the most learned men of the epoch, compares society to a wheel upon which men ride ceaselessly, up and down, gaining and losing status; the force which drives the wheel is education, in particular the mastery of a marketable skill. Through the exercise of a trade, a man earns money, gains status, and ultimately enters the ranks of the rich. Frequently, however, he becomes arrogant in his new status, and he neglects to train his children in a trade. His unskilled offspring inevitably ride the wheel on its downward swing. And so the world turns. A marketable skill offers the only certain riches and the only security. . . .

One hundred and fifty years later, the Florentine Dominican Giovanni Dominici voices exactly the same sentiments. Neither wealth nor inherited status offers security. Only a marketable skill can assure that children "will not be forced, as are many, to beg, to steal, to enter household service, or to do demeaning things." . . .

Although statistics largely elude us, there can be little doubt that medieval society was making substantial investments in education from the twelfth century. . . . The chronicler Giovanni Villani[11] gives us some rare figures on the schools functioning at Florence in the 1330's. The children, both boys and girls, who were attending the grammar schools of the city, presumably between 6 and 12 years of age, numbered between eight and ten thousand. From what we know of the population of the city, better than one out of two school-aged children were receiving formal instruction in reading. Florentine girls received no more formal instruction after grammar school, but of the boys, between 1,000 and 1,200 went on to six secondary schools, where they learned how to calculate on the abacus, in evident preparation for a business career. Another 550 to 600 attended four "large schools" where they studied "Latin and logic," the necessary preparation for entry into the universities and, eventually, for a career in law, medicine, or the Church. Florence, it might be argued, was hardly a typical medieval community. Still, the social investment that Florentines were making in the training of their children was substantial.

Another indicator of social investment in children is the number of orphanages or hospitals devoted to their care, and here the change across the Middle Ages is particularly impressive. The care of the abandoned or orphaned child was a traditional obligation of Christian

[10]Missionary and philosopher, c.1223–c.1315.

[11]Florentine, d.1348.

charity, but it did not lead to the foundation and support of specialized orphanages until late in the Middle Ages. The oldest European orphanage of which we have notice was founded at Milan in 787, but we know nothing at all concerning its subsequent history or that of other orphanages sporadically mentioned in the early sources. The great hospital orders of the medieval Church, which sprang up from the twelfth century, cared for orphans and foundlings, but none initially chose that charity as its special mission.

The history of hospitals in the city of Florence gives striking illustration of a new concern for abandoned babies which emerged in Europe during the last two centuries of the Middle Ages. In his detailed description of his native city, written in the 1330's, Villani boasts that Florence contained thirty hospitals with more than a thousand beds. But the beds were intended for the "poor and infirm," and he mentions no special hospital for foundlings. A century later, probably in the 1420's, another chronicler, Gregorio Dati,[12] . . . composed another description of the marvels of Florence. By then the city contained no fewer than three hospitals which received foundlings and supported them until an age when the girls could marry and the boys could be instructed in a trade. . . .

Even a rapid survey of the foundling hospitals of Europe shows a similar pattern. Bologna seems not to have had an orphanage until 1459, and Pavia not until 1449. At Paris, the first specialized hospital for children, Saint-Esprit en Grèves, was founded in 1363, but according to its charter it was supposed to receive only orphans of legitimate birth. Care of foundlings, it was feared, might encourage sexual license among adults. But the hospital in practice seems to have accepted abandoned babies, and several similar institutions were established in French cities in the fifteenth century.

This new concern for the survival of children, even foundlings, seems readily explicable. Amid the ravages of epidemics, the sheer numbers of orphans must have multiplied in society. Moreover, the plagues carried off the very young in disproportionate numbers. Parents feared for the survival of their lineages and their communities. . . . The frequent creation of foundling hospitals and orphanages indicates that society as a whole shared this concern and was willing to invest in the survival of its young, even orphans and foundlings.

The medieval social investment in children thus seems to have grown from the twelfth century and to have passed through two phases: the first one, beginning from the twelfth century, largely involved a

[12]Florentine writer, businessman, and statesman, 1362–1435.

commitment, on the part of the urban communities, to the child's education and training; the second, from the late fourteenth century, reflected a concern for the child's survival and health under difficult hygienic conditions.

This social investment also presumes an equivalent psychological investment, as well as a heightened attention paid to the child and his development. This is evident, for example, in the rich tradition of pedagogical literature intended for a lay audience, which again dates from the twelfth century. One of the earliest authors to provide a comprehensive regimen of child care was Vincent of Beauvais, who died in 1264. . . . [H]e gives advice on the delivery of the baby; its care in the first hours, days, and months of life; nursing and weaning; the care of older children; and their formal education. Later in the century, Raymond Lull . . . is similarly comprehensive, including passages not only on formal schooling but also on the care and nourishment of the child. "For every man," he explains, "must hold his child dear." . . . The learning of the scholars seems to have spread widely, even among the humble social classes.

These medieval pedagogues also developed a rudimentary but real psychology of children. Vincent of Beauvais recommends that the child who does not readily learn must be beaten, but he warns against the psychological damage which excessive severity may cause. "Children's minds," he explains, "break down under excessive severity of correction; they despair, and worry, and finally they hate. And this is the most injurious; where everything is feared, nothing is attempted." A few teachers . . . wanted to prohibit all corporal punishment at school. For them physical discipline was "contrary to nature"; it "induced servility and sowed resentment, which in later years might make the student hate the teacher and forget his lesson."

The teacher—and on this all writers agree—should be temperate in the use of force, and he should also observe the child, in order to identify his talents and capacities. For not all children are alike, and natural differences must be recognized and developed. Raymond Lull affirms that nature is more capable of rearing the child than the child's mother. The Florentine Giovanni Dominici stresses the necessity of choosing the proper profession for the child. Society, he notes, requires all sorts of occupations and skills, ranging from farmers to carpenters, to bankers, merchants, priests, and "a thousand others." . . .

To read these writers is inevitably to form the impression that medieval people, or some of them at least, were deeply concerned about children. Indeed, Jean Gerson[13] expressly condemns his contem-

---

[13]French theologian, 1363–1429.

poraries, who, in his opinion, were excessively involved with their children's survival and success. In order to gain for them "the honors and pomp of this world," parents, he alleges, were expending "all their care and attention; they sleep neither day nor night and often become very miserly." In investing in their children, they neglected charitable works and the good of their own souls. . . .

Medieval society, increasingly dependent upon the cultivation of sophisticated skills, had to invest in a supporting pedagogy; when later threatened by child-killing plagues, it had to show concern for the survival of the very young. But the medieval involvement with children cannot be totally described in these functional terms. Even as they were developing an effective pedagogy, medieval people were re-evaluating the place of childhood among the periods of life.

One indication of a new sympathy toward childhood is the revision in theological opinion concerning the salvation of the babies who died without baptism. Up until the twelfth century, the leading theologians of the Western church . . . reiterated the weighty opinion of St. Augustine, that such infants were surely damned. In the twelfth century, Peter Abelard and Peter Lombard, perhaps the two most influential theologians of the epoch, reversed the condemnation of unbaptized babies to eternal fires. A thorough examination of the question, however, awaited the work of Thomas Aquinas, the first to use in a technical theological sense the term *limbus puerorum*, the "limbo of children." The unbaptized baby, he taught, suffered only the deprivation of the Beatific Vision.[14] . . .

Aquinas' mild judgment on babies dead without baptism became the accepted teaching of the medieval Church. Only one prominent theologian in the late Middle Ages, Gregory of Rimini,[15] resisted it, and he came to be known as the *tortor puerorum*, the "torturer of children."

No less remarkable is the emergence, from the twelfth century, of a widespread devotion to the Child Jesus. The texts from the early Middle Ages which treat of the Christ Child . . . present Christ as a miniature wonder worker, who miraculously corrects Joseph's mistakes in carpentry, tames lions, divides rivers, and even strikes dead a teacher who dared reprimand him in class. All-knowing and all-powerful, he is the negation of the helpless, charming child. A new picture of the Child Jesus emerges, initially under Cistercian auspices, in the twelfth century. For example, between 1153 and 1157 the English Cistercian Aelred of Rievaulx composed a meditation, "Jesus at the Age of Twelve." Aelred expatiates on the joy which the presence of the

---

[14]The immediate vision of God in Heaven.

[15]D. 1358.

young Christ brought to his elders and companions: ". . . the grace of heaven shone from that most beautiful face with such charm as to make everyone look at it, listen to him, and be moved to affection. . . . Old men kiss him, young men embrace him, boys wait upon him. . . . Each of them, I think, declares in his inmost heart: 'Let him kiss me with the kiss of his mouth.' ". . .

Doubtlessly, the special characteristics of Cistercian monasticism were influential here. Like other reformed orders of the twelfth century, the Cistercians no longer admitted oblates, the boys placed in the monastery at tender ages, who grew up in the cloister with no experience of secular life. The typical Cistercians . . . were raised within a natural family, and many were familiar with the emotions of family life. Grown men when they entered the monastery, they carried with them a distinct mentality—a mentality formed in the secular world and open to secular values. Many doubtlessly had considered and some had pursued other careers before electing the monastic life; they presumably had reflected upon the emotional and spiritual rewards of the married state and the state of parenthood. While fleeing from the world, they still sought in their religious experiences analogues to secular and familial emotions. . . . In celebrating the joys of contemplating a perfect child, they find in their religious experience an analogue to the love and satisfaction which parents feel in observing their growing children. The Cistercian cult of the Child Jesus suggests, in other words, that lay persons, too, were finding the contemplation of children emotionally rewarding.

In the thirteenth century, devotion to the Child Jesus spread well beyond the restricted circle of Cistercian monasticism. St. Francis of Assisi,[16] according to the *Legenda Gregorii*[17] set up for the first time a Christmas crèche, so that the faithful might more easily envision the tenderness and humility of the new-born Jesus. St. Francis, the most popular saint of the late Middle Ages, was thus responsible, at least in legend, for one of the most popular devotional practices still associated with Christmas. . . .

This cult of the Christ Child implies an idealization of childhood itself. "O sweet and sacred childhood," another Cistercian . . . writes of the early years of Christ, "which brought back man's true innocence, by which men of every age can return to blessed childhood and be conformed to you, not in physical weakness but in humility of heart and holiness of life."

How are we to explain this celebration of "sweet and sacred child-

[16]Founder of the Franciscans, c.1182–1226.

[17]*Legends by Gregory.*

hood"? It closely resembles other religious movements which acquire extraordinary appeal from the twelfth century—the cults of poverty, of Christian simplicity, and of the apostolic life. These "movements of cultural primitivism" . . . point to a deepening psychological discontent with the demands of the new commercial economy. The inhabitants of towns in particular, living by trade, were forced into careers of getting and spending, in constant pursuit of what Augustine had called "deceitful riches." The psychological tensions inherent in the urban professions and the dubious value of the proferred material rewards seem to have generated a nostalgic longing for alternate systems of existence, for freedom from material concerns, for the simple Christian life as it was supposedly lived in the apostolic age. Another model for an alternate existence, the exact opposite of the tension-ridden urban experience, was the real or imagined life of the child, who was at once humble and content, poor and pure, joyous and giving joy.

The simple piety of childhood remained an ideal of religious reformers for the duration of the Middle Ages. At their close, both Girolamo Savonarola[18] in the south of Europe and Desiderius Erasmus[19] in the north urged their readers to look to pious children if they would find true models of the Christian life. . . .

Moreover, the medieval cult of childhood extends beyond religious movements and informs secular attitudes as well. . . . Later in the Middle Ages, a Florentine citizen and merchant . . . , reflecting on his own life, calls childhood "nature's most pleasant age. " In his *Praise of Folly*, Erasmus avers that the simplicity and unpretentiousness of childhood make it the happiest time of life. "Who does not know," Folly asks her audience, "that childhood is the happiest age and the most pleasant for all? What is there about children that makes us kiss and hug them and cuddle them as we do, so that even an enemy would help them, unless it is this charm of folly?" Clearly, we have come far from Augustine's opinion, that men would prefer eternal death to life again as a child.

The history of medieval children is as complex as the history of any social group, and even more elusive. This essay has attempted to describe in broad outline the cultural attitudes which influenced the experiences of medieval children, as well as the large social trends which touched their lives. The central movements which, in this reconstruction, affected their fate were the social and economic changes widely evident across Europe from the twelfth century, most especially the rise of a commercialized economy and the proliferation of special skills within society; and the worsening health conditions of the late

[18]Dominican reformer who ruled Florence from 1494 to 1498.
[19]Dutch humanist, c.1466–1536.

Middle Ages, from the second half of the fourteenth century. The growth of a commercialized economy made essential an attentive pedagogy which could provide society with adequately trained adults. And the deteriorating conditions of hygiene across the late Middle Ages heightened the concern for, and investment in, the health and survival of the very young. Paradoxically, too, the growing complexities of social life engendered not truly a discovery but an idealization of childhood: the affirmation of the sentimental belief that childhood is, as Erasmus maintains, a blessed time and the happiest moment of human existence. . . .

Fast, Feast, and Flesh:
The Religious Significance
of Food
to Medieval Women

CAROLINE WALKER BYNUM

In this bold essay, Caroline Walker Bynum explores the religious significance of food for medieval women, a subject she believes scholars have ignored in favor of sex and money. Bynum argues that food as a religious symbol was vitally important to medieval people, who wrote often about eating, gluttony, and fasting and related them to God, sin, and salvation. Her evidence comes from the experience of holy women, some of whom became saints, and all of whom were revered by a society disposed to admire severe asceticism. How did male saints compare to female saints in the Middle Ages? What qualities were each sex likely to have?

These holy women usually performed miracles while abstaining from all food save the holy eucharist. They fasted on communion wafers and, as Bynum illustrates through the life of Lidwina of Schiedam, suffered greatly. The stories of her shedding skin, bones, and intestines; her illness; and her desire to take upon herself the suffering of others—all this seems bizarre to a more materialistic twentieth-century culture. Modern medical and psychological categories such as anorexia do not recapture the intense religiosity of the high and late Middle Ages. These holy women did not have a universal psychological ailment; their behavior reflected historical theological doctrines and the position of women in society. What assumptions in medieval theology and culture associated women with food? How did women use food to control themselves and their world? What cultural explanation does Bynum offer in arguing that food was more significant to women than to men?

How did the clergy, exclusively male, feel about the exploits of holy women? These women, supposedly of a lower order of creation than men, taught the dominant sex much through their fasts from worldly food and their feasts of holy food. Of course, priests alone had the miracle-working power to change ordinary bread into the body of Jesus, the only food that could sustain many holy women. Yet Lidwina's eucharistic visions and hunger, as Bynum shows, involved her in conflict with the clergy. Were Lidwina and other saintly women submissive as women were supposed to be? How did the association of submissiveness and weakness with women relate to society's conception of Jesus, of flesh, and of food?

Caroline Walker Bynum, "Fast, Feast, and Flesh: The Religious Significance of Food to Medieval Women," *Representations* II (1985): 1–16, with editing. (Berkeley: University of California Press).

. . . Scholars have recently devoted much attention to the spirituality of the thirteenth, fourteenth, and fifteenth centuries. In studying late medieval spirituality they have concentrated on the ideals of chastity and poverty—that is, on the renunciation, for religious reasons, of sex and family, money and property. It may be, however, that modern scholarship has focused so tenaciously on sex and money because sex and money are such crucial symbols and sources of power in our own culture. Whatever the motives, modern scholars have ignored a religious symbol that had tremendous force in the lives of medieval Christians. They have ignored the religious significance of food. Yet, when we look at what medieval people themselves wrote, we find that they often spoke of gluttony as the major form of lust, of fasting as the most painful renunciation, and of eating as the most basic and literal way of encountering God. Theologians and spiritual directors from the early church to the sixteenth century reminded penitents that sin had entered the world when Eve ate the forbidden fruit and that salvation comes when Christians eat their God in the ritual of the communion table.

In the Europe of the late thirteenth and fourteenth centuries, famine was on the increase again, after several centuries of agricultural growth and relative plenty. Vicious stories of food hoarding, of cannibalism, of infanticide, or of ill adolescents left to die when they could no longer do agricultural labor sometimes survive in the sources, suggesting a world in which hunger and even starvation were not uncommon experiences. The possibility of overeating and of giving away food to the unfortunate was a mark of privilege, of aristocratic or patrician status—a particularly visible form of what we call conspicuous consumption, what medieval people called magnanimity or largesse. Small wonder then that gorging and vomiting, luxuriating in food until food and body were almost synonymous, became in folk literature an image of unbridled sensual pleasure; that magic vessels which forever brim over with food and drink were staples of European folktales; that one of the most common charities enjoined on religious orders was to feed the poor and ill; or that sharing one's own meager food with a stranger (who might turn out to be an angel, a fairy, or Christ himself) was, in hagiography and folk story alike, a standard indication of heroic or saintly generosity. Small wonder too that voluntary starvation, deliberate and extreme renunciation of food and drink, seemed to medieval people the most basic asceticism, requiring the kind of courage and holy foolishness that marked the saints.

Food was not only a fundamental material concern to medieval people; food practices—fasting and feasting—were at the very heart of the Christian tradition. A Christian in the thirteenth and fourteenth centuries was required by church law to fast on certain days and to receive communion at least once a year. Thus the behavior that defined a Christian was food-related behavior. . . .

Food was, moreover, a central metaphor and symbol in Christian poetry, devotional literature, and theology because a meal (the eucharist) was the central Christian ritual, the most direct way of encountering God. And we should note that this meal was a frugal repast, not a banquet but simply the two basic food stuffs of the Mediterranean world: bread and wine. Although older Mediterranean traditions of religious feasting did come, in a peripheral way, into Christianity, indeed lasting right through the Middle Ages in various kinds of carnival, the central religious meal was reception of the two basic supports of human life. Indeed Christians believed it *was* human life. Already hundreds of years before transubstantiation was defined as doctrine, most Christians thought that they quite literally ate Christ's body and blood in the sacrament. . . .

Thus food, as practice and as symbol, was crucial in medieval spirituality. But in the period from 1200 to 1500 it was more prominent in the piety of women than in that of men. . . . Recent work. . . demonstrates that, although women were only about 18 percent of those canonized or revered as saints between 1000 and 1700, they were 30 percent of those in whose lives extreme austerities were a central aspect of holiness and over 50 percent of those in whose lives illness (often brought on by fasting and other penitential practices) was the major factor in reputation for sanctity. In addition,. . . most males who were revered for fasting fit into one model of sanctity—the hermit saint (usually a layman)—and this was hardly the most popular male model, whereas fasting characterized female saints generally. Between late antiquity and the fifteenth century there are at least thirty cases of women who were reputed to eat nothing at all except the eucharist, but I have been able to find only one or possibly two male examples of such behavior before the well-publicized fifteenth-century case of the hermit Nicholas of Flüe.[1] Moreover, miracles in which food is miraculously multiplied are told at least as frequently of women as of men, and giving away food is so common a theme in the lives of holy women that it is very difficult to find a story in which this particular charitable activity does not occur. The story of a woman's basket of bread for the poor turning into roses when her husband (or father) protests her almsgiving was attached by hagiographers to at least five different women saints.

If we look specifically at practices connected with Christianity's holy meal, we find that eucharistic visions and miracles occurred far more frequently to women, particularly certain types of miracles in which the quality of the eucharist as food is underlined. It is far more common,

---

[1]Swiss saint, 1417–1487.

for example, for the wafer to turn into honey or meat in the mouth of a woman. Miracles in which an unconsecrated host is vomited out or in which the recipient can tell by tasting the wafer that the priest who consecrated it is immoral happen almost exclusively to women. Of fifty-five people from the later Middle Ages who supposedly received the holy food directly from Christ's hand in a vision, forty-five are women. In contrast, the only two types of eucharistic miracle that occur primarily to men are miracles that underline not the fact that the wafer is food but the power of the priest. Moreover, when we study medieval miracles, we note that miraculous abstinence and extravagant eucharistic visions tend to occur together and are frequently accompanied by miraculous bodily changes. Such changes are found almost exclusively in women. Miraculous elongation of parts of the body, the appearance on the body of marks imitating the various wounds of Christ (called stigmata), and the exuding of wondrous fluids (which smell sweet and heal and sometimes *are* food—for example, manna or milk) are usually female miracles.

If we consider a different kind of evidence—the *exempla* or moral tales that preachers used to educate their audiences, both monastic and lay—we find that, according to Frederic Tubach's index [*Index Exemplorum: A Handbook of Religious Tales* (Helsinki 1969)], only about 10 percent of such stories are about women. But when we look at those stories that treat specifically fasting, abstinence, and reception of the eucharist, 30 to 50 percent are about women. The only type of religious literature in which food is more frequently associated with men is the genre of satires on monastic life, in which there is some suggestion that monks are more prone to greed. But this pattern probably reflects the fact that monasteries for men were in general wealthier than women's houses and therefore more capable of mounting elaborate banquets and tempting palates with delicacies.

Taken together, this evidence demonstrates two things. First, food practices were more central in women's piety than in men's. Second, both men and women associated food—especially fasting and the eucharist—with women. There are, however, a number of problems with this sort of evidence. In addition to the obvious problems of the paucity of material and of the nature of hagiographical accounts . . . —there is the problem inherent in quantifying data. In order to count phenomena the historian must divide them up, put them into categories. Yet the most telling argument for the prominence of food in women's spirituality is the way in which food motifs interweave in women's lives and writings until even phenomena not normally thought of as eating, feeding, or fasting seem to become food-related. In other words, food becomes such a pervasive concern that it provides both a literary and a psychological unity to the woman's way of seeing the world. And this cannot be demonstrated by statistics. Let me therefore tell in some detail one of the many stories from the later Middle Ages in which food becomes a leitmotif of stunning complexity and power. It is the story of Lidwina of the town of Schiedam in the Netherlands, who died in 1433 at the age of 53.

Several hagiographical accounts of Lidwina exist, incorporating information provided by her confessors; moreover, the town officials of Schiedam, who had her watched for three months, promulgated a testimonial that suggests that Lidwina's miraculous abstinence attracted more public attention than any other aspect of her life. The document solemnly attests to her complete lack of food and sleep and to the sweet odor given off by the bits of skin she supposedly shed.

The accounts of Lidwina's life suggest that there may have been early conflict between mother and daughter. When her terrible illness put a burden on her family's resources and patience, it took a miracle to convince her mother of her sanctity. One of the few incidents that survives from her childhood shows her mother annoyed with her childish dawdling. Lidwina was required to carry food to her brothers at school, and on the way home she slipped into church to say a prayer to the Virgin. The incident shows how girlish piety could provide a respite from household tasks—in this case, as in so many cases, the task of feeding men. We also learn that Lidwina was upset to discover that she was pretty, that she threatened to pray for a deformity when plans were broached for her marriage, and that, after an illness at age fifteen, she grew weak and did not want to get up from her sickbed. The accounts thus suggest that she may have been cultivating illness— perhaps even rejecting food—before the skating accident some weeks later that produced severe internal injuries. In any event, Lidwina never recovered from her fall on the ice. Her hagiographers report that she was paralyzed except for her left hand. She burned with fever and vomited convulsively. Her body putrified so that great pieces fell off. From mouth, ears, and nose, she poured blood. And she stopped eating.

Lidwina's hagiographers go into considerable detail about her abstinence. At first she supposedly ate a little piece of apple each day, although bread dipped into liquid caused her much pain. Then she reduced her intake to a bit of date and watered wine flavored with spices and sugar; later she survived on watered wine alone—only half a pint a week—and she preferred it when the water came from the river and was contaminated with salt from the tides. When she ceased to take any solid food, she also ceased to sleep. And finally she ceased to swallow anything at all. Although Lidwina's biographers present her abstinence as evidence of saintliness, she was suspected by some during her lifetime of being possessed by a devil instead; she herself appears to have claimed that her fasting was natural. When people accused her of hypocrisy, she replied that it is no sin to eat and therefore no glory to be incapable of eating.

Fasting and illness were thus a single phenomenon to Lidwina. And since she perceived them as redemptive suffering, she urged both on others. We are told that a certain Gerard from Cologne, at her urging, became a hermit and lived in a tree, fed only on manna sent from God. We are also told that Lidwina prayed for her twelve-year-old nephew to be afflicted with an illness so that he would be reminded of God's mercy. Not surprisingly, the illness itself then came from miraculous feeding. The nephew became sick by drinking several drops from a pitcher of unnaturally sweet beer on a table by Lidwina's bedside.

Like the bodies of many other women saints, Lidwina's body was closed to ordinary intake and excreting but produced extraordinary effluvia. The authenticating document from the town officials of Schiedam testifies that her body shed skin, bones, and even portions of intestines, which her parents kept in a vase; and these gave off a sweet odor until Lidwina, worried by the gossip that they excited, insisted that her mother bury them. Moreover, Lidwina's effluvia cured others. A man in England sent for her wash water to cure his ill leg. The sweet smell from her left hand led one of her confessors to confess his own sins. And Lidwina actually nursed others in an act that she herself explicitly saw as a parallel to the Virgin's nursing of Christ.

One Christmas season, so all her biographers tell us, a certain widow Catherine, who took care of her, had a vision that Lidwina's breasts would fill with milk, like Mary's, on the night of the Nativity. When she told Lidwina, Lidwina warned her to prepare herself. Then Lidwina saw a vision of Mary surrounded by a host of female virgins; and the breasts of Mary and of all the company filled with milk, which poured out from their open tunics, filling the sky. When Catherine entered Lidwina's room, Lidwina rubbed her own breast and the milk came out, and Catherine drank three times and was satisfied (nor did she want any corporeal food for many days thereafter). . . .

Lidwina also fed others by charity and by food multiplication miracles. Although she herself did not eat, she charged the widow Catherine to buy fine fish and make fragrant sauces and give these to the poor. The meat and fish she gave as alms sometimes, by a miracle, went much further than anyone had expected. She gave water and wine and money for beer to an epileptic burning with thirst; she sent a whole pork shoulder to a poor man's family; she regularly sent food to poor or sick children, forcing her servants to spend or use for others money or food she would not herself consume. When she shared the wine in her bedside jug with others it seemed inexhaustible. So pleased was

God with her charity that he sent her a vision of a heavenly banquet, and the food she had given away was on the table.

Lidwina clearly felt that her suffering was service—that it was one with Christ's suffering and that it therefore substituted for the suffering of others, both their bodily ills and their time in purgatory. Indeed her body quite literally became Christ's macerated and saving flesh, for, like many other female saints, she received stigmata (or so one—but only one—of her hagiographers claims). . . . Her hagiographers state that the fevers she suffered almost daily from 1421 until her death were suffered in order to release souls in purgatory. And we see this notion of substitution reflected quite clearly in the story of a very evil man, in whose stead Lidwina made confession; she then took upon herself his punishment, to the increment of her own bodily anguish. We see substitution of another kind in the story of Lidwina taking over the toothache of a woman who wailed outside her door.

Thus, in Lidwina's story, fasting, illness, suffering, and feeding fuse together. Lidwina becomes the food she rejects. Her body, closed to ordinary intake and excretion but spilling over in milk and sweet putrefaction, becomes the sustenance and the cure—both earthly and heavenly—of her followers. But holy eating is a theme in her story as well. The eucharist is at the core of Lidwina's devotion. During her pathetic final years, when she had almost ceased to swallow, she received frequent communion (indeed as often as every two days). Her biographers claim that, during this period, only the holy food kept her alive. But much of her life was plagued by conflict with the local clergy over her eucharistic visions and hunger. One incident in particular shows not only the centrality of Christ's body as food in Lidwina's spirituality but also the way in which a woman's craving for the host, although it kept her under the control of the clergy, could seem to that same clergy a threat, both because it criticized their behavior and because, if thwarted, it could bypass their power.

Once an angel came to Lidwina and warned her that the priest would, the next day, bring her an unconsecrated host to test her. When the priest came and pretended to adore the host, Lidwina vomited it out and said that she could easily tell our Lord's body from unconsecrated bread. But the priest swore that the host was consecrated and returned, angry, to the church. Lidwina then languished for a long time, craving communion but unable to receive it. About three and a half months later, Christ appeared to her, first as a baby, then as a bleeding and suffering youth. Angels appeared, bearing the instruments of the passion, and (according to one account) rays from Christ's wounded body pierced Lidwina with stigmata. When she subsequently asked for a sign, a host hovered over Christ's head and a napkin descended onto

her bed, containing a miraculous host, which remained and was seen
by many people for days after. The priest returned and ordered Lidwina
to keep quiet about the miracle but finally agreed, at her insistence, to
feed her the miraculous host as communion. Lidwina was convinced
that it was truly Christ because she, who was usually stifled by food,
ate this bread without pain. The next day the priest preached in church
that Lidwina was deluded and that her host was a fraud of the devil.
But, he claimed, Christ was present in the bread he offered because
it was consecrated with all the majesty of the priesthood. Lidwina
protested his interpretation of her host, but she agreed to accept a
consecrated wafer from him and to pray for his sins. Subsequently
the priest claimed that he had cured Lidwina from possession by the
devil, while Lidwina's supporters called her host a miracle. Although
Lidwina's hagiographers do not give full details, they claim that the
bishop came to investigate the matter, that he blessed the napkin for
the service of the altar, and that the priest henceforth gave Lidwina the
sacrament without tests or resistance.

As this story worked its way out, its theme was not subversive of
clerical authority. The conflict began, after all, because Lidwina wanted
a consecrated host, and it resulted in her receiving frequent communion, in humility and piety. According to one of her hagiographers,
the moral of the story is that the faithful can always substitute "spiritual communion" (i.e., meditation) if the actual host is not given.
But the story had radical implications as well. It suggested that Jesus
might come directly to the faithful if priests were negligent or skepti-
cal, that a priest's word might not be authoritative on the difference
between demonic possession and sanctity, that visionary women might
test priests. Other stories in Lidwina's life had similar implications.
She forbade a sinning priest to celebrate mass; she read the heart of
another priest and learned of his adultery. Her visions of souls in purgatory especially concerned priests, and she substituted her sufferings
for theirs. One Ash Wednesday an angel came to bring ashes for her
forehead before the priest arrived. Even if Lidwina did not reject the
clergy, she sometimes quietly bypassed or judged them.

Lidwina focused her love of God on the eucharist. In receiving it, in
vision and in communion, she became one with the body on the cross.
Eating her God, she received his wounds and offered her suffering for
the salvation of the world. Denying herself ordinary food, she sent that
food to others, and her body gave milk to nurse her friends. Food is
the basic theme in Lidwina's story: self as food and God as food. For
Lidwina, therefore, eating and not-eating were finally one theme. To
fast, that is, to deny oneself earthly food, and yet to eat the broken
body of Christ—both acts were to suffer. And to suffer was to save and
to be saved.

Lidwina did not write herself, but some pious women did. And many of these women not only lived lives in which miraculous abstinence, charitable feeding of others, wondrous bodily changes, and eucharistic devotion were central; they also elaborated in prose and poetry a spirituality in which hungering, feeding, and eating were central metaphors for suffering, for service, and for encounter with God. For example, the great Italian theorist of purgatory, Catherine of Genoa (d. 1510)—whose extreme abstinence began in response to an unhappy marriage and who eventually persuaded her husband to join her in a life of continence and charitable feeding of the poor and sick—said that the annihilation of ordinary food by a devouring body is the best metaphor for the annihilation of the soul by God in mystical ecstasy. She also wrote that, although no simile can adequately convey the joy in God that is the goal of all souls, nonetheless the image that comes most readily to mind is to describe God as the only bread available in a world of the starving. Another Italian Catherine, Catherine of Siena (d. 1380), in whose saintly reputation fasting, food miracles, eucharistic devotion, and (invisible) stigmata were central, regularly chose to describe Christian duty as "eating at the table of the cross the food of the honor of God and the salvation of souls." To Catherine, "to eat" and "to hunger" have the same fundamental meaning, for one eats but is never full, desires but is never satiated. "Eating" and "hungering" are active, not passive, images. They stress pain more than joy. They mean most basically to suffer and to serve—to suffer because in hunger one joins with Christ's suffering on the cross; to serve because to hunger is to expiate the sins of the world. Catherine wrote:

> And then the soul becomes drunk. And after it. . . has reached the place
> [of the teaching of the crucified Christ] and drunk to the full, it tastes the
> food of patience, the odor of virtue, and such a desire to bear the cross
> that it does not seem that it could ever be satiated. . . . And then the soul
> becomes like a drunken man; the more he drinks the more he wants to
> drink; the more it bears the cross the more it wants to bear it. And the
> pains are its refreshment and the tears which it has shed for the memory
> of the blood are its drink. And the sighs are its food.

. . . To the stories and writings of Lidwina and the two Catherines— with their insistent and complex food motifs—I could add dozens of others. Among the most obvious examples would be the beguine Mary of Oignies (d. 1213) from the Low Countries, the princess Elisabeth of Hungary (d. 1231), the famous reformer of French and Flemish religious houses Colette of Corbie (d. 1447), and the thirteenth-century poets Hadewijch and Mechtild of Magdeburg. But if we look closely at the lives and writings of those men from the period whose spirituality is in general closest to women's and who were deeply influenced by wom-

en—for example, Francis of Assisi[2] in Italy, Henry Suso[3] and Johann
Tauler[4] in the Rhineland, Jan van Ruysbroeck[5] of Flanders, or the
English hermit Richard Rolle[6] —we find that even to these men food
asceticism is not the central ascetic practice. Nor are food metaphors
central in their poetry and prose. Food then is much more important to
women than to men as a religious symbol. The question is why?

Modern scholars who have noticed the phenomena I have just
described have sometimes suggested in an offhand way that miraculous abstinence and eucharistic frenzy are simply "eating disorders."
The implication of such remarks is usually that food disorders are
characteristic of women rather than men, perhaps for biological reasons,
and that these medieval eating disorders are different from nine-
teenth- and twentieth-century ones only because medieval people
"theologized" what we today "medicalize." While I cannot deal here
with all the implications of such analysis, I want to point to two problems with it. First, the evidence we have indicates that extended abstinence was almost exclusively a male phenomenon in early Christianity
and a female phenomenon in the high Middle Ages. The cause of
such a distribution of cases cannot be primarily biological. Second,
medieval people did not treat all refusal to eat as a sign of holiness.
They sometimes treated it as demonic possession, but they sometimes
also treated it as illness. Interestingly enough, some of the holy women
whose fasting was taken as miraculous (for example, Colette of Corbie)
functioned as healers of ordinary individuals, both male and female,
who could not eat. Thus, for most of the Middle Ages, it was only in
the case of some unusually devout women that not-eating was both
supposedly total and religiously significant. Such behavior must have a
cultural explanation.

On one level, the cultural explanation is obvious. Food was important to women religiously because it was important socially. In medieval
Europe (as in many countries today) women were associated with food
preparation and distribution *rather than* food consumption. The culture
suggested that women cook and serve, men eat. Chronicle accounts of
medieval banquets, for example, indicate that the sexes were often segregated and that women were sometimes relegated to watching from
the balconies while gorgeous foods were rolled out to please the eyes as
well as the palates of men. Indeed men were rather afraid of women's
control of food. Canon lawyers suggested, in the codes they drew

[2]Founder of the Franciscans, c.1182–1226.
[3]German mystic, c.1295–1336.
[4]German mystic, c.1300–1361.
[5]Flemish mystic, 1293–1381.
[6]Mystic, c.1300–1349.

up, that a major danger posed by women was their manipulation of male virility by charms and potions added to food. Moreover, food was not merely *a* resource women controlled; it was *the* resource women controlled. Economic resources were controlled by husbands, fathers, uncles, or brothers. In an obvious sense, therefore, fasting and charitable food distribution (and their miraculous counterparts) were natural religious activities for women. In fasting and charity women renounced and distributed the one resource that was theirs. Several scholars have pointed out that late twelfth- and early thirteenth-century women who wished to follow the new ideal of poverty and begging . . . were simply not permitted either by their families or by religious authorities to do so. They substituted fasting for other ways of stripping the self of support. Indeed a thirteenth-century hagiographer commented explicitly that one holy woman gave up food because she had nothing else to give up. Between the thirteenth and fifteenth centuries, many devout laywomen who resided in the homes of fathers or spouses were able to renounce the world in the midst of abundance because they did not eat or drink the food that was paid for by family wealth. Moreover, women's almsgiving and abstinence appeared culturally acceptable forms of asceticism because what women ordinarily did, as housewives, mothers, or mistresses of great castles, was to prepare and serve food rather than to eat it.

The issue of control is, however, more basic than this analysis suggests. Food-related behavior was central to women socially and religiously not only because food was a resource women controlled but also because, by means of food, women controlled themselves and their world.

First and most obviously, women controlled their bodies by fasting. Although a negative or dualist concept of body does not seem to have been the most fundamental notion of body to either women or men, some sense that body was to be disciplined, defeated, occasionally even destroyed, in order to release or protect spirit is present in women's piety. Some holy women seem to have developed an extravagant fear of any bodily contact. Clare of Montefalco (d. 1308), for example, said she would rather spend days in hell than be touched by a man. Lutgard of Aywières[7] panicked at an abbot's insistence on giving her the kiss of peace, and Jesus had to interpose his hand in a vision so that she was not reached by the abbot's lips. She even asked to have her own gift of healing by touch taken away. Christina of Stommeln (d. 1312), who fell into a latrine while in a trance, was furious at the laybrothers who rescued her because they touched her in order to do so.

Many women were profoundly fearful of the sensations of their

---

[7]Benedictine nun and mystic, 1182–1246.

bodies, especially hunger and thirst. Mary of Oignies, for example, was so afraid of taking pleasure in food that Christ had to make her unable to taste. From the late twelfth century comes a sad story of a dreadfully sick girl named Alpaïs who sent away the few morsels of pork given her to suck, because she feared that any enjoyment of eating might mushroom madly into gluttony or lust. Women like Ida of Louvain (d. perhaps 1300), Elsbeth Achler of Reute (d. 1420), Catherine of Genoa, or Columba of Rieti (d. 1501), who sometimes snatched up food and ate without knowing what they were doing, focused their hunger on the eucharist partly because it was an acceptable object of craving and partly because it was a self-limiting food. Some of women's asceticism was clearly directed toward destroying bodily needs, before which women felt vulnerable.

Some fasting may have had as a goal other sorts of bodily control. There is some suggestion in the accounts of hagiographers that fasting women were admired for suppressing excretory functions. Several biographers comment with approval that holy women who do not eat cease also to excrete, and several point out explicitly that the menstruation of saintly women ceases. Medieval theology—profoundly ambivalent about body as physicality—was ambivalent about menstruation also, seeing it both as the polluting "curse of Eve" and as a natural function that, like all natural functions, was redeemed in the humanity of Christ. Theologians even debated whether or not the Virgin Mary menstruated. But natural philosophers and theologians were aware that, in fact, fasting suppresses menstruation. . . .

Moreover, in controlling eating and hunger, medieval women were also explicitly controlling sexuality. Ever since Tertullian[8] and Jerome,[9] male writers had warned religious women that food was dangerous because it excited lust. Although there is reason to suspect that male biographers exaggerated women's sexual temptations, some women themselves connected food abstinence with chastity and greed with sexual desire.

Women's heightened reaction to food, however, controlled far more than their physicality. It also controlled their social environment. As the story of Lidwina of Schiedam makes clear, women often coerced both families and religious authorities through fasting and through feeding. To an aristocratic or rising merchant family of late medieval Europe, the self-starvation of a daughter or spouse could be deeply perplexing and humiliating. It could therefore be an effective means of manipulating, educating, or converting family members. In one of the most

[8]Christian theologian, c.160–c.230.
[9]Christian theologian and translator of the Bible, c.347–420.

charming passages of Margery Kempe's[10] autobiography, for example, Christ and Margery consult together about her asceticism and decide that, although she wishes to practice both food abstention and sexual continence, she should perhaps offer to trade one behavior for the other. Her husband, who had married Margery in an effort to rise socially in the town of Lynn and who was obviously ashamed of her queer penitential clothes and food practices, finally agreed to grant her sexual abstinence in private if she would return to normal cooking and eating in front of the neighbors. Catherine of Siena's sister, Bonaventura, and the Italian saint Rita of Cascia (d. 1456) both reacted to profligate young husbands by wasting away and managed thereby to tame disorderly male behavior. Columba of Rieti and Catherine of Siena expressed what was clearly adolescent conflict with their mothers and riveted family attention on their every move by their refusal to eat. Since fasting so successfully manipulated and embarrassed families, it is not surprising that self-starvation often originated or escalated at puberty, the moment at which families usually began negotiations for husbands for their daughters. Both Catherine and Columba, for example, established themselves as unpromising marital material by their extreme food and sleep deprivation, their frenetic giving away of paternal resources, and their compulsive service of family members in what were not necessarily welcome ways. (Catherine insisted on doing the family laundry in the middle of the night.)

Fasting was not only a useful weapon in the battle of adolescent girls to change their families' plans for them. It also provided for both wives and daughters an excuse for neglecting food preparation and family responsibilities. . . . Margaret of Cortona[11] refused to cook for her illegitimate son (about whom she felt agonizing ambivalence) because, she said, it would distract her from prayer.

Moreover, women clearly both influenced and rejected their families' values by food distribution. Ida of Louvain, Catherine of Siena, and Elisabeth of Hungary, each in her own way, expressed distaste for family wealth and coopted the entire household into Christian charity by giving away family resources, sometimes surreptitiously or even at night. Elisabeth, who gave away her husband's property, refused to eat any food except that paid for by her own dowry because the wealth of her husband's family came, she said, from exploiting the poor.

Food-related behavior—charity, fasting, eucharistic devotion, and miracles—manipulated religious authorities as well. Women's eucharistic miracles—especially the ability to identify unconsecrated hosts or

---

[10]Mystic and author of the first autobiography in English, c.1373–c.1433.

[11]Italian saint, c.1247–1297.

unchaste priests—functioned to expose and castigate clerical corruption. The Viennese woman Agnes Blannbekin,[12] knowing that her priest was not chaste, prayed that he be deprived of the host, which then flew away from him and into her own mouth. Margaret of Cortona saw the hands of an unchaste priest turn black when he held the host. Saints' lives and chronicles contain many stories, like that told of Lidwina of Schiedam, of women who vomited out unconsecrated wafers, some-times to the considerable discomfiture of local authorities.

The intimate and direct relationship that holy women claimed to the eucharist was often a way of bypassing ecclesiastical control. Late medieval confessors and theologians attempted to inculcate awe as well as craving for the eucharist; and women not only received ambiguous advice about frequent communion, they were also sometimes barred from receiving it at exactly the point at which their fasting and hunger reached fever pitch. In such circumstances many women simply received in vision what the celebrant or confessor withheld. Imelda Lambertini,[13] denied communion because she was too young, and Ida of Léau,[14] denied because she was subject to "fits," were given the host by Christ. And some women received, again in visions, either Christ's blood, which they were regularly denied because of their lay status, or the power to consecrate and distribute, which they were denied because of their gender. . . . Catherine of Siena received blood in her mouth when she ate the wafer.

It is thus apparent that women's concentration on food enabled them to control and manipulate both their bodies and their environment. We must not underestimate the effectiveness of such manipulation in a world where it was often extraordinarily difficult for women to avoid marriage or to choose a religious vocation. But such a conclusion concentrates on the function of fasting and feasting, and function is not meaning. Food did not "mean" to medieval women the control it provided. It is time, finally, to consider explicitly what it meant.

As the behavior of Lidwina of Schiedam or the theological insights of Catherine of Siena suggest, fasting, eating, and feeding all meant suffering, and suffering meant redemption. These complex meanings were embedded in and engendered by the theological doctrine of the Incarnation. Late medieval theology . . . located the saving moment of Christian history less in Christ's resurrection than in his crucifixion. Although some ambivalence about physicality, some sharp and agon-

---

[12]Nun, d. 1315.
[13]Italian, 1322–1333.
[14]Belgian mystic, d. c.1260.

ized dualism, was present, no other period in the history of Christian spirituality has placed so positive a value on Christ's humanity as physicality. Fasting was thus flight not so much *from* as *into* physicality. Communion was consuming—i.e., becoming—a God who saved the world through physical, human agony. Food to medieval women meant flesh and suffering and, through suffering, salvation: salvation of self and salvation of neighbor. Although all thirteenth and fourteenth-century Christians emphasized Christ as suffering and Christ's suffering body as food, women were especially drawn to such a devotional emphasis. The reason seems to lie in the way in which late medieval culture understood "the female."

Drawing on traditions that went back even before the origins of Christianity, both men and women in the later Middle Ages argued that "woman is to man as matter is to spirit." Thus "woman" or "the feminine" was seen as symbolizing the physical part of human nature, whereas man symbolized the spiritual or rational. Male theologians and biographers of women frequently used this idea to comment on female weakness. They also inverted the image and saw "woman" as not merely below but also above reason. Thus they somewhat sentimentally saw Mary's love for souls and her mercy toward even the wicked as an apotheosis of female unreason and weakness, and they frequently used female images to describe themselves in their dependence on God. Women writers, equally aware of the male/female dichotomy, saw it somewhat differently. They tended to use the notion of "the female" as "flesh" to associate Christ's humanity with "the female" and therefore to suggest that women imitate Christ through physicality.

Women theologians saw "woman" as the symbol of humanity, where humanity was understood as including bodiliness. To the twelfth-century prophet, Elisabeth of Schönau,[15] the humanity of Christ appeared in a vision as a female virgin. To Hildegard of Bingen (d. 1179), " woman" was the symbol of humankind, fallen in Eve, restored in Mary and church. She stated explicitly: "Man signifies the divinity of the Son of God and woman his humanity." Moreover, to a number of women writers, Mary was the source and container of Christ's physicality; the flesh Christ put on was in some sense female, because it was his mother's. Indeed whatever physiological theory of reproduction a medieval theologian held, Christ (who had no human father) had to be seen as taking his physicality from his mother. Mechtild of Magdeburg went further and implied that Mary was a kind of preexistent humanity of Christ as the Logos[16] was his preexistent divinity.

---

[15]German mystic and Benedictine nun, 1129–1164.

[16]In Christian theology, the Word—that is, Christ as God.

Marguerite of Oingt,[17] like Hildegard of Bingen, wrote that Mary was the *tunica humanitatis*, the clothing of humanity, that Christ puts on. And to Julian of Norwich,[18] God himself was a mother exactly in that our humanity in its full physicality was not merely loved and saved but even given being by and from him. . . . Although male writers were apt to see God's motherhood in his nursing and loving rather than in the fact of creation, they too associated the flesh of Christ with Mary and therefore with woman.

Not only did medieval people associate humanity as body with woman; they also associated woman's body with food. Woman was food because breast milk was the human being's first nourishment— the one food essential for survival. Late medieval culture was extraordinarily concerned with milk as symbol. Writers and artists were fond of the theme, borrowed from antiquity, of lactation offered to a father or other adult male as an act of filial piety. The cult of the Virgin's milk was one of the most extensive cults in late medieval Europe. A favorite motif in art was the lactating Virgin. Even the bodies of evil women were seen as food. Witches were supposed to have queer marks on their bodies (sort of supernumerary breasts) from which they nursed incubi.

Quite naturally, male and female writers used nursing imagery in somewhat different ways. Men were more likely to use images of being nursed, women metaphors of nursing. Thus when male writers spoke of God's motherhood, they focused more narrowly on the soul being nursed at Christ's breast, whereas women were apt to associate mothering with punishing, educating, or giving birth as well. Most visions of drinking from the breast of Mary were received by men. In contrast, women (like Lidwina) often identified with Mary as she nursed Jesus or received visions of taking the Christchild to their own breasts. Both men and women, however, drank from the breast of Christ, in vision and image. Both men and women wove together— from Pauline references to milk and meat and from the rich breast and food images of the Song of Songs—a complex sense of Christ's blood as the nourishment and intoxication of the soul. Both men and women therefore saw the body on the cross, which in dying fed the world, as in some sense female. Again, physiological theory reinforced image. For, to medieval natural philosophers, breast milk was transmuted blood, and a human mother (like the pelican that also symbolized Christ) fed her children from the fluid of life that coursed through her veins.

[17]French nun, d. 1310.

[18]English mystic, c.1342–c.1413, sometimes called Dame Juliana.

Since Christ's body itself was a body that nursed the hungry, both men and women naturally assimilated the ordinary female body to it. A number of stories are told of female saints who exuded holy fluid from breasts or fingertips, either during life or after death. These fluids often cured the sick. The union of mouth to mouth, which many women gained with Christ, became also a way of feeding. Lutgard's saliva cured the ill; Lukardis of Oberweimar (d. 1309) blew the eucharist into another nun's mouth; Colette of Corbie regularly cured others with crumbs she chewed. Indeed one suspects that stigmata—so overwhelmingly a female phenomenon—appeared on women's bodies because they (like the marks on the bodies of witches and the wounds in the body of Christ) were not merely wounds but also breasts.

Thus many assumptions in the theology and the culture of late medieval Europe associated woman with flesh and with food. But the same theology also taught that the redemption of all humanity lay in the fact that Christ was flesh and food. A God who fed his children from his own body, a God whose humanity *was* his children's humanity, was a God with whom women found it easy to identify. In mystical ecstasy as in communion, women ate and became a God who was food and flesh. And in eating a God whose flesh was holy food, women both transcended and became more fully the flesh and the food their own bodies were.

Eucharist and mystical union were, for women, both reversals and continuations of all the culture saw them to be. In one sense, the roles of priest and lay recipient reversed normal social roles. The priest became the food preparer, the generator and server of food. The woman recipient ate a holy food she did not exude or prepare. Woman's jubilant, vision-inducing, inebriated eating of God was the opposite of the ordinary female acts of food preparation or of bearing and nursing children. But in another and, I think, deeper sense, the eating was not a reversal at all. Women became, in mystical eating, a fuller version of the food and the flesh they were assumed by their culture to be. In union with Christ, woman became a fully fleshly and feeding self—at one with the generative suffering of God.

Symbol does not determine behavior. Women's imitation of Christ, their assimilation to the suffering and feeding body on the cross, was not uniform. Although most religious women seem to have understood their devotional practice as in some sense serving as well as suffering, they acted in very different ways. Some, like Catherine of Genoa and Elisabeth of Hungary, expressed their piety in feeding and caring for the poor. Some . . . lay rapt in mystical contemplation as their own bodies decayed in disease or in self-induced starvation that was offered for the salvation of others. Many, like Lidwina of Schiedam and Catherine of

Siena, did both. Some of these women are, to our modern eyes, pathological and pathetic. Others seem to us, as they did to their contemporaries, magnificent. But they all dealt, in feast and fast, with certain fundamental realities for which all cultures must find symbols–the realities of suffering and the realities of service and generativity.

The Vision of Death

JOHAN HUIZINGA

The Dutch historian Johan Huizinga's The Waning of the Middle Ages, *first published in 1924, is a classic of historical literature. Believing that Northern European civilization of the fourteenth and fifteenth centuries differed profoundly from that of the Italian Renaissance of the same period, Huizinga explored those areas of late medieval thought and behavior that were decidedly not modern. In analyzing the society of the late Middle Ages, he stressed symbols and cultural forms and their meanings, which twentieth-century people often misunderstand.*

First striking in Sicily in 1347 and spreading rapidly through most of Europe, the pandemic known as the Black Death carried off perhaps one-third of the population in a decade. This plague, the greatest catastrophe in European history, recurred again and again during the next two centuries and only ceased in the eighteenth century. Though some modern health measures, such as quarantine, emerged in response to the plague, medieval people had no effective remedy. They manifested their helplessness in a variety of psychological reactions, ranging from intense pleasure-seeking to extreme religiosity, seen, for example, in new devotions, flagellant movements, and massacres of Jews (who were often considered the cause of God's wrath).

The increased mortality rate, running as high as 60 to 80 percent in some towns, affected art and literature, now intent on depicting death in macabre and gruesome forms. How did art mirror reality? Did the preoccupation with death imply people's acceptance of their own mortality and that of their family members? Or did the emphasis on death in the culture imply a horror of one's own end and a wish to prolong life? To what extent was the late medieval attitude toward death peculiar to that time period?

Note especially Huizinga's description of the cemetery of the Holy Innocents in Paris, where living and dead mixed in unhappy proximity. This is late medieval civilization at its most colorful and bizarre, oscillating between the extremes of a short lifespan continually threatened by dread plague and the promised eternity of life after death.

No other epoch has laid so much stress as the expiring Middle Ages on the thought of death. An everlasting call of *memento mori*[1] resounds through life. Denis the Carthusian, in his *Directory of the Life of Nobles*, exhorts them: "And when going to bed at night, he should consider

---

[1] "Be mindful of death." A "memento mori" is thus a "reminder of death."

Johan Huizinga, *The Waning of the Middle Ages* (Garden City, New York: 1954), 138–151.

how, just as he now lies down himself, soon strange hands will lay his body in the grave." In earlier times, too, religion had insisted on the constant thought of death, but the pious treatises of these ages only reached those who had already turned away from the world. Since the thirteenth century, the popular preaching of the mendicant orders had made the eternal admonition to remember death swell into a sombre chorus ringing throughout the world. Towards the fifteenth century, a new means of inculcating the awful thought into all minds was added to the words of the preacher, namely, the popular woodcut. Now these two means of expression, sermons and woodcuts, both addressing themselves to the multitude and limited to crude effects, could only represent death in a simple and striking form. All that the meditations on death of the monks of yore had produced, was now condensed into a very primitive image. This vivid image, continually impressed upon all minds, had hardly assimilated more than a single element of the great complex of ideas relating to death, namely, the sense of the perishable nature of all things. It would seem, at times, as if the soul of the declining Middle Ages only succeeded in seeing death under this aspect.

The endless complaint of the frailty of all earthly glory was sung to various melodies. Three motifs may be distinguished. The first is expressed by the question: where are now all those who once filled the world with their splendour? The second motif swells on the frightful spectacle of human beauty gone to decay. The third is the death-dance: death dragging along men of all conditions and ages.

Compared with the two others, the first of these themes is but a graceful and elegiac sigh. After having taken shape in Greek poetry, it was adopted by the Fathers,[2] and pervaded the literature of all Christendom, and that of Islam also. . . . The Middle Ages cultivated it with special predilection. We find it in the heavy rhythm of the erudite poetry of the twelfth century:

Where is now your glory, Babylon, where is now the terrible Nebuchadnezzar, and strong Darius and the famous Cyrus? Where is now Regulus, or where Romulus, or where Remus? The rose of yore is but a name, mere names are left to us.

. . . However, the wistfulness of remembrance and the thought of frailty in itself do not satisfy the need of expressing, with violence, the

---

[2]The Fathers of the Church, such as St. Augustine and St. Jerome, were Christian theologians of the first four centuries A.D.

shudder caused by death. The medieval soul demands a more concrete embodiment of the perishable: that of the putrefying corpse.

Ascetic meditation had, in all ages, dwelt on dust and worms. The treatises on the contempt of the world had, long since, evoked all the horrors of decomposition, but it is only towards the end of the fourteenth century that pictorial art, in its turn, seizes upon this motif. To render the horrible details of decomposition, a realistic force of expression was required, to which painting and sculpture only attained towards 1400. At the same time, the motif spread from ecclesiastical to popular literature. Until far into the sixteenth century, tombs are adorned with hideous images of a naked corpse with clenched hands and rigid feet, gaping mouth and bowels crawling with worms. The imagination of those times relished these horrors, without ever looking one stage further, to see how corruption perishes in its turn, and flowers grow where it lay.

A thought which so strongly attaches to the earthly side of death can hardly be called truly pious. It would rather seem a kind of spasmodic reaction against an excessive sensuality. In exhibiting the horrors awaiting all human beauty, already lurking below the surface of corporeal charms, these preachers of contempt for the world express, indeed, a very materialistic sentiment, namely, that all beauty and all happiness are worthless *because* they are bound to end soon. Renunciation founded on disgust does not spring from Christian wisdom.

It is noteworthy that the pious exhortations to think of death and the profane exhortations to make the most of youth almost meet. A painting in the monastery of the Celestines at Avignon, now destroyed, attributed by tradition to the founder, King René himself, represented the body of a dead woman, standing, enveloped in a shroud, with her head dressed and worms gnawing her bowels. In the inscription at the foot of the picture the first lines read:

Once I was beautiful above all women But by death I became like this, My flesh was very beautiful, fresh and soft, Now it is altogether turned to ashes. My body was very pleasing and very pretty, I used frequently to dress in silk, Now I must rightly be quite nude. I was dressed in grey fur and miniver, I lived in a great palace as I wished, Now I am lodged in this little coffin. My room was adorned with fine tapestry, Now my grave is enveloped by cobwebs.

Here the *memento mori* still predominates. It tends imperceptibly to change into the quite worldly complaint of the woman who sees her charms fade, as in the following lines . . . by Olivier de la Marche.

These sweet looks, these eyes made for pleasance, Remember, they will lose their lustre, Nose and eyelashes, the eloquent mouth Will putrefy. . . . If you live your natural lifetime, Of which sixty years is a great deal, Your beauty will change into ugliness, Your health into obscure malady, And you will only be in the way here below. If you have a daughter, you will be a shadow to her, She will be in request and asked for, And the mother will be abandoned by all.

. . . This inability to free oneself from the attachment to matter manifests itself in yet other forms. A result of the same sentiment is to be found in the extreme importance ascribed in the Middle Ages to the fact that the bodies of certain saints had never decayed—that of Saint Rosa of Viterbo, for example. The Assumption of the Holy Virgin exempting her body from earthly corruption was on that account regarded as the most precious of all graces. On various occasions attempts were made to retard decomposition. The features of the corpse of Pierre de Luxembourg were touched up with paint to preserve them intact until the burial. The body of a heretic preacher of the sect of the Turlupins,[3] who died in prison, before sentence was passed, was preserved in lime for a fortnight, that it might be burned at the same time with a living heretical woman.

The importance attached to being buried in the soil of one's own country gave rise to usages which the Church had to interdict strictly as being contrary to the Christian religion. In the twelfth and thirteenth centuries, when a prince or a person of rank died far from his country, the body was often cut up and boiled so as to extract the bones, which were sent home in a chest, whereas the rest was interred, not without ceremony, however, on the spot. Emperors, kings and bishops have undergone this strange operation. Pope Boniface VIII forbade it as "An abuse of abominable savagery, practised by some of the faithful in a horrible way and inconsiderately." Yet his successors sometimes granted dispensations. Numbers of Englishmen who fell in France in the Hundred Years' War enjoyed this privilege. . . .

At the close of the Middle Ages the whole vision of death may be summed up in the word *macabre*, in its modern meaning. Of course, this meaning is the outcome of a long process. But the sentiment it embodies, of something gruesome and dismal, is precisely the conception of death which arose during the last centuries of the Middle Ages. This bizarre word appeared in French in the fourteenth century. . . .

Towards 1400 the conception of death in art and literature took a spectral and fantastic shape. A new and vivid shudder was added to

[3]A fourteenth-century sect that practiced radical mysticism and revolted against the Church.

the great primitive horror of death. The macabre vision arose from deep psychological strata of fear; religious thought at once reduced it to a means of moral exhoration. As such it was a great cultural idea, till in its turn it went out of fashion, lingering on in epitaphs and symbols in village cemeteries.

The idea of the death-dance is the central point of a whole group of connected conceptions. The priority belongs to the motif of the three dead and three living men, which is found in French literature from the thirteenth century onward. Three young noblemen suddenly meet three hideous dead men, who tell them of their past grandeur and warn them of their own near end. Art soon took hold of this suggestive theme. We can see it still in the striking frescoes of the *Campo santo* of Pisa. The sculpture of the portal of the church of the Innocents at Paris, which the duke of Berry had carved in 1408, but which has not been preserved, represented the same subject. Miniature painting and woodcuts spread it broadcast.

The theme of the three dead and three living men connects the horrible motif of putrefaction with that of the death-dance. This theme, too, seems to have originated in France, but it is unknown whether the pictorial representation preceded the scenic or the reverse. . . . [T]he Dance of the Dead has been acted as well as painted and engraved. The duke of Burgundy had it performed in his mansion at Bruges in 1449. . . .

The woodcuts with which the Parisian printer, Guyot Marchant, ornamented the first edition of the *Danse Macabré* in 1485 were, very probably, imitated from the most celebrated of these painted death-dances, namely, that which, since 1424, covered the walls of the cloister of the churchyard of the Innocents at Paris. . . . The woodcuts of 1485 can give but a feeble impression of the paintings of the Innocents, of which they are not exact copies, as the costumes prove. To have a notion of the effect of these frescoes, one should rather look at the mural paintings of the church of La Chaise-Dieu, where the unfinished condition of the work heightens the spectral effect.

The dancing person whom we see coming back forty times to lead away the living, originally does not represent Death itself, but a corpse: the living man such as he will presently be. In the stanzas the dancer is called "the dead man" or "the dead woman." It is a dance of the dead and not of Death. . . . The indefatigable dancer is the living man himself in his future shape, a frightful double of his person. "It is yourself," said the horrible vision to each of the spectators. It is only towards the end of the century that the figure of the great dancer, of a corpse with hollow and fleshless body, becomes a skeleton. . . . Death in person has then replaced the individual dead man.

While it reminded the spectators of the frailty and the vanity of earthly things, the death-dance at the same time preached social equality as the Middle Ages understood it, Death levelling the various ranks and professions. At first only men appeared in the picture. The success of his publication, however, suggested to Guyot the idea of a dance macabre of women. Martial d'Auvergne wrote the poetry; an unknown artist, without equalling his model, completed the pictures by a series of feminine figures dragged along by a corpse. Now it was impossible to enumerate forty dignities and professions of women. After the queen, the abbess, the nun, the saleswoman, the nurse, and a few others, it was necessary to fall back on the different states of feminine life: the virgin, the beloved, the bride, the woman newly married, the woman with child. And here the sensual note reappears, to which we referred above. In lamenting the frailty of the lives of women, it is still the briefness of joy that is deplored, and with the grave tone of the *memento mori* is mixed the regret for lost beauty.

Nothing betrays more clearly the excessive fear of death felt in the Middle Ages than the popular belief, then widely spread, according to which Lazarus, after his resurrection, lived in a continual misery and horror at the thought that he should have again to pass through the gate of death. If the just had so much to fear, how could the sinner soothe himself? And then what motif was more poignant than the calling up of the agony of death? It appeared under two traditional forms: the *Ars moriendi*[4] and the *Quattor Hominum novissima*, that is, the four last experiences awaiting man, of which death was the first. These two subjects were largely propagated in the fifteenth century by the printing-press and by engravings. The Art of Dying, as well as the Last Four Things, comprised a description of the agony of death, in which it is easy to recognize a model supplied by the ecclesiastical literature of former centuries.

Chastellain, in a long-winded poem, *Le Pas de la Mort*,[5] has assembled all the above motifs; he gives successively the image of putrefaction—the lament: Where are the great ones of the earth?—an outline of a death-dance—and the art of dying. . . . Chastellain writes:

> There is not a limb nor a form, Which does not smell of putrefaction. Before the soul is outside, The heart which wants to burst in the body Raises and lifts the chest Which nearly touches the backbone. —The face is discoloured and pale, And the eyes veiled in the head. Speech fails him, For the tongue cleaves to the palate. The pulse trembles and he pants. . . . The bones are disjointed on all sides; There is not a tendon which does not stretch as to burst.

[4]The art of dying.
[5]*The Dance of Death.*

. . . Nowhere else were all the images tending to evoke the horror of death assembled so strikingly as in the churchyard of the Innocents at Paris. There the medieval soul, fond of a religious shudder, could take its fill of the horrible. Above all other saints, the remembrance of the saints of that spot, and of their bloody and pitiful martyrdom, was fitted to awake the crude compassion which was dear to the epoch. The fifteenth century honoured the Holy Innocents with special veneration. Louis XI presented to the church "a whole Innocent," encased in a crystal shrine. The cemetery was preferred to every other place of burial. A bishop of Paris had a little of the earth of the churchyard of the Innocents put into his grave, as he could not be laid there. The poor and the rich were interred without distinction. They did not rest there long, for the cemetery was used so much, twenty parishes having a right of burial there, that it was necessary, in order to make room, to dig up the bones and sell the tombstones after a very short time. It was believed that in this earth a human body was decomposed to the bone in nine days. Skulls and bones were heaped up in charnel-houses along the cloisters enclosing the ground on three sides, and lay there open to the eye by thousands, preaching to all the lesson of equality. . . . Under the cloisters the death-dance exhibited its images and its stanzas. No place was better suited to the simian figure of grinning death, dragging along pope and emperor, monk and fool. The duke of Berry, who wished to be buried there, had the history of the three dead and the three living men carved at the portal of the church. A century later, this exhibition of funeral symbols was completed by a large statue of Death, now in the Louvre, and the only remnant of it all.

Such was the place which the Parisians of the fifteenth century frequented. . . . Day after day, crowds of people walked under the cloisters, looking at the figures and reading the simple verses, which reminded them of the approaching end. In spite of the incessant burials and exhumations going on there, it was a public lounge and a rendezvous. Shops were established before the charnel-houses and prostitutes strolled under the cloisters. A female recluse was immured on one of the sides of the church. Friars came to preach and processions were drawn up there. A procession of children only (12,500 strong, thinks the Burgher of Paris) assembled there, with tapers in their hands, to carry an Innocent to Notre Dame and back to the churchyard. Even feasts were given there. To such an extent had the horrible become familiar.

The desire to invent a visible image of all that appertained to death entailed the neglecting of all those aspects of it which were not suited to direct representation. Thus the cruder conceptions of death, and these only, impressed themselves continually on the minds. The macabre vision does not represent the emotions of tenderness or of consolation. The elegiac note is wanting altogether. At bottom the macabre senti- ment is self-seeking and earthly. It is hardly the absence of the departed dear ones that is deplored; it is the fear of one's own death, and this only seen as the worst of evils. Neither the conception of death the consoler, nor that of rest long wished for, of the end of suffering, of the task performed or interrupted, have a share in the funeral sentiment of that epoch. The soul of the Middle Ages did not know the "divine depth of sorrow." Or, rather, it knew it only in connection with the Passion of Christ.

In all these sombre lamentations about death the accents of true tenderness are extremely rare. They could, however, hardly be wanting in relation to the death of children. And, indeed, Martial d'Auvergne, in his death-dance of women, makes the little girl, when led away by death, say to her mother: "Take good care of my doll, my knuckle-bones and my fine dress." But this touching note is only heard exceptionally. The literature of the epoch knew child-life so little! When Antoine de la Salle, in *Le Reconfort de Madame du Fresne*,[6] wishes to console a mother for the death of her twelve-years-old son, he can think of nothing better than citing a still more cruel loss: the heart-rending case of a boy given as a hostage and put to death. To overcome grief, the only advice he can offer is to abstain from all earthly attachments. A doctrinaire and dry consolation! La Salle, however, adds a second short story. It is a version of the popular tale of the dead child, who came back to beg its mother to weep no more, that its shroud might dry. And here suddenly from this simple story—not of his own invention—there arises a poetical tenderness and beneficent wisdom, which we look for in vain in the thousands of voices repeating in various tones the awful *memento mori*. Folk-tale and folk-song, no doubt, in these ages preserved many sentiments which higher literature hardly knew.

The dominant thought, as expressed in the literature, both ecclesi- astical and lay, of that period, hardly knew anything with regard to death but these two extremes: lamentation about the briefness of all earthly glory, and jubilation over the salvation of the soul. All that lay between—pity, resignation, longing, consolation—remained unex- pressed and was, so to say, absorbed by the too much accentuated and too vivid representation of Death hideous and threatening. Living emotion stiffens amid the abused imagery of skeletons and worms.

---

[6]*The Consolation of Madame du Fresne.*

The Development
of the Concept
# of Civilité

NORBERT ELIAS

The treatise by the Christian humanist Erasmus of Rotterdam, On Civility in
Children *(1530), is the starting point for Norbert Elias in his analysis of manners.
Erasmus wrote to instruct Europeans on their table manners and on control of
bodily functions in public. What does Elias mean by the concept* civilité *and the
term "civilizing process"? Why is Erasmus's treatise so important? What does his
investigation of various areas of human conduct say about the notion of shame in
the Middle Ages and in the sixteenth century?*

*The contrast between the behavior of medieval people at table and the conduct
Erasmus advocated is stark, yet a person today might still feel embarrassed by
the discussion of the proverbial "three winds": burping, sneezing, and farting.
Why did Erasmus stress outward bodily propriety? In the Middle Ages, what was
socially acceptable behavior when eating? What was the "threshold of delicacy"? Of
course, proper behavior was different for the nobility than for the peasantry, as the
attempt was to define manners according to social rank. Part of the difference was
owing to the abundance of the aristocratic table. How, for example, did changes
in utensils affect table manners? How might these changes in table manners relate
to other contemporaneous changes for the aristocracy in education, economic and
political activities, literary and artistic tastes?*

. . . The concept of *civilité* acquired its meaning for Western society at a
time when chivalrous society and the unity of the Catholic church were
disintegrating. It is the incarnation of a society which, as a specific
stage in the formation of Western manners or "civilization," was no less
important than the feudal society before it. The concept of *civilité*, too,
is an expression and symbol of a social formation embracing the most
diverse nationalities, in which, as in the Church, a common language
is spoken, first Italian and then increasingly French. These languages
take over the function earlier performed by Latin. They manifest the
unity of Europe, and at the same time the new social formation which
forms its backbone, court society. The situation, the self-image, and the
characteristics of this society find expression in the concept of *civilité*.

Norbert Elias, *The History of Manners* (NY: Urizen Books, 1978), 53–60, 62–65, 67-70.

The concept of *civilité* received the specific stamp and function under discussion here in the second quarter of the sixteenth century. Its individual starting point can be exactly determined. It owes the specific meaning adopted by society to a short treatise by Erasmus of Rotterdam, *De civilitate morum puerilium* (On civility in children), which appeared in 1530. This work clearly treated a theme that was ripe for discussion. It immediately achieved an enormous circulation, going through edition after edition. Even within Erasmus's lifetime—that is, in the first six years after its publication—it was reprinted more than thirty times. In all, more than 130 editions may be counted, 13 of them as late as the eighteenth century. The multitude of translations, imitations, and sequels is almost without limit. . . .

. . . And a whole genre of books, directly or indirectly influenced by Erasmus's treatise, appeared under the title *Civilité* or *Civilité puérile*.[1] . . .

Here, as so often in the history of words, and as was to happen later in the evolution of the concept *civilité* into *civilisation*, an individual was the instigator. By his treatise, Erasmus gave new sharpness and impetus to the long-established and commonplace word *civilitas*.[2] Wittingly or not, he obviously expressed in it something that met a social need of the time. The concept *civilitas* was henceforth fixed in the consciousness of people with the special sense it received from his treatise. And corresponding words were developed in the various popular languages: the French *civilité*, the English "civility," the Italian *civiltà*, and the German *Zivilität*. . . .

Erasmus's book is about something very simple: the behavior of people in society—above all, but not solely, "outward bodily propriety." It is dedicated to a noble boy, a prince's son, and written for the instruction of boys. . . . [T]he treatise points to attitudes that we have lost, that some among us would perhaps call "barbaric" or "uncivilized." It speaks of many things that have in the meantime become unspeakable, and of many others that are now taken for granted. . . .

Bodily carriage, gestures, dress, facial expressions—this "outward" behavior with which the treatise concerns itself is the expression of the inner, the whole man. Erasmus knows this and on occasion states it explicitly: "Although this outward bodily propriety proceeds from a well-composed mind, nevertheless we sometimes find that, for want of instruction, such grace is lacking in excellent and learned men."

There should be no snot on the nostrils, he says somewhat later. A peasant wipes his nose on his cap and coat, a sausage maker on his

[1]Childish civility.
[2]Civility.

arm and elbow. It does not show much more propriety to use one's hand and then wipe it on one's clothing. It is more decent to take up the snot in a cloth, preferably while turning away. If when blowing the nose with two fingers something falls to the ground, it must be immediately trodden away with the foot. The same applies to spittle.

With the same infinite care and matter-of-factness with which these things are said—the mere mention of which shocks the "civilized" man of a later stage with a different affective molding—we are told how one ought to sit or greet. Gestures are described that have become strange to us, e.g., standing on one leg. . . .

The more one immerses oneself in the little treatise, the clearer becomes this picture of a society with modes of behavior in some respects related to ours, and in many ways remote. We see people seated at table. . . . The goblet and the well-cleaned knife on the right, on the left the bread. That is how the table is laid. Most people carry a knife, hence the precept to keep it clean. Forks scarcely exist, or at most for taking meat from the dish. Knives and spoons are very often used communally. There is not always a special implement for everyone: if you are offered something liquid, says Erasmus, taste it and return the spoon after you have wiped it.

When dishes of meat are brought in, usually everyone cuts himself a piece, takes it in his hand, and puts it on his plate if there are plates, otherwise on a thick slice of bread. . . .

. . . Some put their hands into the dishes when they are scarcely seated, says Erasmus. Wolves or gluttons do that. Do not be the first to take from a dish that is brought in. Leave dipping your fingers into the broth to the peasants. Do not poke around in the dish but take the first piece that presents itself. And just as it shows a want of forbearance to search the whole dish with one's hand . . . neither is it very polite to turn the dish round so that a better piece comes to you. What you cannot take with your hands, take on your *quadra*.[3] . . .

. . . Paintings of table scenes from this or earlier times always offer the same spectacle, unfamiliar to us, that is indicated by Erasmus's treatise. The table is sometimes covered with rich cloths, sometimes not, but always there is little on it: drinking vessels, saltcellar, knives, spoons, that is all. Sometimes we see the slices of bread, the *quadrae*, that in French are called *tranchoir* or *tailloir*. Everyone, from the king and queen to the peasant and his wife, eats with the hands. In the upper class there are more refined forms of this. One ought to wash one's hands before a meal, says Erasmus. But there is as yet no soap for this purpose. Usually the guest holds out his hands, and a page pours water

[3]Plate or slice of bread.

over them. The water is sometimes slightly scented with chamomile or rosemary. In good society one does not put both hands into the dish. It is most refined to use only three fingers of the hand. This is one of the marks of distinction between the upper and lower classes.

The fingers become greasy. . . . It is not polite to lick them or wipe them on one's coat. Often you offer others your glass, or all drink from a communal tankard. Erasmus admonishes: "Wipe your mouth beforehand." You may want to offer someone you like some of the meat you are eating. "Refrain from that," says Erasmus, "it is not very decorous to offer something half-eaten to another." And he says further: "To dip bread you have bitten into the sauce is to behave like a peasant, and it shows little elegance to remove chewed food from the mouth and put it back on the *quadra*. If you cannot swallow a piece of food, turn round discreetly and throw it somewhere."

Then he says again: "It is good if conversation interrupts the meal from time to time. Some people eat and drink without stopping, not because they are hungry or thirsty, but because they can control their movements in no other way. They have to scratch their heads, poke their teeth, gesticulate with their hands, or play with a knife, or they can't help coughing, snorting, and spitting. All this really comes from a rustic embarrassment and looks like a form of madness."

But it is also necessary, and possible, for Erasmus to say: Do not expose without necessity "the parts to which Nature has attached modesty." Some prescribe, he says, that boys should "retain the wind by compressing the belly." But you can contract an illness that way. And in another place: . . . (Fools who value civility more than health repress natural sounds.) Do not be afraid of vomiting if you must; "for it is not vomiting but holding the vomit in your throat that is foul."

With great care Erasmus marks out in his treatise the whole range of human conduct, the chief situations of social and convivial life. He speaks with the same matter-of-factness of the most elementary as of the subtlest questions of human intercourse. In the first chapter he treats "the seemly and unseemly condition of the whole body," in the second "bodily culture," in the third "manners at holy places," in the fourth banquets, in the fifth meetings, in the sixth amusement, and in the seventh the bedchamber. This is the range of questions in the discussion of which Erasmus gave new impetus to the concept of *civilitas*.

. . . The unconcerned frankness with which Erasmus and his time could discuss all areas of human conduct is lost to us. Much of what he says oversteps our threshold of delicacy.

But precisely this is one of the problems to be considered here. In tracing the transformation of the concepts by which different societies have tried to express themselves, in following back the concept of civilization to its ancestor *civilité*, one finds oneself suddenly on the track of the civilizing process itself, of the actual change in behavior that took place in the West. That it is embarrassing for us to speak or even hear of much that Erasmus discusses is one of the symptoms of this civilizing process. The greater or lesser discomfort we feel toward people who discuss or mention their bodily functions more openly, who conceal and restrain these functions less than we do, is one of the dominant feelings expressed in the judgment "barbaric" or "uncivilized." Such, then, is the nature of "barbarism and its discontents" or, in more precise and less evaluative terms, the discontent with the different structure of affects, the different standard of repugnance which is still to be found today in many societies which we term "uncivilized," the standard of repugnance which preceded our own and is its precondition. The question arises as to how and why Western society actually moved from one standard to the other, how it was "civilized." In considering this process of civilization, we cannot avoid arousing feelings of discomfort and embarrassment. It is valuable to be aware of them. It is necessary, at least while considering this process, to attempt to suspend all the feelings of embarrassment and superiority, all the value judgments and criticism associated with the concepts "civilization" or "uncivilized." Our kind of behavior has grown out of that which we call uncivilized. But these concepts grasp the actual change too statically and coarsely. In reality, our terms "civilized" and "uncivilized" do not constitute an antithesis of the kind that exists between "good" and "bad," but represent stages in a development which, moreover, is still continuing. It might well happen that our stage of civilization, our behavior, will arouse in our descendants feelings of embarrassment similar to those we sometimes feel concerning the behavior of our ancestors. Social behavior and the expression of emotions passed from a form and a standard which was not a beginning, which could not in any absolute and undifferentiated sense be designated "uncivilized," to our own, which we denote by the word "civilized." And to understand the latter we must go back in time to that from which it emerged. The "civilization" which we are accustomed to regard as a possession that comes to us apparently ready-made, without our asking how we actually came to possess it, is a process or part of a process in which we are ourselves involved. . . .

. . . What came before Erasmus? Was he the first to concern himself with such matters?

By no means. Similar questions occupied the men of the Middle Ages, of Greco-Roman antiquity, and doubtless also of the related, preceding "civilizations." . . .

The Middle Ages have left us an abundance of information on what was considered socially acceptable behavior. Here, too, precepts on conduct while eating had a special importance. Eating and drinking then occupied a far more central position in social life than today, when they provide—frequently, not always—rather the framework and introduction for conversation and conviviality. . . .

The standard of "good behavior" in the Middle Ages is, like all later standards, represented by a quite definite concept. Through it the secular upper class of the Middle Ages, or at least some of its leading groups, gave expression to their self-image, to what, in their own estimation, made them exceptional. The concept epitomizing aristocratic self-consciousness and socially acceptable behavior appeared in French as *courtoisie*, in English "courtesy," in Italian *cortezia*, along with other related terms, often in divergent forms. . . . All these concepts refer quite directly (and far more overtly than later ones with the same function) to a particular place in society. They say: That is how people behave at court. . . .

. . . What emerges as typical behavior, as the pervasive character of its precepts?

Something, in the first place, that in comparison to later times might be called its simplicity, its naïveté. There are, as in all societies where the emotions are expressed more violently and directly, fewer psychological nuances and complexities in the general stock of ideas. There are friend and foe, desire and aversion, good and bad people.

> You should follow honorable men and vent your wrath on the wicked.

. . . .

> When your companions anger you, my son, see that you are not so hot-tempered that you regret it afterward.

In eating, too, everything is simpler, impulses and inclinations are less restrained:

> A man of refinement should not slurp with his spoon when in company; this is the way people at court behave who often indulge in unrefined conduct.

. . . Noble, courteous behavior is constantly contrasted to "coarse manners," the conduct of peasants.

> Some people bite a slice and then dunk it in the dish in a coarse way; refined people reject such bad manners.

If you have taken a bite from the bread, do not dip it in the common dish again. Peasants may do that, not "fine people."

> A number of people gnaw a bone and then put it back in the dish—this is a serious offense.

Do not throw gnawed bones back into the communal dish. From other accounts we know that it was customary to drop them on the floor. Another precept reads:

> A man who clears his throat when he eats and one who blows his nose in the tablecloth are both ill-bred, I assure you.

Here is another:

> If a man wipes his nose on his hand at table because he knows no better, than he is a fool, believe me.

To use the hand to wipe one's nose was a matter of course. Handkerchiefs did not yet exist. But at table certain care should be exercised; and one should on no account blow one's nose into the tablecloth. Avoid lip-smacking and snorting, eaters are further instructed:

> If a man snorts like a seal when he eats, as some people do, and smacks his chops like a Bavarian yokel, he has given up all good breeding.

If you have to scratch yourself, do not do so with your bare hand but use your coat:

> Do not scrape your throat with your bare hand while eating; but if you have to, do it politely with your coat.

Everyone used his hands to take food from the common dish. For this reason one was not to touch one's ears, nose, or eyes:

> It is not decent to poke your fingers into your ears or eyes, as some people do, or to pick your nose while eating. These three habits are bad.

Hands must be washed before meals:

> I hear that some eat unwashed (if it is true, it is a bad sign). May their fingers be palsied!

. . . If you have no towel, . . . do not wipe your hands on your coat but let the air dry them. Or:

Take care that, whatever your need, you do not flush with embarrassment.

Nor is it good manners to loosen one's belt at table.

All this is said to adults, not only to children. To our minds these are very elementary precepts to be given to upper-class people, more elementary in many respects than what, at the present stage of behavior, is generally accepted as the norm in rural-peasant strata. . . .

This is, if it may so be called, the standard eating technique during the Middle Ages, which corresponds to a very particular standard of human relationships and structure of feeling. Within this standard there is . . . an abundance of modifications and nuances. If people of different rank are eating at the same time, the person of higher rank is given precedence when washing hands, for example, or when taking from the dish. The forms of utensils vary considerably in the course of centuries. There are fashions, but also a very definite trend that persists through the fluctuations of fashion. The secular upper class, for example, indulges in extraordinary luxury at table. It is not a poverty of utensils that maintains the standard, it is quite simply that nothing else is needed. To eat in this fashion is taken for granted. It suits these people. But it also suits them to make visible their wealth and rank by the opulence of their utensils and table decoration. At the rich tables of the thirteenth century the spoons are of gold, crystal, coral, ophite. It is occasionally mentioned that during Lent knives with ebony handles are used, at Easter knives with ivory handles, and inlaid knives at Whitsun. The soupspoons are round and rather flat to begin with, so that one is forced when using them to open one's mouth wide. From the fourteenth century onward, soupspoons take on an oval form. . . .

. . . From the sixteenth century on, at least among the upper classes, the fork comes into use as an eating instrument, arriving by way of Italy first in France and then in England and Germany, after having served for a time only for taking solid foods from the dish. Henri III[4] brought it to France, probably from Venice. His courtiers were not a little derided for this "affected" manner of eating, and at first they were not very adept in the use of the instrument: at least it was said that half the food fell off the fork as it traveled from plate to mouth. As late as the seventeenth century the fork was still essentially a luxury article of the upper class, usually made of gold or silver. What we take entirely for granted, because we have been adapted and conditioned to this social standard from earliest childhood, had first to be slowly and laboriously acquired and developed by society as a whole. . . .

However, the attitude that has just been described toward the "innovation" of the fork shows one thing with special clarity. People who

[4]King of France, 1574–1589.

ate together in the way customary in the Middle Ages, taking meat with their fingers from the same dish, wine from the same goblet, soup from the same pot or the same plate, with all the other peculiarities of which examples have been . . . given—such people stood in a different relationship to one another than we do. . . . Their affects were conditioned to forms of relationship and conduct which, by today's standard of conditioning, are embarrassing or at least unattractive. What was lacking in this *courtois* world, or at least had not been developed to the same degree, was the invisible wall of affects which seems now to rise between one human body and another, repelling and separating, the hall which is often perceptible today at the mere approach of something that has been in contact with the mouth or hands of someone else, and which manifests itself as embarrassment at the mere sight of many bodily functions of others, and often at their mere mention, or as a feeling of shame when one's own functions are exposed to the gaze of others, and by no means only then.

The Family
in Renaissance Italy

DAVID HERLIHY

During the fourteenth and fifteenth centuries, a cultural flowering known as the Renaissance took place in Italy. David Herlihy studies primarily Florence, the center of the Renaissance and a leading city in Europe, in order to understand the nature of the family in Renaissance Italy. He finds that three factors— demography, environment, and wealth—affected the long-term development of the family.

Population trends, especially after the Black Death, shifted during the Renaissance. How did those changes influence the size of households and the number of servants? Note that Herlihy is very careful to make comparisons whenever possible between urban and rural families. In other words, environment influenced the structure of the family and the functions it performed. Families in cities differed from their counterparts in the countryside, not only in size, but also in the establishment of new families, remarriage, and the very functions the family performed. Wealth likewise shaped the family in determining whom to marry, household size, and age at marriage. What does Herlihy mean when he argues that demography, environment, and wealth led to a crisis of the Renaissance family?

Herlihy next discusses the composition of the Italian household, particularly in regard to marriage and children. Age at marriage seems to provide much information about family structure. Why was there such a disparity in Florence between the age of first marriage for women and for men? Why did the situation differ in rural areas? Why did some men and women remain unmarried? What was their fate? Why did some women prefer to remain widows rather than remarry? How did marriage patterns affect the prevalence of prostitution and homosexuality? Children were very important to the Renaissance family, though the relationship between mother and child was unlike that between father and child. The fathers cared for their children's future, especially their sons', often leaving some posthumous instructions specifying their upbringing. Mothers, closer in age to their offspring and tending to survive their husbands, influenced their children in areas of special concern to women. In this way, Herlihy believes that the character of the Renaissance was determined considerably by female education of the young. Thus he accords singular importance to the family and holds its peculiar structure responsible in large part for the cultural awakening of the Renaissance.

. . . Sociologists and historians once assumed that the typical family in traditional Europe (that is, in Europe before the Industrial Revolution) was large, stable and extended, in the sense that it included other relatives besides the direct descendants and ascendants of the head and his wife. The sources of Renaissance Italy rather show that there is no such thing as a traditional family, or, in different terms, a family with unchanging characteristics. The family in ca. 1400 was perceptibly different from what it had been in ca. 1300, and was to be different again in the sixteenth century. Moreover, the rural family varied in marked respects from the city household, and the poor—can this be surprising?—lived differently from the rich. How precisely did the times, location and wealth affect the Renaissance household?

In Italy as everywhere in Europe, the population between the thirteenth and the sixteenth centuries experienced powerful, even violent, fluctuations. These directly affected the households in their average size and internal structure. The history of population movements in late medieval and Renaissance Italy may be divided into four periods, with distinctive characteristics: (1) stability in numbers at very high levels, from some point in the thirteenth century until ca. 1340; (2) violent contraction, from ca. 1340 to ca. 1410, to which the terrible Black Death of 1348 made a major but not exclusive contribution; (3) stability at very low levels, from approximately 1410 to 1460; (4) renewed expansion, which brought the Italian population to another peak in the middle sixteenth century.

To judge from Tuscan evidence, the population in our second period (ca. 1340 to ca. 1410) fell by approximately two-thirds. A city of probably 120,000 persons in 1338, Florence itself counted less than 40,000 in 1427. In some remote areas of Tuscany, such as the countryside of San Gimignano, losses over the same period surpassed 70 percent. The region of San Gimignano was in fact more densely settled in the thirteenth century than it is today.

It is difficult for a modern reader even to grasp the dimensions of these losses; for every three persons living in ca. 1300, there was only one to be found alive in ca. 1410, in many if not most Italian regions. And the population, stable at low levels from approximately 1410, shows no signs of vigorous growth until after 1460. The subsequent expansion of the late fifteenth and early sixteenth centuries was particularly notable on the fertile plain of the Po river in Northern Italy and in the Veneto (the region of Venice). Verona, near Venice, for example, had fewer than 15,000 inhabitants in 1425, but reached 42,000 by 1502, nearly tripling in size. Venice itself reached approximately 170,000 persons by 1563; it was not to reach that size again until the twentieth century. Rome and Naples were also gaining rapidly in population. Florence too was growing, but at a moderate rate. In 1562 Florence counted slightly fewer than 60,000 inhabitants, which made the city only a third larger than it had been in 1427. Florence, in sum, even in this period of growth, was losing relative position among the major cities of Italy.

Inevitably, the collapse in population, subsequent stability, then growth affected the average size of the households. At Prato, for example, a small region and city 20 miles west of Florence, the average size of the rural household was 5.6 persons in 1298, and only 5 in 1427. Within the city of Prato, average household size similarly fell from 4.1 persons in 1298 to only 3.7 in 1427. By the late fourteenth and fifteenth centuries, the urban household widely across northern Italy was extremely small: 3.8 persons per household at Florence in 1427; 3.6 at Pistoia in the same year; 3.5 at Bologna in 1395; and 3.7 at Verona in 1425.

The acute population fall and the ensuing period of demographic stability at low levels (to ca. 1460) also affected the internal structure of the households. The demographic catastrophes, especially the plagues and famines, left within the community large numbers of incomplete or truncated households—those which lacked a married couple and included only widowers, widows, bachelors or orphaned children. At Florence in 1427, the most common of all household types found within the city counted only a single person; these one-member households represented some 20 percent of all urban households. The numerous, small, severely truncated and biologically inactive families (in the sense that they could produce no children) may be regarded as the social debris, which the devastating plagues and famines of the epoch left in their wake.

The renewed demographic expansion from about 1460 in turn affected average size and the internal structure of the household. Average household size at Verona, only 3.7 persons in 1425, reached 5.2 persons only thirty years later, in 1456, and was 5.9 persons in 1502. Within the city of Florence, average household size gained from 3.8 persons in 1427 to 4.8 persons in 1458 to 5.2 persons in 1480, and reached 5.7 members in 1552. Within the Florentine countryside, average household size similarly grew from 4.8 persons in 1427, to 5.3 in 1470, to 5.8 in 1552.

Several factors explain this increase in average household size in both city and countryside, during this period of demographic growth after 1460. As the plague and famine lost their virulence, the numbers of very small, highly truncated and biologically inactive families diminished within the community. Families were also producing larger numbers of children (perhaps we should say, of surviving children).

Paradoxically, however, the large households of the late fifteenth and sixteenth centuries also indicate an effort to slow the rate of population growth. In a rapidly growing community, average household size tends to remain relatively low, as sons and daughters leave the paternal home at an early age to marry, and the community contains many young, hence small, families. But no community can allow its population to grow without limit, and in traditional society the principal means of slowing or stopping growth was to prevent young persons from marrying, or marrying young. These young persons remained in their parents' house for long periods, thus increasing average household size. Many of them, especially males, remained unmarried even after the death of their parents, living as bachelors in households headed by an older, married brother. Within the city of Florence, for example, in 1427 some 17.1 percent of the households included a brother or sister of the household head, but 26.1 percent did so in 1480. We have no exact figures from the sixteenth century, but the percentage was doubtlessly even larger. The Florentine household, in other words, was much more laterally extended in the sixteenth century than it had been in 1427. The effort to slow or stop population growth, more than the growth itself, accounts for the larger size and more complex structure of the Italian household in the late fifteenth and sixteenth centuries.

Another factor which contributed to these shifts in average household size was the changing servant population. The drastic fall in the population in the late fourteenth century made labor scarce and forced wages upward, and this meant that households before 1460 could afford to support comparatively few servants. At Verona in 1425, for example, some 7 percent of the urban population were employed as household servants. After 1460, as the population once more was growing, wages tended to decline, and households could afford to support larger numbers of retainers. By 1502 at Verona, servants constituted 12.3 percent of the urban population. The numbers of servants grew especially large in the city of Florence, where, by 1552, 16.7 percent of the urban population were employed in household service; nearly half the urban households (42 percent) had at least one domestic, and one Florentine citizen employed no fewer than 57 servants. This growth in the number of servants has great social and cultural importance. It meant that the Italian urban family of some means could live with considerably greater comfort and elegance in ca. 1500—during the height of the Renaissance—than had been possible a hundred years before.

By the sixteenth century, the typical Italian household was large in size and complex in structure; it included numerous children, servants, and lateral relatives of the head. Sociologists and historians used to consider this extended household characteristic of traditional European

society. Today, we can discern that this type of household was characteristic only of particular periods and circumstances in the varied history
of the Italian family.

The location of the household, its surroundings or environment,
also exerted a powerful influence upon its internal structure. Unlike
the long-term demographic trend, this factor exerted a largely uniform
influence over time. In most periods and places, the rural household
was larger than its urban counterpart. At Prato in 1298, the average
household size was 5.6 in rural areas and 4.1 in the city; at Florence in
1427, the comparable figures are 4.8 in the countryside and 3.8 in the
city. However, the changes we have already considered—particularly
the great growth in the number of servants, which was more characteristic of the cities than of rural areas—tended to reduce these contrasts in
the sixteenth century. In 1552, the average size of the urban household
at Florence was 5.7 persons; it was 5.8 in the countryside.

Average household size, however, reveals very little about the internal character of the family. No matter what their relative size, the
households of the countryside remained fundamentally different from
those of the city. Perhaps the most evident contrast was this: almost
invariably, the rural household contained at least one married couple;
households headed by a bachelor, widow, widower or orphans were
rarely found in rural areas. In the cities, on the other hand, bachelors
and widows frequently appeared at the head of households at all periods. Households which lacked sexually active partners were therefore
common in the city, but rare in the countryside. So also, the number of
children supported in urban households tended to be below the number
found in rural homes. . . .

These contrasts point to fundamental differences in the functions
of the family in the countryside and the city. In the countryside, the
family fulfilled both biological and economic functions: the procreation
and rearing of children, and the maintenance of a productive enterprise,
the family farm. In Italy, as everywhere in medieval Europe, a peasant
economy dominated the countryside. In the peasant economy, the
basic unit of labor was not so much the individual but the family.
A single man or woman did not have the capacity to work an entire
farm, but needed the help of a spouse and eventually children. The
young peasant who wished to secure his own economic independence
consequently had to marry. For the same reason, if a peasant or his wife
were widowed, he or she tended to remarry quickly, unless a young
married couple was already present in the household, for the farm could
be successfully worked only through family labor. In rural areas there
were consequently very few truncated households, that is, those which
did not contain at least one married couple. The rural environment
encouraged marriage, not only for biological but for economic reasons.

Conversely, those residents of the countryside who did not wish to marry or remarry were strongly drawn to the cities.

Within the cities, the family of course continued to perform its biological functions of rearing children, but its economic functions were very different. The young man seeking to make his fortune in most urban trades or professions often found a wife more of a burden than a help. He frequently had to serve long years at low pay as an apprentice. He had to accumulate diligently his earnings and profits; capital alone permitted him one day to pursue his trade in his own right and name. Such a man could not usually contemplate marriage until his mature years, when he was economically established; even then, the urban family was not cemented, as was the rural household, by close participation in a common economic enterprise.

The urban environment, in other words, tended to be hostile to the formation of new households, and added little to their inner strength. Moreover, at the death of a spouse, his or her partner was not under the same pressures to remarry, as was the rural widower or widow who needed help in farming. Urban communities consequently contained far greater numbers of adult bachelors and widows than could be found in the rural villages. The urban environment was often hostile to the very survival of lineages. Both inside and outside of Italy, the city frequently proved to be the graveyard of family lines. . . .

The third factor which strongly influenced the character of the household was wealth or social position, but this influence was exerted in complex ways. In some respects, wealth reinforced the environmental influences reviewed above. Thus, in the cities, rich young men tended to approach marriage even more cautiously than their poorer neighbors. Marriage among the wealthy involved the conveyance of substantial sums of money through the dowry. Marriage also called for the sealing of family alliances, which affected the political and social position of all parties involved. The high stakes associated with marriage frequently led the wealthy young man (or his family) to search long for a suitable bride, and to protract the negotiations when she was found. Marriage, in other words, was not lightly regarded, or hastily contracted, among the rich. Moreover, if death should dissolve the marriage, the surviving partner, particularly the widow, usually controlled enough wealth in her own name to resist pressures to remarry. Bachelors and widows were therefore especially numerous among the wealthy. The poorer families of the city, in approaching marriage, had less reason for caution and restraint.

In the countryside, on the other hand, the wealthy peasant usually owned a large farm, which could only be worked with the aid of a wife and family. The rich inhabitant of the city looked upon marriage in the light of future advantages—the dowry and the family connections it would bring him; the substantial peasant needed family labor to make himself rich in harvests as well as land. Among the rural rich there were consequently few families headed by a bachelor or widow. Poorer inhabitants of the countryside—peasants who possessed less than an entire farm and who worked primarily as agricultural laborers—were less eager to take a wife, who, with children, might excessively tax already scant resources. Wealth, in sum, facilitated marriage in rural areas, while obstructing it within the city.

We must note, however, that there are important exceptions to the rule we have just enounced. In Tuscany, and widely in central Italy, there existed large numbers of sharecroppers, called *mezzadri*, who leased and worked entire farms in return for half the harvest. The owner of the farm provided his *mezzadro* with most of the capital he needed—cattle, tools, seed, fertilizer and the like. With few possessions of his own, the sharecropper usually appeared in the tax rolls as very poor, but he still required a wife and family to help him in his labors. In other words, the need to recruit a family of workers, rather than wealth itself, was the critical factor in encouraging marriages among the peasants.

Besides reinforcing environmental influences, wealth had another effect upon households, which was common to both cities and countryside. In both environments, almost invariably, rich households tended to be larger than poor households. And they were more abundantly supplied with all types of members: they supported relatively more children, more servants and more lateral relatives of the head. For example, if we consider only those households in the city of Florence in 1427 with a male head between age 43 and 47, the average size for the richer half of the urban households was 6.16 persons; it was 4.57 among the poorer half. In rural areas too, and in other periods, wealth exerted a similar, strong influence upon the size and complexity of households. It was as if the family head of the Renaissance, in both city and countryside, equipped himself with as large a household as his resources could reasonably support.

The marked influence of wealth upon household size had some paradoxical effects.   Considerations of property . . . prompted rich young men in the city to marry late, and some did not marry at all; but once married, the rich were prolific in producing children. . . . The urban poor were far less hesitant in entering marriage, but the poor urban family was also far less successful than the rich in rearing children.   Probably the children of the deprived fell victim, in greater relative numbers than the children of the privileged, to the rampant diseases of the age.   Poor parents certainly had strong reasons for exercising restraint in procreating children, and they probably limited the number of their offspring in other ways—through primitive methods of birth control and through the abandonment of babies they could not support. In the countryside, on the other hand, wealth tended to encourage both early marriage and high fertility among those who married.

Our consideration of these three factors—the long-term demographic trend, environment and wealth—which strongly influenced the Renaissance family brings us to the following conclusion. The huge losses and slow recovery in the population in the late Middle Ages precipitated a major crisis within the Italian household, as it did in many other social institutions. Frequent deaths undermined the durability and stability of the basic familial relations—between husband and wife, and parents and children. High mortalities threatened the very survival of numerous family lines. The crisis was especially acute within the city, the environment of which was already basically hostile to the formation of households and to their cohesiveness. . . .

This grave crisis did, however, increase awareness of the family and its problems. Writers of the age were led to examine, and at times to idealize, familial relationships and the roles which father, mother and children played within the household. They sought to determine when young men should marry, how brides should be chosen, and how children should be trained, in order to assure the happiness and especially the survival of the family. . . .

Against this background, we can now look in more detail at the Renaissance household. Specifically, we shall examine what sociologists call the "developmental cycle" of the household—how it was formed through marriage, grew primarily through births, and was dissolved or transformed through deaths.

Perhaps the most distinctive feature of the Renaissance marriage was the great age difference which separated the groom from his bride. At Florence in 1427–28, in 55 marriages reported in the *Catasto*,[1] the average age difference between the bride and groom was 13.6 years. Demographers can also estimate age of first marriage from the proportions of the population remaining single at the various age levels, through somewhat complicated calculations we need not rehearse here. By this method, the average age of first marriage for women in the city of Florence in 1427 can be estimated at 17.9 years; for men it is 29.9 years.

In this, the city of Florence presents an extreme example of a common pattern. In the Florentine countryside in 1427, the estimated age of first marriage for women, based on the proportions remaining single,

[1]1427 census in Florence.

was 18.3 years, and for men 25.6 years. The age difference between the spouses, 7.3 years, was less than in the city, but still considerable. In the city of Verona in 1425, the age difference was also smaller—7 years—but still extended.

The three factors of environment, wealth and long-term demographic trend affected the formation of new households and inevitably therefore the age of first marriage. However, the age of first marriage for men was far more sensitive to all these influences than the marriage age for women. The typical bride was never much older than 20 years, and was usually much younger. The age of first marriage for men varied over a much wider range of years, from 25 to 35 and at times perhaps to 40. According to a Florentine domestic chronicler writing in the early 1400's, Giovanni Morelli, his male ancestors in the thirteenth century were prone to postpone their first marriage until age 40. . . . In the period before the devastating plagues,[2] when the mean duration of life was relatively extended, men would be forced to wait long before they would be allowed to marry. The medieval community had already reached extraordinary size in the thirteenth century and could ill support continued, rapid growth.

It is at all events certain that the great plagues and famines of the fourteenth century lowered the average age at which men first entered marriage. Thus, in 1427 in the city of Florence, the average age of first marriage for men was approximately 30 years, which compared to Morelli's estimate of 40 years for the thirteenth century. Subsequently, as the plagues grew less virulent, and lives became longer, the age of first marriage for men again moved upward. In 1458, for example, the estimated age of first marriage for Florentine men was 30.5 years, and it was 31.4 years in 1480.

The age of first marriage for women moved upward and downward in the same direction as that of men, but, as we have mentioned, over a shorter range of years. (The estimated age of first marriage for Florentine women was 17.9 years in 1427, 19.5 in 1458 and 20.8 in 1480.) The reasons for this relative inelasticity in marriage age for women seem to have been preeminently cultural: Italian grooms of the Renaissance, under almost all circumstances, no matter what their own age, preferred brides no older than 20.

So also, between city and countryside, the differences in age of first marriage for men (29.9 and 25.6 years respectively in 1427) were much greater than the differences in age of first marriage for women (17.9 and 18.3 years respectively). Women were slightly older at first marriage in rural areas, perhaps because the agricultural labors they were to perform required physical maturity. Again within the city, the

[2]That is, before 1348.

richest Florentine males in 1427, from households with an assessment of over 400 florins, entered marriage for the first time at an estimated age of 31.2 years; their poorest neighbors, from households with no taxable assets, were considerably younger at first marriage—only 27.8 years. But rich girls and poor girls married for the first time at nearly the same ages—17.9 and 18.4 years respectively. Rich girls tended to be slightly younger, perhaps because their worried fathers wanted to settle their fate as quickly as possible. But almost all Florentine brides, in every corner of society, were remarkably young, at least by modern standards.

We should further note that in those segments of society where men married late (that is, in the towns, and particularly among the wealthy) many men, perhaps 10 percent, did not marry at all, but remained as bachelors, usually in the households of married relatives. On the other hand, girls who did not marry either entered domestic service— an option not open to girls from well-to-do households—or joined a religious order. There were almost no lay spinsters in urban society, apart from servants.

How does this pattern of marriage compare with modern practices? Sociologists now identify what they call a "west European marriage pattern," which is apparently found in no other, non-Western society. This pattern is distinguished by late marriages for both men and women, and by the presence in the population of many adult men and women who do not marry at all. How "modern" were the men and women of the Renaissance? Clearly, within the cities, male behavior already corresponded closely to this modern pattern; men married late and some did not marry at all, especially among the wealthy. The women of the Renaissance, on the other hand, even within the cities, were far from modern in their marital behavior; they married young and those who did not marry rarely remained in the lay world. Renaissance Italy, in other words, was not the birthplace of the modern marriage pattern, at least not for women.

The long span of years, which separated the groom from his bride, had distinctive effects upon both the character of the Renaissance household and upon the larger society. The young girl had little voice in selecting her mate, and usually no competence to choose. The first weeks of marriage must have been traumatic for these child brides. . . . But the position and status of these young matrons thereafter improved, for several reasons. The husbands were older, occupied men; many were already past the prime of their years. The brides, themselves only reaching maturity, rapidly assumed chief responsibility for the management of their households. . . . For many women, ultimate liberation would come with the deaths of their much older husbands. At the death of the husband, the dowry returned to the widow;

the large sum of money which had taxed her family's resources at her marriage now could make her a woman of means, independent enough to resist a second marriage if she did not want it. As a widow with some property, she was free from male domination in a way she had never been as a child and a wife. The years of childhood, of service as a wife, were hard but often abbreviated for the lady of the Renaissance; and time worked in her favor.

Within the larger society, especially within the cities, the tendency for males to postpone marriage meant that the community would contain large numbers of unattached young men, who were denied legitimate sexual outlets for as long as two decades after puberty. Erotic tensions thus ran high within the city, and the situation inevitably promoted both prostitution and sodomy, for which the Renaissance cities enjoyed a merited reputation. The typical triad of many contemporary stories and dramas—the aged husband, beautiful young wife, and clever young man intent on seducing her—reflects a common domestic situation. These restless young men, uninhibited by responsibilities for a wife and family, were also quick to participate in the factional and family feuds and battles which were frequent occurrences in Renaissance social history. . . .

Delayed marriage for men inevitably affected the treatment and the fate of girls. Because of high mortalities and the inevitable shrinking of the age pyramid, there were fewer eligible and willing grooms, at approximately age 30, than prospective brides, girls between 15 and 20. The girls, or rather their families, had to enter a desperate competition for grooms, and this drove up the value of dowries to ruinous levels. . . . Since prospective brides outnumbered available grooms, many girls had no statistical chance of finding a husband. For most of them, there would be no alternative but the convent. A great saint of the fifteenth century, Bernardino of Siena, once described these unhappy girls, placed in convents because they were too poor, too homely, or too unhealthy to be married, as the "scum and vomit of the world."

The acts by which the marriage was contracted were several. The formal engagement usually involved the redaction of a notarial contract, which stipulated when the marriage should occur and how the dowry should be paid. The promise of marriage would often be repeated solemnly in church. On the wedding day, the bride and groom would often attend a special Mass, at which they received the Church's blessing. But that blessing, or even the presence of a priest, was not required for a legitimate marriage until the Council of Trent[3] in the

---

[3]Church council, 1545–1563.

sixteenth century made it obligatory for Catholics. The central act in
the wedding ceremony was a procession, in which the groom led his
bride from her father's house to his own. Through this public display,
society recognized that this man and this woman would henceforth live
together as husband and wife. The groom then usually gave as lavish
a feast as his resources would allow, which sometimes lasted for days.

. . . Given the character of the marriage, the typical baby was
received by a very young mother and a much older father. Within
the city of Florence in 1427, the mean age of motherhood was approximately 26.5 years . . . ; the mean age of fatherhood was 39.8 years. The
age differences between mothers and fathers were again, less extreme
in the countryside or in other Italian towns, but still must be considered
extended.

The great differences in the average ages of fathers and mothers affected the atmosphere of the home and the training of
children. . . . The mature, if not aged, fathers would have difficulty
communicating with their children, and many would not live to see
their children reach adulthood. One reason the male heads of family
placed moral exhortations in their *ricordi*[4] is that they feared that they
would not survive long enough to give much advice . . . to the younger
generation.

This distinctive situation placed the wife and mother in a critical
position between the old generation of fathers and the children. Much
younger and more vigorous than her husband, usually destined for
longer and more intimate contact with her children, she became a prime
mediator in passing on social values from old to young. Understandably, many of the educational tracts, which proliferate in Italy from the
early fifteenth century, are directed at women. One of the first of them,
Dominici's *Governance and Care of the Family*, . . . beautifully describes
both what Florentine mothers did, and what the author, a Dominican
friar, wished them to do. Mothers, according to the friar, spent the
days pampering and playing with their young children, fondling and
licking them, spoiling them with beautiful toys, dressing them in elegant clothes, and teaching them how to sing and dance. An effeminiz-
ing influence seems evident here, which was not balanced by a strong
masculine presence within the home. The friar recommends that the
mothers rather impart spiritual values to their children; in telling them
how to do this, he shows the new fifteenth-century awareness of the
psychology of children. The home should contain a play altar, at which
the young could act out the liturgy, and pictures of Christ and St.
John represented as playful children, to whom real children will feel

[4]Diaries.

immediate rapport. Clearly, Dominici did not regard the child simply as a miniature adult, without a mind and psychology of his own.

Two conclusions seem appropriate here. The Renaissance household, with an aged, occupied and often absent husband and a young wife, was not ideally equipped to give balanced training to its children. But this deficiency seems to have increased the concern for the proper education of children. . . . [W]omen continued to dominate the training of young children, and inevitably they inculcated in them qualities which they admired—a taste for refined manners and elegant dress, and a high esthetic sensibility. In the sixteenth century, a character in the *Book of the Courtier*, by Baldassare Castiglione, then the most popular handbook of good manners, attributes all gracious exercises—music, dancing and poetry—to the influence of women. The gentleman of the Renaissance was fashioned to the tastes of women; so also was much of the culture of the age.

Births also helped shape the total society. Here, an important factor was the differences in relative fertility among the various segments of the community. The rural population, as we have mentioned, tended to be more prolific than the urban, and the rich, while slow to marry, still reproduced themselves more successfully than the poor. Differences in fertility rates inevitably generated flows of people from some parts of society to others. Thus, differential fertility between city and countryside assured that there would be constant immigration from rural areas into the towns. . . . This immigration had important social effects. It appears to have been selective, as the city especially attracted the skilled and the highly motivated. At Florence, many of the cultural leaders of the Renaissance . . . were of rural or small-town origins. The urban need for people promoted the careers of these gifted men. On the other hand, by introducing them into a milieu which made their own reproduction difficult, immigration also tended over the long run to extirpate the lines of creative individuals. It was not an unmixed blessing.

Within the cities, the wealthier families, in spite of the male reluctance to enter marriage, still tended to produce more children than the poor. Many of these children would be placed in convents or enter careers in the Church, but some would face a difficult decision. Either they would have to accept a social position lower than their parents, or they would have to seek to make their fortunes outside of their native city, even outside of Italy. . . . Many were forced therefore to wander through the world in search of fortune. Demographic pressures, in other words, required that even the sons of the wealthy adopt an entrepreneurial stance. This helps explain the ambitions and high energy of the Florentines and other Italians, and the prominence they achieved all over Europe, in many fields, in the Renaissance period.

The final event in the history of a marriage was death, and we can deal with death more briefly, as we have already referred to its central role in the social history of the epoch. Death was everywhere present during the Renaissance, and the ravages it perpetrated were at the root of the crisis of the family, which was most severe in the late fourteenth and early fifteenth centuries. Here, we shall note only the distinctive reactions of the surviving partner in a marriage to the death of a spouse. For reasons already discussed, in the countryside it was typical for both widows and widowers quickly to remarry, if they were of suitable age. But in the city, the behavior of widowed men and women was quite different. The urban widower, who as a young man had usually waited long before entering his first marriage, quickly sought out a new wife. The widow, on the other hand, who as a young girl had been rushed into wedlock, delayed remarriage, and many widows did not remarry at all. The cities of the Renaissance consequently contained numerous male bachelors and widows, but very few spinsters and widowers. The mature male, who once had married, found it difficult to live without the continuing companionship of a woman. But the woman, after she had lost a husband, felt little compulsion to remarry. . . .

IV

Early Modern Europe

In one sense, history is the solving of problems. Two of the classic problems have been the difficulty of defining the term "modern" and, following from that, the difficulty of determining when the modern world began. Wrangling over these problems persists, with little agreement. The Italians of the Renaissance were the first to broach the subject, seeing themselves, with no little immodesty, as the first modern people, more closely akin to the ancient world than to their immediate ancestors, whom they called Gothic and barbaric. Renaissance Italy saw the centuries after the fall of Roman civilization as the Middle Ages, a period between the classical world of Greece and Rome and fifteenth-century Italy. In the nineteenth century, historians began a debate over whether Renaissance Italy was modern, protomodern, or perhaps still essentially medieval. The debate continues today, part of the larger problem of periodization. Are there periods in history, or do historians arbitrarily classify certain centuries as periods, distinct eras?

As a way out of the dilemma, the term "early modern Europe" has come frequently to be favored, possibly because its chronological boundaries are so nebulous that historians can include within it very different cultures. Sometimes the early modern period in Europe refers to 1400–1789, thus encompassing Renaissance Italy, or 1500–1789, omitting both the Renaissance and the French Revolution. On the other hand, all categories of early modern Europe contain the sixteenth and seventeenth centuries, the period that the following selections describe.

These were the centuries when Italian humanism spread beyond the Alps, becoming Northern or Christian humanism. This is the era of the Protestant Reformation, Catholic Counter-Reformation, European exploration overseas, and the beginnings of political absolutism. It is the age of Michelangelo, Cervantes, Shakespeare, and Milton. But this was also a premodern society, characterized by tradition, relative immobility, and privilege. This society was still predominantly rural, though urban centers increased in size. Capitalism like-

wise grew, though this was surely not its heyday. Monarchy remained the political ideal and reality, though there were some calls for socialist or republican governments. The religion was Christian, though Christianity changed dramatically. In sum, the early modern era in Europe was a period of the confluence of old and new, a period of rapid change in some areas, but not a period of desire for or expectation of change, as the modern Western world is. Some historians refer to this time as an age of crisis, because so much was called into question and so many institutions, beliefs, and conventions were shaken.

The following selections show dramatically a life that could be described in the words of the English philosopher, Thomas Hobbes, as "poor, nasty, brutish, and short." Condemned to hunger and cold, wracked by diseases, intensely religious if not fanatical, often violent, subject to increasing supervision by church and state, sixteenth- and seventeenth-century Europeans could, moreover, expect a lifespan less than half that of ours today.

Population Structures

HENRY KAMEN

In this selection, Henry Kamen discusses the subjects of distance, time and population in the sixteenth and seventeenth centuries. This was the great period of European voyages of exploration, of the conquest of other civilizations (such as the Aztec and Incan), and the spread of Christianity by missionaries around the world, from the Western Hemisphere to Japan to India. As Europeans came to know the world, they conquered distance, but what about time?

Travel across the oceans took so long and was therefore so dangerous that only the most courageous, desperate, or foolhardy dared to undertake such voyages. Even in Europe communication was very slow; Kamen points out the speed—if that is the right word—at which mail traveled in this, the first era of European postal systems. What were the implications of the sluggish pace of communications for government administrators and for businessmen? Time seemed to move especially slowly for those involved in ocean crossings or dependent on overland transport. They needed to be fortified with the virtue of patience. Only a few by the seventeenth century were becoming slaves to the clock, a technological marvel that hardly mattered to the huddled masses. What notion of time affected the daily lives of workers?

Finally, time was involved in the population structure. Kamen relies on statistical information provided by demographers to bring home the point that Europeans had, compared to the modern world, precious little time allotted to them. The figures are striking. Infant mortality was horrendous: 20–25 percent of children died by their first birthday. Another 25 percent would not reach the age of 10. Yet Europe swarmed with children, because life expectancy was short in all groups. Why, if the average life expectancy was perhaps 28 to 34, did people wait so long to marry? What were the implications of the late age of first marriage? What was the so-called Western European marriage pattern?

Lastly, Kamen compared rich and poor families and looks at birth control. How did Europeans control fertility or cope with unwanted children? How did these patterns vary by social class?

. . . By the early sixteenth century the traders, adventurers, and explorers of the Atlantic seaboard had immeasurably extended the horizons of Europeans. The brief and fragmentary medieval contacts between Europe and Asia were replaced in the Renaissance epoch by direct

Henry Kamen, *The Iron Century: Social Change in Europe*, 1550–1660, 2d ed. (London: A.D. Peters & Co. Ltd. , 1976) 11–16, 25–31.

and profitable exchanges between the traders of Europe and the Asian monarchies. . . . Spices, particularly pepper and ginger, became the chief source of wealth of the Portuguese crown, which in the first half of the sixteenth century pioneered the European discovery of the East Indian territories and China and Japan. It was the Portuguese Magellan,[1] who had spent seven years in the Indies, who eventually passed over into the service of Spain and helped to give the latter a definitive role in the struggle for overseas possessions. Between them these two small nations, some nine million in population, opened up the globe. . . .

. . . After mid century the great collections of travel literature, notably the Venetian Ramusio's[2] *Delle navigazioni* (1550)[3] and Hakluyt's[4] *Principall Navigations* (1589), began to dispel old myths about the overseas territories and presented the literate public with realities far removed from the tales of bisexual monsters and dog-headed men with which their fathers had been regaled.

Trade and exploration were the first stage, largely limited to the early century, of Europe's discovery of the outside world. In that early period the sense of wonder was still paramount: many realized with a shock that Asia and America frequently outdid any marvels that Europe might offer. Antonio Pigafetta, who sailed with Magellan in 1519 on the first European circumnavigation of the globe, claimed to have heard that the emperor of China was 'the greatest in all the world'. Cortés,[5] writing to his own emperor after entering Tenochtitlán[6] in 1521, claimed of Moctezuma's[7] palaces that 'there is not their like in all Spain'. The great temple, he said, was one 'whose size and magnificence no human tongue could describe', and the city itself he called 'the most beautiful thing in the world'. . . .

In the course of the century this awareness of Europe's modest part in world civilization was superseded by a more aggressive attitude. Confident in his own superiority, the European moved forward into the colonial epoch. The aggressiveness was in part fed by the conviction that Christianity must be taken to the heathen. The most remarkable achievements in this respect were of men like St Francis Xavier (d. 1552), whose global vision took him to Goa, Malabar, Malacca,

---

[1]Ferdinand Magellan, c.1480–1521.

[2]The humanist, historian, and geographer Gian Battista Ramusio, 1485–1557.

[3]*Of Navigations.*

[4]Richard Hakluyt (c.1522–1616), English geographer.

[5]Hernando Cortés (1485–1547), Spanish conqueror of the Aztec Empire.

[6]Capital of the Aztecs, now Mexico City.

[7]Emperor of the Aztecs c.1502–1520.

Japan and the Chinese coast; and of Fray Toribio de Motolinía, who in 1524 landed in Mexico with eleven other Franciscans to begin the first large-scale conversion ever undertaken by Christians outside Europe. In part, however, the attitude sprang from an assumption of inherent racial superiority. 'How can we doubt', wrote the Spanish humanist Sepúlveda[8] in 1547, 'that these people—so uncivilised, so barbaric, contaminated with so many impieties and obscenities—have been justly conquered by a nation so humane and excelling in every virtue?' This may be compared with the words of Jan Pieterz Coen, seventeenth-century creator of the Dutch East Indies. 'May not a man in Europe', he asked a critic of his policies, 'do what he likes with his cattle? Even so does the master here do with his men, for these with all that belongs to them are as much the property of the master as are brute beasts in the Netherlands.' European perception of the outside world was thus rooted in a supreme confidence. . . . And in tune with this confidence came the growing urge to dominate, as stated firmly in 1590 by the Jesuit José de Acosta when, applauding the possession by Spain of America, he affirmed that this was entirely 'in accord with the desire of Providence that certain kingdoms rule others'.

Not the least amazing feature of the expansion of Europe was the conquest of distance. A look at the distances covered by the ships trading to Asia round the Cape, the voyages made by the English settlers to north America, the territory traversed by Francis Xavier or Pizarro,[9] might lead to the suspicion that technological progress had made it possible. Yet, for all the improvements in nautical science, time was barely attacked, and the endurance of man alone was a decisive factor in the conquest of distance.

Water, horse or coach were the three means of transport, and their efficiency varied. Over long distances the sea was beyond all doubt the quickest method of communication, but over smaller overland areas the horse was faster and more reliable, making it the obvious basis for the nascent postal services of Europe. Governments took a special interest in improving the quality of the postal service, which, however, remained very expensive and therefore used less by private individuals than by the state and by merchants. In any case, there was no significant increase in speed during the early modern period. Uncertainty of conditions meant that in the sixteenth century the post from Antwerp to Amsterdam normally took from three to nine days, and to Gdansk from twenty-four to thirty-five days. An English regulation of 1637 specified that mail was to travel in summer at 7 miles an

[8]Juan Ginés de Sepúlveda, 1490–1573.
[9]Spanish conqueror of the Inca Empire (in Peru).

hour and in winter at 6. A generation later, in 1666, the average speed of letters was not more than 4 miles an hour. . . .

Outside Europe the vastness of distance required measurement in terms of endurance rather than time. The heroes were those like Columbus, who informed Queen Isabella[10] in 1503 that 'the world is small: I mean that it is not as large as people say it is'. Few would have agreed. The expedition of Magellan and Sebastián del Cano, which set out from Seville with five ships in 1519 and returned in 1522 with only one vessel containing eighteen men, after having sailed round the world, was proof of the high cost of any attempt to make the globe smaller. When Francis Drake[11] made the same voyage fifty-five years later the difficulties were still prohibitive: he had five ships when he set sail from Plymouth in 1577 and only one when he returned in 1580. The long absence is deceptive, for in most voyages far longer periods were spent in harbour than at sea. The ships of the American passage, the *carrera de Indias*,[12] took on the average seventy-five days to cross from Seville to Vera Cruz, and 130 days to cross back; the entire journey, however, including long waits in Vera Cruz and Havana, might mean that a ship leaving Seville in July one year did not normally return before October in the subsequent year. The fortitude of the explorers was acclaimed by the historian Cieza de León, who asked what other race but the Spaniards could have penetrated 'through such rugged lands, such dense forest, such great mountains and deserts, and over such broad rivers'? We can reply that the Russians in Siberia, the Puritans in New England, the Dutch and Portuguese in Africa and Asia, the French in Canada, were each in their own way, and often with methods that few would approve, bringing the outside world closer to Europe and thereby conquering the great gulf imposed by time and space.

The government of a world empire was made peculiarly difficult for Philip II[13] by the inability to communicate speedily with his administrators. 'I have not heard anything from the king about the affairs of the Netherlands since 20 November last', complained the governor of that region, Requeséns, from Antwerp on 24 February 1575. Businessmen no less than politicians had an investment in overcoming distance and time. Any delay in the payment of bills of exchange, the arrival of the galleons, the shipment of perishable cargo, might spell ruin. Yet when all the evidence for the urgent demands of these men

[10]Isabella I, the Catholic, Queen of Castille and Léon (1474–1504), Queen of Aragon (1479–1504), and wife of Ferdinand V.

[11]English navigator and naval hero, 1540–1596.

[12]The trade between Spain and South America.

[13]King of Spain, 1556–1598.

of the world is considered, there can be little doubt that they were only a minority group. Time was not yet a universal pacemaker, and the age appears to move at a casual pace, regulated only by the movements of the sun, the cycle of the seasons, and an occasional clock.

Clocks were a relative novelty in the early sixteenth century. The population still took its division of the hours and minutes from the Church: the day was measured by liturgical hours, church bells tolled their passing and called the faithful to prayer. Protestantism helped to liberate time from its clerical dress, and clocks completed the process of secularization. By the end of the sixteenth century the clock industry was booming, particularly when the clockmakers from Catholic countries fled as refugees to Protestant states. In 1515 there were no clockmakers in Geneva, after 1550 they came as refugees from France, and by 1600 the city had twenty-five to thirty master clockmakers and an unknown number of apprentices. In the mathematical universe of early seventeenth-century intellectuals, clocks played an essential part. In contrast to the genial pace of earlier decades, . . . the seventeenth century began the subjection of humanity to the clock. It was the astronomer Kepler[14] who looked upon the universe and pronounced it 'similar to a clock', Boyle[15] who considered it 'a great piece of clockwork'.

Clocks and watches remained the preserve of a minority. Industrial time was measured by daylight hours, a winter working day being shorter than a summer one by about two hours, with wages consequently lower. In sixteenth-century Antwerp, building workers had a seven-hour day in winter but a twelve-hour day in summer; winter wages were one-fifth lower. Concepts like 'from sunrise to sunset' were written into work regulations, but were inevitably imprecise. Only a few trades had their hours of work laid down by the clock rather than by daylight: in 1571 the printers of Lyon complained because their working day was timed to begin at 2 a.m. and ended only at 8 p.m. For most workers, especially on the land, imprecision of time took strict discipline out of work. Rest from labours was both recognized and encouraged. In the diocese of Paris at the beginning of the seventeenth century there were fifty-nine obligatory religious holidays, which together with the Sundays made up well over 100 days a year. It was normal in much of Catholic Europe not to work for nearly a third of the year. La Fontaine[16] commented at the time that 'on nous ruine en fêtes,'[17] but the system

[14]Johannes Kepler, 1571-1630.

[15]Robert Boyle (1627–1691), English chemist.

[16]French poet, 1621–1695.

[17]"We are being ruined by holidays."

was not necessarily as harmful as it might appear: in a largely agricultural economy, there was not enough work to employ people continuously, so that holidays provided a festive alternative to what might otherwise have been days of unemployment. All classes, not merely the leisured part of the population, accepted this casual attitude to time. There were, however, objections when attempts were made to change the calendar. In France, the king in 1563 decreed that the year should start in January instead of at Easter; the Parlement of Paris[18] refused to register the edict until January 1567, a refusal which made the year 1566 only eight months long. A definitive international reform of the calendar did not come until 1582, when pope Gregory XIII abolished ten days from the year; most Protestant countries refused to accept the change, which led to the operation of a dual calendar in Europe. . . .

Early modern European society was dominated by death. Life expectancy at birth was alarmingly low: in the seventeenth-century nobility the average male expectation of life at birth was 28 years, the female expectation 34 years. In the English peerage in 1575–1674 the average male expectation at birth was 32 years, the female 34.8. . . . The lot of the poorer people, for whom records are more difficult to come by, was inevitably worse. A study covering 3700 children of all classes born in Paris at the end of the seventeenth century arrives at an overall life expectancy of 23 years.

These figures are statistical abstracts, but are borne out by the all too real data for infant mortality. In the demographic system of early modern Europe it was almost a rule that one out of every four or five children born failed to survive the first year of life: in England the average was a fifth of all children, in France a quarter. Survival beyond infancy continued to be extremely hazardous. In the Castilian villages of Simancas, Cabezon and Cigales in the sixteenth century, up to 50 per cent of children died before their seventh year; in the nearby city of Palencia the figure was 68 per cent. In England less than two-thirds of all children born survived to the age of 10, in northern France barely a half. Almost one child in two in early modern Europe failed to live to the age of 10, and two live births were required to produce one human adult. The example of the Capdebosc family in the Condomois (France) is instructive. Jean Dudrot de Capdebosc married Margaride de Mouille in 1560. They had ten children, of whom five died before their tenth year. Odet, the eldest son, married Marie de la Crompe in 1595: of their eight children five did not reach their tenth year. Jean, the eldest, married twice. Jeanne, his first wife, had two children, one of whom died at 9 years, the other at five weeks. Marie, the second wife, had

---

[18]A sovereign judicial court with jurisdiction over approximately one-half of France.

thirteen children in the twenty-one years 1623–45. Of them, six died in infancy, one was killed in war, two became nuns. Of the thirty-three children born to this prolific family during the century, only six founded a family. The principal reason: infant mortality.

Because life was short, the Europe of around 1600 was predominantly youthful. Children and young people must have been everywhere more in evidence than the aged. Sebastian Franck claimed (1538) that 'the whole of Germany is teeming with children'. . . . In Geneva in 1561–1600 the average population age was as low as 23, rising to 27.5 in 1601–1700. . . .

The predominance of youth in the population had important cultural effects. Young men, whose numbers often exceeded those of women, played a leading role in communal activities: at harvest time, in festivities, at weddings. Organized youth groups–called 'abbeys' in southern France, 'cencerradas' in southern Spain–were to be found both in villages and big cities (Lyon in the sixteenth century had some twenty 'abbeys'), and gave scope to the disorderly propensities of the young. Despite the large numbers of young people they did not, as was once thought, marry young. Limited evidence for Spain tends to suggest that in the sixteenth and early seventeenth centuries girls married at the age of 20, men at about 25. In Altopascio (Tuscany) in the seventeenth century girls married when just over 21. These ages are exceptional. Over most of western Europe women's first marriage occurred between the ages of 24.5 and 26.5; the men were usually two to three years older. Among the élite, the age at marriage tended to be lower, since an early and profitable wedding helped to secure property: in the sixteenth century daughters of the Genevan bourgeoisie wed at about 22 years, English noblewomen at just over 20. The lower orders, on the other hand, probably delayed marriage until they could afford to set up their own family unit; though some couples . . . were allowed to live together after betrothal.

The relatively long wait for marriage raises interesting questions about how a young person who remained unmarried until the age of 29 spent his sexual energy. Sexual dalliance short of intercourse appears to have been tolerated quite freely among the common people of western Europe. None the less, illegitimacy rates were fairly low: in England in twenty-four parishes studied, the rate was 2.6 per cent of live births; in Spain the level at Talavera de la Reina was 3 per cent, though in Galicia it rose to some 5.6 per cent. Communal prejudice against mothers of illegitimate children were strong enough to restrict levels. On the other hand, the rate of premarital conception was everywhere quite high, and more in the cities than in the countryside. In the seventeenth century the rate in Amiens was nearly 6 per cent of first births, in Lyon up to 10 per cent; in one village in Galicia (Spain) 7.5 per cent of children were born within seven months of marriage. German towns appear to have had a high level, up to 21 per cent for Oldenburg in 1606–1700. England provides the most startling evidence: one-fifth of all first births in the sixteenth and seventeenth centuries were conceived before marriage, and in some villages as many as one-third.

Of course, not everyone married. It has been suggested that different marriage patterns existed in east and west Europe: in the 'west European pattern' a high proportion of women, possibly up to one-fifth, abstained completely from marriage; in the east, virtually all women married. At any given moment in the west, and thanks to religious ideals (convents, for example), economic disability, widowhood or simply the unavailability of men, up to half of all women up to 50 years old might not be married. Although in general the population was fairly balanced between male and female the men too would suffer difficulties in finding mates: Rome in 1592 had only fifty-eight women for every 100 men, and in Nördlingen during the Thirty Years War the authorities allowed unlimited immigration to women . . . but restricted entry of males.

Marriage, moreover, was seldom for life. Thanks to the high mortality rate, the average couple could look forward to a relatively short married life: at Basel in the 1660s the mean length of a marriage was just over twenty years. A nuclear family would thus be thrown adrift by the untimely death not only of half the children but also of one parent. It became the rule rather than the exception to re-marry, though poorer and older women had less hope of doing so, which explains the high proportion of widows in the rural Mediterranean. In the rich Genevan élite in 1550–99, 26 per cent of marriages by men were re-marriages; in the village of Pedralba (Valencia) in the seventeenth century one marriage in three was a re-marriage. In Crulai (Normandy) a fifth of all male and a tenth of all female marriages were re-marriages; in this village one widower out of two, and one widow out of six, married again. In one French peasant parish in the seventeenth century, we are told by a contemporary,

> When a husband loses his wife or a wife her husband, the surviving spouse at once invites everyone to a meal: this sometimes takes place in the house where the corpse is lying, and the guests laugh, drink, sing and make arrangements for remarrying their host or hostess. The widower or widow receives proposals, and gives reasons for acceptance or rejection: it is only rarely that the party comes to an end before the arrangement has been concluded.

The relative brevity of married life, and the very high infant mortality, meant that the balance of birth over death was very precariously maintained. Enormous importance must therefore be attached to the fertility rate at this period. In almost every town, deaths normally exceeded births, and population levels could only be maintained by continuous immigration. . . .

Female fertility was radically affected by late marriage, which meant that girls started reproducing some ten years after they were able to. One historian has referred to this as preindustrial Europe's natural system of birth-control. When we bear in mind that most women had borne their last child by about 40 . . . , it can be seen that the average reproductive period of women at the time was fifteen years, less than half the span of a woman's normal fertility. The inevitable result was few children. Age-specific fertility rates show that women marrying in the age-group 25 to 29 years tended to produce about four children; in older age groups the rate declined. . . .

This fairly low reproductive rate, in a society where a high proportion of women never married, created a distinctive family pattern. In twentieth-century Europe the economically privileged classes and nations tend to have small families, the poorer communities tend to have large ones. In preindustrial Europe precisely the opposite held good: the poor had fewer children, the rich could afford to have more. In the sixteenth-century village of Villabañez (Old Castile) families seldom had more than four children; in Córdoba in 1683 58 per cent of families had no more than two children, 32 per cent had no more than four. In France the average number of children was just over four per family. In late sixteenth-century Norwich the poor had 2.3 children per family, the richer burgesses had 4.2. Europe was thus far from having the large families usually associated with preindustrial communities. . . .

The absolute dependence of fertility on the age of the mother, is solid proof that birth-control was not widely practised. At the same time, however, there were mechanisms in existence that controlled fertility. It has been widely argued that late marriage in itself was a conscious method of control (though against this thesis one might cite the evidence of Spain, where a lower marriage age did not result in a different pattern of fertility). Breast-feeding, which delays a mother's possibility of conceiving, remained normal practice; but the evidence at least from French towns shows that a high proportion of mothers from the élite and artisan classes gave their infants out to be wet-nursed, and this increased their ability to conceive while reducing that of the wet-nurses. The most commonly practised method of controlling unwanted children was exposure after birth; most such abandoned infants were illegitimate, but several also were left by parents too poor to care for them. The practice of leaving babies on the steps of churches and hospitals grew regularly throughout the early modern period and led to the establishment of foundlings' hospitals in the major European cities. By the end of the seventeenth century the number of foundlings had attained alarming proportions: the hospital in Madrid had 1400 infants in its care in 1698, and in the same decade the hospital in Paris was taking in over 2000 a year.

The best documented cases of birth-control refer not to the rural but to the urban population and élites. Henri Estienne referred in 1566 to women who utilized 'preservatives that prevent them becoming pregnant'. . . . By the next century, according to a confessor's manual published in Paris in 1671, priests were instructed to inquire in the confessional whether the faithful had 'employed means to prevent generation', and whether 'women during their pregnancy had taken a drink or some other concoction to prevent conception'. At the same period contraceptive and abortive practices were known in Spain, to judge by confessors' manuals and the prosecutions undertaken by the Inquisition. A more scientific, though necessarily indirect, guide to contraceptive practices is the study of birth intervals: lengthy intervals, such as those of forty-nine months or more found in all social classes in early eighteenth-century Geneva, are clear testimony that controls were practised; but it is less certain that the practices involved anything more than careful abstention. Very gradually, the unspeakable came to be spoken, and birth-control was recognized to exist. . . .

The Early History of
Syphilis: A Reappraisal

ALFRED W. CROSBY, JR.

Too often historians have described the voyages of Columbus and their aftermath in terms of how Europeans affected the Americas through exploration and settlement. In his important book, The Columbian Exchange. Biological and Cultural Consequences of 1492, *Alfred W. Crosby, Jr., offers a more balanced perspective by showing that the opening up of the Western Hemisphere affected life—human, animal, and plant—on both sides of the Atlantic. Although the balance sheet is mixed, Crosby believes that the bad outnumbered the good. Thus, maize, manioc, and potatoes increased the amount of food, improved the diet, and so led to a rise in the population of Europe. On the other hand, smallpox and measles decimated the American Indians, and the Spaniards began the breakdown of ecological stability in the New World.*

In this selection, Crosby discusses syphilis, the New World's revenge on the Old World. Against those who argue that syphilis had been present in Europe before Columbus, Crosby maintains that it first came to Europe in the 1490s. What arguments does the author make to support this claim? How did syphilis spread in Europe once it had arrived? In other words, what groups of people were primarily responsible for infecting others with that loathsome disease?

What exactly did syphilis do to people physically? Crosby stresses that the disease changed over time. How did people cope with it? What cures were available? Syphilis affected social relations even as it infected bodies. How did the relations of men and women—how did love-making—change as a result of this new virus? Bedeviled by herpes and AIDS, our own age might seem analogous to the sixteenth century.

The New World gave much in return for what it received from the Old World. In the writings of Desiderius Erasmus,[1] one can find mention of nearly every significant figure, event, crusade, fad, folly, and misery of

[1]Dutch humanist, c.1466–1536.

Alfred W. Crosby, Jr., *The Columbian Exchange. Biological and Cultural Consequences of 1492* (Westport: Greenwood Press, 1972), 122–27, 141–42, 145–60.

the decades around 1500. Of all the miseries visited upon Europe in his lifetime, Erasmus judged few more horrible than the French disease, or syphilis. He reckoned no malady more contagious, more terrible for its victims, or more difficult to cure . . . or more fashionable! . . .

The men and women of Erasumus's generation were the first Europeans to know syphilis or so they said, at least. The pox, as the English called it, had struck like a thunderbolt in the very last years of the fifteenth century. But unlike most diseases that appear with such abruptness, it did not fill up the graveyards and then go away, to come again some other day or perhaps never. Syphilis settled down and became a permanent factor in human existence.

Syphilis has a special fascination for the historian because, of all mankind's most important maladies, it is the most uniquely "historical." The beginnings of most diseases lie beyond man's earliest rememberings. Syphilis, on the other hand, has a beginning. Many men, since the last decade of the fifteenth century, have insisted that they knew almost exactly when syphilis appeared on the world stage, and even where it came from. "In the yere of Chryst 1493 or there aboute," wrote Ulrich von Hutten,[2] one of Erasmus's correspondents, "this most foule and most grevous dyseasse beganne to sprede amonge the people." Another contemporary, Ruy Díaz de Isla,[3] agreed that 1493 was the year and went on to say that "the disease had its origin and birth from always in the island which is now named Española." Columbus had brought it back, along with samples of maize and other American curiosities.

. . . In fact, the matter of the origin of syphilis is doubtlessly the most controversial subject in all medical historiography. . . .

Until the most recent decades there were only two widely accepted views of the provenance of syphilis: the Columbian theory and its antithesis, which stated that syphilis was present in the Old World long before 1493. Now the Unitarian theory has appeared, which postulates that venereal syphilis is but one syndrome of a multi-faceted world-wide disease, treponematosis. But before we examine this newest challenge to the veracity of Ulrich von Hutten and Díaz de Isla and the other Columbians, let us deal with the older argument: was venereal syphilis present on both sides of the Atlantic in 1492 or only on the American?

The documentary evidence for the Old World seems clear. No unequivocal description of syphilis in any pre-Columbian literature of the Old World has ever been discovered. . . .

The physicians, surgeons, and laymen of the Old World who wrote

[2]German humanist, 1488–1523.
[3]Sixteenth-century writer of medical books.

about venereal syphilis in the sixteenth century recorded, with few exceptions, that it was a new malady; and we have no reason to believe they were all mistaken. . . . Spaniards, Germans, Italians, Egyptians, Persians, Indians, Chinese, and Japanese . . . agreed that they had never seen the pox before. It is very unlikely that they were all mistaken on the same subject at the same time.

. . . The variety of names given it and the fact that they almost always indicate that it was thought of as a foreign import are strong evidence for its newness. Italians called it the French disease, which proved to be the most popular title; the French called it the disease of Naples; the English called it the French disease, the Bordeaux disease, or the Spanish disease; Poles called it the German disease; Russians called it the Polish disease; and so on. Middle Easterners called it the European pustules; Indians called it the disease of the Franks (western Europeans). Chinese called it the ulcer of Canton, that port being their chief point of contact with the west. The Japanese called it Tang sore, Tang referring to China; or, more to the point, the disease of the Portuguese. . . . [I]t was not until the nineteenth century that . . . "syphilis," minted in the 1520s, became standard throughout the world.

Another indication of the abrupt appearance of the pox is the malignancy of the disease in the years immediately after its initial recognition in Europe. The classic course of a new disease is rapid spread and extreme virulence, followed by a lessening of the malady's deadliness. The most susceptible members of the human population are eliminated by death, as are the most virulent strains of the germ, in that they kill off their hosts before transmission to other hosts occurs. The records of the late fifteenth and early sixteenth centuries are full of lamentations on the rapid spread of syphilis and the horrible effects of the malady, which often occurred within a short time after the initial infection: widespread rashes and ulcers, often extending into the mouth and throat; severe fevers and bone pains; and often early death. The latter is a very rare phenomenon in the initial stages of the disease today, and most who do die of syphilis have resisted the disease successfully for many years. Ulrich von Hutten's description of syphilis in the first years after its appearance indicates a marked contrast between its nature then and its "mildness" today:

> There were byles, sharpe, and standing out, hauying the similitude and quantite of acornes, from which came so foule humours, and so great stenche, that who so ever ones smelled it, thought hym selfe to be enfect. The colour of these pusshes [pustules] was derke grene, and the slight therof was more grevous unto the pacient then the peyne it selfe: and yet their peynes were as thoughe they hadde lyen in fire.

. . . The most convincing of all evidence for the abrupt arrival of the French disease in the Old World in approximately 1500 is the physical remains, the bones of the long dead. No one has ever unearthed pre-Columbian bones in the Old World which display unequivocal signs of syphilitic damage. . . .

Several anti-Columbian theorists have brushed aside all the above arguments by hypothesizing that syphilis had existed in the Old World prior to the 1490s, but in a *mild* form. Then, in the 1490s the causative organism mutated into the deadly *Treponema pallidum*, and syphilis began to affect the deep body structures and became a killer. This hypothesis cannot be disproved and it comfortably fits all the facts, but it cannot be proved, either. . . .

Where did syphilis come from? If it came from America, then we may be nearly certain that it came in 1493 or shortly after. Let us consider the physical evidence first. Is there a contrast here between the Old and New Worlds? The answer becomes more and more unequivocally affirmative as the archeologists and paleopathologists disinter from American soil an increasing number of pre-Columbian human bones displaying what is almost surely syphilitic damage. . . .

The documentary evidence for the Columbian provenance of venereal syphilis is obviously shaky. We cannot say, moreover, that the evidence provided by the paleopathologists is utterly decisive, but when the two are combined—when archivists and gravediggers join hands to claim that America is the homeland of *Treponema pallidum*—it becomes very difficult to reject the Columbian theory. . . .

Is venereal syphilis a separate and distinct disease, once endemic to only one part of the world, or is it merely a syndrome of a disease which has always been worldwide, but happens to have different symptoms and names in different areas? Those who accept the Unitarian theory, as it is called, claim that that which is called syphilis, when transmitted venereally, is really the same malady as the nonvenereal illnesses called yaws in the tropics, bejel in the Middle East, pinta in Central America, irkinja in Australia, and so on. The manner in which this ubiquitous disease, named "treponematosis" by the Unitarians, manifests itself in man is somewhat different in different areas, because of climatic and cultural differences, but it is all one disease. If this is true, then all the squabble about deformation of forehead bones here and not there, ulcers on the sex organs now and not then, and on and on, is completely irrelevant. As E. H. Hudson, the foremost champion of the Unitarian theory, puts it, "Since treponematosis was globally distributed in prehistoric times, it . . . is idle to speak of Columbus' sailors bringing syphilis to a syphilis-free Europe in 1493." . . .

In fact, such is the paucity of evidence from the fifteenth and sixteenth centuries that the Unitarian theory is no more satisfactory than the Columbian. We simply do not know much, and may never know much about the world distribution of the treponemas in the 1490s. . . .

There are only two things of which we can be sure. One, the only pre-Columbian bones clearly displaying the lesions of treponematosis or one of that family of disease are American. . . . Two, several contemporaries did record the return of venereal syphilis with Columbus. . . .

The Columbian theory is still viable. Even if it is unequivocally proved that all the treponematoses are one, the Columbians can simply claim that treponematosis was exclusively American in 1492. There is no unquestionable evidence that any of the treponematoses existed in the Old World in 1492. . . .

It is not impossible that the organisms causing treponematosis arrived from America in the 1490s in mild or deadly form, and, breeding in the entirely new and very salubrious environment of European, Asian, and African bodies, evolved into both venereal and nonvenereal syphilis and yaws. If this is true, then Columbus ranks as a villain with the serpent of the Garden of Eden.

A less presumptuous theory is that the treponematoses were one single disease many thousands of years ago. Then, as man changed his environment and habits, and especially when he crossed the Bering Straits into the isolation of the Americas, the differing ecological conditions produced different types of treponematosis and, in time, closely related but different diseases. . . .

. . . It seems logical to believe that if deadly diseases crossed the Atlantic from east to west, then there must have also been a similar countercurrent. The most likely candidate for the role of America's answer to the Old World's smallpox is venereal syphilis. The theory of the origin of the treponematoses offered in this chapter squares with all Darwin tells us about evolution, and allows the American Indians and Columbus the dubious honor of incubating and transporting venereal syphilis. It is this hypothesis which, in the current state of medical and historical research, seems to hold the most promise as a vehicle for future inquiry and speculation.

Having finished with the polemics of syphilis, let us turn to the first century of its recorded history. By the fifteenth century, treponematosis had evolved into several related maladies in the desert-isolated jungles, isolated plateaus, different islands, and continents of the world. Then came one of the greatest technological advances: European innovations in shipbuilding, seamanship and navigation. . . . A great mixing of peoples, cultural influences, and diseases began.

The various treponematoses spread out from their hearthlands, mixing and changing under new ecological conditions in a way that will probably always confound medical historians. The evidence that comes down to us from that time is sparse and confused. . . .

Europeans drew the world together by means of ocean voyages. . . . The epidemiology of syphilis has a special characteristic: it is usually transmitted by sexual contact and spreads when a society's or a group's allegiance to marital fidelity fails. Sailors, by the nature of their profession, are men without women, and therefore men of many women. If we may assume that the nature of sailors in the sixteenth century was not radically different than in the twentieth, then we can imagine no group of the former century more perfectly suited for guaranteeing that venereal syphilis would have worldwide distribution. . . . European sailors carried it to every continent but Antartica and Australia before Columbus was in his grave.

Venereal syphilis arrived in Barcelona in 1493, according to Díaz de Isla, but we have no other news of it in Spain for several years. Why? First, because of the paucity of documentation. Second, because syphilis spreads by venereal contact, and not by touch, breath, or insect vectors, as do the traditional epidemic diseases of smallpox, typhus, plague, and so on. In a stable society its spread will be steady but not extremely fast. . . . Imagine 1,000 people, one of whom is syphilitic. He infects two others, who infect two others each, in turn. The number of the diseased goes up steadily: 1, 2, 4, 8, 16, 32, and so on. In the early stages the disease's advance is rapid, but the victims are few and below the threshold of society's attention. The disease's spread does not accelerate, it is passed on from one to another no more rapidly than before, but 32 becomes 64, 64 leads to 128, 128 is suddenly 256—and society abruptly decides that its existence is threatened by epidemic, long after the initial arrival of syphilis.

Venereal syphilis will only spread with the rapidity of plague or typhus when a society is in such chaos that sexual morality breaks down. Such a sad state of affairs is usually the product of war. Women are without protection or food, and have only their bodies to sell. The men of the armies have a monopoly of force, most of the wealth and food—and no women.

The first recorded epidemic of syphilis took place in Italy in the mid-1490s. In 1494 Charles VIII of France,[4] in pursuit of his claims to the throne of Naples, crossed the Alps into Italy with an army of about 50,000 soldiers of French, Italian, Swiss, German, and other origins. The campaign was not one marked by full-scale battles, but the army, trailing its column of the usual camp followers, engaged in the usual practices of rape and sack anyway. The Neapolitans, retreating toward

[4]King of France, 1483–1498.

their city, laid the countryside to waste. Charles, once ensconced in Naples, discovered that the Italians, appalled by his success, were putting aside their personal conflicts and forming a coalition against him. Ferdinand[5] and Isabella,[6] anxious to prevent the establishment of French hegemony in Italy, were sending Spanish troops. Charles packed his bags and marched back to France, and the whole process of battle, rape, and sack was repeated in reverse.

Syphilis, hitherto spreading slowly and quietly across Europe, flared into epidemic in Italy during this invasion, just as the epidemiology of the malady would lead one to expect. It is probable that there was also a rapid spread of typhus, another traditional camp follower. It was in Italy that the truth of Voltaire's[7] epigram was first demonstrated: "Depend upon it, when 30,000 men engage in pitched battle against an equal number of the enemy, about 20,000 on each side have the pox."

Charles arrived back at Lyon in November 1495, where he disbanded his army; and its members, with billions of treponemas in their blood streams, scattered back to their homes in a dozen lands or off to new wars. With the dispersal of that army, the lightning advance of syphilis across Europe and the rest of the Old World became inevitable.

Syphilis had already appeared in Germany by the summer of 1495, for in August Emperor Maximilian[8] of the Holy Roman Empire issued a mandate at Worms calling it the "evil pocks" and blaming it on the sin of blasphemy. In the same year Swiss and Frenchmen recorded its arrival with horror. The pox reached Holland and England no later than 1496. Greece knew it in the same year, and Hungary and Russia in 1499. . . .

The epidemic rolled on into Africa, where "If any Barbarie be infected with the disease commonly called the Frenche pox, they die thereof for the most part, and are seldom cured"; and appeared in the Middle East as early as 1498, with a similar result. The Portuguese, among the earliest to receive the infection, probably carried it farthest, around the Cape of Good Hope. It appeared in India in 1498 and sped on ahead of the Portuguese to Canton by 1505. In a decade it advanced from the Caribbean to the China Sea, at once a tribute to man's nautical genius and social idiocy.

We are lucky in our attempt to trace the early history of syphilis in that shame was not attached to the disease at the beginning. . . . As

---

[5]Ferdinand V, the Catholic, King of Castille and Léon (1474–1504, ruling jointly with his wife, Isabella I). As Ferdinand II, King of Aragon (1479–1516) and as Ferdinand III, King of Naples (1504–1516).

[6]Isabella I, the Catholic, Queen of Castille and Léon (1474–1504), Queen of Aragon (1479–1504), and wife of Ferdinand V.

[7]French author, 1694-1778.

[8]1493–1519.

if to illustrate the frankness of the age, Ulrich von Hutten, the great humanist, wrote a gruesomely detailed tract on his own sufferings, gratuitously mentioning that his father had the same disease, and dedicated the whole to a cardinal! . . .

The plentiful documentation enables the venerologist of an antiquarian bent to trace not only the history of the epidemic but the history of its remedies and of the character of the disease itself. The best analysis of the latter is by Jean Astruc.[9] . . . He breaks down the early history into five stages.

1. 1494–1516. In this period the first sign of the disease in a patient was small genital ulcers, followed by a widespread rash of various character. . . . As the disease spread through the victim's body, palate, uvula, jaw, and tonsils were often destroyed. Large gummy tumors were common, and the victim suffered agonizing pains in muscles and nerves, especially at night. General physical deterioration followed and often culminated in early death.

2. During the period 1516 to 1526 two new symptoms were added to the syphilis syndrome: bone inflammation, characterized by severe pain and eventual corruption of the bone and marrow; and the appearance in some sufferers of hard genital pustules, resembling warts or corns.

3. A general abatement of the malignancy of the disease marked the period 1526 to 1540. The number of pustules per sufferer decreased, and we hear more of gummy tumors. Inflamed swelling of the lymph gland in the groin became common. Loss of hair and teeth became common, but this may have been caused by mercury poisoning, mercury having been used as a remedy.

4. From 1540 to 1560 the diminution of the more spectacular symptoms of the malady continued. Gonorrhea, which by this time and for centuries afterward was confused with syphilis, became "the most common, if not perpetual symptom" in the early states of syphilis.

5. Between 1560 and 1610 the deadliness of the malady continued to decline, and only one new symptom was added: noise in the ears.

By the seventeenth century syphilis was as we know it today: a very dangerous infection, but not one that could be called explosive in the nature of its attack on the victim. . . .

If one wished to create a disease to encourage the proliferation of quacks and quack remedies, one could do no better than syphilis; and this was particularly true in the sixteenth century. The disease was new and no traditional remedies for it existed. Its symptoms were hideous, persuading sufferers to try any and all cures. Syphilis is a malady characterized by periods of remission and latency . . . and so if

[9]Eighteenth-century venerologist.

the quack does not kill with his cure, he can often claim success—for a time, at least. The quacks cured by searing the pustules with hot irons, and prescribed an unbelievable assortment of medicines to swallow and to apply, the latter including even boiled ants' nest, along with the ants. . . .

The two most popular remedies for syphilis in the sixteenth century were mercury and guaiacum. The first came into use very soon after the appearance of the pox, both in Europe and Asia. . . . [I]t proved to be the only generally effective means of arresting syphilis for the next four hundred years. Before the middle of the sixteenth century, mercury was being rubbed on, applied to the body in plasters and swallowed in pills.

Unfortunately, mercury was overused, and in many cases the cure was successful but the patient died of it. The humoral theory of disease, which dominated European thinking at the time, taught that illness came as the result of an imbalance among the four humors. Syphilis could be cured if the body could be obliged to bleed, defecate, sweat out, and spit out the excess of the offending humor: phlegm, in this case. The most obvious symptom of mercury poisoning is the constant dribbling of saliva, even to the amount of several pints a day. What, thought the sixteenth-century physician, could be more desirable? The body is purging itself of that which is making it sick. Out came the offending excess, often along with gums, teeth, and assorted interior fragments of the body. . . .

. . . Many other remedies were tried in its place—China root, sassafras, sarsaparilla, and so on—but only one displaced mercury as the cure, if only for a time. This was guaiacum, a decoction of the wood of a tree of the West Indies, which became the most popular panacea of the 1520s. The wood had much to recommend it. It came from America, as did the disease; and this is, of course, the way a thoughtful God would arrange things. It was a very impressive wood, extremely hard and so heavy that "the leaste pece of its caste into water, synketh streyght to the bottom," which indicated that it must have additional miraculous properties. A decoction of it caused the patient to perspire freely, a very desirable effect, according to humoral theory. . . .

The prevalence of syphilis and the wood's effectiveness not only against it but also against "goute in the feete, the stone, palsey, lepre, dropsy, falling evyll, and other diseases," drove its price to dizzy heights. Like a poor man's soup bone, the sawdust of guaiacum was boiled up again and again for those not lucky enough or wealthy enough to buy the first decoction. Counterfeit guaiacum flooded the market and pieces of the wood were hung in churches to be prayed to by the most impecunious syphilitics. . . .

. . . Murmurs, soon rising to shouts, of the wood's ineffectiveness began to be voiced in the 1530s. . . . The fad of the Holy Wood from the New World returned a few generations later, and the use of it never quite died out—it was not removed from the British Pharmacopoeia until 1932—but its reputation as *the cure* had evaporated. Europe returned to China root, sassafras, prayer, and, especially, mercury. . . .

. . . In an age in which the Pope had to rescind an order expelling all prostitutes from Rome because of the loss of public revenue that resulted, the new venereal disease inevitably spread to every cranny of Europe and became, like smallpox or consumption, one of the permanently resident killers. The English doctor, William Clowes, stated in the 1580s that one out of every two he had treated in the House of St. Bartholomew had been syphilitic, and that "except the people of this land do speedily repent their most ungodly life and leave this odious sin, it cannot be but the whole land will shortly be poisoned with this most noisome sickness."

However, *Treponema pallidum* brought some good in its train, though those who benefited from it were few. Physicians, surgeons and quacks found a source of wealth in the pox. . . .

. . . When man is both helpless and foolish in the presence of horror, as is often the case in matters pertaining to venereal disease, he finds solace in jokes. There was a great deal of joking about the French disease in the sixteenth century. . . .

Erasmus mentions syphilis a number of time. In one of his *Colloquies* he announces to the world that "unless you're a good dicer, an infamous whoremonger, a heavy drinker, a reakless spendthrift, a wastrel and heavily in debt, decorated with the French pox, hardly anyone will believe you're a knight.". . .

To most, however, the pox was no subject for laughter, but an unmitigated disaster. It was no respecter of rank, and thus had a direct and dismal effect on political and church history. . . . Two dynasties whose members were not noted for monogamous behavior died out in that age, the House of Valois[10] and the House of Tudor.[11] As usual, little can be proved, but the inability of queens to give birth to living children makes one suspect that syphilis played a role in the demise of these families, and thus in the political turmoil of their realms. There is little doubt that Francis I,[12] famous for having "lost all save life and

[10]Royal dynasty in France, 1328–1589.

[11]Royal dynasty in England, 1485–1603.

[12]King of France, 1515–1547.

honor" in the battle of Pavia, lost both in the end to the pox. And there is little doubt that one and possibly two of the husbands of Mary Queen of Scots,[13] and, therefore, possibly the woman herself, had the disease. . . .

The pox's full impact, however, can never be measured if we restrict ourselves to economics, literature, politics, and religion. *Treponema pallidum* was chiefly a social villain, one of the most evil of the whole age of Erasmus, Shakespeare, and Francis I. The fear of infection tended to erode the bonds of respect and trust that bound men and women together. The prostitute's chance of Christian forgiveness faded. "If I were judge," roared Luther,[14] "I would have such venemous syphilitic whores broken on the wheel and flayed because one cannot estimate the harm such filthy whores do to young men." And those less obviously offensive suffered, also, from the terror engendered by the new plague. The sick and the stranger found closed doors where once they had found hospitality. Friendships were altered by a new coolness, as men began in some degree to limit their contacts with any who might conceivably have been touched by the pox.

We find little bits of information indicating the change. Public baths went out of style, for it was widely realized that many as innocent of promiscuity as newborn babes had contracted the French disease in such places. The use of the common drinking cup fell out of style. The kiss, a customary gesture of affection between friends as well as lovers, came under suspicion. . . .

What was the effect of syphilis on general human contact? Consider that one of the crimes—false or no—of which Cardinal Woolsey[15] was accused in his arraignment before Parliament in 1529 was that he, "knowing himself to have the foul and contagious disease of the great pox . . . came daily to your grace [Henry VIII],[16] rowning in your ear, and blowing upon your most noble grace with his perilous and infectious breath, to the marvellous danger of your highness." . . .

It is obvious that in no area did syphilis wreak more havoc than in relations between men and women. No civilization has ever satisfactorily solved the problem of sex. Even if there were no such thing as venereal disease, the sex relationship would still produce distrust, fear, and pain, as well as confidence, love, and comfort. Add to the normal emotional difficulties of the sex relationship not just the possi-

[13]Mary Stuart, Queen of Scotland, 1542–1567.

[14]Martin Luther, German Protestant reformer, 1483–1546.

[15]Lord Chancellor of England, 1515–1529.

[16]King of England, 1509–1547.

bility of the pains of gonorrhea but the danger of a horrible and often fatal disease, syphilis. Where there must be trust, there must now also be suspicion. Where there must be a surrender of self, there must now also be a shrewd consideration of future health. . . .

Gabriello Falloppio, in his book of syphilis, *De Morbo Gallico*[17] (1564), suggested that after sexual intercourse a man should carefully wash and dry his genitals. The age of the canny lover had arrived.

[17]*Of the French Disease.*

Life in Renaissance France

LUCIEN FEBVRE

Historians, not to mention theologians and anthropologists, have long debated whether human nature changes over time. Are people intrinsically good or bad; have they had the same emotional makeup for thousands of years; have humans in the past loved, hated, and felt as we do? These are questions that address the very essence of what it means to live in a historical age. Using sixteenth-century France as an example, Lucien Febvre argues that people do differ from their ancestors. Frenchmen of the Renaissance, an era of economic expansion, cultural and intellectual brilliance, and religious strife, were very unlike their modern descendants.

Febvre describes twentieth-century Frenchmen as urban, sedentary, and refined. How does he contrast these descriptions with the characteristics of the Renaissance French? What evidence does he cite to argue that neither the nobility nor the monarch lived comfortably or sedately?

Febvre describes carefully the relationship between city and countryside. Where did the city end and the country begin? If the division between urban and rural was not clearly delineated, the dichotomy between day and night was quite dramatic. The sixteenth century had not yet conquered night. What implications did this feature, darkness nearly untouched by light, have for life during the Renaissance?

People did not look as we do today. A coarse, unvarying diet, with few stimulants, affected energies and attitudes. For example, what were their ideas on beauty? In closing, Febvre recites a marvelous anecdote about four middle-class men sitting and talking at a table. What do their conversation and subsequent actions tell us about sixteenth-century people?

. . . I know that man's essential nature is unchanging through time and space. . . . But that is an assumption, and I might add, a worthless assumption for a historian. . . . The men of the early sixteenth century must be the object of our attention if we wish to try to understand what the Renaissance was, what the reformation was. It would be an impossible task to try to "recreate" them, to build them up into their real unity, an impossible task and an unnecessary one. Let us be less ambitious. By way of introduction it should be enough to evoke them, projecting onto the screen of our imaginations some typical silhouettes. . . .

Lucien Febvre, *Life in Renaissance France* (Cambridge: Harvard University Press, 1977), 2–12, 14–23.

Twentieth-century man, the Frenchman of the twentieth century, can be defined in many ways, but essentially, taken in terms of his physical existence, his material life, three points stand out: he is urban, sedentary, and refined. We are urban, living an urban life in the city, the modern big city which is not merely a place where there is a greater agglomeration of people more densely packed than elsewhere, but a place where man is not the same as elsewhere. Age distribution, for example, is not the same in the city as in the country. Proportionally there are fewer children and fewer old people than adults, who, having spent their childhood elsewhere, often leave the city in retirement, adults who come to the city to spend the strength of their youth and their maturity. All ties between us and the land have been broken, except perhaps for a short time during vacations. The land seen through urban eyes is a place of rest and relaxation and beauty rather than hard physical labor.

We are sedentary. We may talk much about travel and go rushing about by car or by plane; that is only further proof of our need to be sedentary. The ever-increasing speed of such machines, their flexibility, their ease of access, in fact, the comfort they provide, make it possible for us to take long trips without ever really leaving home. How rare it is nowadays to find the ordinary man more than two or three days" journey from his home.

Man has become urban, sedentary, and refined as well. What a large place the word "comfort" has come to occupy in our language, modern comfort in which we take such pride. What implications the word has, of convenience and material ease: a light turned on or off at the flick of a finger, an indoor temperature independent of the seasons, water ready to flow hot or cold, as we wish, anytime, anywhere. All these, and a thousand other marvels as well, fail to astonish us. Yet they affect the physical temper of our bodies, help us to avoid certain diseases and make us prey to others. They influence our work habits, our leisure time, our customs and conventions, and all the ways of thinking and feeling which are the result of these things. Can we really claim then that they are merely exterior, merely accident, not worth noting or discussing? We are tied to all this technology, it has a hold on us, it makes us serve it, odd, rooted spirits as we are. We are slaves three times over to the insatiable hungers we ourselves have created. In that sense, the men of the sixteenth century were free.

The people who lived in the sixteenth century, in the France of Charles VIII,[1] of Louis XII,[2] of François I,[3] were not urban; they lived

---

[1]King of France, 1483–1498.

[2]King of France, 1498–1515.

[3]King of France, 1515–1547.

on the land. There were no big cities in the modern sense of the word. It is true that foreigners, and the French themselves, sang the praises of their cities. They spoke of Paris as one of the wonders of the world. Yet what were these cities really like? We see the sixteenth-century city laid out before us in old prints, in cosmographies, in collections of maps. . . . The city lay surrounded by crenelated walls, flanked by round towers. A sunken road led to the narrow gate protected by a drawbridge guarded night and day by watchful soldiers. To the right, a crude cross. Straight ahead on a hill top, a huge gibbet, pride of the citizens, where the bodies of hanged men were left to mummify. Often over the gate, impaled on a spike, hung a head or an arm or a leg, some hideous slice of human flesh carved by the hangman: justice at work in a thick-skinned society.

The sunken road leading to the gate was muddy. Past the gate the street widened as it followed a capricious route through the town. A filthy stream ran down its center, fed by rivulets of liquid manure seeping from nearby manure heaps. It was a muddy slough in the rain, a desert of choking dust in the heat of the sun, in which urchins, ducks, chickens, and dogs, even pigs in spite of repeated edicts to control them, all wallowed together.

Entering the city we see that each family has its own house, as in the country. As in the country, each house has a garden behind it, where boxwood borders mark out the vegetable patches. And again as in the country, because city life is the barest modification of country life, each house has an attic with a window for raising and storing hay, straw, grain, and all kinds of winter provisions. Each house has its oven where the mistress and the female servants bake every week. Each house has its press near the cellar, filled every October with the fumes of new wine. Finally, each house has its stable with saddle and draft horses, and its barn with cows and oxen and sheep, led away in the morning when the neighborhood shepherd blows his horn, and brought home again in the evening.

The city was permeated by the country. The country even penetrated into the houses. The city man received his country tenants in his home, peasants who came periodically, bringing their master what his land had produced, laying baskets heavy with their rustic bounty on the polished tiles of the floor. The lawyer received his clients in his study, their arms filled with hares and rabbits, chickens or ducks. The country penetrated city bedrooms in the summertime when the floor was strewn with flowers or leaves and the unused fireplaces were filled with greenery to keep the rooms cool and sweetsmelling. In the winter the floor tiles were covered with a thick layer of country straw to help keep men and animals warm. The country made its presence felt even in everyday language, which was filled with allusions to the fields.

Seasons began with the singing of the cricket, the blooming of the violet, the ripening of the wheat. The city, filled with orchards, gardens, and green trees, was nothing but a slightly more densely populated countryside. Life there was scarcely more rushed or more complex than in the villages. The city had no hold on its inhabitants.

The great majority of people did not live in cities. Nor were all those who lived on the land peasants. All the noblemen of France in those days had homes in the country. Some of them lived in chateaux, often admirable buildings. But let us turn away for a moment from the classical façades, the sculptures, the finely carved marble, and look instead at these fine houses with the eye of a prospective tenant. Each room leads to the next, all huge, all monotonously square: a wall in front, a wall behind, windows in the left wall, windows in the right. To go from one end of the house to the other, one must pass in turn through all the rooms in the series. This was not only the case in France. In his diverting *Memoirs*, Benvenuto Cellini[4] explains the rather colorful origin of the disfavor in which he tells us he was held by the Grand Duchess of Tuscany. When Cosimo dei Medici[5] in his palace in Florence sent for his favorite sculptor, Benvenuto Cellini had to drop whatever he was doing and rush to his master. Quickly, nearly running, he would burst through the door and climb the stairs. On his way to see the Duke he would go from room to room, crossing each in turn. But these rooms were not all merely ceremonial chambers; there were also private ones, even very private ones used by the Grand Duchess herself. And from time to time it happened that these rooms were not empty when he passed through them, so that the artist was forced, in passing, to bow before some noble and powerful person whose attention at that moment was fully occupied with other things, and to whom the sudden appearance of the artist in these most private apartments must have seemed highly disagreeable. But Cellini had no choice; the Grand Duke was waiting and this was the only possible route.

That took place in Florence, in the Uffizi,[6] in Florence which by comparison with France at the same time was a model of delicacy and refinement. Now consider what the real level of comfort in a French chateau must have been. For one thing, people must have lived through the winter shivering, their teeth chattering. We may admire the huge fireplaces which sometimes extend over the whole of one wall of the great square rooms, and we are quite right to do so. We are in

---

[4]Italian sculptor and metalsmith (1500–1571), brought to France by Francis I.

[5]Cosimo the Great, Duke of Florence from 1537 and Grand Duke of Tuscany (1569–1574).

[6]Palace built for Cosimo dei Medici, now one of the world's great art museums.

a position to admire them, standing as tourists in the chateau where central heating has since been installed. In the sixteenth century they were also admired, but the people who did so kept their furlined coats and their warm hats on. In vain did an army of woodcarriers bring in load after load of branches and logs to be added to fire after fire. All the brightly burning (or smoking) fireplaces of Chambord or Blois would not meet the requirements of us modern sybarites. Far from the fire it was freezing; and when the flames crackled and rose, close to the fire it was hot enough to fry you. People were cold, always cold, even inside their homes.

Their homes were simply an extension of the countryside, without the sharp contrast of home's welcoming warmth. Can we really believe that the ideas of such people about home and hearth, about the family, would be the same as those held today by people drunk with warmth, slaves to central heating? Now try for a moment to imagine modern man without any ideas or feelings about his house, his home. What a void this would create! . . .

In any case, the list of such chateaux is short: Blois, Chenonceaux, Azay, Amboise, Oiron, Bonnivet. They are the exception. The ordinary dwelling for the gentleman who was not a prince was a manor house. And in the manor, people spent most of their time in a single room, the kitchen. Generally, meals were eaten there. (French houses almost never had a special room for dining until the eighteenth century. Even Louis XIV,[7] on ordinary occasions, ate his meals at a square table placed in front of the window in his bedroom. The noblemen of the sixteenth century, having fewer pretensions, generally ate in the kitchen.) This room is called, in the dialect of some provinces, the "heater." That is the giveaway. It was warm in the kitchen, or at least, less cold than elsewhere. There was always a fire. The aromatic steam coming from the stew-pot made the air a bit heavy perhaps, but warm, and all told, welcoming. Fresh straw spread on the floor kept people's feet warm. People gathered in the kitchen where they lived elbow to elbow, and they relished this kind of closeness. Like all peasants, they hated to be alone. The more the merrier. The sixteenth century did not have our modesty. It knew nothing of our need to be alone. The beds of the day are evidence of this, great big things in which several people would sleep at once without embarrassment or scruples. Individual bedrooms are a modern idea. "Whatever for?" our forefathers would have asked. Setting apart a room for each activity is another modern notion. The kitchen was the gathering place for everyone, and everything, or almost everything, was done there.

[7]King of France, 1643–1715.

The lord of the manor and his wife were there in their high-backed wooden chairs next to the fire. Their children, both boys and girls, sat on benches. Their guests were received there, the parish priest, their tenants, and their servants. Bustling servants laid or cleared the table under the vigilant eye of their mistress. Farmers, plowmen, day laborers coming in from the fields at day's end heavy with fatigue and with mud, sank into their seats to eat their meager fare. Adding to the confusion were the animals: chickens and ducks who made their home beneath the table, hunting birds perched on the shoulders of the hunters, dogs crouched at their masters' feet, grooming themselves as they lay stretched out in the straw or searching out their fleas under the cover of the women's skirts or roasting themselves before the fire.

Slowly, methodically, respectfully, people ate the coarse food put before them. Bread was rarely made from wheat. Thick floury soup, mush made of millet or groats were served in place of potatoes or pasta. Generally each person at the table was given a large thick slice of somewhat stale dense bread. On this, using three fingers, the diner scooped up whatever he might choose from the central serving dish. Very little red meat was eaten except at weddings and other special occasions. Salt pork appeared from time to time, but there were many meatless days, and fast days, and days of abstinence, and Lent as well, so strictly observed that people often undermined their health. When there was meat it was game or fowl. The sixteenth century did not know the stimulation provoked by red meat, by flesh food accompanied by alcohol and wine; it did not know the illusion of strength and power which modern man obtains from his usual food, nor the instant stimulation of the nervous system which, thanks to coffee, even the most humble know today. The closest equivalent in the sixteenth century was spices, whose use was limited only by their enormous cost. People who used neither alcohol nor tobacco nor coffee nor tea and who only rarely ate red meat got their stimulation from spices, setting themselves aflame with ginger and pepper and nutmeg and carefully concocted mustards.

All told, people spent very little time in the house. They came to eat or to take refuge when life and work in the fields was cut short by a heavy rain, and at night. Night too was different; man had not yet learned to conquer the darkness. The kitchen and bedrooms were lit most usually by the dancing flames in the fireplace. Lamps were, in general, nasty, sooty little things which sputtered or smoked and spread their stench through the room. We can scarcely imagine what one of those big kitchens must have been like after three or four hours of habitation by twenty or so people still in work clothes, not to count the animals who lived there. The room would fill with musty, lingering odors of men and beasts and past meals, the acrid odor of sputtering wicks and the smell of muck-spattered leggings drying in front of the fire. Imagine a boy who wants to settle in his nook to read or to study under such conditions. How can he amidst all this disorder? The kitchen is not for reading except maybe four or five times a year when it is raining hard and no one knows what else to do. As a last resort someone reads aloud a few chapters from an old romance. From time to time, late in the evening when everyone else is in bed, the master brings his account book up-to-date, carefully detailing what was owed him as well as his expenses. Real life for this man and those like him was life out-of-doors, riding over the fields and vineyards, the meadows and woods. They oversaw their land while they hunted or hunted while overseeing their land. Real life was going to a fair or a market, exchanging a few words with the peasants there in a shared language about shared interests which, needless to say, were neither political nor metaphysical. On Sundays and holidays the lord, who considered from a certain point of view was nothing but a kind of superior peasant, started the dance by taking the girls once around the floor, and if need be played at bowls, archery, or wrestling.

But what about the court, you will ask, the brilliant court of François I, if not earlier, that of Charles VIII or Louis XII? Let us have a look at the court. The word itself is impressive, evoking magnificent visions: great gilded rooms glowing with the light of a thousand candles, filled with lords and ladies who themselves live in sumptuous chateaux. . . . [T]he outward setting and the fashions change. But the court surely always remains just that, the court, a place of privilege above all, and display, where powerful people, whose every costume costs a fortune, gather to live in ostentatious luxury and comfort in the midst of a continual whirl of banquets, receptions, and other entertainments. Lazy and useless lives no doubt, yet not totally free of all signs of wit, clever remarks, now and then, little verses or biting epigrams.

Very well. But against this image must be set the work of patient scholars who have gathered and classified the letters and documents of the royal chancellery. From these we can reconstruct, day by day, for all the thirty years of the reign of François I, the activities of the sovereign. Suppose we open the collection at random to 1533. The king was just over forty. He was already starting to turn gray; his eyes were becoming heavy; his nose was growing longer. The ladies of Paris and elsewhere had left a heavy mark on the king. And the earlier misfortune of Pavia[8] had broken many an enchantment.

On the first of January, 1533, François I was in Paris, at the Louvre. He had spent all of December there. He was to spend all of January and February there. Three months in the same place! That was most unlike the king's usual habits. He soon reverted to another pattern.

[8]French defeat by the Spanish in 1525. Francis I was captured at the battle.

In March the king set off. First he made a tour of the Valois and the Soissonais. On the seventh of March he was at La Ferté-Milon; on the ninth at the Abbey of Longpont; on the tenth, at F'ere-en-Tarendois; on the fifteenth at Soissons; on the seventeenth at Coucy. Then he turned northward. François spent the twentieth at Marle and la F'ere; the twenty-first at Ribémont; the twenty-second at Guise; the twenty-fourth at Marle again. Then he turned toward Champagne. On the twenty-eighth he arrived at Saint-Marcoul de Corbeny; the next day he was at Cormicy, and the day following at Reims. That city, in which the kings of France were crowned, did not hold him long. By the third of April he had arrived in Château-Thierry by the way of F'ere-en-Tarendois. He stayed there for three days. By the seventh he was at Meaux, but by then it was Holy Week and the king remained at Meaux for the Easter celebrations. It was not until the nineteenth that he came to Fontainebleau to spend a week. On the twenty-sixth he was at Gien, having come by way of Montargis and Châtillon-sur-Loign. Then he set off toward Bourges, arriving on the second of May for three days, after which he set off again toward Moulins where he spent four days after touring the Bourbonnais: Issoudoun, Meillant, Cérilly, Bourbon-l'Archambault. With an intermediate stop at Roanne, the king made his way to Lyon by the twenty-sixth of May. And there he stopped. He spent a month in Lyon, not, of course, without making numerous excursions to other places nearby. At the end of June he left the city, crossed the Forez, and entered Clermont-Ferrand on July tenth. Next he wandered about the Auvergne from Riom to Issoire to Vic. A week later he was in Velay. By the seventeenth he had come as far as Polignac; by the eighteenth he was at le Puy for two days; the twenty-fourth at Rodez; the twenty-fifth on the road to Toulouse, the city where he spent the first week of August. By August ninth he was at Nîmes; on the twenty-ninth he began a twelve-day stay at Avignon; by September fifteenth he was in Arles; the twenty-first at Martigues; the twenty-second at Marignane. On the fourth of October he entered Marseilles. We need follow him no further; it is clear that we shall have had more than enough of these endless lists of dates and places long before François I had his fill of travel. Was this the life of a king or of a knight-errant, wandering always, up hill and down dale? . . .

The court followed the king. It followed him on the highway, through the woods, along the rivers and across the fields, more like a train of perpetual tourists than a court. Or, more exactly, it was like a troop doing a day's march. The advance party would move out ahead to set up "camp" before the king arrived: the quartermaster, the official charged with finding and allocating housing for everyone; and a whole tribe of cooks, specialists in sauces, roasts, and pastries. Riding old nags usually acquired through the generosity of the king, they hurried through the dawn to that night's stopping place. It might be a simple village house, a gentleman's manor, or the palace of some important nobleman. Or, if need be, from time to time the king would be content to spend the night in the big tent which a sturdy mule bore on its back, following all the peregrinations of the king. The tent might be set up anywhere, in a clearing, in the midst of the fields or meadows, as the whims of the master dictated.

Once the advance party had moved out, the body of the court began to leave also. First the king and his guards, officers, and gentlemen of his household: as he passed through a village the church bells would ring, and the priests would come running to the roadside. The peasants who saw the royal cortege approach from the distance as they worked in the fields would run toward it. There, in the midst of a splendid group of mounted men, they saw the king, either on horseback himself or riding in a litter that lurched with each step taken by the stout mules drawing it. Behind the king came the ladies of the court, ladies who did a day's march alongside the men. Following the example of the king, they too lived like soldiers on a campaign. Constant travel may eventually become a way of life which one comes to enjoy or even to feel a kind of nostalgia for; nonetheless it is not an easy life or a restful one, not suited to frail women of delicate constitution.

The ladies of the court were not frail. Their portraits have been preserved for us thanks to the popularity of pencil drawings in the sixteenth century. Collections of these portraits . . . are to be found in the most far-flung lands. What disappointments await us in the pages of such collections. The written words of contemporaries are filled with a thousand sincere-sounding compliments. And here are the ladies of unparalleled beauty preserved, for example, in the Montmor collection in the Library at Aix-en-Provence, once attributed to Madame de Boissy, wife of the head of the king's household. The portraits have manuscript captions. First we come to Madame de Chateaubriand, mistress of the king, of Bonnivet, and others too, none of whom was ashamed of the association. . . . Looking at the portrait of so famous a beauty we find a rather fleshy blond woman with a wide, flat face and rather ordinary shoulders. The caption leaves us with a shred of hope: "Formed better by nature than by pencil," it says. We find Madame de l'Estrange. Her name in the madrigals of the day inevitably rhymed with "face d'Ange" (angel face); her face now seems to have been whittled from some cheap, intractable wood. And Diane de Poitiers, who was the delight of the son, Henri II,[9] after having been the joy of the father, François I, surely must have been an extraordinary woman to be able to extend her reign from one sovereign to the next, especially when the two men

[9]King of France, 1547–1559.

were so unlike on another. "A beautiful sight, an honest companion," says the caption under her portrait in the Montmor collection. . . . As for her looks, however, we see an astute face with a sharp nose, premature bags under the eyes, and a wide, thin-lipped mouth. This is the evidence not merely of one portrait, but of five of six drawn between 1525 and 1550, so that no effort of the will can make our own esthetic sense coincide with that of our ancestors: for us that face holds neither charm nor distinction nor grace nor beauty.

It is odd that these depictions of great ladies or princesses or court favorites almost never convey a sense of breeding or nobility. Or perhaps what breeding there is seems surprisingly rustic and casual. But in all fairness, how could they have refined their features or simply preserved the freshness of their looks while exposing themselves constantly, on horseback, to the out-of-doors, to the cutting wind, to the driving rain and snow, traveling for weeks and weeks without real rest, without anything more than improvised lodging? The ladies of the court were a sad sight as they followed the king; the oldest dozing in their litters, the others rocked by the rhythmic step of their mares or packed into wagons without springs so that the wheels transmitted every bump in the road. Relief might come when they all piled into a rented or borrowed barge, to drift between the flat banks of some river or stream.

Twelve thousand horses, three or four thousand men, not counting the women (who were by no means all of the respectable sort): the court was like a little army, privately outfitted, self-sufficient, living an independent existence. It brought its own merchants of all sorts, protected and regulated by the chief provost, granted the sole right to supply the courtiers. There were butchers and poultrymen, fishmongers and greengrocers, fruiterers and bakers; wine merchants prepared to sell both wholesale and retail; purveyors of hay and straw and oats. There was a whole tribe of servants to aid in the hunt: to care for the dogs and falcons; to see to the nets and traps. Another group was needed to see to the feeding of the court: two mares carrying bottles of wine intended for the king's table and that of his chamberlains and the head of his household; cooks and their apprentices who on certain days established by tradition would entertain the king with dances. And there were the couriers and fast riders, hardy horsemen who were always ready to ride at top speed to the nearest coast from the depths of Auvergne or Burgundy, seeking oysters or mussels or fish for the king's table on meatless days.

Ambassadors were brought to despair by the unsettled life of the court. One of them, Mariano Giustiniano, was ambassador in 1535, that is, two years after the period we have just been examining in detail. To the Senate in Venice he wrote the following report: "My tenure as ambassador lasted forty-five months . . . I traveled constantly . . . Never during that time did the court remain in the same place for as long as two weeks." It should be said that of all those who followed the peregrinations of the court, the diplomats suffered the most. The king did his best to avoid contact with these observers, interested by profession in unearthing hidden secrets, and he led them a merry chase in doing so. He was careful never to inform them of the court's itinerary; he would invent a hunt or a sudden excursion as an excuse to flee their company. They, on the other hand, were professionally obliged to be as close as possible to the person of the king.

The nobles were less assiduous. Those who followed the royal party for more than a month or two were rare indeed. Most of those who already belonged to the world of the court came each year to spend a few weeks with the king. They left their land and their homes intending to return, and in fact, they did so as soon as they could. There they recovered and settled once more into a familiar society, while from the north to the south, from the east to the west, from the Ardennes to Provence, from Brittany to Lorraine, the king of France, on horseback, continued his rounds, begun at his coronation and ended by his death.

What has been said so far has brought us to no conclusion. No conclusion is wanted, for the aim of these pages has been to present to the reader, by way of introduction, a few images of life in sixteenth-century France, images of the time of Louis XII and François I, striking images. They show us in action, so to speak, people performing timeless acts, going through the eternal circle of all human life. But if I am not entirely mistaken, the reader has also seen, and I suppose felt, as he was reading, that this eternal circle did not follow quite the same course in the sixteenth century as it does today.

. . . Concrete man, living man, man in flesh and blood living in the sixteenth century and modern man do not much resemble each other. He was a country man, a nomad, a rustic, and in all these we are far form him. When we see him before us in the strength of his manhood at the age of forty, what dangers has he not surmounted, what challenges has he not overcome? Above all, he survived. He lived through his first sixteen years during which, regularly, at the very least half of all children died. Family account books yield an eloquent record of this grim fact. They are punctuated nearly every three lines by the death of a child, like the tolling of a funeral bell. Later, our sixteenth-century man escaped death by that combination of mortal scourges known in a word as the plague, which killed several thousand people each year, spreading occasionally to epidemic proportions when it would decimate entire populations.

However middle class, however bourgeois, we may assume him to be, however far by profession from arms and military, he had nonetheless risked his life a hundred times as a soldier. When the enemy was at the gates of his city about to besiege it, he ran to the ramparts with his halberd and his helmet to fight alongside the others. He risked his life equally when he traveled, as all men of the sixteenth century did, whether they were lawyers or merchants or journeymen making their tour of the kingdom, or students heading across the Alps to the schools of Padua or Pavia. They all wrote their wills before leaving home. As he approached the nearby woods, the traveler would observe the dark copse spreading up the hillside, offering a hiding place for the brigand waiting for the opportunity to attack the unaccompanied or unarmed as they passed. In the wretched inn which he reached just as night fell, the exhausted traveler found sinister vagrants and black-handed charcoal burners; men whose motions were brusque and whose faces gave rise to disquieting suspicions came stealthily into the room to drink themselves sodden. The traveler spent the night standing guard in his miserable room, without fire or lamp to give him light, his sword unsheathed and placed across the crude wooden table he had pushed against the door to keep it closed. By dawn he had had enough; he fled without further ado, pleased to find that thieves had not made off with his horse.

Life was a perpetual combat to be waged against man, the seasons, and a hostile and ill-controlled nature. A person who was victor in such a combat, who arrived at maturity without too many accidents or misadventures, had a tough skin, a thick hide, literally as well as figuratively. If a vein of great sensitivity or delicacy lay hidden beneath the surface toughness we have no way of knowing it. History must limit itself to recording appearances. In the sixteenth century, appearances are neither gracious nor soft. One, two, five children in a family died in infancy, carried off by unknown diseases ill-distinguished or ill-diagnosed and generally ill-cared-for. The family record book simply notes the death and the date. Then the writer, father of the child, passes on to more notable events: a hard frost in April killing the autumn's fruit in the bud, an earthquake signaling great catastrophes. His wife might be respected for her virtue and her fecundity, and praised, perhaps, for the skill with which she ran the home. But when she died, leaving her husband too few children, five or six at most, he married again as soon as he could because it was important to have a dozen, more if possible. On the other hand, if a peasant in the country had been left a widow and remarried, she would not take her children by the first marriage; they were left to shift for themselves as servants or beggars by the roadside.

Thomas Platter,[10] in his memoirs, evokes a life enormously far from

[10]Sixteenth-century Swiss educator.

our own although we are separated from him by scarcely more than seven or eight normal lifetimes. Thomas Platter tells us, as though he were speaking of something entirely ordinary, without registering the least surprise, that as his father died when he was still an infant, his mother remarried soon thereafter. This caused the immediate dispersion of her children, so that Platter simply did not know how many brothers and sisters he had. With effort he could recall the names of two sisters and three brothers and something of what became of them. About the others he remembered nothing. He himself was taken in by an aunt. He never again heard from his mother. . . .

Indeed, the things which are nearest and dearest to us today— home, hearth, wife, and children—seem to have been regarded by the man of the sixteenth century as merely transitory goods which he was always prepared to renounce. On occasion he would renounce them without any very real or serious reason for doing so, impelled by an unconscious need to wander, the sprouting of seeds planted by generations of crusading and errancy. One of the constant companions of any historian of the sixteenth century is the *Colloquies* of Erasmus,[11] a small but rich mirror of the times. In it we find scenes such as this; Four men are sitting at a table. They are middle-class, peaceful, sedentary, married, well-established men who have come together as old friends to share a glass of wine. Perhaps they have shared a glass too many and the wine has gone to their heads. One of them suddenly bursts out: "Any friend of mine will follow me; I'm going on a pilgrimage to Santiago de Compostella."[12] A drunken impulse. The second man speaks in turn: "As for me, I'm not going to Santiago, I'll go all the way to Rome." The third and fourth friends make peace in the group, suggesting a compromise. First they will go to Santiago and then, from there, to Rome. All four of them will go, and they pass a glass of wine to drink to their pilgrimage. The pact has been sealed, the vows made. There is no going back on it, so they leave. One of the pilgrims dies in Spain; the second in Italy. The third is left dying in Florence by the fourth who returns home alone a year later, worn out, prematurely aged and ruined. The story is not fiction; it depicts the customs of a time which is no longer ours.

These are the things we should try to remember when we wish to understand the "things of the sixteenth century." We must remember that we are all, like it or not, hothouse products; the man of the sixteenth century grew in the open air.

[11]Dutch humanist, c.1466–1536.

[12]City in northwest Spain containing the reputed tomb of the apostle James. After Rome, Santiago was the most popular European site for Medieval pilgrims.

Mutiny and Discontent in the Spanish Army of Flanders, 1572–1607

GEOFFREY PARKER

During its Golden Age in the sixteenth century, Spain was the most powerful state in Europe. Spain ruled much of the New World, the Duchy of Milan, southern Italy, Sicily, Sardinia, Portugal (from 1580 to 1640) and Portuguese possessions overseas, the province of Franche Comté in what is now France, and, finally, the Low Countries. Consisting of present day Belgium, the Netherlands, and Luxembourg, the seventeen provinces of the Low Countries had a long tradition of local autonomy, as evidenced in their provincial estates, vibrant cities (Antwerp, Amsterdam, Bruges, Brussels, Ghent), and relatively tolerant religious opinions. Part of the Duchy of Burgundy since the fourteenth century, the Low Countries had prospered under Duke Charles, native born, who became King of Spain in 1516 and Holy Roman Emperor in 1519. His son, Philip II of Spain (1556–1598), was not from the Low Countries and looked upon the local political freedoms and religious diversity with growing distaste. Philip was an autocratic ruler and a fervent Catholic. He aimed to reduce the independent governmental traditions of the Low Countries and to crush Protestantism there. To these ends he introduced the Inquisition and circumvented the local estates.

In response, the nobility in the Low Countries revolted and Protestants rioted throughout the provinces, pillaging Catholic churches. Philip then sent in the Duke of Alva and more soldiers. Alva confiscated property, killed thousands of Protestants, and supported the Inquisition. His iron-fisted rule nearly succeeded in eliminating resistance. Only William, Prince of Orange, managed to sustain the Dutch Revolt. Eventually, the ten southern provinces remained in Spanish hands and only the seven northern provinces, later known as the United Provinces, achieved independence from Spain.

Alva and, later, the Prince of Parma were successful in retaining the southern provinces (now Belgium) because Spain possessed the strongest army in Europe, undefeated in battle for a century (until 1643). At the same time, troubles in the army contributed to Spain's failure to subdue the entire Dutch Revolt.

Military history has traditionally focused on battles and strategies, but here Geoffrey Parker explores the life of the common soldier, his frustrations and aims. What was the soldier's life like? What provoked a mutiny? What purpose did the mutineers hope to accomplish? How did the soldiers behave during a mutiny? How did the mutinies affect the policies of the Spanish government?

Geoffrey Parker, "Mutiny and Discontent in the Spanish Army of Flanders 1572–1607," *Past and Present* 58 (February 1973): 38–52.

The mutineers, after all, revolted against their king and during a war. Were they traitors? Were their mutinies justified? Where do our sympathies lie? Were there similarities between the revolts of soldiers and those of civilians in early modern Europe?

In early modern times, Sir George Clark once wrote, "The history of armies was one of the hinges on which the fate of Europe turned". The broad outlines of this history have long been known—a spectacular growth in the size of armies (with perhaps a million men under arms in 1706), in the scale, duration and cost of warfare, and in the professionalism of the troops—but until recently the quality of life experienced by the soldiers of early modern Europe has been largely ignored. Now, thanks to the survival of copious documentary and literary sources, a detailed picture is beginning to emerge. Clearly conditions were extremely hard, especially on active service. The soldiers spent much of their time sleeping beneath hedgerows or in makeshift shelters of branches or canvas; they were permanently subject to a brutal and arbitrary discipline; and there was always a high risk of mutilation or violent death. Worst of all the men were often left without wages and sometimes without food as well.

It is surprising that the troops endured these harsh and humiliating surroundings for so long. Only when there was a serious deterioration in living standards did they protest: first isolated acts of defiant disobedience occurred, then desertion *en masse*, and finally mutiny. These disorders are important for the historian not only because they lay bare the problems and pressures of the soldier's everyday life, but because they could give rise to serious political and domestic repercussions. A major munity, for example, might jeopardize the outcome of a war and could provoke unrest and even rebellion at home. Governments were always highly sensitive to the morale of their troops and many a political decision was influenced by the level of discipline (or indiscipline) among the armed forces. . . .

. . . Few fighting forces could boast of as many mutinies or of mutinies better organized than the Army of Flanders, a heterogeneous body of some 70,000 men drawn largely from the Habsburg states in Germany, the Netherlands, Italy and Spain. This army was permanently at war between 1572 and 1607 and during this period it was shaken by no less than forty-six mutinies, mainly concentrated in two cycles: five between 1572 and 1576 and thirty-seven between 1589 and 1607—an average of over two a year. Some mutinies were relatively insignificant, involving only a hundred men and lasting just a few weeks, but the major military revolts involved three or four thousand men and took a year, and sometimes two or three years, to pacify.

There was already a strong tradition of organized mutiny among the Spanish troops on foreign service: several regiments had mutinied successfully in Italy during the 1520s and in the Netherlands during the 1550s. Sooner or later, when conditions became unbearable, the suggestion would be made that the time for protest had come again. In the middle of the night a group of discontented soldiers (often sworn comrades) would beat the alarm on their drums to assemble the troops and propose a mutiny. This was the critical stage of every sedition. Not all attempts at mutiny succeeded: on a number of occasions the ringleaders miscalculated the feelings of their comrades and were isolated, arrested and shot. For an appeal to mutiny to succeed, there had to be a general consensus among the troops that the proposed disobedience was entirely justified. Normally this meant that major Spanish mutinies only took place at the end of a campaign or after a battle, not before. Thus in April 1574 the High Command feared the outbreak of a mutiny among the Spanish veterans, who were owed three years' arrears of wages, when they were ordered to take the field against the invading army of Count Louis of Nassau. The Spaniards responded well however, and made a forced march of over two hundred miles to Mook, a town on the Maas south of Nijmegen. There, despite acute hunger (they had received no rations for three days), they fought and totally defeated the invaders (whose leaders, including Count Louis, were killed). Only then, as they stood elated on the field of victory, was the decision taken to mutiny for their just arrears—thirty-seven months' backpay. The veterans had performed their obligations to the full; they now felt that it was high time for the government to reciprocate.

Once any group of soldiers had decided to mutiny, the officers and anyone else who would not join the movement were expelled from the camp. Regular officers were allowed to remain only if they agreed to waive their rank and serve on the same footing as everyone else. Troops from other units not caught up in the initial sedition, even those speaking a different language, were always free to join. Thus at the mutiny of Zichem, which began with four hundred Italians in July 1594, thirteen different languages were spoken by the 2,800 veterans involved by the time it ended in July 1596. However neither the linguistic dissonance nor the distinctions of class and rank prevented the mutineers from united and purposeful action to achieve their ends.

The mutineers always elected their own officers. There was an *electo* or leader, a council to advise him and commissars to carry out his orders. Every man owed unswerving, blind obedience to these elected chiefs. All insubordination was punished with death. On the whole, the leaders were ordinary soldiers. Some were educated but most were only semi-literate and a few could not even write their names. Almost all came from the rank and file. The soldiers did not have enough confidence in the officers and gentleman-rankers who joined the mutiny to entrust their entire destiny to them. Sometimes the *electo* or some of his advisers were N.C.O.s . . . , men accustomed to command and used to dealing with higher authorities, but often they were just privates with long service and correspondingly long pay-arrears.

Having established their rudimentary political organization the mutineers turned their attention to self-defence. They had to secure control of a strongly-fortified town or village, either by suborning its garrison (not a difficult feat when most garrisons were scandalously underpaid) or by direct assault and capture, so that they could safely defy the government without fear of counter-attack. Occupation of a fortified centre, preferably close to a political frontier, also enabled the mutineers to compel the neighbouring countryside to provide regular "contributions" and food. Next, with defence and future income assured, the *electo* and his advisers got down to the business of negotiating with the government for the satisfaction of their claims. On the whole, these were not unreasonable and they were articulated with a surprising degree of sophistication in lengthy petitions.

> First of all we ask and beg Your Excellency to give the order for us to be paid all the arrears of wages which are justly ours.
> We ask Your Excellency, for the service of God and the good of all the soldiers, to ask His Majesty . . . [to provide] a wage which will allow the soldiers to feed and clothe themselves, for now the price of everything has increased so excessively that our wages are not enough even to buy food. We ask that while this matter is being discussed with His Majesty, Your Excellency should order victuals to be sold at a reasonable price which will allow the soldiers to live.
> [We ask] that no Governor, Colonel or Captain should punish a soldier arbitrarily without the case first being considered by the Judge-Advocate, nor should degrading punishments like flogging be administered if the offence does not merit them.
> Many soldiers have suffered and died because there was nowhere for them to be cured when they were sick. Most of them would have recovered if there had been medical assistance. We therefore ask Your Excellency to give us some help in this [and set up a field hospital].

Payment for services rendered, food at a price men could afford, no punishment without trial, basic medical care for soldiers in daily danger of death—these demands of the mutinous Spanish regiments in 1574 were hardly excessive. Their other grievances were equally reasonable. They asked that surgeons and chaplains should be provided to serve with the front-line units "because many soldiers have died unconfessed for lack of anyone to cure or confess them"; that soldiers captured by the enemy should be exchanged for prisoners-of-war in Spanish hands; and that the arrears of soldiers who died in service should be paid to their next-of-kin.

In all mutinies the payment of overdue wages was the principal point at issue. The amounts involved were certainly substantial. Whereas the wage-arrears claimed by the mutineers of the English Parliamentary forces[1] were calculated in weeks, those of the soldiers in the Spanish Netherlands ran into months. The mutineers of Antwerp in 1574, whose grievances are quoted above, were owed thirty-seven months' wages. The light cavalry mutinied in 1576 for seventy-two months' arrears—a total of six years' pay. A group of mutineers at Namur in 1594 claimed (with some exaggeration however) that the government owed them "a hundred months' pay". . . . These enormous outstanding arrears were the result of the chaotic structure of the army's finances. In the sixteenth century the Spanish Army in the Netherlands very rarely issued a general pay to all its forces. With 70,000 men under arms, it seldom had the money to do so. Instead the government lived from hand to mouth, issuing a month's wages here, two or three months' there, in an effort to keep at least the front-line units content. Inevitably this meant that, for some of the time, some of the units were left with no pay at all. It was in these "neglected" units that mutinies began.

The government's financial embarrassments also influenced the duration of most mutinies. When the numbers involved in a mutiny ran to two thousand men and more, immediate settlement of the mutineers' claim was out of the question. A special consignment of bullion had to be solicited from the central government in Spain (which at all times provided at least 75 per cent of the army's money). The mutiny of Antwerp in 1574 cost over one million florins to settle (£100,000 sterling at Elizabethan exchange rates). The first mutiny at Diest in 1590–1 cost 750,000 florins, the second in 1599–1601 1.3 million florins and the third in 1606–7 a further million. Amounts of this magnitude were not easy for the central government to find, on top of all its other commitments. It could sometimes take a year. While the Army's commanders waited for the money to come from Spain, a sort of interim agreement was worked out. The High Command promised to provide the mutineers with a regular sum . . . every month until their

---

[1]In the 1640s, during the Puritan Revolution.

outstanding arrears could be settled in full. In return the mutineers agreed to stop collecting contributions of their own from the countryside and promised to act as the official garrison of the town they had occupied. They also undertook to come to the assistance of loyal troops if these were in danger. Thus the mutineers of La Chapelle led the forces which relieved the beleaguered garrison of La F'ere in 1596, and the mutineers of Diest fought in the forefront of the battle of Nieuwpoort (July 1600). They were still commanded by their *electo* however.

Mutual assistance of this kind sometimes hastened the final settlement of the mutineers' claims, but in a sense it was superfluous. Whether or not there was co-operation, almost every mutiny by troops of the Army of Flanders ended in complete success: each mutineer was paid in full and in cash.

Compared with their financial claims, the other grievances of the mutineers were easily dealt with. All demanded a full and free pardon for their actions during the mutiny; some asked to transfer to another unit (perhaps to escape retribution at the hands of their officers), while others demanded a safe-conduct to leave the Netherlands with their just rewards. Even the last presented no problem: the High Command was only too pleased to be rid of men who had displayed a talent for organizing and directing discontent. There were also the specific grievances of 1574–5, noted above, calling for the provision of cheap food, for a proper judicial system to protect the troops against the arbitrary power of their officers, for a hospital, field medicine and chaplains. The justice of these grievances was recognized and they were redressed by the High Command during the 1580s. A regular network of military judges and special courts grew up under a Judge-Advocate-General while a hierarchy of chaplains was instituted under a Vicar-General. At the same time a permanent military hospital was opened at Mechelen (it had 330 sick-beds by the 1630s) and each regiment was provided with a team of surgeons and barbers. In the 1590s the troops began to receive their daily bread (or rather a three-pound loaf every two days) and their clothes on credit, the cost being subsequently deducted from their wages. These welfare services were established largely on the initiative of Alexander Farnese, the prince of Parma,[2] and they were important. They answered many of the complaints of the first generation of mutineers. However they left virtually untouched the central grievance: unpaid wages. Revolts among the troops therefore continued to occur, and they continued to last a long time.

This longevity of the mutinies of the Army of Flanders posed a number of special problems for the troops involved. Above all they had

[2](1545–1592), appointed governor-general of the Netherlands in 1578.

to take steps to secure their internal discipline and morale, and to display to the outside world their corporate solidarity and their capacity to remain on strike until their demands were met. This was not easy. However justified and sophisticated the mutineers' behaviour might seem, the Army's commanders remained convinced that they were dealing with "lackeys and labourers", "canaille"[3], "pay-grabbers and vagabonds", "the vilest and most despicable people in the kingdom", "low-born people who must be frightened and chastised for the sake of the future" and so on. The motives of such men were naturally assumed to be the basest possible: "They do not mutiny through privation but for the hell of it and to steal whatever is going" wrote one observer; "[In time] necessity turns to corruption . . . [and the soldiers] mutiny many times rather because they want to do so than because they have any just cause for it" wrote another. There was no lack of evidence to give support to this hostile view. There were indeed certain soldiers who mutinied almost once a year to secure their wage arrears, while many had been involved in more than three mutinies during their military career by 1609 (when they were all expelled from the Army). In every mutiny there were also extremists. Their influence was responsible for some of the violence and some of the threatening flysheets which appeared in the early stages of each disturbance. . . .

Yet in the end almost everyone paid tribute to the discipline and self-control of the mutineers. With a few uevastating exceptions (like the sack of Aalst and Antwerp in 1576) there was little unprovoked violence and even the most rapacious and sadistic officers were left relatively unscathed by their men. The *electo* of almost every mutiny published and enforced a strict legal code known as the Ordinance. The mutineers of Pont-sur-Sambre in 1593, Italians and Walloons, issued an Ordinance of twenty-one clauses on the first day of their mutiny, imposing severe penalties for theft and assault, for luxury and blasphemy. No wilful damage to persons or property in the neighbourhood of the mutineers" camp was permitted; instead a careful assessment of local resources was made and a contribution-system organized, payable fortnightly in cash to the mutineers' treasurer. The same strict discipline characterized most of the mutineers' military enterprises. Marching under their elected leaders and fighting beneath their own banner, they were a match for anyone. On occasion they displayed suicidal courage: at Antwerp in 1576 (the "Spanish Fury") and again at Tienen in 1604 the mutineers, without waiting to make a breach with artillery, simply made a furious charge with scaling ladders on the walls of the obstreperous town. No officer would have dared to ask his men to undertake such a murderous mission. As Cardinal Bentivoglio, papal nuncio in

[3]Rabble.

the Netherlands, grudgingly affirmed: "Never has disobedience been seen which produced greater obedience".

A considerable part of the self-restraint and the foolhardy courage stemmed from the mutineers' conviction that they were right. A sense of the patent justice of their claims pervades almost all their known writings. The letters sent in their names to the government, the *carteles* or flysheets they circulated among themselves, the pamphlets they published all emphasized the righteousness of their cause. "Anyone can see that we ask only for what is just and for what we so richly deserve" ran a flysheet composed by the mutineers of Antwerp in 1574 (they were owed thirty-seven months' wages at the time). These mutineers even devised their own slogan: "Let us say with a loud voice that four-letter word which sounds so sweet in the ears of poor soldiers who have served so well: *TODO, TODO, TODO* (all, all, all)". These men knew that they had earned their pay. They believed that their arduous and dangerous service over the years entitled them to a living wage and gave them the right to live.

The same sense of legitimacy underlay the self-confident tone which the mutineers adopted in their formal contacts with the outside world. To begin with, each mutiny had its own secretary who drafted the *electo's* epistles and orders, carefully retaining a copy for the mutineers' archive. The secretary was also custodian of the official seal of the mutiny, used to authenticate correspondence, which usually bore some symbolic emblem or motto. Thus the mutineers of Zichem in 1594 had a seal which showed a queen bee followed by a swarm of drones encircled by the inscription *MENS EADEM OMNIBUS* ("the same mind in all"). The three thousand mutineers of Hoogstraten in 1602 went even further and commissioned a special banner, inappropriately displaying the Virgin and Child, with the slogan *PRO FIDE CATHOLICA ET MERCEDE NOSTRA* ("for the Catholic faith and our reward"). They also dressed in green to distinguish themselves from the red badges of Spain and the orange of the States-General,[4] they printed a pamphlet in several languages to justify their actions to the world and, like the mutineers of Zichem before them, they styled themselves "The Republic of Hoogstraten". By such means the mutineers attracted the attention of contemporaries—even playwrights: the mutineers of the 1590s were the subject of an entire play by Luis Vélez de Guevara (*Los amotinados de Flandes*,[5] written in 1633)—and they earned the respect of their superiors. The government felt obliged to address its correspondence to "The magnificent gentlemen, the honourable soldiers of the mutinied regiments", while abject commanders began their letters with engag-

---

[4]The assembly of the Netherlands, composed of delegates from the provinces.
[5]*The Mutineers of Flanders.*

ing paternalism "Magnificent and honoured sons" and concluded "Your good father to love and serve you". The mutineers thus achieved an ambition of the humble and the humiliated of all societies: they were acknowledged to be "somebody".

Yet all this ostentation was a means not an end. Liable to attack by forces still loyal to the government, sometimes even driven to seek asylum with the Dutch, the mutineers valued every artifice which might bolster their morale and impress the government with their collective solidarity. The mutineers of Hoogstraten or Zichem did not want to organize an independent city-state: they just wanted to be paid. Payment in full of outstanding wages was invariably followed by an immediate "return to work".

Like most civilian revolts of the early modern period, the military mutinies of the Spanish army reveal no evidence of any revolutionary purpose or politically conscious agitators. There is not a hint that any mutineers dreamed of overturning the established order, none that they even wished to influence the government towards making peace. The military proletariat in ferment with its elected leaders may bear a superficial resemblance to a soviet with its revolutionary committee, but there were no Levellers[6] in the Army of Flanders and no Putney Debates.[7] The mutineers were indeed more like strikers: they wanted to receive the wages they had already earned and a formal promise of better conditions of service in the future.

Nevertheless, the mutinies of the Spanish army in the Netherlands certainly did not lack political significance. Because they tied down the government's élite troops and involved such vast amounts of money, the outbreak of a major military revolt usually paralysed the army for a whole campaign, sabotaging any offensive and jeopardizing the security of loyal but isolated towns. In certain circumstances a mutiny could undermine the very foundations of the government's authority. In 1574 the Spanish Governor-General of the Netherlands, Don Luis de Requesens, lamented that the mutiny of his most seasoned troops at Antwerp called into question the whole basis of Spanish power. Speaking to a confidant,

He insisted that it was not the prince of Orange[8] who had lost the Low Countries but the soldiers born in Valladolid and Toledo, because the mutineers had driven money out of Antwerp and destroyed all credit and

[6]Radicals emerging during the seventeenth-century Puritan Revolution in England who favored popular democracy, religious toleration, and equality before the law.

[7]Debate in Putney, England, in 1647 between the Levellers and conservatives in the Parliamentary army.

[8]The leader of the Dutch forces in revolt against Spain.

reputation, and he believed that within eight days His Majesty would not have anything left here.

The outbreak of peasant revolts all over the south Netherlands (the consequence of an almost complete harvest failure) appeared to bear out the Governor's pessimistic view, but eventually the discontent died down and Requesens's prophesy was not fulfilled until 1576, in the wake of another major military revolt.

After a siege lasting eight months the Spanish field army forced the surrender of the seaport of Zierikzee in Zeeland (21 June 1576). Once again, the troops had manifestly done their duty; now the cry went up for wage-arrears (forty months in some cases). The government in Brussels was in an impossible position. Requesens had died in March and the caretaker administration (the Council of State) which took over had neither the authority nor the funds to control the army. The king of Spain[9] had already declared himself bankrupt (September 1575) and was unable to send any money to the Netherlands. There was thus no means of offering to the troops the pecuniary satisfaction which they desired and deserved—and the troops knew it! In July they abandoned their hard-won conquests in Zeeland and streamed south in search of plunder and pay. On 25 July a group of three thousand Spaniards made a surprise attack on the loyal town of Aalst (Alost) in Flanders and sacked it with unusual brutality. The reaction was swift and firm: the very next day the caretaker government published an edict which declared all mutineers to be outlaws who could be killed at will. Peasants in a number of villages were armed by their lords and organized into vigilante groups to protect their communities. Any troops in the neighbourhood were attacked. Stragglers and isolated detachments were regularly ambushed and even full companies of cavalry were set upon. To the propertied classes, total anarchy appeared dangerously near. The States of Brabant held an emergency meeting at Brussels and decided to levy troops on their own authority for protection against the mutineers and the peasants alike. They also summoned the estates of the other provinces to join them, and within a month the self-appointed States-General had opened formal peace talks at Ghent with representatives from Holland and Zeeland, the provinces in revolt since 1572. A tentative agreement to suspend hostilities, taken without reference to the king or the Council of State, was reached on 30 October—the "Pacification of Ghent". This made the position of the mutineers critical. Outlawed, attacked and now isolated by a cease-fire, the Spanish veterans decided on a perilous course of action. Only

[9]Philip II, 1556–1598.

the city of Antwerp was rich enough to satisfy their financial demands and secure enough to guarantee their defence. Therefore on Sunday, 4 November, the Spaniards carried out a surprise attack on the city. Beneath their banner, which displayed Christ on the Cross on one side and the Madonna on the other, the mutineers stormed the city and sacked it. Eight thousand civilians were killed, often in the most barbarous manner, and perhaps one thousand houses were destroyed in this desperate action, known to posterity as the "Spanish Fury".

The terrible holocaust perpetrated by "the soldiers born in Valladolid and Toledo" destroyed the last vestiges of the king's authority in the Netherlands. On 8 November the "Pacification of Ghent" was ratified by representatives of almost all the provinces of the Low Countries, again without reference to the king, bringing the war to an end. The sack of the richest city in northern Europe convinced every Netherlander that peace had to be secured immediately and at all costs. Philip II's mutinous troops might have taken Antwerp, but they had lost the Netherlands in doing so.

Fortunately for Spain the circumstances of 1576 were unique. No subsequent group of mutineers repeated the outrages of the Spaniards at Antwerp; never again was a loyal town sacked by the troops who were supposed to be defending it as Aalst and Antwerp had been. However the collective protests of the troops of the Army of Flanders continued to influence the strategic and political developments of the war. The outbreak of a mutiny among the forces in the field sabotaged the Spanish offensives of 1589, 1593 and 1600; the mutiny of the troops detailed to relieve Groningen in 1594 and Grave in 1599 led to the loss of these important towns; a major mutiny at Diest in 1607 seriously undermined Spain's bargaining position in the negotiations with the Dutch for a cease-fire. Even minor mutinies alarmed the High Command, and with some justice. A number of mutinous garrisons ended their disobedience by selling to the Dutch the places entrusted to their keeping...and the government was always frightened that others, starved of their wages, would do the same. There was also the constant fear that a "general mutiny" of the whole army would break out, as it had in 1576, threatening to bring civil revolution in its wake. Many political decisions were of necessity taken with this threat in mind.

. . . In war-torn England too, the fear that the disorders of the soldiers would provoke social anarchy, which appeared a very real possibility in 1645–7, was a leading factor in shaping Parliament's attitude towards its discontented armed forces. This is, of course, not the only similarity. Both series of military upheavals sprang initially from economic pressure (delay in the payment of wages at a time of high prices) and not from political or social aspirations; both were organized overwhelmingly by the rank-and-file, not by dissident officers or professional agitators; and both followed a recognizable pattern of behaviour which was on the whole moderate and non-violent, culminating in the presentation of a formal petition demanding the redress of legitimate, limited grievances.

The same pattern of collective protest may be observed elsewhere. The mutinies of Queen Elizabeth's[10] forces in Ireland and the Netherlands are an obvious parallel; so are those of the Habsburg troops in Hungary during the "long" Turkish war (1593–1606). The widespread unrest in the Swedish army in Germany in 1633, 1635 and 1647-8 bore an unusually close resemblance to the mutinies of the Army of Flanders and the English Parliamentary armies discussed above because, besides the similarity of organization and aims, they had serious political repercussions: the insubordination of the troops in the 1630s ruined the prestige won for Sweden by Gustavus Adolphus's[11] victories, and in the 1640s it delayed the signing of the peace of Westphalia.[12] Even certain eighteenth-century mutinies clearly belong in the same category, for instance the revolts of the sailors aboard the English fleet in 1797.

Despite the obvious superficial differences, the same pattern of collective protest clearly underlay many of the civilian uprisings of the early modern period as well. Many recent studies have emphasized the moderate demands, the conservative or atavistic motivation, the strict code of behaviour and the self-discipline which characterized popular revolts in France, England and Italy during the sixteenth, seventeenth and eighteenth centuries. This broad similarity need not surprise us. Although some men became permanent, professional soldiers, most did not. At the end of a war the majority of the armed forces were demobilized; in wars of long duration anything between 8 and 80 percent of an army's strength might desert every year and have to be replaced. There was thus a continual interchange of personnel between military and civilian society which would facilitate the transfer of habits and attitudes from one to the other. . . .

[10]Elizabeth I, Queen of England, 1558–1603.

[11]Protestant King of Sweden who defeated the Catholic, imperial forces in Germany during the Thirty Years' War (1618–1648).

[12]1648 treaties that ended the Thirty Years' War.

Who Were the Witches?

CHRISTINA LARNER

During the European witch craze or witch hunt, which lasted from approximately 1450 to 1650, perhaps 100 thousand people were executed by burning, strangulation, or hanging. Fifty thousand died in the slaughter in Germany alone. Countless others were exiled or sentenced to prison, often after having been tortured. Some were even acquitted and returned to their community to be treated as outcasts.

In the last twenty years, the witch craze has interested a number of historians, whose research has added greatly to our knowledge of the alleged witches and those who persecuted them. But there is still much that is not clear. For example, why did the craze begin during the Renaissance and Scientific Revolution, supposed periods of intellectual advance? Certainly the belief in witches was not new, yet the so-called medieval "Dark Ages" witnessed no hunt for witches. Some scholars locate the origins of the craze in folklore, theology, heresy, and changes in the law. Some look to the practice of ceremonial magic among socially prominent individuals or the development of a fictitious stereotype of a small, secret sect of night-flying witches who met regularly and, with the aid of the devil, engaged in ritual murder, cannibalism, incest, and other antihuman activities, and strove to destroy Christian society.

The reasons for the rather sudden end of the craze in the mid-seventeenth century are not clear, either. The overwhelming majority of Europeans continued to believe in the reality of the devil and witches long after courts ceased prosecuting for witchcraft. Did judges experience a crisis of conscience, unsure of their ability to determine if the person before them was a witch? Did the Scientific Revolution's conception of a universe operating through natural law convince those in control of the mechanisms of persecution that Satan's personal intervention would contradict the regularity of nature and was therefore impossible? Or, perhaps, did the fires of the great witch hunt run their course, with Europeans suffering burn-out, exhaustion from the constant fear of witches and of each individual's fear that someday he, too, might be accused?

In this selection, Christina Larner addresses another question that has been central to the scholarly debate over the craze: Who were the accused witches? She is concerned with understanding the typical witch in the Scottish trials, but note her comparisons to witches in England, Germany, France, and Switzerland. She discusses the accused's economic and marital status, personal character, and private life. Above all, Larner seeks to understand why 80 percent of those accused of witchcraft in Scotland were women. To what extent was witch hunting really woman hunting? (And, by the way, why were males accused at all?) The witch in Scotland was considered to be an enemy of God, society, and the state. Why were men, who controlled the courts, so disposed to see women as such enemies?

Christina Larner, *Enemies of God*. (Baltimore: The John Hopkins University Press, 1981), pp. 89-102.

> *It has been suggested that early modern Europe was the most misogynistic (woman-hating) period of European history. Why was there this hatred? How responsible was it for the persecution of women? During this era, more women were killed for witchcraft than for all other capital crimes put together. The witch craze has much to teach us about European society and about the relations between the sexes.*

The witches of Scotland were typical of the witches of rural Europe. They were predominantly poor, middle-aged or elderly women. . . .

. . . The average witch was the wife or widow of a tenant farmer, probably fairly near the bottom of the social structure. If she was categorized in the records at all it was as spouse. . . . It is evident from the accusations that the quarrels which generated them were about the exchange of goods and services in a tenant and sub-tenant economy.

It is hard to speak with great certainty in the absence of more detailed local research on one of the major witchcraft areas such as Fife or East Lothian, but the impression given is slightly different from the English scene, where it is clear that the witches were ninety-three per cent women, and that they were absolutely at the bottom of the social heap. They were the wives or widows of wage labourers; they were on the poor law; they were beggars. The Scottish ones appear on average to be slightly further up the stratification scale. Those really at the bottom of the Scottish scale were the large but unknown number of people who were in a sense outside the system. They were the criminals, paupers, gypsies, entertainers, and wandering wage labourers, all generally summed up under the title of vagabond. . . . In the present state of knowledge it looks as though, while a few belonged to the class of outsiders: wage labourers, servants, and the dispossessed, many of the accused witches had a more or less stable domicile and might be related to people in the neighbourhood who had a formal stake in the feudal structure. The majority, however, appear to have been at the bottom of the formal feudal structure itself; they had at least a house with a kailyard,[1] some were part wage-earner, part tenant-farmer; others were sub-tenants and tenants in a farm-toun.[2] In other words they had a position in society, albeit a lowly and often semi-dependent one, and they did not mean to drop out. Unless someone had a fixed position in the community their reputation was not likely to have a chance to grow. Exceptions of course were those who were banished for witchcraft and

[1] A vegetable garden.
[2] A hamlet centered on land divided among four or more families.

who had to move for that reason, or whose reputation travelled with them. . . .

Suspects were then from the settled rather than the vagabond or outcast poor, and they were predominantly women. Witchcraft was, as elsewhere in Europe, overwhelmingly a woman's crime. It was also in Scotland almost the only woman's crime in this period. . . .

. . . The number of male witches fluctuated, but overall amounted to about one fifth of the whole. If one leaves aside those decades in which the numbers are too low for percentages to have much significance it becomes clear that the proportion of men dropped fairly sharply during the major panics. In the quieter periods the proportion of male suspects was from twenty per cent to twenty-seven per cent; during the epidemics it dropped to eleven per cent to twelve per cent. When demand rose, the supply was more definitely female. The trend, which is the opposite of what Midelfort found for south-western Germany,[3] is quite marked but it is not clear how it should be interpreted. It looks as though male witches needed time to build up a reputation, and that during a crisis, when an instant supply of witches was required, accusers were more likely to resort to classic stereotypes. It looks also as though convicted witches, under pressure to name accomplices, felt they were more likely to convince if they named other women.

Whatever one may make of this fluctuation, however, it is clear that overall the figure for men is higher than Macfarlane found for Essex.[4] . . . Midelfort for south-western Germany and Monter for Switzerland[5] found the overall proportions similar to those of Scotland. The very low proportion of male witch suspects found in England seems rather unusual. The substantial proportion of male witches in most parts of Europe means that a witch was not defined exclusively in female terms. If she were the problem would be simpler, but the two principal characteristics of the witch, malice and alleged supernatural power, are human rather than female characteristics, yet as least four out of five persons to whom they are ascribed are women. Witchcraft was not sex-specific but it was sex-related.

There are two distinct problems about this. The first is that of why witchcraft in Europe was so strongly sex-related. The second is what bearing this sex-relatedness had on outbreaks of witch-hunting. It is

[3]H.C. Erik Midelfort, *Witchhunting in Southwestern Germany, 1562–1684* (Stanford: Stanford University Press, 1972).

[4]A. Macfarlane, *Witchcraft in Tudor and Stuart England* (London: Routledge and Kegan Paul Ltd., 1970).

[5]E.W. Monter, *Witchcraft in France and Switzerland* (Ithaca: Cornell University Press, 1976).

argued here that the relationship between women and the stereotype of witchcraft is quite direct: witches are women; all women are potential witches. The relationship between witch-hunting and woman hunting, however, is less direct. Witches were hunted in the first place as witches. The total evil which they represented was not actually sex-specific. Indeed the Devil himself was male. Witch-hunting was directed for ideological reasons against the enemies of God, and the fact that eighty per cent or more of these were women was, though not accidental, one degree removed from an attack on women as such.

So far as the woman stereotype is concerned witches were seen to be women long before there was a witch-hunt. The stereotype rests on the twin pillars of the Aristotelean view of women as imperfectly human—a failure of the process of conception—and the Judaeo-Christian view of women as the source of sin and the Fall of Man. Since witchcraft involved a rejection of what are regarded as the noblest human attributes women were the first suspects. Women were intrinsically and innately more prone to malice, sensuality, and evil in general, and were less capable of reasoning than men were, but were nevertheless to be feared by men. There are a number of ingredients in this fear: through their life-bearing and menstruating capacities they are potential owners of strange and dangerous powers. . . .

Women are feared as a source of disorder in patriarchal society. Not only are menstruating women to be feared. So too are women as child bearers. It is only by exhibiting total control over the lives and bodies of their women that men can know that their children are their own. They are feared too in the sexual act. The fact that they are receptive, not potent, and can receive indefinitely, whether pleasurably or not, has generated the myth of insatiability. Because it was thought that women through these insatiable lusts might either lead men astray or hold them to ridicule for their incapacity, witches were alleged to cause impotence and to satisfy their own lusts at orgies with demons, animals, and such human males as could also be seduced. James VI was giving a version of the prevailing view when he argued as to why women were more disposed to witchcraft than men:

> The reason is easie: for as that sexe is frailer then men is, so is it easier to be intrapped in these grosse snares of the Devill, as was well proved to be true, by the Serpents deceiving of Eve at the beginning, which makes him the homelier with that sex ever since.

It is perhaps worth noting that the stereotype of the witch is the mirror-opposite of the stereotype of the saint. The witch, through a special relationship with the Devil, performs impious miracles; the saint, through a special relationship with God, performs pious miracles. In the peak period for saints (thirteenth to fourteenth centuries) sanctity was sex-related to males in much the same proportion as witchcraft was later to females. The female stereotype is in fact so strong that in some periods the words woman and witch were almost interchangeable. In twelfth-century Russia when the authorities were looking for witches they simply rounded up the female population. . . .

The presence of up to twenty per cent of males in the European witch-hunt has a variety of explanations. Monter found that male witches in his survey tended to predominate in areas which had a history of confusing witchcraft and heresy. Midelfort found that male suspects tended to be accused of other crimes as well. Urban male suspects could be a source of income to the authorities. This has some parallels with Scotland. . . . The Scottish male suspects . . . have so far all turned out to be either husband or brother of a female suspect, a notorious villain as on the continent, or, in a few cases, a solitary cunning man.[6] The difference between Scotland and England in the proportion of males accused can be accounted for by the fact that the English had very few multiple trials in which male relatives might be embroiled, and the fact that in England cunning folk normally escaped being accused of witchcraft.

Although it can be argued that all women were potential witches, in practice certain types of women were selected or selected themselves. In Scotland those accused of witchcraft can be described, though not with precision, under four heads: those that accepted their own reputation and even found ego-enhancement in the description of a "rank witch' and the power that this gave them in the community; those that had fantasies of the Devil; those who became convinced of their guilt during their inquisition or trial; and those who were quite clear that they were innocent, and who either maintained their innocence to the end or confessed only because of torture or threat of torture. They are all equally interesting in relation to the image of the witch in the community, but those who embraced the role of witch are also interesting in relation to the actual attraction of witchcraft for women.

This attraction of witchcraft is clear when we ask why the witches were drawn from the ranks of the poor. Apart from the obvious fact that it was socially easier to accuse those who were least able to defend themselves witchcraft had a particular attraction for the very poor. It has been pointed out by Thomas[7] that the English witches, who were

---

[6]A cunning man (or woman) practiced so-called white witchcraft, which involved predicting the future, healing, preparing love potions, and recovering lost objects.

[7]Keith Thomas, *Religion and the Decline of Magic* (New York: Charles Scribner's Sons, 1971).

more clearly than the Scottish ones at the bottom of the stratification ladder, were people who felt themselves to be totally impotent. The normal channels of expression were denied to them, and they could not better their condition. Witchcraft, Thomas suggests, was believed to be a means of bettering one's condition when all else had failed. The fear of witchcraft bestowed power on those believed to be witches. A reputation for witchcraft was one possible way of modifying the behaviour of those more advantageously positioned. More than that, it was a direct way of providing benefits for themselves. Although the Demonic Pact does not loom very large in English witchcraft it is made something of a centerpiece by Thomas in the psychology of the self-conscious witch. Those who committed . . . the "mental crime' of the Demonic Pact (that is those who not only consciously believed that they were committing effective acts of malefice, the social crime, but also that they were able to do this because of their relationship with the Devil in the Demonic Pact) also revealed in their confessions the exact nature of the promises which the Devil had made to them. We have moved a long way in rural pre-industrial England and Scotland from the classic aristocratic pacts of the Dr. Faustus type where great creative gifts are on offer in return for the individual immortal soul of the human concerned. The economic value to the Devil of the soul of a seventeenth-century peasant was not so great. With these people, in whom hope is expressed in the most circumspect of terms, we are in the world of relative deprivation. Seventeenth-century English women at the margins of society did not expect that their soul would qualify them for silk and riches. Instead they said that the Devil promised them mere freedom from the extremes of poverty and starvation. He told them, typically, "that they should never want".

The witches of Scotland used exactly the same terminology as those of England, but since the Pact loomed much larger they used it more habitually and more extensively. The Devil's promises were much the same from the time when the pact is first mentioned in Scottish cases until it faded from the collective imagination. John Feane in 1591 related that the Devil had promised him "that he should never want". In 1661 it was the same. The Devil promised Margaret Brysone "That she should never want", Elspeth Blackie, "that she should want nothing", and likewise Agnes Pegavie and Janet Gibson. Bessie Wilson was told by the Devil, "thee art a poor puddled (overworked) body. Will thee be my servant and I will give thee abundance and thee sall never want", and Margaret Porteous was told even more enticingly, that "she should have all the pleasure of the earth". . . . English witches in their exchanges with the Devil were sometimes offered small sums of money which sometimes then turned out to be worthless. . . .

Equally good indicators of their expectations and sense of the economically possible are the more elaborate confessions which include descriptions of witches' meetings. The food and drink said to have been available at these meetings varied a bit; very occasionally it was said to have been unpalatable, usually in circumstances in which the Devil was also perceived as being generally unkind to his servants and beating them up for failures in wickedness. More often it fell within the range of normal peasant fare: oatcakes and ale. Sometimes it was the fare of the landed class: red wine, wheaten cake, and meat.

There are other suggestions than hope of alleviating poverty as to why women might be attracted to witchcraft. . . . In situations of domestic stress and tension in which men resort to violence, women use witchcraft. The female witches in the seventeenth-century Scottish courts may be the equivalent of the males accused of slaughter and murder. This is to assume what is sometimes forgotten in analyses which involve oppressor and oppressed, that women are not more virtuous than dominant males any more than the poor are more virtuous than dominant landlords. They are merely less powerful. . . . Women may turn to cursing to give vent to aggression or exercise power. They may fantasize about the Devil to bring colour to their lives.

The women who sought or involuntarily received the accolade of witch were poor but they were not in Scotland always solitary. The women who were the classic focus of witch accusations were frequently, it turns out, impoverished not because they were widows or single women with no supporters or independent means of livelihood, but were simply married to impoverished men. . . . About half of those whose status is recorded were in fact married at the time of their arrest. Some were solitaries, but solitariness as such does not appear to have been an important element in the composition of a Scottish witch. Nor does ugliness appear to have been of very much importance. . . . The stereotype of the ugly, old woman certainly existed in Scotland, but there is little evidence connecting this stereotype with actual accused witches.

So far as personal as opposed to social characteristics go we are left with the variable of character. This is a notoriously difficult concept to deal with historically. One can sometimes identify character traits in particular individuals. But it is usually hard to say whether these are deviant in terms of standard behaviours of the period. . . . We may observe some of the personal characteristics of the witch; we do not know whether they are characteristic of all seventeenth-century Scottish women near the bottom of the socio-economic hierarchy. . . .

When all this is said, however, the essential individual personality trait does seem to have been that of a ready, sharp and angry tongue. The witch had the Scottish female quality of smeddum: spirit, a refusal to be put down, quarrelsomeness. No cursing: no malefice; no witch.

The richness of language attributed to witches is considerable. Helen Thomas of Dumfries was accused by Agnes Forsyth in August 1657 of having said, "Ane ill sight to you all, and ane ill sight to them that is foremost, that is Agnes Forsyth." . . . Agnes Finnie of the Potterrow in Edinburgh, who was accused in 1642, was alleged to have said that "she should gar the Devil take a bit of the said Bessie Currie", and to John Buchanan at Lambarr, "John, go away, for as you have begun with witches so you shall end with them." . . .

The witch may have been socially and economically in a dependent position, but the factor which often precipitated accusations was the refusal to bring to this situation the deference and subservience which was deemed appropriate to the role. In her dealings with relative equals too she was likely to be just as aggressive.

It is one thing, however, to produce a static ideal-type of the commonest features of the witch. She is a married middle-aged woman of the lower peasant class and she has a sharp tongue and a filthy temper. The problem as with so many stereotypes is that its explanatory force is limited in that not only did a considerable number of Scottish witches not fit the stereotype; an even larger number of people who did, and who lived in the danger zones for witch accusation and prosecution, were never accused or identified in this way. . . .

Without the collective rulemaking by which witchcraft was reconstructed as an offence against society in 1563 and the nature of it redefined during the 1590–91 treason trials, there could have been no Scottish witch-hunt. It is possible to develop this argument further and say there would have been no demonic witches. There were, essentially, no demonic witches in the Highlands and Islands during the period of the hunt, and none in the rest of Scotland before the late sixteenth century. There were plenty of specialists. There were charmers, healers, sooth-sayers, poisoners, owners of the evil eye, and there were cursers. Many of these, particularly the successful cursers, would have been called witches. The difference between them and the seventeenth-century east-coast and lowland witch was two-fold: in the first place, the meaning of the label changed to something at once more precise and more universally anti-social: the new witch was not only the enemy of the individual or even of the locality; she was the enemy of the total society, of the state, and of God; in the second place . . . the new organizational processes both created a demand for the production of witches and at the same time made the production more rewarding to the community. It was these factors that generated activity on the . . . level . . . of interpersonal relations.

In the process of building up a reputation in a community there was one important element which provides a link between the static description of the social and personality types which were most likely to attract accusations of witchcraft, and the identification of those individuals who actually ended up in the courts. This was the accused's friends, relatives, and associates. There was nothing like a link with someone already suspected to set the labelling process going. . . . Evil powers were believed to be transmitted from parent to child (a belief which sits uneasily with the demonic pact). Those cases that have come to light tend to be the ones where mother and daughter were executed together (partly because it is otherwise difficult to identify the relationship when the mother retained her own name while passing her husband's on to the daughter). . . .

Other relationships had their effect as well. In 1629, the sheriff of Haddington was given a commission to try John Carfra, Alison Borthwick, his wife, and Thomas Carfra, his brother. They were also charged with having consulted with Margaret Hamilton and Bernie Carfra, who was, no doubt, another relative, and who had already been burnt for witchcraft. Husband and wife teams were quite common. In West Lothian, in February, 1624, Elspet Paris was tried along with her husband, David Langlandis, and the following month William Falconner, his sister Isobell Falconner, and his wife Marioun Symsoun were tried with a group of other witches. In the same area, in Kirkliston, near Edinburgh, in 1655, William Barton and his wife were strangled and burnt. Mere acquaintanceship however would do perfectly well. When Elspeth Maxwell was tried at Dumfries in 1650 it was alleged that she had been an associate of a woman who had been burnt three years before, and this was a very common item in the depositions. Yet these links and associations are still only an occasional factor in the making of witches. The build up of reputation seems normally to have taken some time, and to have been a dynamic process of social interaction between witch and neighbours with steady mutual reinforcement. . . .

The length of time over which a reputation could be built up varied greatly, a factor which lends support to the suggestion that many reputed witches could live with the reputation for a lifetime and die in their beds, even during the seventeenth century. Some witches who were eventually accused had lived with the label long enough to have acquired a title. In Inverkeithing, in 1631, Walker the Witch was active. Janet Taylor, who was banished from Stirling in 1634 was known as the Witch of Monza. Others had names which simply identified a peculiarity which could make them socially marginal. "Deiff Meg", whose deafness clearly contributed to her reputation, was tried with four others in Berwick in 1629. . . .

Others had a long term reputation without acquiring any special title, and with or without such a title many lived with the reputation for years before they were eventually brought to trial. Janet Wright of

Niddry, near Edinburgh, was said in 1628 to have been by her own confession for the last eighteen or nineteen years "a consulter with the devil has resaved his marks, renunced her baptism and givin herselfe over to the devill's service"; and William Crichtoun of Dunfermline in 1648 "being straitlie posed and dealt with by the ministers and watchers, he came to a confession of sundrie things, and that he hade made a paction with the Devill to be his servand 24 yeirs and more since". . . .

When we turn from the selection of the individual back to the classic characteristics, however, there still remains a problem. What is the relationship between the type of person accused of witchcraft and the growth of witchcraft prosecutions? There is some evidence to suggest that the relationship is a direct one. Witch-hunting *is* woman-hunting or at least it is the hunting of women who do not fulfil the male view of how women ought to conduct themselves. . . .

If we turn to the sphere of ideology the case for witch-hunting being seen as a woman-hunt is more convincing. The stereotype of the witch was not that of the child-woman; it was that of the adult, independent woman. The religion of the Reformation and the Counter Reformation demanded that women for the first time become fully responsible for their own souls. Indeed preachers went out of their way to refer to "men and women' in their sermons. The popularization of religion, however, took away from women with one hand what it gave to them with the other, for the particular form of religion was strongly patriarchal. The ritual and moral inferiority of women was preached along with their new personal responsibility. The status of women became ambiguous under the terms of the new ideology.

Witchcraft as a choice was only possible for women who had free will and personal responsibility attributed to them. This represented a considerable change in the status of women in Scotland at least. Up to the time of the secularization of the crime of witchcraft their mis-demeanours had been the responsibility of husbands and fathers and their punishments the whippings thought appropriate to children. As witches they became adult criminals acting in a manner for which their husbands could not be deemed responsible. The pursuit of witches could therefore be seen as a rearguard action against the emergence of women as independent adults. The women who were accused were those who challenged the patriarchal view of the ideal woman. They were accused not only by men but also by other women because women who conformed to the male image of them felt threatened by any iden-tification with those who did not.

. . . [W]hile witch-hunting and woman-hunting are closely con-nected they cannot be completely identified as one and the same phenomenon. The relationship is at one degree removed. The demand for ideological conformity was simply a much wider one than that aspect of it that concerned the status of women. . . . The pursuit of witches was an end in itself and was directly related to the necessity of enforcing moral and theological conformity. The fact that a high proportion of those selected in this context as deviants were women was indirectly related to this central purpose.

The Rites of Violence: Religious Riot in Sixteenth-Century France

NATALIE Z. DAVIS

Eight religious wars rocked the kingdom of France from 1562 to 1598. Spurred by the grandiose ambitions of the leading aristocratic families and fueled by the religious fervor so characteristic of the Protestant and Catholic Reformations, these civil wars became international wars as Spain sought, and nearly succeeded, to dismember her northern neighbor. The devastation was enormous, as Huguenot (French Protestant) and Catholic armies crisscrossed France. Indeed, by the late 1580s, there were three competing factions: Protestant, ultra-Catholic (receiving support from Spain), and those Frenchmen who placed the state above religion. No wonder, then, that in this ungodly four decades of turmoil, violence and brutality were endemic.

Natalie Davis explores one aspect of violent behavior in late sixteenth-century France: the religious riot. Her article is evidence of the influence of anthropology on history, for she seeks to discover the meaning of the patterns of riot behavior. Davis does not see the riots as class warfare; they drew legitimacy from religious rituals and beliefs. Most notorious of these riots was the St. Bartholomew's Day Massacre of 23–24 August 1572, when Catholics killed perhaps two to three thousand Huguenots in Paris and, later, approximately ten thousand in other parts of France. Davis goes beyond this well-known event to the dynamics of religious riots throughout the kingdom. In attempting to locate common denominators of the many outbreaks of sectarian violence during this very religious period in history, Davis raises important questions. What claims to legality did the rioters have? We are often tempted to dismiss rioters out of hand as lawbreakers, but sixteenth-century participants in crowd violence had quite another perspective. Who participated in the riots? The very poor, hoping to profit from the occasion, or better-placed social groups, committed sincerely to specific goals?

What goals did rioters have? Did they simply lash out at random, unreflective as they acted? Were they organized and did they plan their acts of desecration, brutality, and death?

Davis's examination of the idea of pollution places us in the midst of the religious crowd. Sixteenth-century Catholics were certain that Protestants (who in turn believed the same about Catholics) profaned God and the community by their actions and even by their very existence. Was there not, then, an obligation, a duty to society and to God to remove the uncleanliness and profanation? How

Natalie Zemon Davis, "The Rites of Violence: Religious Riot in Sixteenth-Century France" *Past and Present* 59 (May 1973): 51–91.

*could a sincere Christian in the sixteenth century permit defilement by others
who threatened to overturn society, to rupture what should be, according to both
Catholics and Protestants, a society unified by the one faith and only one faith?
French people did not believe in the virtue of religious toleration. In fact, religious
toleration was thought to be injurious to God and to God's plan. What were the
differences between Catholic and Protestant riots? How did the belief systems of
each religion determine the types of violence practiced by its adherents? Finally,
when did the riots most often occur?*

*In conclusion, we are left with great insight as to the mentality of these
religious people, for we know of their greatest fears and the steps they were
prepared to take to alleviate those fears. Were they justified? And was such violence
extraordinary or usual in Reformation France?*

These are the statutes and judgements, which ye shall observe to do in the
land, which the Lord God of thy fathers giveth thee . . . Ye shall utterly
destroy all the places wherein the nations which he shall possess served
their gods, upon the high mountains, and upon the hills, and under every
green tree:

And ye shall overthrow their altars, and break their pillars and burn
their groves with fire; and ye shall hew down the graven images of their
gods, and destroy the names of them out of that place [Dueteronomy xii.
1–3].

Thus a Calvinist pastor to his flock in 1562.

If thy brother, the son of thy mother, or thy son, or thy daughter, or the
wife of thy bosom, or thy friend, which is as thine own soul, entice thee
secretly, saying Let us go serve other gods, which thou hast not known,
thou, nor thy fathers . . . Thou shalt not consent unto him, nor hearken
unto him . . . But thou shalt surely kill him; thine hand shall be first upon
him to put him to death, and afterwards the hand of all the people. . . .

If thou shalt hear say in one of thy cities, which the Lord thy God
hath given thee to dwell there, saying, Certain men, the children of Belial
are gone out from among you, and have withdrawn the inhabitants of
their city, saying Let us go and serve other gods, which ye have not
known . . . Thou shalt surely smite the inhabitants of that city with the edge
of the sword, destroying it utterly and all that is therein [Deuteronomy xiii.
6, 8–9, 12–13, 15].

And [Jehu] lifted up his face to the window and said, Who is on my
side? Who? And there looked out to him two or three eunuchs. And he
said, Throw her down. So they threw [Jezebel] down: and some of her
blood was sprinkled on the wall, and on the horses: and he trode her under

foot . . . And they went to bury her: but they found no more of her than the skull and the feet and the palms of her hands . . . And [Jehu] said, This is the word of the Lord, which he spake by his servant Elijah . . . saying, In the portion of Jezreel shall dogs eat the flesh of Jezebel: and the carcase of Jezebel shall be as dung upon the face of the field [II Kings ix. 32–3, 35–7].

Thus in 1568 Parisian preachers held up to their Catholic parishioners the end of a wicked idolater. Whatever the intentions of pastors and priests, such words were among the many spurs to religious riot in sixteenth-century France. By religious riot I mean, as a preliminary definition, any violent action, with words or weapons, undertaken against religious targets by people who are not acting *officially and formally* as agents of political and ecclesiastical authority. As food rioters bring their moral indignation to bear upon the state of the grain market, so religious rioters bring their zeal to bear upon the state of men's relations to the sacred. The violence of the religious riot is distinguished, at least in principle, from the action of political authorities, who can legally silence, humiliate, demolish, punish, torture and execute; and also from the action of soldiers, who at certain times and places can legally kill and destroy. In mid sixteenth-century France, all these sources of violence were busily producing, and it is sometimes hard to tell a militia officer from a murderer and a soldier from a statue-smasher. Nevertheless, there are occasions when we can separate out for examination a violent crowd set on religious goals. . . .

. . . We may see these crowds as prompted by political and moral traditions which legitimize and even prescribe their violence. We may see urban rioters not as miserable, uprooted, unstable masses, but as men and women who often have some stake in their community; who may be craftsmen or better; and who, even when poor and unskilled, may appear respectable to their everyday neighbours. Finally, we may see their violence, however cruel, not as random and limitless, but as aimed at defined targets and selected from a repertory of traditional punishments and forms of destruction. . . .

. . . My first purpose is to describe the shape and structure of the religious riot in French cities and towns, especially in the 1560s and early 1570s. We will look at the goals, legitimation and occasions for riots; at the kinds of action undertaken by the crowds and the targets for their violence; and briefly at the participants in the riots and their organization. We will consider differences between Protestant and Catholic styles of crowd behaviour, but will also indicate the many ways in which they are alike. . . .

What then can we learn of the goals of popular religious violence? What were the crowds intending to do and why did they think they must do it? Their behaviour suggests, first of all, a goal akin to preaching: the defence of true doctrine and the refutation of false doctrine through dramatic challenges and tests. "You blaspheme", shouts a woman to a Catholic preacher in Montpellier in 1558 and, having broken the decorum of the service, leads part of the congregation out of the church. "You lie", shouts a sheathmaker in the midst of the Franciscan's Easter sermon in Lyon, and his words are underscored by the gunshots of Huguenots waiting in the square. "Look", cries a weaver in Tournai, as he seizes the elevated host from the priest, "deceived people, do you believe this is the King, Jesus Christ, the true God and Saviour? Look!" And he crumbles the wafer and escapes. "Look", says a crowd of image-breakers to the people of Albiac in 1561, showing them the relics they have seized from the Carmelite monastery, "look, they are only animal bones". And the slogan of the Reformed crowds as they rush through the streets of Paris, of Toulouse, of La Rochelle, of Angoulême is "The Gospel! The Gospel! Long live the Gospel!"

Catholic crowds answer this kind of claim to truth in Angers by taking the French Bible, well-bound and gilded, seized in the home of a rich merchant, and parading it through the streets on the end of a halberd. "There's the truth hung. There's the truth of the Huguenots, the truth of all the devils". Then, throwing it into the river, "There's the truth of all the devils drowned". And if the Huguenot doctrine was true, why didn't the Lord come and save them from their killers? So a crowd of Orléans Catholic taunted its victims in 1572: "Where is your God? Where are your prayers and Psalms? Let him save you if he can". Even the dead were made to speak in Normandy and Provence, where leaves of the Protestant Bible were stuffed into the mouths and wounds of corpses. "They preached the truth of their God. Let them call him to their aid".

The same refutation was, of course, open to Protestants. A Protestant crowd corners a baker guarding the holy-wafer box in Saint Médard's Church in Paris in 1561. "Messieurs", he pleads, "do not touch it for the honour of Him who dwells here". "Does your God of paste protect you now from the pains of death?" was the Protestant answer before they killed him. True doctrine can be defended in sermon or speech, backed up by the magistrate's sword against the heretic. Here it is a defended by dramatic demonstration, backed up by the violence of the crowd.

A more frequent goal of these riots, however, is that of ridding the community of dreaded pollution. The word "pollution" is often on the lips of the violent, and the concept serves well to sum up the dangers which rioters saw in the dirty and diabolic enemy. A priest brings ornaments and objects for singing the Mass into a Bordeaux jail. The

Protestant prisoner smashes them all. "Do you want to blaspheme the Lord's name everywhere? Isn't it enough that the temples are defiled? Must you also profane prisons so nothing is unpolluted?" "The Calvinists have polluted their hands with every kind of sacrilege men can think of", writes a Doctor of Theology in 1562. Not long after at the Sainte Chapelle,[1] a man seizes the elevated host with his "polluted hands" and crushes it under foot. The worshippers beat him up and deliver him to the agents of Parlement.[2]. . .

One does not have to listen very long to sixteenth-century voices to hear the evidence for the uncleanliness and profanation of either side. As for the Protestants, Catholics knew that, in the style of earlier heretics, they snuffed out the candles and had sexual intercourse after the voluptuous Psalmsinging of their nocturnal conventicles. . . . But it was not just the fleshly licence with which they lived which was unclean, but the things they said in their "pestilential" books and the things they did in hatred of the Mass, the sacraments and whole Catholic religion. As the representative of the clergy said at the Estates[3] of Orléans, the heretics intended to leave "no place in the Kingdom which was dedicated, holy and sacred to the Lord, but would only profane churches, demolish altars and break images".

The Protestants' sense of Catholic pollution also stemmed to some extent from their sexual uncleanness, here specifically of the clergy. Protestant polemic never tired of pointing to the lewdness of the clergy with their "concubines". It was rumoured that the Church of Lyon had an organization of hundreds of women, sort of temple prostitutes, at the disposition of priests and canons; and an observer pointed out with disgust how, after the First Religious War,[4] the Mass and the brothel re-entered Rouen together. One minister even claimed that the clergy were for the most part Sodomites. But more serious than the sexual abominations of the clergy was the defilement of the sacred by Catholic ritual life, from the diabolic magic of the Mass to the idolatrous worship of images. The Mass is "vile filth"; "no people pollute the House of the Lord in every way more than the clergy". Protestant converts talked of their own past lives as a time of befoulment and dreaded present "contamination" from Catholic churches and rites.

Pollution was a dangerous thing to suffer in a community, from

[1] A Gothic church in Paris, built in the thirteenth century to house relics.

[2] The Parlement of Paris, a sovereign judicial court with jurisdiction over approximately one-half of France.

[3] The Estates in French provinces were assemblies that maintained relations with the central government and dealt with provincial affairs.

[4] 1562–1563.

either a Protestant or a Catholic point of view, for it would surely provoke the wrath of God. Terrible wind storms and floods were sometimes taken as signs of His impatience on this count. Catholics, moreover, had also to worry about offending Mary and the saints; and
though the anxious, expiatory processions organized in the wake of
Protestant sacrilege might temporarily appease them, the heretics were
sure to strike again. It is not surprising, then, that so many of the acts
of violence performed by Catholic and Protestant crowds have . . . the
character either of rites of purification or of a paradoxical desecration,
intended to cut down on uncleanness by placing profane things, like
chrism, back in the profane world where they belonged. . . .

For Catholic zealots, the extermination of the heretical "vermin"
promised the restoration of unity to the body social and the guarantee
of its traditional boundaries:

> *And let us all say in unison:*
> *Long live the Catholic religion*
> *Long live the King and good parishioners,*
> *Long live faithful Parisians,*
> *And may it always come to pass*
> *That every person goes to Mass,*
> *One God, one Faith, one King.*

For Protestant zealots, the purging of the priestly "vermin" promised
the creation of a new kind of unity within the body social, all the
tighter because false gods and monkish sects would no longer divide
it. Relations within the social order would be purer, too, for lewdness
and love of gain would be limited. As was said of Lyon after its "deliv-
erance" in 1562:

> . . . .
> *When this town so vain*
> *Was filled*
> *With idolatry and dealings*
> *Of usury and lewdness,*
> *It had clerics and merchants aplenty.*
>
> *But once it was purged*
> *And changed*
> *By the Word of God,*
> *That brood of vipers*
> *Could hope no more*
> *To live in so holy a place.*

Crowds might defend truth, and crowds might purify, but there
was also a third aspect to the religious riot—a political one. . . .

. . . When the magistrate had not used his sword to defend the faith and the true church and to punish the idolators, then the crowd would do it for him. Thus, many religious disturbances begin with the ringing of the tocsin, as in a time of civic assembly or emergency. Some riots end with the marching of the religious "wrongdoers" on the other side to jail. In 1561, for instance, Parisian Calvinists, fearing that the priests and worshippers in Saint Médard's Church were organizing an assault on their services . . . , first rioted in Saint Médard and then seized some fifteen Catholics as "mutinous" and led them off, "bound like galley-slaves", to the Châtelet prison.

If the Catholic killing of Huguenots has in some ways the form of a rite of purification, it also sometimes has the form of imitating the magistrate. The mass executions of Protestants at Merindol and Cabri³eres in Provence and at Meaux in the 1540s, duly ordered by the Parlements of Aix and of Paris as punishment for heresy and high treason, anticipate crowd massacres of later decades. The Protestants themselves sensed this: the devil, unable to extinguish the light of the Gospel through the sentences of judges, now tried to obscure it through furious war and a murderous populace. Whereas before they were made martyrs by one executioner, now it is at the hands of "infinite numbers of them, and the swords of private persons have become the litigants, witnesses, judges, decrees and executors of the strangest cruelties".

Similarly, *official* acts of torture and *official* acts of desecration of the corpses of certain criminals anticipate some of the acts performed by riotous crowds. The public execution was, of course, a dramatic and well-attended event in the sixteenth century, and the wood-cut and engraving documented the scene far and wide. There the crowd might see the offending tongue of the blasphemer pierced or slit, the offending hands of the desecrator cut off. There the crowd could watch the traitor decapitated and disemboweled, his corpse quartered and the parts borne off for public display in different sections of the town. The body of an especially heinous criminal was dragged through the streets, attached to a horse's tail. The image of exemplary royal punishment lived on for weeks, even years, as the corpses of murderers were exposed on gallows or wheels and the heads of rebels on posts. . . . [C]rowds often took their victims to places of official execution, as in Paris in 1562, when the Protestant printer, Roc Le Frere, was dragged for burning to the Marché aux Pourceaux, and in Toulouse the same year, when a merchant, slain in front of a church, was dragged for burning to the town hall. "The King salutes you", said a Catholic crowd in Orléans to a Protestant trader, then put a cord around his neck as official agents might do, and led him off to be killed.

Riots also occurred in connection with judicial cases, either to hurry the judgement along, or when verdicts in religious cases were considered too severe or too lenient by "the voice of the people". Thus in 1569 in Montpellier, a Catholic crowd forced the judge to condemn an important Huguenot prisoner to death in a hasty "trial", then seized him and hanged him in front of his house. . . . And in 1561 in Marsillargues, when prisoners for heresy were released by royal decree, a Catholic crowd "rearrested" them, and executed and burned them in the streets. . . .

The seizure of religious buildings and the destruction of images by Calvinist crowds were also accomplished with the conviction that they were taking on the rôle of the authorities. When Protestants in Montpellier occupied a church in 1561, they argued that the building belonged to them already, since its clergy had been wholly supported by merchants and burghers in the past and the property belonged to the town. . . .

To be sure, the relation of a French Calvinist crowd to the magisterial model is different from that of a French Catholic crowd. The king had not yet chastised the clergy and "put all ydolatry to ruyne and confusyon", as Protestants had been urging him since the early 1530s. Calvinist crowds were using his sword as the king *ought* to have been using it and as some princes and city councils outside of France had already used it. Within the kingdom before 1560 city councils had only *indicated* the right path, as they set up municipal schools, lay-controlled welfare systems or otherwise limited the sphere of action of the clergy. During the next years, as revolution and conversion created Reformed city councils and governors (such as the Queen of Navarre) within France, Calvinist crowds finally had local magistrates whose actions they could prompt or imitate.

In general, then, the crowds in religious riots in sixteenth-century France can be seen as sometimes acting out clerical rôles—defending true doctrine or ridding the community of defilement in a violent version of priest or prophet—and as sometimes acting out magisterial rôles. Clearly some riotous behaviour, such as the extensive pillaging done by both Protestants and Catholics, cannot be subsumed under these heads; but just as the prevalence of pillaging in a war does not prevent us from typing it as a holy war, so the prevalence of pillaging in a riot should not prevent us from seeing it as essentially religious. . . .

So long as rioters maintained a given religious commitment, they rarely displayed guilt or shame for their violence. By every sign, the crowds believed their actions legitimate.

One reason for this conviction is that in some, though by no means all, religious riots, clerics and political officers were active members of the crowd, though not precisely in their official capacity. In Lyon in 1562, Pastor Jean Ruffy took part in the sack of the Cathedral of

Saint Jean with a sword in his hand. Catholic priests seem to have been in quite a few disturbances, as in Rouen in 1560, when priests and parishioners in a Corpus Christi parade[5] broke into the houses of Protestants who had refused to do the procession honour. . . .

On the other hand, not all religious riots could boast of officers or clergy in the crowd, and other sources of legitimation must be sought. Here we must recognize what mixed cues were given out by priests and pastors in their sermons on heresy or idolatry. . . . However much Calvin[6] and other pastors opposed such disturbances (preferring that all images and altars be removed soberly by the authorities), they nevertheless were always more ready to understand and excuse this violence than, say, that of a peasant revolt or of a journeymen's march. Perhaps, after all, the popular idol-smashing was due to "an extraordinary power (*vertu*) from God.". . .

The rôle of Catholic preachers in legitimating popular violence was even more direct. If we don't know whether to believe the Protestant claim that Catholic preachers at Paris were telling their congregations in 1557 that Protestants ate babies, it is surely significant that . . . Catholic preachers did blame the loss of the battle of Saint Quentin[7] on God's wrath at the presence of heretics in France. . . . And if Protestant pastors could timidly wonder if divine power were not behind the extraordinary force of the iconoclasts, priests had no doubts that certain miraculous occurrences in the wake of Catholic riots were a sign of divine approval, such as a copper cross in Troyes that began to change colour and cure people in 1561, the year of a riot in which Catholics bested Protestants. . . .

In all likelihood, however, there are sources for the legitimation of popular religious riot that come directly out of the experience of the local groups which often formed the nucleus of a crowd—the men and women who had worshipped together in the dangerous days of the night conventicles, the men in confraternities, in festive groups, in youth gangs and militia units. It should be remembered how often conditions in sixteenth-century cities required groups of "little people" to take the law into their own hands. Royal edicts themselves enjoined any person who saw a murder, theft or other misdeed to ring the tocsin and chase after the criminal. Canon law allowed certain priestly rôles to laymen in times of emergency, such as the midwife's responsibility

[5]A Roman Catholic festival instituted in the thirteenth century to honor the Blessed Sacrament (the body of Jesus).

[6]John Calvin (1509–1564), French Protestant theologian, founder of Calvinism and religious leader of Geneva.

[7]Spanish victory over the French in 1557.

to baptize a baby in danger of dying, while the rôle of preaching the Gospel was often assumed by Protestant laymen in the decades before the Reformed Church was set up. . . .

. . . [T]he occasion for most religious violence was during the time of religious worship or ritual and in the space which one or both groups were using for sacred purposes. . . .

Almost every type of public religious event has a disturbance associated with it. The sight of a statue of the Virgin at a crossroad or in a wall-niche provokes a Protestant group to mockery of those who reverence her. A fight ensues. Catholics hide in a house to entrap Huguenots who refuse to doff their hats to a Virgin nearby, and then rush out and beat the heretics up. Baptism: in Nemours, a Protestant family has its baby baptized on All Souls' Day[8] according to the new Reformed rite. With the help of an aunt, a group of Catholics steals it away for rebaptism. A drunkard sees the father and the godfather and other Protestants discussing the event in the streets, claps his sabots and shouts, "Here are the Huguenots who have come to massacre us". A crowd assembles, the tocsin is rung, and a three-hour battle takes place. Funeral: in Toulouse, at Easter-time, a Protestant carpenter tries to bury his Catholic wife by the new Reformed rite. A Catholic crowd seizes the corpse and buries it. The Protestants dig it up and try to rebury her. The bells are rung, and with a great noise a Catholic crowd assembles with stones and sticks. Fighting and sacking ensue.

Religious services: a Catholic Mass is the occasion for an attack on the Host or the interruption of a sermon, which then leads to a riot. Protestant preaching in a home attracts large Catholic crowds at the door, who stone the house or otherwise threaten the worshippers. . . .

But these encounters are as nothing compared to the disturbances that cluster around processional life. Corpus Christi Day, with its crowds, coloured banners and great crosses, was the chance for Protestants *not* to put rugs in front of their doors; for Protestant women to sit ostentatiously in their windows spinning; for heroic individuals, like the painter Denis de Vallois in Lyon, to throw themselves on the "God of paste" so as "to destroy him in every parish in the world". Corpus Christi Day was the chance for a procession to turn into an assault on and slaughter of those who had so offended the Catholic faith, its participants shouting, as in Lyon in 1561, "For the flesh of God, we must kill all the Huguenots". A Protestant procession was a parade of armed men and women in their dark clothes, going off to services at their temple or outside the city gates, singing Psalms and spiritual songs that to Catholic ears sounded like insults against the Church and

---

[8]Commemoration of the souls of the departed, celebrated on 2 November.

her sacraments. It was an occasion for children to throw stones, for an exchange of scandalous words—"idolaters", "devils from the Pope's purgatory", "Huguenot heretics, living like dogs"—and then finally for fighting. . . .

The occasions which express most concisely the contrast between the two religious groups, however, are those in which a popular festive Catholicism took over the streets with dancing, masks, banners, costumes and music—"lascivious abominations", according to the Protestants. . . .

As with liturgical rites, there were some differences between the rites of violence of Catholic and Protestant crowds. . . .

. . . [T]he iconoclastic Calvinist crowds . . . come out as the champions in the destruction of religious property ("with more than Turkish cruelty", said a priest). This was not only because the Catholics had more physical accessories to their rite, but also because the Protestants sensed much more danger and defilment in the *wrongful use of material objects*. . . .

In bloodshed the Catholics are the champions (remember we are talking of the actions of Catholic and Protestant crowds, not of their armies). I think this is due not only to their being in the long run the strongest party numerically in most cities, but also to their stronger sense of *the persons of heretics* as sources of danger and defilment. Thus, injury and murder were a preferred mode of purifying the body social.

Furthermore, the preferred targets for physical attack differ in the Protestant and Catholic cases. As befitting a movement intending to overthrow a thousand years of clerical "tyranny' and "pollution", the Protestants' targets were primarily priests, monks and friars. That their ecclesiastical victims were usually unarmed (as Catholic critics hastened to point out) did not make them any less harmful in Protestant eyes, or any more immune from the wrath of God. Lay people were sometimes attacked by Protestant crowds, too, such as the festive dancers who were stoned at Pamiers and Lyon, and the worshippers who were killed at Saint-Médard's Church. But there is nothing that quite resembles the style and extent of the slaughter of the 1572 massacres. The Catholic crowds were, of course, happy to catch a pastor when they could, but the death of any heretic would help in the cause of cleansing France of these perfidious sowers of disorder and disunion. . . .

. . . [T]he overall picture in these urban religious riots is not one of the "people" slaying the rich. Protestant crowds expressed no preference for killing or assaulting powerful prelates over simple priests. As for Catholic crowds, contemporary listings of their victims in the 1572 massacres show that artisans, the "little people", are represented in significant numbers. . . .

. . . Let us look a little further at what I have called their rites of violence. Is there any way we can order the terrible, concrete details of filth, shame and torture that are reported from both Protestant and Catholic riots? I would suggest that they can be reduced to a repertory of actions, derived from the Bible, from the liturgy, from the action of political authority, or from the traditions of popular folk justice, intended to purify the religious community and humiliate the enemy and thus make him less harmful.

The religious significance of destruction by water or fire is clear enough. The rivers which receive so many Protestant corpses are not merely convenient mass graves, they are temporarily a kind of holy water, an essential feature of Catholic rites of exorcism. . . .

Let us take a more difficult case, the troubling case of the desecration of corpses. This is primarily an action of Catholic crowds in the sixteenth century. Protestant crowds could be very cruel indeed in torturing living priests, but paid little attention to them when they were dead. (Perhaps this is related to the Protestant rejection of Purgatory and prayers for the dead: the souls of the dead experience immediately Christ's presence or the torments of the damned, and thus the dead body is no longer so dangerous or important an object to the living.) What interested Protestants was digging up bones that were being treated as sacred objects by Catholics and perhaps burning them, after the fashion of Josiah in I Kings. The Catholics, however, were not content with burning or drowning heretical corpses. That was not cleansing enough. The bodies had to be weakened and humiliated further. To an eerie chorus of "strange whistles and hoots", they were thrown to the dogs like Jezebel, they were dragged through the streets, they had their genitalia and internal organs cut away, which were then hawked through the city in a ghoulish commerce.

Let us also take the embarrassing case of the desecration of religious objects by filthy and disgusting means. It is the Protestants . . . who are concerned about objects, who are trying to show that Catholic objects of worship have no magical power. It is not enough to cleanse by swift and energetic demolition, not enough to purify by a great public burning of the images, as in Albiac, with the children of the town ceremonially reciting the Ten Commandments around the fire. The line between the sacred and the profane was also re-drawn by throwing the sacred host to the dogs, by roasting the crucifix upon a spit, by using holy oil to grease one's boots, and by leaving human excrement on holy-water basins and other religious objects.

And what of the living victims? Catholics and Protestants humiliated them by techniques borrowed from the repertory of folk justice. Catholic crowds lead Protestant women through the streets with muzzles on—a popular punishment for the shrew—or with a crown of thorns. A form of charivari[9] is used, where the noisy throng humiliates its victim by making him ride backward on an ass. . . . In Montauban, a priest was ridden backward on an ass, his chalice in one hand, his host in the other, and his missal at an end of a halberd. At the end of his ride, he must crush his host and burn his own vestments. . . .

These episodes disclose to us the underlying function of the rites of violence. As with the "games" of Christ's tormentors, which hide from them the full knowledge of what they do, so these charades and ceremonies hide from sixteenth-century rioters a full knowledge of what they are doing. Like the legitimation for religious riot . . . , they are part of the "conditions for guilt-free massacre". . . . The crucial fact that the killers must forget is that their victims are human beings. These harmful people in the community—the evil priest or hateful heretic— have already been transformed for the crowd into "vermin" or "devils". The rites of religious violence complete the process of dehumanization. So in Meaux, where Protestants were being slaughtered with butchers' cleavers, a living victim was trundled to his death in a wheelbarrow, while the crowd cried "vinegar, mustard". And the vicar of the parish of Fouquebrune in the Angoumois was attached with the oxen to a plough and died from Protestant blows as he pulled.

What kinds of people made up the crowds that performed the range of acts we have examined in this paper? First, they were not by and large the alienated rootless poor that people the pages of Norman Cohn's *Pursuit of the Millennium*. A large percentage of men in Protestant iconoclastic riots and in the crowds of Catholic killers in 1572 were characterized as artisans. Sometimes the crowds included other men from the lower orders. . . . More often, the social composition of the crowds extended upward to encompass merchants, notaries and lawyers, as well as clerics. . . .

In addition, there was significant participation by two other groups of people who, though not rootless and alienated, had a more marginal relationship to political power than did lawyers, merchants or even male artisans—namely, city women and teenaged boys. . . .

Finally, as this study has already suggested, the crowds of Catholics and Protestants, including those bent on deadly tasks, were not an inchoate mass, but showed many signs of organization. Even with riots that had little or no planning behind them, the event was given some structure by the situation of worship or the procession that was the occasion for many disturbances. In other cases, planning in advance led to lists of targets, and ways of identifying friends or fellow rioters. . . .

That such splendor and order should be put to violent uses is

---

[9]Davis defines this elsewhere as "a noisy, masked demonstration to humiliate some wrongdoer in the community."

a disturbing fact. Disturbing, too, is the whole subject of religious violence. How does an historian talk about a massacre of the magnitude of St. Bartholomew's Day? One approach is to view extreme religious violence as an extraordinary event, the product of frenzy, of the frustrated and paranoic primitive mind of the people.

A second approach sees such violence as a more usual part of social behaviour, but explains it as a somewhat pathological product of certain kinds of child-rearing, economic deprivation or status loss. This paper has assumed that conflict is perennial in social life, though the forms and strength of the accompanying violence vary; and that religious violence is intense because it connects intimately with the fundamental values and self-definition of a community. The violence is explained not in terms of how crazy, hungry or sexually frustrated the violent people are (though they may sometimes have such characteristics), but in terms of the goals of their actions and in terms of the rôles and patterns of behaviour allowed by their culture. Religious violence is related here less to the pathological than to the normal.

Thus, in sixteenth-century France, we have seen crowds taking on the rôle of priest, pastor or magistrate to defend doctrine or purify the religious community, either to maintain its Catholic boundaries and structure, or to re-form relations within it. We have seen that popular religious violence could receive legitimation from different features of political and religious life, as well as from the group identity of the people in the crowds. The targets and character of crowd violence differed somewhat between Catholics and Protestants, depending on their perception of the source of danger and on their religious sensibility. But in both cases, religious violence had a connection in time, place and form with the life of worship, and the violent actions themselves were drawn from a store of punitive or purificatory traditions current in sixteenth-century France.

In this context, the cruelty of crowd action in the 1572 massacres was not an exceptional occurrence. St. Bartholomew was certainly a bigger affair than, say, the Saint Médard's riot, it had more explicit sanction from political authority, it had elaborate networks of communication at the top level throughout France, and it took a more terrible toll in deaths. Perhaps its most unusual feature was that the Protestants did not fight back. But on the whole, it still fits into a whole pattern of sixteenth-century religious disturbance.

This inquiry also points to a more general conclusion. Even in the extreme case of religious violence, crowds do not act in a mindless way. They will to some degree have a sense that what they are doing is legitimate, the occasions will relate somehow to the defence of their cause, and their violent behaviour will have some structure to it— here dramatic and ritual. But the rites of violence are not the rights of violence in any *absolute* sense. They simply remind us that if we try to increase safety and trust within a community; guarantee that the violence it generates will take less destructive and less cruel forms, then we must think less about pacifying "deviants" and more about changing the central values.

Insanity in Early
Modern England

MICHAEL MACDONALD

Insanity, as Michael MacDonald reminds us, is not the same for all times and places, but is culturally defined. Definitions of what constitutes madness reflect the values of a society. Thus, in England, interpretations of madness and the treatment accorded the insane changed between the sixteenth-century Protestant Reformation and the eighteenth-century Industrial Revolution. What were the most significant of these changes? How do developments in English society explain the increased attention given to the mentally ill?

Many early modern Englishmen looked to family life as a cause of mental disorder. Why? Even the government held the institution of the family to be a primary concern in its efforts to deal with the insane. Thus the Court of Wards and Liveries acted rather honestly and "sanely" when it adjudicated the estates of lunatics. How did the government's behavior toward poor lunatics come to be intertwined with the problem of poverty? Just as the state had the poor locked up in workhouses, so by the eighteenth century did governments, as well as private citizens, establish asylums for the insane. Why did society now condone the confinement of these groups of people who formerly had enjoyed a measure of freedom?

There was great competition in England among those who thought they understood mental disorders. Proponents of magic, religion, and science, which interacted and overlapped in the seventeenth century, disagreed on the causes and treatment of insanity. Should we be more surprised that remedies and explanations offered by physicians did not work or that the élite of England gradually came to accept the claims of medical science? At least supernatural explanations for madness, if perhaps misguided, did not normally harm the mentally disturbed. Exorcisms and faith healing, for example, may have had therapeutic value. On the other hand, medical remedies employed techniques that were seen to be, as MacDonald says, "unpleasant, ineffective, and theoretically insupportable." Why did the ruling classes put their faith in those secular priests, the physicians? How did irrationality come to typify the attitude toward the mentally ill, cruelly treated and incarcerated, during the eighteenth-century "Age of Reason"?

Madness is the most solitary of afflictions to the people who experience it; but is the most social of maladies to those who observe its

Michael MacDonald, *Mystical Bedlam: Madness, Anxiety, and Healing in Seventeenth-Century England* (Cambridge, England: Cambridge University Press, 1981), 1–11.

effects. Every mental disorder alienates its victims from the conventions of action, thought, and emotion that bind us together with the other members of our society. But because mental disorders manifest themselves in their victims' relationships with other men and women, they are more profoundly influenced by social and cultural conditions than any other kind of illness. For this reason the types of insanity people recognize and the significance they attach to them reflect the prevailing values of their society; the criteria for identifying mental afflictions vary between cultures and historical periods. The response to the insane, like the reaction to the sufferers of physical diseases, is also determined by the material conditions, social organization, and systems of thought that characterize a particular culture and age. The methods of caring for mentally disturbed people, the concepts that are used to explain the causes of their maladies, and the techniques that are employed to relieve their anguish are all determined more by social forces than by scientific discoveries, even today. Two central problems, therefore, confront historians of insanity. First, they must show how ideas about mental disorder and methods of responding to it were adapted to the social and intellectual environment of particular historical periods. Second, they must identify changes in the perception and management of insanity and explain how they were related to broader transformations in the society.

The history of mental disorder in early modern England is an intellectual Africa. Historians and literary scholars have mapped its most prominent features and identified some of its leading figures, but we still have very little information about the ideas and experiences of ordinary people. Both the unfortunates who actually suffered from mental afflictions and the men and women who tried to help them still inhabit *terra incognita*. Their story, the social history of insanity between the Reformation and the Industrial Revolution, falls into two distinct eras divided by the cataclysm of the English Revolution. During the late sixteenth and early seventeenth centuries, the English people became more concerned about the prevalence of madness, gloom, and self-murder than they had ever been before, and the reading public developed a strong fascination with classical medical psychology. Nevertheless, conventional beliefs about the nature and causes of mental disorders and the methods of psychological healing continued to reflect the traditional fusion of magic, science, and religion that typified the thinking of laymen of every social rank and educational background. The enormous social and psychological significance of the family shaped contemporary interpretations of insane behavior and determined the arrangements that were made to care for rich and poor lunatics alike. . . . During the century and a half following the great upheaval of the English Revolution, the governing classes embraced secular interpretations of the signs of insanity and championed medical methods of curing mental disorders. They shunned magical and religious techniques of psychological healing. Private entrepreneurs founded specialized institutions to manage mad people, and municipal officials established public madhouses. The asylum movement eventually transferred the responsibility for maintaining lunatics out of the family and into the asylum. Madmen were removed from their normal social surroundings and incarcerated with others of their kind; lunatics lost their places as members of a household and acquired new identities as the victims of mental diseases.

Interest in insanity quickened about 1580, and madmen, melancholics, and suicides became familiar literary types. Scientific writers popularized medical lore about melancholy, and clergymen wrote treatises about consoling the troubled in mind. Gentlemen and ladies proclaimed themselves melancholy; physicians worried about ways to cure the mentally ill; preachers and politicians denounced sinners and dissenters as melancholics or madmen. Anxious intellectuals claimed that self-murder was epidemical, and they argued about its medical and religious significance. . . . Heightened concern about the nature and prevalence of mental disorders was fostered by the increasing size and complexity of English society. Population growth and economic change increased the numbers of insane and suicidal people and overburdened the capacity of families and local communities to care for the sick and indigent. Renaissance humanism set new standards of conduct for the nobility, and the turbulent and incomplete triumph of Protestantism fragmented English society into religious groups with sharply differing views about how people ought to behave. The adequacy of traditional codes of conduct was subjected to intense criticism by learned reformers and religious zealots, and both humanist intellectuals and Puritan clergymen were naturally concerned about the causes and significance of abnormal behavior. Although they often looked to the same sources for ideas about insanity, one can say in general that religious conservatives elaborated classical medical psychology, whereas Puritan evangelists revitalized popular religious psychology and set it in a Calvinist theological framework.

In spite of the increased interest in insanity and the growing controversy about its religious implications, the perception and management of mental disorders did not change fundamentally before 1660. Contemporary ideas about the varieties of mental maladies and their characteristic signs were rooted in ancient science and medieval Christianity, and the typology of insanity was similar all over Western Europe. Within the broad framework of medical and religious thought, however, popular stereotypes of mental disorder were adapted to fit English conditions. For example, widely held beliefs about the behavior of mad and troubled people and the immediate causes of their misery reflected the psychological significance of the family in the lives of ordinary villages. Descriptions of the symptoms of violent madness placed great emphasis on irrational threats toward members of one's immediate family. Traditional legal prohibitions against suicide aimed to prevent it by emphasizing the responsibility of potential self-murders for their family's welfare. Common complaints about the causes of overwhelming anxiety and despair included unrequited love, marital strife, and bereavement. This preoccupation with the family was the consequence of its elemental importance in English society. The household was the basic social unit, and at every level of society it performed a myriad of functions. Within the walls of great houses and cottages children were reared and educated, the sick and infirm were nursed and maintained, estates were managed and goods were manufactured. Most households were very small. Except among the wealthy, whose entourages often included dozens of servants, clients and kin, households normally consisted only of a married couple, their young children, and, in many cases, a servant or apprentice. The small size of domestic groups and the high rate of geographical mobility in early seventeenth-century England greatly enhanced the part that the nuclear family played in the emotional lives of people of low and middling status.

The social importance of the family was also recognized in the arrangements for maintaining mad and troubled people. Only a handful of the insane in a nation of five million souls were cast into an asylum before the English Revolution. Bedlamites[1] swarmed through the imaginations of Jacobean playwrights and pamphleteers, but the famous asylum was in truth a tiny hovel housing fewer than thirty patients. Bethlem Hospital was the only institution of its kind, and its inmates languished there for years, living in squalid conditions without adequate medical treatment. Private institutions to house the insane did not begin to proliferate until the last half of the seventeenth century, municipal asylums to rival Bedlam were not founded in major cities for another century, and county lunatic hospitals were not established until after 1808. Tudor and Stuart governments responded to increasing concern about insanity by refurbishing traditional institutions to help families bear the burden of harboring a madman. The welfare of rich lunatics was guarded by the Court of Wards and Liveries, which exercised the crown's feudal right to manage the affairs of minors who inherited land as tenants-in-chief. Children, idiots, and lunatics were

---

[1]Bedlam and Gedlamites are names derived from Bethlem Hospital in London.

siblings in the eyes of the law, because they all lacked the capacity to reason and so could not be economically and legally responsible.

The Court of Wards was notorious for selling its favors to the highest bidder, allowing guardians who purchased wardships to ruin their charges' estates and bully them into profitable marriages. But toward lunatics the court behaved with uncharacteristic delicacy, repudiating rapacity in favor of family and legitimacy. King James[2] instructed the court to ensure that lunatics "be freely committed to their best and nearest friends, that can receive no benefit by their death, and the committees, bound to answer for...the very just value of their estates upon account, for the benefit of such lunatic (if he recover) or of the next heir." The order was obeyed. The court usually appointed relatives or friends of mad landowners to see that they were cared for and their property preserved. Naturally, there were some sordid struggles for the guardianship of rich lunatics, and sometimes men hurled false accusations of insanity at wealthy eccentrics in hopes of winning a rich wardship. But the court was unusually scrupulous about investigating chicanery when it concerned lunatics, and abuses appear to have been rare. Before a landowner was turned over to a committee of guardians, a jury of local notables was assembled to certify that he had been too mad to manage his estates for a year and more. Such juries relied on common sense and common knowledge to establish that a person was insane, but their chief preoccupation was to discover whether he could perform the necessary economic chores to preserve the family property.

The court and the men who acted as inquisitors and guardians on its behalf behaved more virtuously toward the estates of lunatics than those of minor heirs because there was little profit in the wardship of the insane. Lunacy was regarded as a temporary state and the law decreed that when the madman recovered he should have restored to him all of his property, save the amount the guardians expended for his care. And because lunatics were unreasoning creatures, they could not contract marriages, perhaps the most valuable aspect of the wardship of minors. Legal rules and low incentive to break them effectively protected the rights of insane landowners, and when the Court of Wards was abolished during the Revolution cries were heard that lunatics were now vulnerable to the greed of unscrupulous guardians as never before. . . .

The chief concern of the crown's policy toward insane landowners was to preserve the integrity of their estates so that their lineages would not be obliterated by the economic consequences of their madness. Paupers had no property or social standing to protect, but the Tudor

[2]James I, 1603–1625.

and Stuart state tried also to assist poor lunatics by providing financial relief for their families. After 1601 the government obliged parishes to treat impoverished madmen as "deserving poor," people who, like orphans and cripples, were unable to work through no fault of their own. . . . These allowances were paid out of the funds from local taxation for poor relief, and they were intended to prevent humble families from starvation and fragmentation because the lunatic's labor was lost. A 1658 order by Lancashire justices to provide for Isabell Breatherton illustrates the way the system worked in practice:

> It is ordered by this court that the . . . churchwardens and overseers of the poor within the parish of Wimwick shall . . . take into consideration the distracted condition of Isabell, wife of James Breatherton of Newton and provide for her or allow unto her said husband weekly or monthly allowances as her necessity requires, so as she may be kept from wandering abroad or doing any hurt or prejudice either to herself or otherwise.

As the population grew and the economy became more specialized in the sixteenth and seventeenth centuries, poverty became a major social problem. Municipal governments experimented with new kinds of institutions, such as hospitals and workhouses, in an attempt to find some solution to the increasingly alarming situation, and the crown began slowly to imitate some features of these experiments. In 1609, for example, counties were ordered to establish houses of correction to confine the able-bodied poor and train them for gainful employment; compliance was slow, but by the 1630s every shire[3] had such an institution. Lunatics were sometimes housed in these local Bridewells,[4] but it appears that incarceration was regarded as an exceptional and undesirable expedient. Lancashire officials were reluctant to confine madmen to the county's house of correction if they could avoid it, preferring to leave them in the care of their families whenever possible. For the poor as for the rich, therefore, the Tudor and early Stuart state left the care and management of the insane largely in the hands of their families and attempted to lessen the social and economic impact of lunacy by helping families either directly through the Court of Wards or indirectly through the parishes.

Early seventeenth-century methods of explaining the natural and supernatural causes of insanity and relieving the suffering of its victims were marked by a traditional mingling of magical, religious, and scientific concepts. Individual cases of mental disorder might be

[3]A district in England coinciding roughly with a modern county.
[4]Jails, named after the London house of correction.

attributed to divine retribution, diabolical possession, witchcraft, astrological influences, humoral imbalances,[5] or to any combination of these forces. Cures were achieved (in theory) by removing the causes of the sufferer's disturbance, and the means to combat every kind of malign effect were dispensed by a bewildering array of healers. Insane men and women were treated by specialists, such as humanistic physicians, who practiced a single method of psychological healing, or they were consoled by eclectics, such as medical astrologers or clerical doctors, who combined remedies from several systems of therapy. The profusion of causal explanations for insanity and of healing methods was not simply the result of the inchoate state of the medical profession. It was also a practical manifestation of the popular confidence that magic, religion, and science could be reconciled. Medieval and Renaissance cosmology provided a systematic model for making such a reconciliation, and on a less sophisticated plane popular religious thought fused religious and magical beliefs.

Classical medical psychology became very popular among the educated classes during the sixteenth and seventeenth centuries. It was disseminated by the physicians, who were increasingly articulate and well-organized, and by humanist intellectuals, who were often clerics and medical amateurs. . . . Although the remedies sanctioned by natural scientific theories were no more effective than religious or magical treatments for mental disorder, the medical approach eventually prevailed over supernatural explanations for the causes of madness. In the early seventeenth century the natural and supernatural approaches coexisted uneasily, championed by rival groups of professionals, to be sure, but not yet incompatible to many minds. Humanistic physicians battled to secure a monopoly over the care of sick and insane people and to make their trade proof against the interloping of clerical doctors, apothecaries, surgeons, astrologers, and village wizards. . . .

. . . Medical practice was a natural extension of ministers' duty to relieve the afflictions of their flocks, and a great many rural rectors and vicars provided various kinds of medical services for their parishioners. Medicine was an essential aspect of the astrologers' art, and occultists of every degree of rank and learning, from highly educated university graduates to illiterate village wise folk, used astrology as a tool for medical diagnosis and prognostication. The doctors could do little to prevent clergymen from practicing their craft, because the church and the universities had the power to license medical practitioners, and neither was likely to concur that learned clerks who practiced medicine

---

[5]Physicians believed that sickness was caused by an imbalance among the four humors (yellow bile, black bile, phlegm, and blood).

were as culpable as ignorant quacks. Humanistic physicians could not possibly supply all the medical needs of the English people, and so long as clerical doctors, and indeed astrologers and cunning men and women,[6] did not slaughter their patients and garnered reputations for effective treatments, the authorities were inclined to grant them licenses to practice medicine legally. In London and its suburbs, however, the College of Physicians were empowered to fine unlicensed practitioners, and the privilege was used to harass popular astrologers and empirics. . . . The doctors' efforts to persuade the public that scientific medicine was the only legitimate basis for healing made little headway before the English Revolution: Professional eclecticism and therapeutic pluralism continued to characterize the treatment of physically ill and mentally disturbed people.

During the course of the seventeenth century, religious controversy and the shock of revolution accelerated the triumph of medical explanations for insanity among the governing classes. The Anglican hierarchy repudiated popular demonology for theological reasons, only to discover that Jesuits and Puritans eagerly took up the struggle against the Fiend and his minions. Radical Protestants developed new means for casting out devils and uplifting downcast hearts and used them to proselytize as well as to console. They insisted that misery, anxiety, and sadness were the emblems of sin, the normal afflictions of the unregenerate, and they taught that the surest means to overcome them was spiritual self-discipline and godly fellowship. Insanity was the epitome of conduct unguided by a pious and responsible personality. . . . The Puritans produced a literature of anxious gloom in which despair normally preceded conversion, and they naturally bruited about their ability to relieve such suffering. During the Revolution the sects—especially the Quakers—employed their powers of exorcism and spiritual healing to prove by miracles their divine inspiration and refute the charges of the "hireling priests." The orthodox elite seized the healer's gown in which the radicals clothed themselves and turned it inside out, calling religious enthusiasm madness and branding the vexations of tender consciences religious melancholy.

These events coincided with remarkable achievements in physical science and anatomy, and they helped to accomplish the end that physicians had been unable to attain by propaganda and persecution. They prompted the ruling elite to embrace secular explanations for mental disorders and to repudiate magical and religious methods of healing them. The secularization of the elite's beliefs about insanity affected

---

[6]Cunning men and women practiced so-called white witchcraft, which involved predicting the future, healing, preparing love potions, and recovering lost objects.

their notions about the nature of mental diseases as well as the causes of such afflictions. . . . The educated classes' gradual rejection of traditional religious ideas about suicide in favor of the medical theory that it was the outcome of mental disease was also fostered by orthodox hatred of religious enthusiasm. Throughout the eighteenth century dissenting sects continued to exorcise people who believed that they were possessed by the Devil. Anglican spokesmen argued that the age of miracles was long past, and the Devil rarely if ever swayed the minds and inhabited the bodies of people in modern times. This argument corroded the traditional stereotype of suicide, which depicted self-murder as a religious crime, committed at the instigation of the Devil, who often appeared personally to urge his victims on to self-destruction.

The rejection of the supernatural beliefs and thaumaturgy of the sectaries fostered scorn for religious and magical therapies. Although the methods of psychological healing practiced by the Dissenters[7] were often effective, the governing classes abandoned them in favor of medical remedies for mental disorders, techniques that were widely recognized to be unpleasant, ineffective, and theoretically insupportable. Magical remedies against supernatural harm, such as astrological amulets, charms, and exorcisms, were discarded by reputable practitioners. By the end of the seventeenth century a loose hierarchy of prestige had been established among the various types of healers who treated insanity, and at its apex were the humanistic physicians, who viewed madness and gloom as natural disorders. The dominance of secular interpretations of insanity among the eighteenth-century governing classes was embodied in the asylum movement. Beginning about 1660, scores of entrepreneurs founded private madhouses to care for the insane, and beginning about a century later, some municipal governments established receptacles for pauper lunatics. The therapeutic practices of the new asylums were based mainly on medical theories and remedies. . . .

The governing classes' repudiation of supernatural explanations of the signs and causes of insanity and their rejection of magical and religious therapies were not readily accepted by the mass of the English people. Throughout the eighteenth century ordinary villagers continued to believe that witches and demons could drive men mad and that the Devil could possess the minds and bodies of his victims. They sought the help of a ragtag regiment of increasingly disreputable astrologers and folk magicians to protect them against these evils. The exorcisms and religious cures of the Non-conformist sects,[8] and particularly of the Methodists, appealed to the strong popular attachment

---

[7]Those who rejected Anglicanism, the state religion.
[8]The Dissenters from Anglicanism (Church of England).

to traditional supernaturalism. The deepening abyss between elite attitudes toward insanity and popular beliefs was not simply the consequence of the enlightened scientism of the educated classes. Medical theories about mental disorders were contradictory and controversial; medical therapies were notoriously difficult to justify either theoretically or empirically. They appealed to an elite sick of sectarian enthusiasm because they lacked the subversive political implications that religious psychology and therapy had acquired during the seventeenth century. As the eighteenth century progressed, more and more people were subjected to incarceration in madhouses and to medical brutality. The abolition of family care for lunatics and the abandonment of therapeutic pluralism were the consequences of religious conflict, political strife, and social change. The lunacy reformers of the early nineteenth century drew an exaggerated, but nevertheless genuinely horrified, picture of the terrible suffering that the asylum movement and rise of medical psychology inflicted on the insane. . . .

"Environment and Pollution." Jean Gimpel. From *The Medieval Machine: The Industrial Revolution of the Middle Ages*. New York, 1976. Reprinted by permission of Holt, Rinehart and Winston, Publishers.

"Medieval Children." David Herlihy. From *Essays on Medieval Civilization*, Bede Karl Lackner and Kenneth Roy Phillip, eds. Used by permission of the Walter Prescott Webb Memorial Lecture Committee, University of Texas at Arlington. (Originally the copyright read: Austin and London: University of Texas Press, 1978. They are now distributed by Texas A&M University Press.)

"Fast, Feast and Flesh: The Religious Significance of Food to Medieval Women." Caroline Walker Bynum. From *Representations* No. 11 (California: the University of California Press, 1985).

"The Vision of Death." Johan Huizinga. From *The Waning of the Middle Ages* (1924). Reprinted by permission of St. Martin's Press Inc. and Edward Arnold (Publishers) Ltd., London and Baltimore.

"The Development of the Concept of Civilité." Norbert Elias. From *The History of Manners*, trans. by Edmund Jephcott. Reprinted by permission of Pantheon Books, 1978.

"The Family in Renaissance Italy." David Herlihy. (Copyright 1974 by The Forum Press, Inc. Arlington Heights, Il.), pp. 4–12. Reprinted by permission of the publisher, The Forum Press.

"Population Structures." Henry Kamen. From *The Iron Century: Social Change in Europe, 1500–1650*. New York and Washington, 1971, pp. 3–18. Permission granted by Henry Kamen and A.D. Peters and Co. Ltd.

"The Early History of Syphilis: A Reappraisal." Alfred W. Crosby, Jr. From *The Columbian Exchange: Biological and Cultural Consequences of 1492* (Greenwood Press, Westport, CT, 1972), 122–27, 141–42, 145–60. Copyright 1972 by Alfred W. Crosby, Jr. Reprinted by permission of the publisher.

"Life in Renaissance France." Lucien Febvre. From *Life in Renaissance France*, Marian Rothstein, ed. and tr., Cambridge, Mass.: Harvard University Press, copyright 1977 by the President and Fellows of Harvard College. Reprinted by permission of the publishers.

"Mutiny and Discontent in the Spanish Army of Flanders, 1572–1607." Geoffrey Parker. The Past and Present Society, 175 Bamburg Rd, Oxford, England. This article is here reprinted in abridged form, with the permission of the Society and the author, from *Past and Present: a Journal of Historical Studies*, no. 58, Feb. 1973, pp. 38–52.

"Who Were the Witches?" Christina Larner. From *Enemies of God*. Baltimore: The Johns Hopkins University Press, 1981, pp. 89–102. Copyright 1981 by Christina Larner.

"The Rites of Violence: Religious Riot in Sixteenth-Century France." Natalie Z. Davis. The Past and Present Society, 175 Bambury Road, Oxford, England. This article is here reprinted in abridged form, with the permission of the Society and the author, from *Past and Present: a Journal of Historical Studies*, no. 59, May 1973, pp. 51–91. This article also appears in Chapter 6 of Natalie Zemon Davis's *Society and Culture in Early Modern France*, Stanford University Press, 1975.

"Insanity in Early Modern England." Michael MacDonald. From *Mystical Bedlam: Madness, Anxiety, and Healing in Seventeenth-Century England*. Cambridge, England and New York: Cambridge University Press, 1981, pp. 1–11.